RELIGIOUS STUDIES

LORRAINE ABBOTT

WITH STEVE CLARKE

EDITED BY GORDON W M KAY

DYNAMIC LEARNING

HODDER
EDUCATION
AN HACHETTE UK COMPANY

Dedication

For Ellie, Lucy and Holly

'We do not learn for school but for life'

Cicero

Acknowledgements

Dylan, Harriett and Beth for their constant enthusiasm, engagement and questioning.

Every effort has been made to trace all copyright holders, but if any have been inadvertently overlooked the Publishers will be pleased to make the necessary arrangements at the first opportunity.

All text and photo credits can be found on the back page of this title.

Although every effort has been made to ensure that website addresses are correct at time of going to press, Hodder Education cannot be held responsible for the content of any website mentioned in this book. It is sometimes possible to find a relocated web page by typing in the address of the home page for a website in the URL window of your browser.

Hachette UK's policy is to use papers that are natural, renewable and recyclable products and made from wood grown in well-managed forests and other controlled sources. The logging and manufacturing processes are expected to conform to the environmental regulations of the country of origin.

Orders: please contact Hachette UK Distribution, Hely Hutchinson Centre, Milton Road, Didcot, Oxfordshire, OX11 7HH. Telephone: +44 (0)1235 827827. Email education@ hachette.co.uk
Lines are open from 9 a.m. to 5 p.m., Monday to Friday. You can also order through our website: www.hoddereducation.co.uk

ISBN: 978 1 4718 6524 4

First published in 2016 by:

Hodder Education,
An Hachette UK Company
Carmelite House
50 Victoria Embankment
London EC4Y 0DZ

www.hoddereducation.co.uk

Impression number   10 9 8 7 6

Year   2021

Cover photo © Viktoria Rodriguez/EyeEm/Getty Images

Illustrations by DC Graphic Design Limited and Oxford Designers & Illustrators

Typeset in DIN Regular 11/13pt by DC Graphic Design Limited

Printed and bound by CPI Group (UK) Ltd, Croydon, CR0 4YY

A catalogue record for this title is available from the British Library.

Contents

INTRODUCTION — **v**

Christianity — **1**

Introduction — 2

1 Beliefs and teachings — **5**

The nature of God — 5

The concept of a God as a Trinity of persons — 8

Biblical accounts of Creation — 12

The problem of evil and suffering and a loving and righteous God — 21

Jesus Christ — 25

The incarnation, crucifixion, resurrection and ascension — 34

The concept of salvation — 37

Eschatological beliefs and teachings — 40

2 Practices — **43**

Worship — 44

Sacraments — 51

Prayer — 54

The role and importance of pilgrimage — 60

Celebrations — 64

The role of the Church in the local community and living practices — 71

Mission — 81

The role of the Church in the wider world — 85

Let's revise — 91

Islam — **93**

Introduction — 94

3 Beliefs and teachings — **97**

Core beliefs — 97

Nature of Allah — 100

Prophethood (Risalah) — 103

Books (Kutub) — 112

Angels (Malaikah) — 114

Eschatological beliefs — 116

Life after death (Akhirah) — 119

4 Practices **124**

The importance of practices 124

Public acts of worship 126

Private acts of worship 133

Zakah 134

Sawm 136

Hajj 139

Festivals and special days 145

Jihad 150

Let's revise 152

Religion, philosophy and ethics in the modern world
from a Christian perspective 153

5 Relationships and families **154**

Relationships 155

Men and women 180

Christian understandings of equality 186

Let's revise 193

6 The existence of God **195**

The question of God 195

The nature of reality 209

Experiencing God 218

Let's revise 240

7 Religion, peace and conflict **242**

Violence and conflict 243

Peace and peacemaking 261

Forgiveness and reconciliation 268

Let's revise 281

**8 Dialogue within and between religious and non-religious
beliefs and attitudes** **283**

Challenges for religion 283

Dialogue within and between religious groups 319

Dialogue within and between religious and non-religious groups 332

Let's revise 337

GLOSSARY **339**

INDEX **340**

Introduction

This book has been written specifically to support the OCR Religious Studies GCSE course.

There are two parts to the GCSE:

- **Part 1** Beliefs and Teachings and Practices
- **Part 2** Religion, philosophy and ethics in the modern world from a religious perspective.

Part 2 is divided into four themes:

1 Relationships and families.
2 The existence of God, gods and the ultimate reality.
3 Religion, peace and conflict.
4 Dialogue between religious and non-religious beliefs and attitudes.

Part 1 of this book is from the perspective of Christianity and Islam and Part 2 from the perspective of Christianity.

About the exams

Part 1, the Beliefs and Teachings and Practices are examined by **two one** hour exams; one for **each** of the two religions you have studied. There will be **two** questions on each exam paper and you have to answer both of them.

Part 2, the philosophical and ethical themes, are examined by **a two hour** exam paper. There is a question on each of the four themes and you must answer all **four** questions.

The exams for Part 1 are worth 50% of the marks and so is the exam for Part 2.

The Exam for Part 1

Each of the two questions in each Part 1 exam paper is broken up into **five** questions.

Questions (a) (b) and (c) These questions are each worth 3 marks.

Your response to these questions must have three points.

The question might ask for three things, for example: *Give three reasons why a Christian would want to be baptised.*

The question might ask you to describe one thing, for example: *Describe* **one** *Christian teaching about why there is sin in the world.*

- In this case you must state a teaching then show further detail and development for the second and third marks.

The question might ask a more general question, for example: *What do Christians mean when they describe God as 'personal'?*

- In this case you could give three examples of what Christians mean or one with development.

Question (d) These questions are worth 6 marks.

Usually the questions will ask you to explain something, for example: *Explain why Christians consider Easter to be an important festival in the Christian Church.*

- You should show a deep understanding of the reasons which a Christian might give for Easter being important to them.
- A response might start with reference to the resurrection of Jesus and then explain why that is of significance to Christians in terms of belief and their hopes for salvation and for life after death.

Question (e) These questions are worth 15 marks.

You will be given a statement to discuss. You must refer to different views about the issue **within** the religion you have studied and you must engage and comment on them. It is best to treat these discussion questions as a short essay.

- So you need first of all to explain the issue in the stimulus; then describe and explain different views within the religion about the issue comparing them with each other.
- You should come to some sort of judgement or conclusion about the discussion to sum it up. **You do not need to give a personal point of view.**
- You might however, have a personal view which you could use as a thread running through the discussion and against which you might compare other views but the requirement is to discuss the views of different Christian / Muslim groups within that religion.
- In the discussion, where possible, you should show how these views are based on sources of wisdom and authority. For example you might be able to refer to texts from the Bible or teachings of the churches for Christianity or texts from the Qur'an or Hadith for Islam.

The Exam for Part 2

Each of the four questions in each Part 2 exam paper is broken up into **four** questions.

Question (a) These questions are each worth 3 marks

These questions are similar to the 3 mark questions for the Part 1 exam.

Question (b) These questions are worth 6 marks.

These will ask for factual knowledge and will ask you to describe or outline something. For example, outline the philosophical argument from design for the existence of God.

Question 4 This question examines the Dialogue theme. There is special instruction for question (b): *'In your response you must consider that religious traditions in Great Britain are diverse, but mainly Christian.'*

- So at some point in your response, you have to show that you know and understand this. For example in a question about interfaith dialogue, you could start by saying that whilst Christianity is the dominant religion of Great Britain, there are many other faiths with many millions of followers, so interfaith dialogue is important because of the diverse nature of British society.

Question (c) These questions are worth 6 marks.

These questions are similar to the (d) question in the Part 1 exams. They will ask you to explain views or compare views about a topic.

In this question examiners will be assessing your ability to refer to sources of wisdom and authority.

- For example, you might be able to refer to texts from the Bible or teachings of the churches for Christianity, or texts from the Qur'an or Hadith for Islam.
- Explain why religious experiences are important to some Christians.

Question (d) These questions are worth 15 marks.

You will be given a statement to discuss but the task is slightly different to the discussion task in the Part 1 Exam.

The instruction on the exam paper is to: *Explain and evaluate the importance of points of view from the perspective of Christianity'.*

- This means that, for example, if the topic is about euthanasia, you might refer to and comment on different Christian views, also non-religious / non-Christian views. If you do refer to non-religious / non-Christian views you must comment on how Christians might regard the non-religious views.
- You do **not** need to try to develop a personal point of view, which is different from any of the views within the religion. If you do express a personal view, you must justify it with evidence and argument.
- You might for example have a personal view which you could use as a thread running through the discussion and against which you might compare other views

There is also an instruction on the exam paper that you must: *Draw on your learning from across your course of study, including reference to beliefs, teachings and practices within Christianity.*

- This means that where possible, you should show that there are beliefs, teachings or practices which could be the basis of Christian attitudes. In the case of a discussion about euthanasia, for example, you could refer to what you learned in Part 1 about the sanctity of life from the first three chapters of Genesis.

Command words

Questions will start with one of these words.

Part 1 Exam

Questions (a) (b) (c) Name / State / Give

Question (d) Explain / Compare

Question (e) Discuss

Part 2 Exam

Question (a) Name / State / Give

Question (b) Describe / Outline

Question (c) Explain / Compare

Question (e) Discuss

You will find more detail about the command words in the back of the OCR Specification.

BELIEFS AND TEACHINGS AND PRACTICES

Christianity

Introduction

Who are Christians?

Christianity is thought to be the largest religion in the world today, with a following of about 2.4 billion people. Since the origin of the religion in the first century CE, Christian teachings and beliefs have developed and it is now a diverse faith that has its roots in the life and teaching of Jesus Christ.

Christian beliefs

There are, of course, some things that all Christians have in common. One of these is that they are all followers of Christ or, more accurately, followers of Jesus of Nazareth, to whom they give the title 'Christ'.

Christians believe that there is only one God, who is all-powerful, all-loving and created the universe. Most Christians, however, believe that God has three parts: the Father, the Son (Jesus) and the Holy Spirit.

Jesus

Jesus of Nazareth lived in Palestine in the first century CE and was crucified around 30CE. Jesus' followers, or disciples, were initially Jewish people like him who had been with him during his life. They believed that he rose from the dead three days after his crucifixion, a belief that supported their claim that he was divine as well as human. These people believed him to be the long-awaited Messiah. Messiah was translated as 'Christ' in Greek, and so they became known as Christians.

Christians believe that Jesus died for the sins of humanity and that because of his death Christians can hope to spend eternity with God in heaven. Jesus also provides an example for Christians to follow when living their lives.

Sources of authority

By the middle of the first century CE many of the people who had known Jesus had died. This meant that it became important to create a record of Jesus' life before the memory was lost. These writings became known as the 'gospels', which means good news. The writings of the first Christians became known as the New Testament; this collection of writings, along with the Old Testament, make up the Bible. The Bible is a key source of wisdom and authority for all Christians; it, like being a follower of Jesus, is something all Christians have in common. However, different Christians might interpret it in different ways; some might believe it is the actual word of God and that everything in it is absolutely true. Others believe that it was written in a certain time period and needs to be interpreted for today's world.

To deal with disagreements about beliefs, statements of belief – known as creeds – were created. The word 'creed' is from the Latin word *credo*, meaning 'I believe'. The Apostles' Creed and the Nicene Creed, which was finalised in 381CE, are both still recited by many Christians in their regular worship. These creeds are also important sources of wisdom and authority for Christians.

The sources of wisdom a Christian might refer to depends on the denomination they belong to. For most Protestants, the Bible is the most important – and possibly the only – source of wisdom and authority. For some other Protestant Christians, religious experiences – such as being filled with the Holy Spirit – are also a source of authority and wisdom. For Roman Catholics, the history of the Church, and the statements of the Pope and Church Councils, are important, as well as the Bible. In the Eastern Orthodox Churches, it is the voice of the patriarchs (the highest ranking Bishops in the Orthodox Churches), along with the Bible and ancient traditions, that are sources of authority.

Denominations

There are thousands of different Christian denominations, or groups. It is usually possible to point to the source of authority or wisdom that leads to different groups holding different beliefs. Sometimes a difference of belief or practice is based on different interpretations of what the Bible says.

The first major divergence in Christianity was the result of a disagreement in 1054CE about exactly what the words of the Nicene Creed meant. This became known as the East–West Schism. The Christians in the East of the Roman Empire considered themselves to be correct in their beliefs and took on the name of 'Orthodox', which in Greek means correct or straight beliefs, while those in the West continued to accept the authority of Rome and became known as Roman Catholics.

In the Roman Catholic Church a further divergence, known as the Reformation, occurred in the sixteenth century CE. It began as a protest in Germany, which then spread throughout many parts of Europe, against what many Christians believed was misuse of the power of the Roman Catholic Church. Christians who broke away from the authority of Rome at this time became known as Protestants. In England this development coincided with the reign of King Henry VIII who, having failed to obtain a divorce from the Pope to enable him to marry Anne Boleyn, separated the Church in England from the Roman Catholic Church and took on the role of Head of the Church in England. This led to the creation of a Church quite separate from the Roman Catholic Church, which became the official or established Church of England, of which the monarch is the head.

In the years that followed the Reformation, many other Protestant denominations were formed, which led to the diversity of Christianity today. In Britain the members of these denominations, such as Baptists and Presbyterians, refused to conform to the organisation and pattern of worship of the Church of England and so became known as non-conformists. Other denominations – such as the Methodists, the Quakers and The Salvation Army – expressed their own interpretation of the faith. During the last three centuries, Christian missionaries from many denominations have spread Christianity around the world, leading to the existence of Christianity in all its diverse forms in almost every country in the world.

The differences of belief that led to the diversity of Christianity today often caused very serious and violent reactions in the past. Today, however, Christians are generally tolerant of the diversity in their religion.

Practices

Prayer and worship are important to Christians as a way of communicating with and showing their feelings towards God. The way they do these things, though, will depend on the denomination they are part of and on their individual preferences. Sacraments are rituals where Christians feel they receive God's blessing; examples of this include baptism and the Eucharist. Christians also hold services to mark special occasions in the lives of individuals, as well as to celebrate Christian festivals. Pilgrimage to holy sites is another way Christians might choose to show their faith. Christians try to follow the example set by Jesus during his lifetime, and this includes showing compassion and helping those in need; for some it also means sharing their faith with those around them and trying to encourage others to become Christian.

1 Beliefs and teachings

Topic checklist ✔

- ✔ Nature of God
- ✔ Concept of God as a Trinity of persons
- ✔ Biblical accounts of Creation
- ✔ The problem of evil and suffering and a loving and righteous God
- ✔ Jesus Christ
- ✔ The incarnation, crucifixion, resurrection and ascension
- ✔ The concept of salvation
- ✔ Eschatological beliefs and teachings

Key concepts 🔑

Christians believe that there is only one God, but that he is made up of three 'persons'. These three persons are known as the Father, the Son and the Holy Spirit. God is seen as the creator of the world, but Christians have different interpretations of what this may mean. All Christians agree, however, that God is loving and powerful despite the suffering that goes on in this world. The greatest evidence of God's love, they believe, was when He took human form and revealed Himself on Earth as Jesus. Jesus' life fulfils God's promise of salvation and reveals more about what Christians believe will happen after death.

To discuss 💬

Look at the timeline.

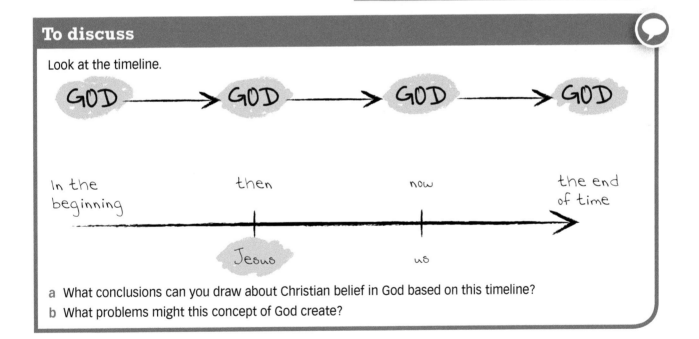

a What conclusions can you draw about Christian belief in God based on this timeline?
b What problems might this concept of God create?

The nature of God

Christianity is known as a monotheistic religion because it teaches that there is only one God. Christians believe that this God is eternal – He is without a beginning or end, unlike humans who are born and who die. God is outside time; the word for this is 'atemporal'. Time is part of the world that God Himself created, and so He is in control of both time and space. God is omniscient, which means He knows everything. He is able to see the whole of time, the past, the present and the future. His knowledge is therefore perfect. Existing outside time and space means that he is transcendent and above all created things.

Christianity, however, also teaches that God is immanent, which means He is involved with the world and human lives. In acting in this way God is able to demonstrate His benevolence (love and kindness) towards humans as well as, at times, His judgement. In the Bible God is often shown to be in a relationship with people through prayer, visions and the presence of the Holy Spirit. So Christianity understands Him to be a personal God.

God is omnipotent; He is all-powerful. This means He can do anything. So He had the power to create the universe, to perform miracles and to become a human being incarnate as Jesus Christ. Because He is good and loving, however, He cannot do anything that is evil, and He does not lie. Such actions would not be in God's nature and so wouldn't be possible.

Christians believe that God's perfect nature and omniscience ensure that He is a fair and righteous judge of humans. God sees all that humans do, say and think. He has set rules for humans to follow, and Christians believe that He provided a perfect example of the right way to live when He came into the world as Jesus. So when humans fall short of God's standards, He will judge them, and this will have eternal consequences for them after death. God, however, is also forgiving to those who seek His forgiveness.

Although all Christians believe God has these characteristics, different groups emphasise some more than others. For example, the characteristic of God as judge was strongly favoured by the Church in the fourteenth and fifteenth centuries, while more recently the forgiving and loving characteristics of God have been emphasised by some Protestant denominations.

Stretch what you know

Boethius was a sixth-century CE Christian philosopher. While imprisoned and awaiting execution he wrote *The Consolation of Philosophy*. In this writing he explores how God can justly punish people after death if He knows the future. If our future is known by God and humans are simply acting out the plans that God has for them, then how can people really control what they do? Surely if this is the case, then God would be wrong to punish humans for something they really had no choice in.

Boethius had a solution to this problem. He believed God was omniscient, but that humans also had free will. He argued that God's foreknowledge does not cause future events to happen. Rather, because God is atemporal, He sees all events simultaneously. To God there is no past, present or future; it is all the immediate. Boethius says: 'his knowledge, too, transcends all temporal change and abides in the immediacy of his presence.' Humans therefore remain completely free in their choices, and God is right to punish or reward humans for their actions.

a Why did Boethius think there might be a problem in believing in both God's omniscience and human free will?

b Explain how Boethius was able to sustain belief both in human free will and in God's omniscience.

c Explain to what extent you agree with Boethius' argument.

Tasks

1 On a piece of paper, draw nine identical hexagons and cut them out. On each hexagon write one of the characteristics of God and include an emoji to symbolise the meaning of that characteristic:

a Benevolent   d Eternal   g Personal

b Omnipotent   e Transcendent   h Forgiving

c Omniscient   f Immanent   i Judgemental

2 Now put the hexagons together. Every time one side of a hexagon touches another, explain the link between the touching characteristics. Stick these into your book once you have arranged them effectively. For example:

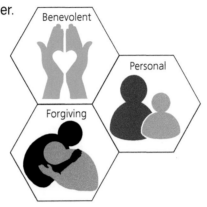

3 Now annotate your hexagons by drawing arrows to at least three different sides that touch and adding a Bible verse to each.

4 Using only your annotated hexagons, write an explanation of the Christian beliefs about the nature of God.

5 Based on your understanding of the Christian beliefs about the nature of God, explain how you think such beliefs would affect a Christian's daily life.

Different views on the nature of God

The Plymouth Brethren are a Christian denomination that focus very much on the holiness of God and his purity. Their understanding of the Bible teaching about God means that they believe only those who are part of the Brethren are able to truly know the oneness of God. The brethren live, as far as possible, lives separate from the rest of the world to remove themselves from evil. This follows their understanding of Bible passages such as 1 John 2:15–17:

'Do not love the world or anything in the world. If anyone loves the world, love for the Father is not in them…the world and its desires pass away, but whoever does the will of God lives forever.'

In a similar way the Amish live in their own communities, separating themselves from the pollution of sin in the world. However the Amish believe that whilst God, in his love has provided salvation through the death and resurrection of Jesus they also believe that they must practice life of salvation by works. They believe that God is forgiving (Matthew 6:12) but they also believe that living in accordance with the laws and commands present in the Bible is necessary for salvation. This way of understanding God's judgment of humans is linked to teachings such as the parable of the sheep and the goats (Matthew 25:31–46).

Bible bitz

'Let all creation rejoice before the Lord, for he comes, he comes to judge the earth. He will judge the world in righteousness and the peoples in his faithfulness.'
(Psalm 96:13)

'But the Lord is the true God; he is the living God, the eternal King. When he is angry, the earth trembles; the nations cannot endure his wrath.'
(Jeremiah 10:10)

'"I am the Alpha and the Omega," says the Lord God, "who is, and who was, and who is to come, the Almighty."'
(Revelation 1:8)

'Praise be to the God and Father of our Lord Jesus Christ, the Father of compassion and the God of all comfort, who comforts us in all our troubles, so that we can comfort those in any trouble with the comfort we ourselves receive from God.'
(2 Corinthians 1:3–4)

'For God so loved the world that he gave his one and only Son, that whoever believes in him shall not perish but have eternal life.'
(John 3:16)

'For you are great and do marvellous deeds; you alone are God.'
(Psalm 86:10)

'And forgive us our sins'
(Matthew 6:12)

'You shall have no other gods before me'
(Exodus 20:3)

This emphasis on works for salvation is different from many free churches such as Hillsong. Hillsong church focuses on the grace of God for forgiveness, and does not believe that anything a person has done can lead to salvation as a reward. Hillsong churches believe that God's forgiveness is a revelation of his benevolence and it is a gift. A simple belief and acceptance of this is all they believe is required for salvation (John 3:16).

Free churches such as Baptist churches teach that God is directly accessible by all believers. They do not believe that priests are necessary to intercede between humans and God in any way, unlike the Catholic Church where priests do fulfill this role, for example in confession and Eucharist. The Free Church emphasis is on the personal and accessible nature of God. This relationship they believe is exhibited in Jesus' teaching for example when Jesus teaches the disciples to pray using the phrase 'abba' to speak to God, abba means 'daddy' and shows this close personal relationship. Furthermore the Bible speaks of Christians being 'priests and kings' (1 Peter 2:9), for free churches this is further reason to emphasise God as immanent.

The concept of God as a Trinity of persons

The word 'trinity' means triad or three united as one. The Bible presents God as a Holy Trinity, as being one God but having three distinct parts:

- The Father
- The Son
- The Holy Spirit.

Each of these is God and there is only one God. For example, in Matthew 28 Jesus instructs the apostles to baptise 'in the name of the Father, the Son and the Holy Spirit', or in 2 Corinthians 13 Paul prays for God's grace to be present with the Church through the Father, the Son and the Holy Spirit. Each person of the Trinity is distinct. All persons of the Trinity are equal; they have the perfect, complete relationship.

Each person in the Trinity – Father, Son and Holy Spirit – fulfils a different role. The Father is often referred to simply as God, and the Son is identified by Christians as Jesus. Both God the Father and the Holy Spirit are unseen, while Christians believe that Jesus, the Son, was the human form of God who lived on Earth over 2,000 years ago and who then returned to heaven after his resurrection.

To discuss

Look at the diagram of the Trinity.

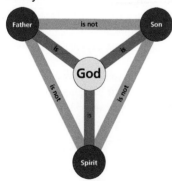

a What can you say about God based on this diagram?

b Discuss why Christianity is monotheistic (believes in one God) and not polytheistic (believes in many gods).

God the Father

Christians believe that God the Father is the creator of the universe. This is expressed in the Apostles' Creed, one of the first statements of belief, which can be found in the Church of England's *Alternative Service Book*:

'I believe in God, the Father almighty, creator of heaven and earth.'

In the Bible Christians are taught to speak to God using the phrase 'Abba, Father' (Romans 8:15). Abba, a word from the Aramaic language that Jesus spoke, may be understood as similar to calling God 'Daddy' – a way of showing the close, loving relationship that Christians may have with the creator, like with a loving parent.

God as Father also conveys a sense of safety and protection for those who are His followers. This can be seen in Proverbs 18:10, where the righteous are said to be safe in God's strength.

God the Son

Jesus is believed to be God in human form. In the Apostles' Creed it says:

'I believe in Jesus Christ, God's only Son, our Lord, who was conceived by the Holy Spirit, born of the Virgin Mary...'

Christians believe that Jesus was not conceived naturally but was placed in Mary by the Holy Spirit. They believe that Jesus was free of all sin because he was not made by two humans, unlike all other humans. Although the idea is a very difficult one, Jesus is understood to be completely human but also completely God. God came to Earth in the form of Jesus for three main purposes:

1 To reveal Himself to people, showing His love and power and teaching them how He wants people to live. This is explained in the section about Jesus Christ (p.25–27).
2 To sacrifice Himself on the cross, receiving God's punishment for human sin in order for repentant people to be forgiven. This is explained in the sections about salvation (p.37) and the crucifixion (p.36).
3 To rise from the dead to show that God has power over death, that He is eternal, and that Christians, too, may have an everlasting life in heaven after death. This is explained in the sections about the resurrection (p.40) and eschatological beliefs (p.40).

God the Holy Spirit

In the New Testament of the Bible the spirit of God is often referred to using the Greek word *paraclete*. The word paraclete means one who comes alongside someone else. The Holy Spirit is understood to be the part of God that is with Christians as their constant guide and comforter. The Holy Spirit's presence in the lives of believers is described in the Bible in Acts 2:4, when it

Shamrock

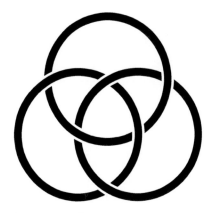
Borromean rings

Triskelion
♎ These symbols are often used to show the trinity and the idea of three in one

9

comes to Jesus' followers at the feast of Pentecost after Jesus has died and ascended to heaven:

'All of them were filled with the Holy Spirit and began to speak in other tongues as the Spirit enabled them.'

Although Jesus had gone, the disciples now knew the Spirit of God was with them, as Jesus had promised.

Christians today believe that the Spirit helps them to live in the way that God requires, helping them to understand His teaching and giving them the promise of life with Him in heaven after death.

Do all Christians believe in the Trinity?

The belief that God is a Trinity of persons is held by almost all people who call themselves Christians. The Trinity is a vital way of explaining both how God could become human as Jesus and also how His power is felt in the world today through the Holy Spirit.

There are some denominations, however, that think belief in the Trinity leads to the idea that there is more than one God and so puts the monotheism of Christianity in danger. They see it as going against the second of the Ten Commandments in Exodus 20:3 ('You shall have no other gods before me.'). Because of this, Unitarians such as the Christadelphians do not believe in the Trinity.

The Nicene Creed

The Nicene Creed is one of the most widely accepted statements of faith among Christian Churches. It is used by Catholics, Anglicans and most Protestant Churches. The final form was agreed at the Council of Constantinople in 381CE (a process that began at the Council of Nicea in 325CE, hence the name Nicene Creed). The First Council of Nicea was, the first ecumenical meeting of Christians. The contemporary version of the Nicene Creed is shown here:

We believe in one God, the Father, the Almighty,
maker of heaven and earth, of all that is seen and unseen.

We believe in one Lord, Jesus Christ,
the only Son of God, eternally begotten of the Father,
God from God, light from light, true God from true God,
begotten, not made, one in Being with the Father.
Through him all things were made.
For us and for our salvation he came down from heaven,
By the power of the Holy Spirit he was born of the Virgin Mary and became man.
For our sake he was crucified under Pontius Pilate;
He suffered, died and was buried.
On the third day he rose again in fulfilment of the Scriptures;
He ascended into heaven and is seated at the right hand of the Father.
He will come again in glory to judge the living and the dead,
and his kingdom will have no end.

We believe in the Holy Spirit, the Lord, the giver of life,
who proceeds from the Father (and the Son)
Who with the Father and the Son is worshipped and glorified.
Who has spoken through the prophets.

We believe in one holy catholic and apostolic Church.
We acknowledge one baptism for the forgiveness of sins.
We look for the resurrection of the dead, and the life of the world to come.
Amen.

To discuss

a What does the Nicene Creed say God has done 'for our sake'?

b What do you understand by the following phrases?
- 'the only Son of God, eternally begotten of the Father'
- 'God from God, light from light, true God from true God'

c Why do you think the early Christian Church came together to write a statement of faith?

d What purpose do you think the creed may have today when recited in church services?

Stretch what you know

Christians had many arguments about how to express and explain their beliefs about God, Jesus and the Holy Spirit and how they related to each other. The Nicene Creed was written to ensure all Christians really did understand that Jesus Christ was truly both God and man. Some Christians, however, found it hard to see what it meant for Jesus as the Son of God to be fully God and also a real historical person called Jesus. One famous early Christian said:

'For we do not hold that which the heretics imagine: that some part of the being of God was converted into the Son, or that the Son was procreated by the Father from non-existent substances, that is, from a being outside himself, so that there was a time when he, the Son, did not exist.'

(Origen, The Fundamental Doctrines 4:4:1, 225CE)

a Explain the belief that Origen is rejecting.

b Explain how the claim of the heretics in this quote would affect Christian teaching.

Biblical accounts of Creation

Genesis 1

In the beginning God created the heavens and the earth. Now the earth was formless and empty, darkness was over the surface of the deep, and the Spirit of God was hovering over the waters.

And God said, 'Let there be light,' and there was light. God saw that the light was good, and he separated the light from the darkness. God called the light 'day,' and the darkness he called 'night.' And there was evening, and there was morning – the first day.

And God said, 'Let there be a vault between the waters to separate water from water.' So God made the vault and separated the water under the vault from the water above it. And it was so. God called the vault 'sky.' And there was evening, and there was morning – the second day.

And God said, 'Let the water under the sky be gathered to one place, and let dry ground appear.' And it was so. God called the dry ground 'land,' and the gathered waters he called 'seas.' And God saw that it was good.

Then God said, 'Let the land produce vegetation: seed-bearing plants and trees on the land that bear fruit with seed in it, according to their various kinds.' And it was so. The land produced vegetation: plants bearing seed according to their kinds and trees bearing fruit with seed in it according to their kinds. And God saw that it was good. And there was evening, and there was morning – the third day.

And God said, 'Let there be lights in the vault of the sky to separate the day from the night, and let them serve as signs to mark sacred times, and days and years, and let them be lights in the vault of the sky to give light on the earth.' And it was so. God made two great lights – the greater light to govern the day and the lesser light to govern the night. He also made the stars. God set them in the vault of the sky to give light on the earth, to govern the day and the night, and to separate light from darkness. And God saw that it was good.

And there was evening, and there was morning – the fourth day.

And God said, 'Let the water teem with living creatures, and let birds fly above the earth across the vault of the sky.' So God created the great creatures of the sea and every living thing with which the water teems and that moves about in it, according to their kinds, and every winged bird according to its kind. And God saw that it was good. God blessed them and said, 'Be fruitful and increase in number and fill the water in the seas, and let the birds increase on the earth.' And there was evening, and there was morning – the fifth day.

And God said, 'Let the land produce living creatures according to their kinds: the livestock, the creatures that move along the ground, and the wild animals, each according to its kind.' And it was so. God made the wild animals according to their kinds, the livestock according to their kinds, and all the creatures that move along the ground according to their kinds. And God saw that it was good.

Then God said, 'Let us make mankind in our image, in our likeness, so that they may rule over the fish in the sea and the birds in the sky, over the livestock and all the wild animals, and over all the creatures that move along the ground.'

So God created mankind in his own image, in the image of God he created them; male and female he created them.

God blessed them and said to them, 'Be fruitful and increase in number; fill the earth and subdue it. Rule over the fish in the sea and the birds in the sky and over every living creature that moves on the ground.'

Then God said, 'I give you every seed-bearing plant on the face of the whole earth and every tree that has fruit with seed in it. They will be yours for food. And to all the beasts of the earth and all the birds in the sky and all the creatures that move along the ground – everything that has the breath of life in it – I give every green plant for food.' And it was so.

God saw all that he had made, and it was very good. And there was evening, and there was morning – the sixth day.

Genesis 2

Thus the heavens and the earth were completed in all their vast array.

By the seventh day God had finished the work he had been doing; so on the seventh day he rested from all his work. Then God blessed the seventh day and made it holy, because on it he rested from all the work of creating that he had done.

This is the account of the heavens and the earth when they were created, when the Lord God made the earth and the heavens.

Now no shrub had yet appeared on the earth and no plant had yet sprung up, for the Lord God had not sent rain on the earth and there was no one to work the ground, but streams came up from the earth and watered the whole surface of the ground. Then the Lord God formed a man from the dust of the ground and breathed into his nostrils the breath of life, and the man became a living being.

Now the Lord God had planted a garden in the east, in Eden; and there he put the man he had formed. The Lord God made all kinds of trees grow out of the ground – trees that were pleasing to the eye and good for food. In the middle of the garden were the tree of life and the tree of the knowledge of good and evil.

A river watering the garden flowed from Eden; from there it was separated into four headwaters. The name of the first is the Pishon; it winds through the entire land of Havilah, where there is gold. (The gold of that land is good; aromatic resin and onyx are also there.) The name of the second river is the Gihon; it winds through the entire land of Cush. The name of the third river is the Tigris; it runs along the east side of Ashur. And the fourth river is the Euphrates.

The Lord God took the man and put him in the Garden of Eden to work it and take care of it. And the Lord God commanded the man, 'You are free to eat from any tree in the garden; but you must not eat from the tree of the knowledge of good and evil, for when you eat from it you will certainly die.'

The Lord God said, 'It is not good for the man to be alone. I will make a helper suitable for him.'

Now the Lord God had formed out of the ground all the wild animals and all the birds in the sky. He brought them to the man to see what he would name them; and whatever the man called each living creature, that was its name. So the man gave names to all the livestock, the birds in the sky and all the wild animals.

But for Adam no suitable helper was found. So the Lord God caused the man to fall into a deep sleep; and while he was sleeping, he took one of the man's ribs and then closed up the place with flesh. Then the Lord God made a woman from the rib he had taken out of the man, and he brought her to the man.

The man said,

'This is now bone of my bones and flesh of my flesh;

she shall be called 'woman,' for she was taken out of man.'

That is why a man leaves his father and mother and is united to his wife, and they become one flesh.

Adam and his wife were both naked, and they felt no shame.

(Genesis 1–2)

To discuss

Read Genesis 1 and 2 with a partner.

a How does God bring into existence everything, including the animals?

b How does this compare to the way that He brings into existence Adam and Eve?

c What do you think is significant about the differences?

According to Genesis 1 God created the world over six days and on the seventh day he rested

The account of Creation in Genesis 1

In the Bible, God is shown to be the one who brings the world into existence. While there are different interpretations of the Creation stories (or narratives) in the Bible, all Christians agree that God caused the universe to exist. The main accounts of Creation are found in Genesis 1–3 and in John 1.

At the start of the Genesis account of Creation, God brings order to chaos and his Spirit is present, 'hovering over the waters'. This image of the Spirit 'hovering' is meant to give the same idea as a bird sitting over a nest of eggs, caring for them, to bring them to life. In the same way, the Spirit is preparing to bring life into the world. By speaking aloud God then brings all things into existence, starting with light itself. Over six days, through the power of His Word, the Earth takes form and is filled with plants and creatures. The Moon, Sun and stars are also called into being at His spoken command. As soon as God commands something, it happens, for example:

'God said "let the land produce vegetation" … And it was so.'

(v.11–13)

Everything in Creation demonstrates God's power and purpose. All that God creates is described as 'good', and once Creation is completed God describes it as 'very good'. Nothing in Creation is bad or evil. God also names parts of nature, for example 'God called the dry land earth' (v.10). This shows God's authority over Creation. It is on day five that the world is ready for living creatures, as land, sea, sky and plants are all present. The final part of God's Creation in Genesis 1 is the creation of humans.

The creation of humans

Humans are created as distinct from the rest of Creation,

'Then God said, "Let us make mankind [humanity] in our image, in our likeness."'

(v.26)

This, according to some Christians, is one of the first reference to the Trinity in the Bible, because the word 'our' in the statement suggests that the Father, Son and Holy Spirit are speaking together.

Humanity, unlike any other part of Creation, is being made in the image or likeness of God. But humanity is also given a purpose: to 'rule over the fish of the sea and the birds of the air, over the livestock, over all the earth, and over all the creatures that move along the ground' (v.26–27). Humans are given this responsibility to look after and care for the Earth, acting as God's stewards. They are accountable to God in a way that no other part of Creation is. God also creates them as male and female to have children and to be blessed by God (v.29–30).

The account of Creation in Genesis 2

Genesis 2 provides a second account of Creation, this time starting with the creation of Adam and Eve. The name 'Adam' means humanity, and the name 'Eve' means beginning. This account is in the form of a story and contrasts with Genesis 1, which is written in a poetic style. By starting with the creation of Adam and Eve, the writer shows the importance of humanity within God's Creation. God is described much like a potter shaping clay as He creates Adam from the dust of the ground and breathes life into him. It is only after God has breathed life into Adam that Adam becomes a living being.

In Genesis 2 God is portrayed as displaying human qualities not seen before in Biblical descriptions of Him. The word for describing God by using human characteristics is 'anthropomorphic', for example when God 'breathed into his [Adam's] nostrils the breath of life'. This very physical description of how God brought Adam to life by His breath, which can also be translated as 'spirit', shows God's unique relationship with humanity.

In Genesis 2 God also gives Adam one rule – that he should not eat fruit from a particular tree:

'[you] must not eat from the tree of the knowledge of good and evil, for when you eat from it you will certainly die.'

He can, however, eat from any other plant, including the tree of life. This is the first law given by God to humanity and it carries with it a punishment if it is broken. Adam, however, is given a free choice to make. He can choose to obey or disobey God; this ability to choose is known as free will. God, aware of man's need for a helper, creates Eve from Adam's rib.

The role of the Spirit in Creation

The Spirit is the agent of God in creation. In Psalm 33:6 it says:

'By the word of the LORD the heavens were made, And by the breath of His mouth all their host.'

One of the names of the Holy Spirit is the breath of God and this passage demonstrates the creative work of the Spirit. In Job the Spirit's creative work extends to man also:

'The Spirit of God hath made me, and the breath of the Almighty hath given me life.'

In this passage the Holy Spirit is not only the creator of the physical form of man but also the life giver.

Tasks

1 Using words or images, record the six days of Creation found in Genesis 1.
2 Describe the different way in which, according to Genesis 2, God created humanity compared to the rest of creation.
3 Explain the way in which the Holy Spirit is seen in this chapter.

The role of the Word in Creation

The Greek term for the Word is 'Ho Logos', and it is the name given to the Son of God, God incarnate, Jesus.

The Word is present with God before the creation of the world and the Word is God. This clearly demonstrates Jesus as one of the three persons of the Trinity, distinct but one.

It is through Him that life was given. God is the one and only source of life; without God there would be no life.

In the beginning was the Word, and the Word was with God, and the Word was God. He was with God in the beginning. Through him all things were made; without him nothing was made that has been made. In him was life, and that life was the light of all mankind. The light shines in the darkness, and the darkness has not overcome it. . . .

The Word became flesh and made his dwelling among us. We have seen his glory, the glory of the one and only Son, who came from the Father, full of grace and truth.

(John 1:1–5, 14)

This clearly shows that God the Son was directly involved in the creation of the world.

This is a reference to Jesus' incarnation.

This is referring to humanity's choice to disobey God, as seen in Genesis 3. Instead of receiving the light, which is the life given by the Word, humanity chooses disobedience that resulted in death.

To discuss

In John 1 verse 14 it says, 'The Word became flesh'.

a What can you say about the existence of the Word based upon this verse?

b Based upon your existing knowledge of the Trinity, whom is this verse referring to?

c What role does the Word have in Creation? How do you know this?

Biblical account of The Fall

Genesis 3

Now the serpent was more crafty than any of the wild animals the Lord God had made. He said to the woman, 'Did God really say, "You must not eat from any tree in the garden"?'

The woman said to the serpent, 'We may eat fruit from the trees in the garden, but God did say, "You must not eat fruit from the tree that is in the middle of the garden, and you must not touch it, or you will die."'

'You will not certainly die,' the serpent said to the woman. 'For God knows that when you eat from it your eyes will be opened, and you will be like God, knowing good and evil.'

When the woman saw that the fruit of the tree was good for food and pleasing to the eye, and also desirable for gaining wisdom, she took some and ate it. She also gave some to her husband, who was with her, and he ate it. Then the eyes of both of them were opened, and they realised they were naked; so they sewed fig leaves together and made coverings for themselves.

Then the man and his wife heard the sound of the Lord God as he was walking in the garden in the cool of the day, and they hid from the Lord God among the trees of the garden. But the Lord God called to the man, 'Where are you?'

He answered, 'I heard you in the garden, and I was afraid because I was naked; so I hid.'

And he said, 'Who told you that you were naked? Have you eaten from the tree that I commanded you not to eat from?'

The man said, 'The woman you put here with me – she gave me some fruit from the tree, and I ate it.'

Then the Lord God said to the woman, 'What is this you have done?'

The woman said, 'The serpent deceived me, and I ate.'

So the Lord God said to the serpent, 'Because you have done this, 'Cursed are you above all livestock and all wild animals! You will crawl on your belly and you will eat dust all the days of your life. And I will put enmity between you and the woman, and between your offspring and hers; he will crush your head, and you will strike his heel.'

To the woman he said, 'I will make your pains in childbearing very severe; with painful labour you will give birth to children. Your desire will be for your husband, and he will rule over you.'

To Adam he said, 'Because you listened to your wife and ate fruit from the tree about which I commanded you, "You must not eat from it," 'Cursed is the ground because of you; through painful toil you will eat food from it all the days of your life. It will produce thorns and thistles for you, and you will eat the plants of the field. By the sweat of your brow you will eat your food until you return to the ground, since from it you were taken; for dust you are and to dust you will return.'

Adam named his wife Eve, because she would become the mother of all the living.

The Lord God made garments of skin for Adam and his wife and clothed them. And the Lord God said, 'The man has now become like one of us, knowing good and evil. He must not be allowed to reach out his hand and take also from the tree of life and eat, and live forever.' So the Lord God banished him from the Garden of Eden to work the ground from which he had been taken. After he drove the man out, he placed on the east side of the Garden of Eden cherubim and a flaming sword flashing back and forth to guard the way to the tree of life.

[Genesis 3]

The Fall

In Genesis 1–2 God creates the world and the first humans and tells them not to eat from the Tree of Knowledge. In Genesis 3 Adam and Eve use the free will that God has given them. The serpent, a creature described as 'crafty', questions God's command to Adam and Eve not to eat the fruit of the Tree of Knowledge of Good and Evil. Eve repeats God's command not to eat the fruit back to the serpent, but he is persistent and challenges what God has said by claiming that if they eat the fruit from the forbidden tree they will 'surely not die' (v.4). Furthermore, the serpent suggests that God wants to prevent Adam and Eve gaining the same knowledge as God. Eve is tempted by the way the fruit looks and by the possibility of gaining greater knowledge by eating it. She chooses to eat the fruit and also to share some with Adam. Adam and Eve have now disobeyed God and this disobedience is called sin. So by eating the forbidden fruit, sin has entered the world for the first time. This is known as original sin – the first occasion mankind disobeyed God. This event broke the perfect relationship that had existed between God and humanity.

God is once again given human characteristics by being depicted anthropomorphically, in this case walking in the garden (v.8). Adam and Eve instantly try to hide from him. They already know that what they have done is wrong and they show a sense of guilt. Their sinfulness is clear when God questions them. Adam blames Eve and Eve blames the serpent; neither of them accepts responsibility for their actions. After giving out punishments for this disobedience, God then sends Adam and Eve out from the Garden of Eden so that they can no longer take from the fruit of the tree of life and live forever.

The result of the Fall

'The Fall' is the term Christians use to describe this move by humans out of a perfect relationship with God and to disobedience and a broken relationship. Many Christians believe that the Fall has affected the entire human race. They believe that every person born since the Fall is affected by this original sin. Many Christians believe that original sin means that all humans are born out of relationship with God and in need of His salvation to bring them back into the relationship. Original sin means that unless the price of the sin is paid, which is known as redemption, a person has no hope of eternal life in heaven with God.

Tasks

1 Describe the way in which God punishes Adam and Eve for their sinfulness. Refer to Genesis 3:14–19 in your answer.

2 What evidence might Christians point to as the effect of sin in the world today?

3 How might someone who is not religious explain the effects that you have given in your previous answer?

4 To what extent do you agree that sinful behaviour has an effect upon the world that you live in?

Different and divergent interpretations of the Genesis Creation story

Christians have different ways of understanding the Creation story in Genesis. All Christians, however, agree that:

- God created the universe.
- God acted out of love and goodness; He cares for His creation, even in its broken and sinful state.
- Human beings are made in God's image but are sinful and lack His perfection.

Literal interpretations of the Creation story

Some Christians take Genesis 1–3 literally. They believe that the Bible is God's actual words and that the accounts in this section of Genesis provide an accurate historical account of the creation of the world and the Fall. These Christians are taking what is known as a Creationist approach. They reject any science that suggests that the world was not made in six days. Some creationists argue that the world is approximately 5,700 years old. This date is calculated by working back through the events in the Bible. Ultimately these Christians argue that the Bible is inspired by God and that God's Word is infallible, unlike human knowledge, and as such it should be taken as an absolute truth.

The Creation story as a myth

Many Christians interpret the Genesis accounts as myths. A myth is a story that is used to convey important truths but is not meant to be taken literally. There are many reasons to support the view that these accounts are mythological, including the apparent differences between both the style and the order of the accounts given in Genesis 1 and 2. Also, scientific evidence has shown that the universe is billions of years old, rather than several thousand years old, so the Genesis accounts cannot be literally true.

Many of these Christians would also say that any attempt to match the Genesis accounts – which were written hundreds of years before science had developed – to scientific evidence, is unhelpful and also unnecessary. The details of ancient myths do not need to be taken literally but they do give us some very important truths about the uniqueness of humans and the possibility of humans having a relationship with God.

This approach leads some Christians to a view known as Theistic Evolution. They believe that life developed through the process of evolution, which is when characteristics beneficial to a species' survival are passed on from one generation to the next, resulting over time in different forms of life developing. They also believe, however, that evolution was a process started by God and that it is the mechanism by which God brings about life.

To discuss

a How would you represent, through a piece of art, the work of the Holy Spirit in Genesis 1?

b What would you want your piece of art to suggest to people about creation?

You may find it useful to research the way other artists have tried to represent the spirit's work in Creation as you plan your responses to these two tasks.

The Creation story as compatible with science

Other Christians do not think that the days that are referred to in Genesis 1 need to be taken literally. This is because they say that God's time is not the same as our time. This view would suggest that each day of the week in the Creation story actually represents a longer period of time, maybe even billions of years. This makes the Creation account more compatible with the evidence provided by science about the age and development of life on the Earth.

Stretch what you know

Henry Morris (1918–2006) was a prominent supporter of Creationism, the belief that the world was created as it says in the Bible. He wrote several books to defend his position. His starting point was the view that the Bible is literally true and cannot be wrong. That means that he did not believe the Bible had any mistakes, and that he believed it was written by God and was meant to be taken literally. From this starting point Morris developed his views, which include a rejection of the claim that dinosaurs lived millions of years ago.

a Find out more about Morris' theology; you may find this web link helpful:
http://creation.com/recent-creation-is-a-vital-doctrine

b Now investigate Intelligent Design and Irreducible Complexity. Present your findings in a diagram, cartoon or essay.

c Explain whether Morris' theology is compatible with what you have found out about the Intelligent Design approach.

You may find this web link helpful in your research:
www.intelligentdesign.org

⋂ How Christians understand the accounts of Creation is based on their interpretation of the Bible

The problem of evil and suffering and a loving and righteous God

To discuss

a Divide the events shown in the photos on this page into two groups: those showing moral evil and those showing natural evil.

b Do you think humans bear the greatest responsibility for either of these types of evil, or do you think God or the devil is to blame for all evil? Give reasons for your answer.

c What could humans do to reduce suffering?

d At times of disaster people often ask, 'Why do innocent people suffer?' What questions would you like to ask God about suffering and evil in our world?

🎧 The terrible atrocities carried out in concentration camps like Auschwitz during the Second World War caused many people to question their faith in God

Evil and sin

The Genesis account of Creation describes the Fall, when Adam and Eve exercised their free will and made the choice to give in to temptation and eat the fruit from the Tree of Knowledge of Good and Evil, even though God had forbidden this. This was the first sin in the world, and as a result of this first sin, the perfect relationship between humans and God was broken. Christians believe that original sin caused humans to lose their immortality, and because of this all humans will one day die. This belief is seen when Paul writes to the Romans and explains to them that:

'…sin entered the world through one man, and death through sin, and in this way death came to all men, because all sinned.'

Suffering caused by death is therefore a direct result of original sin. When humans today continue to disobey God, their sin is seen as creating further suffering in the world.

Evil is a word used to describe everything that is the opposite of good. Some thinkers have said that it is good gone wrong or a complete lack of goodness. Some people have thought of evil as a force that works against everything good and have personified it in the form of the devil or Satan. Satan was expelled from heaven by God when he sinned (Isaiah 14:12). The Bible says that Satan acts to tempt humans and this leads them to disobey God. This in itself leads to evil and suffering in the world. He is described as a dangerous enemy to Christians, the destroyer and leader of a host of demons who help him in his attacks against God's people (Ephesians 6:11). Whilst people can resist the devil, as Jesus did in the desert (Matt.4:1–11), he still causes suffering that may test their faith (1 Peter 5:8–9).

The existence of evil is a philosophical as well as a religious issue, so it is also an area of study in the Philosophy and Ethics themes for this course.

Natural and moral Evil

Evil is often divided into two categories: natural evil and moral evil. Natural evil is suffering created through no direct fault of humans. This includes all natural disasters – such as earthquakes, floods and tornadoes – that bring devastation and tragedy to innocent people. Moral evil is when suffering is caused by the actions of human beings, for example the immeasurable suffering caused when Adolf Hitler tried to kill the entire Jewish people in Europe in the 1930s and 1940s.

The problem of Evil

Mackie's inconsistent triad shows the problem of evil. If God is omnibenevolent (all loving), then He would care enough to stop the suffering caused by evil, but He hasn't, so maybe He is not omnipotent (all powerful).

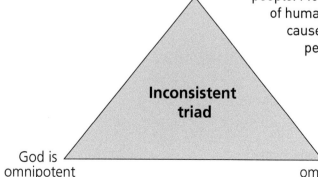

Evil exists

Inconsistent triad

God is omnipotent

God is omnibenevolent

🎧 Mackie's inconsistent triad

On the other hand, if He is omnipotent and has the power to stop suffering but He hasn't, maybe He doesn't care enough, so He is obviously not omnibenevolent. It seems that it is impossible to hold on to a belief in an omnipotent and omnibenevolent God when evil and suffering exist in the world.

Christians have proposed responses to this problem. These responses are called theodicies, and one of the first attempts was by a Christian called Irenaeus, who lived during the second century CE.

Irenaean theodicy

Irenaeus argued that God allows evil and suffering to exist. The world was deliberately created with both good and evil in order that humans would be able to choose and learn what is right and good. This has become known as the soul-making theodicy because it basically suggests that it is through suffering that we learn and develop spiritually, just as it is through good and bad experiences that a child learns to be a responsible adult. God allows suffering because He wants our souls to develop.

Irenaeus also believed that God would not interfere with human decisions because this would affect human free will. For Irenaeus, the Fall was just a stage in the human learning process and was not the complete disaster that it might at first seem. If God gives people the freedom to choose between right and wrong, which is known as free will, then sometimes they will choose evil – but they will learn from it and choose the better path in the future. As long as they are open to learning from their actions they can get to heaven.

Augustinian theodicy

Saint Augustine offered an alternative explanation (theodicy) to the problem of evil, which starts with the understanding that God made a perfect Creation as recorded in Genesis. There is no evil in God's creation. Augustine argues that evil is in fact the absence of goodness. Evil is when something good becomes corrupted and lacks its intended perfection. Augustine explains that when Adam and Eve make a bad use of their free will in the Garden of Eden by eating the fruit that God told them not to, evil enters the perfectly good creation.

So it is through human free will that evil comes into existence. This is known as the Fall, which is covered on page 18. This event of the Fall means that all humans inherit a sinful nature described as original sin. God does not intervene to stop Adam and Eve making their bad choice, because by doing so humans would no longer have free will and would be like robots rather than people who have the power to make decisions.

God does provide humans with the opportunity of salvation from their sin and the possibility of an eternal afterlife in His presence. He does this through the sacrifice of His son Jesus Christ. Humans remain free to accept or reject God's offer of salvation.

♪ Irenaeus

Tasks

1 Describe the difference between natural evil and moral evil.

2 State how the existence of these two types of evil creates a problem for the Christian concept of God.

3 Summarise two Christian theodicies that respond to the problem of evil.

4 For each theodicy, identify and explain at least three weaknesses that you think it has.

5 Imagine that God is on trial for doing nothing about evil and suffering in the world. Using your work from the questions in this box, prepare a speech in God's defence and a speech to convict Him.

What do Christians today think about evil and suffering?

The different views that have been explained in this section are still found today among different Christian groups. The problem of evil is probably one of the greatest barriers to belief in God for many people. This aspect of it will be discussed in the philosophy theme about belief in God (p.207).

Some conservative Christians see suffering in the way Augustine did, as a natural result of the sinful nature of humans. In this view, war, famine and disease all come from the evil that is within humans. But this does not explain why a loving God allows natural evils such as earthquakes or tidal waves, nor does it really explain why innocent people suffer.

Other Christians see the world as a test. Human evil is something humans are responsible for and should be able to deal with, especially if they are followers of Jesus' teachings about loving others. Without natural disasters there would be no opportunity for people to show their love for others, as they are able to do when people are in need.

Others take the view that, like in all things, God has a purpose here that humans may not fully understand. Suffering has a purpose, therefore, which is not fully understood, but it is an opportunity to share in the suffering that Jesus himself experienced.

To discuss

a Discuss what suffering is represented through this photo.

b To what extent would you say this is an example of natural evil?

c Discuss whether you think the photographer had a moral responsibility to do anything more than just take this photo.

Jesus Christ

🎧 'At that time Jesus came from Nazareth in Galilee and was baptised by John in the Jordan'

(Mark 1:9)

🎧 'he [Jesus] began to teach in the synagogue, and many who heard him were amazed ... they asked ... What are these remarkable miracles he is performing?'

(Mark 6:2)

🎧 'Just then his disciples returned and were surprised to find him talking with a woman'

(John 4:37)

🎧 'Then Jesus said to her, "Your sins are forgiven."'

(Luke 7:48)

🎧 'Going a little farther, he fell with his face to the ground and prayed, "My Father, if it is possible, may this cup be taken from me. Yet not as I will, but as you will."'

(Matthew 26:39)

To discuss

a The way Jesus lived provides an example that Christians seek to follow. From the images above, what may Jesus' actions in these situations suggest to Christians about how they should live?

b Why do you think Christians today seek to follow Jesus' example more than the example of any other person in the Bible or within Christianity?

Jesus' life

The account of Jesus' life is found in the four Gospels in the New Testament. They don't give much detail of him or of his life and each Gospel has a different perspective on him. They focus instead on the things he said, what he did and on what happened to him, which made Christians realise that he was much more than just a good man. His disciples used words or titles to describe him that show they considered him to be God's chosen one. Titles such as Messiah (Christ), Son of God, Lord and Saviour show that he was, for them, like God Himself.

So for Christians, Jesus' life and example are important because they give them a pattern for their own lives. Jesus is also important because, as the Son of God, his death is the sacrifice that provides the means by which humans can be brought back into the relationship with God, which was broken by the sinful behaviour both of Adam and Eve and of humans throughout history.

🎧 'Without the shedding of blood there is no forgiveness of sins'
(Hebrews 9:22)

Jesus as the Son of God

Christians believe that Jesus was God incarnated, which means God in human form. Christians believe that his conception was not natural, but that he was conceived by the Holy Spirit. This means that Jesus was not formed like any other human as the result of sexual intercourse. Instead, Christians believe that the Holy Spirit caused Mary to become pregnant without the need for a human father. The Old Testament contains prophecies about God coming to Earth – Jesus' miraculous conception and birth fulfil these prophecies.

Jesus as the Messiah

Jesus is often referred to as the 'Messiah', which means anointed one. Kings were anointed with oil to show they had been chosen by God, so by using the title Messiah, Christians are referring to Jesus as King or Lord. They believe he was sent by God to be the saviour of humanity.

The Jews had been waiting a long time for the arrival of the Messiah. They had many different ideas about what he would be like, but most Jews hoped he'd be like one of the old kings of Israel. Many Jews expected that he would help them to fight and destroy the Romans. Jesus is anointed with oil in Mark 14:3–9 and in Caesarea Philippi Jesus is called the Christ (Mark 8:27). This is significant to Christians because whilst Jesus' life fulfilled the Old Testament prophecies he came as the Messiah for all people, not just the Jews. His kingdom and rule was not a military one but a spiritual one, through his life Christians believe their relationship with God can be restored and he can then rule in their hearts and lives.

Jesus as Lord and Saviour

Christians refer to Jesus as their saviour. The Bible teaches that after the Fall, the relationship between humans and God was broken, and since then all humans have been born with original sin. Jesus was sent to Earth by God the Father to take the punishment for all human sin and to restore the broken relationship between God and humanity. In the book of Romans it says that the punishment for sin is death. Jesus therefore came to Earth to die and his death was enough to pay for all human sin. His death was sufficient payment for human sin because he himself was perfect and was not affected by original sin.

Jesus didn't just die for human sin but he was also able to beat death and return to life. He had the power to do this because, as God in human form, he was not just fully human, he was also fully God.

The result of Jesus' death and resurrection was forgiveness from God, allowing His relationship with humans to be restored. Christians believe that Jesus has made it possible for them to spend eternity in heaven after their physical death. Christians worship Jesus and try to follow his example as they live out their lives. They recognise him as their Lord.

The Hebrew word for Lord is elohim and in the New Testament Paul teaches that declaring Jesus as Lord is the route to salvation (Romans 10:9). The title of elohim is a plural word and it shows that Jesus was one with God the Father, God the Holy Spirit and in complete control of the universe. This is significant to Christians because in acknowledging Jesus is Lord means that they recognise his divine authority and they are willing to submit to his rule in their lives.

Stretch what you know

The Bible tells us that before Jesus was born, the Jews were waiting for a Messiah to come. God had promised his coming to the Jewish people. The Jews had various ideas what the Messiah would be like but the most popular belief was that he would be a military leader or king. They hoped for a Messiah who would help them to overcome the Romans. Many Jews believed his coming would begin a time of peace. Of course, not everyone recognised Jesus as the Messiah and other people at the time claimed to be the Messiah as well.

a Read the Old Testament prophecies about Jesus in the 'Bible bitz' box below. What do they reveal about the coming Messiah?

b Research the Essenes and find out what they expected of the coming Messiah.

c How do the Essenes' expectations, the biblical prophecies and Jesus' actual life compare?

Tasks

1 State the differences between Jesus' conception and the conception of all other humans.

2 Describe the effect this conception had on Jesus' nature.

3 Why was it important that Jesus' nature was different from the rest of humanity, who are affected by original sin?

4 Explain the relationship between sin, salvation and the death of Christ.

Bible bitz

'The blind will be able to see, and the deaf will hear. The lame will leap and dance'
(Isaiah 35:5–6)

'Look your king is coming to you! He comes triumphant and victorious, but humble and riding on a donkey'
(Zechariah 9:9)

'May the kings of Tarshish and of distant shores bring tribute to him'
(Psalm 72:10)

'Therefore the Lord will give you a sign: The virgin will conceive and give birth to a son, and will call him Immanuel [which means God with us]'
(Isaiah 7:14)

'…He was pierced for our transgressions, he was crushed for our sins; the punishment that brought us peace was on him, by his wounds we are healed'
(Isaiah 53:5)

The importance of Jesus' example and teachings to Christians

The Sermon on the Mount is recorded in Matthew 5–7. It contains many of Jesus' teachings about how Christians should live in order to please God. The Sermon can be divided into six sections:

1 The Beatitudes (5:3–16)
2 Jesus and the law (5:17–48)
3 True discipleship (6:1–18)
4 True righteousness (6:19–7:12)
5 The narrow gateway (7:13–23)
6 Building on solid foundations (7:24–29)

1 The Beatitudes

The word 'beatitudes' means blessings. In this passage in the Bible, Jesus describes the attitudes or qualities that God wants His followers to develop and that He will bless. These qualities include meekness, mercy and peacefulness.

Tasks

Find out about the work of Martin Luther King, Mother Teresa or Oscar Romero. Summarise their life and explain how they demonstrated the qualities promoted by Jesus in the Beatitudes.

'Jesus said:

"Blessed are the poor in spirit,
for theirs is the kingdom of heaven.

Blessed are those who mourn,
for they will be comforted.

Blessed are the meek,
for they will inherit the earth.

Blessed are those who hunger and thirst for righteousness,
for they will be filled.

Blessed are the merciful,
for they will be shown mercy.

Blessed are the pure in heart,
for they will see God.

Blessed are the peacemakers,
for they will be called children of God.

Blessed are those who are persecuted because of righteousness, for theirs is the kingdom of heaven.

"Blessed are you when people insult you, persecute you and falsely say all kinds of evil against you because of me. Rejoice and be glad, because great is your reward in heaven, for in the same way they persecuted the prophets who were before you."'

(Matthew 5:3–12)

In the first three Beatitudes Jesus is helping his followers to see that by knowing their needs they are able to be better, truer people. They will be more open to God, knowing their needs and being able to receive from Him. They are then, in turn, better able to share God's love through their actions, as they care for others. An example of a Christian who clearly demonstrated these qualities is Mother Teresa and her work in the slums of Kolkata.

Beatitudes four to seven all focus on searching for God and truth and righteousness. Seeking to be 'pure in heart' means to be God-focused in all you do, and not to be distracted by selfishness. Martin Luther King's work to bring about equality in America is a good example of this quality.

The final Beatitudes concentrate on suffering as a result of doing what is right in the eyes of God. If a Christian suffers because they are being faithful to God, they are 'happy' because they are being true to themselves and living with integrity. This is, however, not an easy thing to do, but it will be rewarded in heaven.
An example of a Christian who suffered for doing what was right is Oscar Romero. He stood up for the poor in El Salvador, but was assassinated for taking this stand.

2 Jesus and the law

Moses originally brought the law of God to the Israelites. Jesus' teaching does not replace this law but it changes the way that believers should understand it. Jesus was teaching that obedience to the law must come from a person's heart. He looks at how what a person is thinking is as bad as the actions a person does. The reason for this is that God knows all our thoughts as well as our deeds, and also because it is a person's thinking and emotions that will then influence their actions. For example, in verses 21–26 Jesus considers the command 'do not murder.' Jesus explains that anger that is about hate for someone else is as unacceptable as murder. In the same way that murder robs a human of their God-given value, so does anger. Anger may also lead to murder and so Jesus condemns it.

Jesus also addresses the issue of adultery in this section of the sermon (5:27–30). In the same way that an inner feeling can lead to murder so, Jesus says, lust can lead to adultery. Lust means wanting to use someone's body for sexual pleasure, rather than loving them completely. It focuses on physical pleasure rather than the whole of a relationship. Adultery is the act of having a sexual relationship with someone other than one's husband or wife, which is damaging to the trust in a marriage and goes against God's commands. Jesus says lust is the act of committing 'adultery in the heart.'

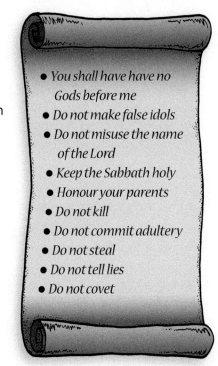

- *You shall have have no Gods before me*
- *Do not make false idols*
- *Do not misuse the name of the Lord*
- *Keep the Sabbath holy*
- *Honour your parents*
- *Do not kill*
- *Do not commit adultery*
- *Do not steal*
- *Do not tell lies*
- *Do not covet*

🎧 God gave Moses the ten commandments, but Jesus taught that it was thoughts as well as actions that were important

Divorce

'It has been said, "Anyone who divorces his wife must give her a certificate of divorce." But I tell you that anyone who divorces his wife, except for sexual immorality, makes her the victim of adultery, and anyone who marries a divorced woman commits adultery.'

(Matthew 5:31–32)

Oaths

'Again, you have heard that it was said to the people long ago, "Do not break your oath, but fulfil to the Lord the vows you have made." But I tell you, do not swear an oath at all: either by heaven, for it is God's throne; or by the earth, for it is his footstool; or by Jerusalem, for it is the city of the Great King. And do not swear by your head, for you cannot make even one hair white or black. All you need to say is simply "Yes" or "No"; anything beyond this comes from the evil one.'

(Matthew 5:33–37)

Revenge and love for enemies

In the final section of the Sermon that is concerned with the law, Jesus presents a challenging interpretation to the law of Moses, based on love. In this section Jesus tells his followers not just to love their neighbours – that is, those people they are on good terms with – but also to love their enemies. In the Old Testament

To discuss 💬

Explain what you think Jesus is teaching about divorce and oaths in this section of the Sermon on the Mount.

the Israelites were told not to 'bear grudges' (Leviticus 19:18). All humans are made in God's image according to Christianity; every human therefore has the capacity to sin and the need to be loved and forgiven. Jesus extends this to include a person's enemies. Jesus demonstrates exactly this love when he is prepared to die on the cross for human sinfulness. Other Christians throughout history have also put this love into practice. For example, Christian communities in Rwanda restoring relationships with those who participated in mass killings during the attempted genocide in 1994.

3 True discipleship (5:1–18)

In this section, Jesus focuses on what it means to be a true follower. He dismisses outward acts of religion that are done for show in order that others may think a person is righteous. He gives examples of those who tell others about their own goodness of giving to the needy, or who pray so that everyone can see them. Instead, Jesus requires true disciples to be sincere in all they do, keeping their fasting and charity private, known only to themselves and God. In this way they are not doing things to receive praise from humans, instead they are doing them to serve and please God.

> **To discuss**
>
> Christians pray for forgiveness as they themselves forgive others.
>
> a Read what Jesus says about forgiveness in Matthew 18:21–35.
>
> b Explain what Jesus means in this section of teaching.

'This, then, is how you should pray:

Our Father in heaven,
hallowed be your name,
your kingdom come,
your will be done,
on earth as it is in heaven.
Give us today our daily bread.
And forgive us our debts,
as we also have forgiven our debtors.
And lead us not into temptation,
but deliver us from the evil one.

For if you forgive other people when they sin against you, your heavenly Father will also forgive you. But if you do not forgive others their sins, your Father will not forgive your sins.'

(Matthew 6:9–15)

Jesus wants people's prayers to be straight and to the point, not ornate and complicated as if such things will make a person more spiritual. He gives a pattern for prayer in what is now known as the **Lord's Prayer**.

This is a prayer that many Christians continue to use today, but the Lord's Prayer also offers a structure for believers to base their own prayers on. It starts with worship of God, then it moves on to request that God meet their daily needs. This is not about praying for what a person wants, or worrying about the next day, it is about simply trusting God for the present. Next, Jesus includes a section of repentance and asking for God's forgiveness. The forgiveness being asked for should also be reflected in the believer's own life, as they should have forgiven others around them who have upset them or who owe them.

4 True righteousness (6:19–7:12)

Wealth (6:19–24)

In this section, Jesus requires his followers to take seriously their commitment to the faith. He warns believers not to build up treasures on Earth or to worry about their earthly needs; instead he wants them to have faith that God will provide for them.

Jesus teaches that true riches are spiritual 'treasures', which cannot be destroyed by moths or even stolen by other people. The qualities that he has presented in the Beatitudes represent some of these 'heavenly treasures'. Jesus wants believers to understand that a person cannot worship both God and money. Either God is whom they worship, in which case worldly wealth should not be important, or they worship money, in which case they cannot be God-focused. Jesus is not saying that money itself is evil or wrong, he is saying that the *love of* money is wrong. This is because it becomes an idol that may lead to selfishness and greed.

Judging others (7:1–6)

In this section on righteousness Jesus wants people to understand that no person is perfect and so no person is in any position to judge anyone else. Jesus teaches that if people judge others, then God will use the same standards to judge them. Unlike God, human judgment is flawed and limited; no one would want to receive such a judgement. This should be a clear warning, therefore, against judging others in this way. Jesus uses this analogy to make his point:

'Why do you look at the speck of sawdust in your brother's eye and pay no attention to the plank in your own eye? How can you say to your brother, "Let me take the speck out of your eye," when all the time there is a plank in your own eye? You hypocrite, first take the plank out of your own eye, and then you will see clearly to remove the speck from your brother's eye.'

(Matthew 7:3–5)

His point is clear: until a person is perfect, they are in no fit state to judge the sin of someone else. Instead, a person should focus on how they can become closer to God and more obedient to Him.

5 The narrow gateway (7:13–23)

In this section, Jesus warns believers about the difficulties of being a Christian. He uses the image of a narrow gate and pathway compared to a broad and wide pathway. The broad pathway leads to destruction. This represents a life that is lived without any attention to the laws of God as presented in the Sermon on the Mount so far. While this is perhaps an easier way of living, it will ultimately not lead to God's blessing or to a place in heaven. In contrast, the life a believer seeks to follow is challenging; there may be persecution, there are God's laws and His command to love even enemies. Following this narrow pathway is difficult during the time the believer lives on this Earth but it will lead to rewards in heaven, which will be eternal.

To discuss

'Has someone wronged you recently? Resist the urge to judge that person. Instead, pray that God might use you to reach the offender.'

(Warren Wiersbe)

How does what Warren Wiersbe says link up with the teaching of Jesus in the Sermon on the Mount?

Tasks

'Jesus says "Not everyone who says to me, 'Lord, Lord,' will enter the kingdom of heaven, but only the one who does the will of my Father who is in heaven."'

(Matthew 7:21)

Explain what you think Jesus meant when he said this. Can you link it to any other sections of the teachings in the Sermon on the Mount?

6 Building on solid foundations (7:24–29)

'"Therefore everyone who hears these words of mine and puts them into practice is like a wise man who built his house on the rock. The rain came down, the streams rose, and the winds blew and beat against that house; yet it did not fall, because it had its foundation on the rock. But everyone who hears these words of mine and does not put them into practice is like a foolish man who built his house on sand. The rain came down, the streams rose, and the winds blew and beat against that house, and it fell with a great crash."

When Jesus had finished saying these things, the crowds were amazed at his teaching, because he taught as one who had authority, and not as their teachers of the law.'

(Matthew 7:24–29)

Jesus' example

Jesus' example and teachings are central to Christian beliefs because it is through Jesus that God chose to reveal Himself in physical form. Through Jesus' life and teaching Christians are able to see how they should try live in obedience to God. Jesus spent time with those whom the rest of society rejected or who were considered worthless. Jesus himself declared that these were whom he came for when he said, 'I have not come to call respectable people, but outcasts' (Mark 2:17). Jesus was demonstrating that God's kingdom was open to anyone. Christians believe that God values all people and that a relationship with Him is possible for anyone. Jesus demonstrated this by his actions and not just by his preaching. He ate with unpopular tax collectors (Luke 19:1–10), he helped people with leprosy (Matthew 8:3) and he forgave prostitutes (John 8). Christians understand that they too must care for those in society who are rejected.

Jesus often helped people in need. Often he did miraculous things, such as healing the sick, raising the dead and feeding the hungry. He commanded his twelve disciples to go and do the same (Matthew 10:8). Christians today continue to work to respond to the needs of people. This may be through providing a service, such as visiting the sick, getting involved in local **food banks** or perhaps volunteering in a soup kitchen.

Jesus' actions were accompanied by his teachings. He said that the greatest commandment was to:

'Love the Lord your God with all your heart and with all your soul and with all your mind.' This is the first and greatest commandment. And the second is: 'Love your neighbour as yourself.'

(Matthew 22:37–38)

Jesus' teaching centres around sacrificial love, which is love that places God, others, and even enemies, above yourself. The word used in the New Testament for this kind of love is **agape**. It is a sacrificial love that voluntarily suffers discomfort, and even death for the benefit of other people without expecting anything in return.

Tasks

In this section (7:24–29), the rock represents the teachings of Jesus in the Sermon on the Mount.

1 Summarise the teachings of Jesus in the Sermon on the Mount.

2 Provide two examples of how Jesus' teachings in the Sermon on the Mount could be applied in the world today.

3 Why do you think Jesus' teaching, especially in this sermon, is so important to Christians today?

4 'Jesus' teachings are too unrealistic to be of any use in the modern world.' Discuss this statement. Consider different perspectives. You must include Christian views as well as your own opinion.

How Christians follow Jesus' example

Christians will show this love and practise it just as Jesus did. Because they must practise agape love, Jesus requires his followers to forgive each other, to help people when they are in need and to work to achieve peace.

Christians aim to share the message of Jesus both through preaching and through their actions, exactly as Jesus did. Jesus spoke of the coming of the Kingdom of God. This is a reference to a future time when God will reign and there will be peace, but also to the change that comes into people's hearts when they repent of their sin and place God first in their hearts. Christians work towards the creation of God's Kingdom. Jesus even taught his disciples to pray to God and ask that His 'Kingdom come; his will be done, on earth as it is in heaven' (Matthew 6:10). Christians want to share this message as they want to see people become believers and part of God's Kingdom. Sharing Jesus' message and persuading others to become believers is known as evangelism (see p.331).

Different Christian beliefs about Jesus

In the same way that the Creation stories in Genesis are interpreted differently by different groups of Christians, so it is with aspects of Jesus' life and the beliefs that Christians have about him. While all Christians believe that Jesus was both God and man, modern scientific knowledge makes it difficult to believe in a virgin birth, healing miracles, nature miracles and the resurrection.

As a result, some liberal Christians will look for the meaning behind events such as these. The miracles, for example, are just like parables and are meant to teach us about how Jesus put Christian love (agape) into action.

Conservative Christians, however, and especially those who believe the Bible is actually the literal Word of God rather than just containing the words of God, will say that God can do anything as He is all-powerful. This means that anything is possible, including a virgin birth and miracles.

To discuss

- ■ wwjd bracelets – wwjd stands for the question 'What would Jesus do?'

- a Discuss why some Christians may choose to wear a wwjd bracelet.

- b To what extent do you think referring to Jesus' example would help a Christian when responding to issues in this century, for example responding to immigration, terrorism or euthanasia?

Link it up

'When Jesus came down from the mountainside, large crowds followed him.

A man with leprosy came and knelt before him and said, "Lord, if you are willing, you can make me clean." Jesus reached out his hand and touched the man. "I am willing," he said. "Be clean!" Immediately he was cleansed of his leprosy.'

(Matthew 8:1–3)

a What does this account in Matthew demonstrate about Jesus' love?

b Look up the healing accounts in Mark 5:21–42. What more do you understand about Jesus' love from these events?

c How may these examples help Christians understand Jesus' command to 'love your neighbour'?

The incarnation, crucifixion, resurrection and ascension

The incarnation

For Christians, Jesus is not just a good human being whose example it is worth following. For Christians he is God made man – God incarnate. His incarnation means that he is not affected by the original sin that all human beings are born with as a result of the Fall. The Fall refers to the first sin of Adam and Eve when they disobeyed God and ate the fruit of the forbidden tree (see p.18).

Jesus' life on Earth provides the perfect example of how God wants every person to live. Jesus did more than that, though. Christians believe that Jesus as God incarnate was able to perform miracles during his time on Earth. Christians believe that this not only demonstrated that he was God, because he had power over diseases and over nature itself when he calmed a storm, but it provided a glimpse of heaven, a place where there is no pain, suffering or physical harm.

One of the main purposes of Jesus' incarnation, however, was to die, to take the punishment for human sin. Jesus takes the punishment for the sin of humankind and restores the broken relationship between God and humanity. The crucifixion and resurrection of Jesus are at the centre of the Christian faith.

The crucifixion

Jesus was crucified, which means he was nailed to a wooden cross and left to hang there until death. As a form of execution, crucifixion is extremely unpleasant and it was regularly used by the Romans (who sentenced Jesus to his death). It is a public death and was designed to be slow and painful so the crucified person's suffering would act as a deterrent to other criminals.

Jesus suffered the full pain of a human death, and Christians believe that Jesus can understand human suffering because he suffered during his crucifixion. The crucifixion is the low point in the story of Jesus' life because it seems as if evil has won over good; Christians, however, also believe that Jesus' crucifixion was an **atonement** sacrifice. His death had a purpose that benefits all humans; this idea will be explained in the next section.

The Old Testament contained prophesies about a Messiah (see page 26), Jesus' life, his suffering and death on the cross fulfilled many of these prophesies. The Gospel writers identified Jesus as the Messiah.

The resurrection

Jesus, however, did not remain dead. Three days after his crucifixion Christians believe that he rose from the dead. Paul records in his first letter to the Christians in Corinth that Jesus was seen alive by 500 people after his death (1 Corinthians 15:3–9).

To discuss

Look back at the characteristics of God on pages 5–6. Which of these characteristics do you feel are demonstrated by the life and death of Jesus?

To discuss

■ The women coming to Jesus' tomb found the stone rolled away from the entrance and the tomb empty

In what way does this image try to demonstrate Jesus' incarnation?

Bible bitz

'Does not Scripture say that the Messiah will come from David's descendants and from Bethlehem, the town where David lived?'

(John 7:42)

The four Gospels all have an account of how his tomb was empty when women went to embalm his body on the Sunday after his death, and that he then appeared and spoke to them. His rising from the dead is known as the resurrection and demonstrates Jesus' power over death itself. He was free from the original sin that leads to death and eternal separation from God, and so Christians believe that he was able to rise back to life. Jesus' resurrection is evidence that he was God incarnate; no other human being has power over life and death in this way.

The first Christians believed Jesus' resurrection proved not only that he was truly God and man, but also that God had approved of his sacrifice and that it was sufficient to pay the debt of human sin. Christians find hope in the resurrection, as they believe that they too will be raised to life after death to share eternity in heaven with Jesus. This is confirmed when Jesus says to one of his followers, 'I am the resurrection and the life; he who believes in me will live even if he dies' (John 11:25).

The ascension

Forty days after Jesus' resurrection, the book of Acts in the New Testament records that Jesus rose (ascended) back up to heaven:

'…he [Jesus] was taken up to heaven as they [the disciples] watched him, and a cloud hid him from their sight.'

(Acts 1:9)

Christians have different understandings of Jesus' **ascension**. At the time many people believed that heaven was above the Earth and hell was below. Many Christians at the time, and today, understand this ascension account to be Jesus literally returning back up to heaven. The account can also be understood symbolically, however. The rising up of Jesus represents his success of good over evil, and that he lives alongside God and reigns with Him.

❂ 'Now the first covenant had regulations for worship and also an earthly sanctuary. A tabernacle was set up. In its first room were the lampstand and the table with its consecrated bread; this was called the Holy Place. Behind the second curtain was a room called the Most Holy Place'

(Hebrews 9:1–3)

Certainly, Jesus' ascension signified the end of his life and work on Earth. His work in heaven continues: Jesus said he was going to prepare a place for believers (John 14:2). Christians understand this to be their future home in heaven after their death. Also, in the letter to the Hebrews it talks about Jesus acting as a high priest (Hebrews 4:14–16). The high priest used to offer sacrifices to God in the Temple for the sins of the Jews (see p.37). Jesus had now stepped into this place and no more sacrifice was needed; his was the final sacrifice. This means Christians believe they can pray to God with confidence, knowing that they are forgiven and back in relationship with Him.

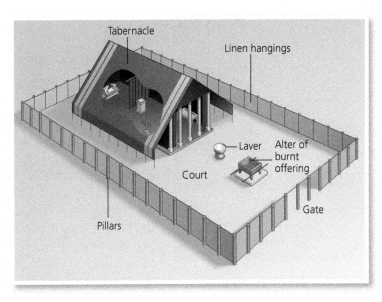

Link it up

a Look up the following passages in the Bible and identify which parts of the Apostles' Creed they each relate to:
  - Mark 15:21–41
  - Matthew 28:1–10
  - Luke 1:26–35.

b Summarise each of these Bible passages in your own words.

c Explain why each of these passages is important to the Christian faith.

The Apostles' Creed

The Apostles' Creed was formerly believed to have been written by the twelve apostles. It is now believed, however, that it was probably developed between the second and ninth centuries. It was created as a way of summing up Christian doctrine and challenging any heresies.

I believe in Jesus Christ, his only Son, our Lord,
who was conceived by the Holy Spirit,
born of the Virgin Mary,
suffered under Pontius Pilate,
was crucified, died, and was buried;
On the third day he rose again;
he ascended into heaven,
he is seated at the right hand of the Father,
and he will come to judge the living and the dead.

I believe in the Holy Spirit,
the holy catholic Church,
the communion of saints,
the forgiveness of sins,
the resurrection of the body,
and the life everlasting.
Amen.

↻ Cross signifies the belief that death was not the end

↻ Christians believe that Jesus died on the cross for the sins of all humans

Different Christian beliefs about the incarnation, crucifixion, resurrection and ascension

The crucifixion, the resurrection and the ascension are events in the life of Jesus, but for Christians the events are not just historical. They see them as having a huge significance for humans because they are examples of God working in the world. Some conservative Christians take the view that the events actually took place as described, while others may see the ascension, for example, as metaphorical. Different groups of Christians may emphasise one of these events more than others. For example, the use of a crucifix in worship by some Christians allows them to focus on the meaning of the death of Jesus and on his sacrifice and suffering. The empty cross found in Protestant churches emphasises the idea that the cross was not the end and that Jesus rose from the dead.

The concept of salvation

Christians believe that because Adam and Eve sinned in the Fall, the human relationship with God had been broken and something had to be done to repair the relationship. Humans have to be saved from punishment for their sins. The Christian message is that this saving process, or salvation, was done by God Himself, by becoming human as Jesus (the incarnation) and died as a sacrifice in the place of humans. This is known as the atonement. Atonement is a word to describe something that makes amends or pays for having done something wrong.

Atonement

Before Jesus the Jews aimed to live in such a way as to fulfil all of their religious laws. In the time of Moses an agreement was made between God and the Jewish nation, that God would care for them if they obeyed His laws. This agreement was known as the Covenant, and the Ten Commandments are part of this. As a result of sin, however, people fell short of God's requirements.

God provided a way for the Jewish people to atone (make amends) for this sin through the regular offering of the atonement sacrifice on the Day of Atonement. The Day of Atonement happened once every year, as recorded in Leviticus:

'On this day shall atonement be made for you, to cleanse you; from all your sins you shall be clean before the Lord.'

(Leviticus 16:30)

On this day the high priest would enter the innermost part of the Temple, called 'the Holy of Holies', by going through the heavy veil that separated it from the rest of the Temple. The priest was seen to be entering into the presence of God Himself. There he would make an animal sacrifice. The blood of the animal would bring atonement or reconciliation between humans and God on that day. On that day the people of God would stand pure before God, just as Adam and Eve had been before the Fall. As they went on into another year, however, they would once again sin and so the Day of Atonement had to be an annual event.

Christians use this background of Jewish practice to help them understand the significance of Jesus' death on the cross. Christians believe that the priests were temporary, standing in until the time of the true High Priest: Jesus. Jesus entered heaven, which is the true presence of God, just as the priest entered the Holy of Holies, but his sacrifice when he died was once and for all. In the letter to the Hebrews in the New Testament the writer makes it clear that Jesus' sacrifice was superior to the sacrifices of animals, and that, by the sacrifice of Jesus, a new agreement (covenant) had been created between God and mankind:

'By that will we have been sanctified through the offering of the body of Jesus Christ once for all.'

(Hebrews 10:9–10)

To discuss

a In many images artists show Jesus bleeding on the cross. Using the Hebrews quote to help you, discuss why artists may do this.

b If forgiveness for sin in the Old Testament required animal sacrifice, how does Jesus' death fulfil the requirements of the Hebrews' verse to bring about forgiveness?

c In the Old Testament regular sacrifices were made as the people kept sinning and needing God's forgiveness. Jesus' death on the cross happened only once, but Christians believe it was sufficient to bring about forgiveness without the need for any more sacrifices. What reasons can you give for this?

The law

In the past religious law had condemned people; it had shown that they were sinful and imperfect. Everyone failed to obey all of the laws or commandments. No one could meet God's standards. Hebrews 9:26 tells Christians that Jesus' sacrifice was once and for all, and that humans could be forgiven and made right with God even if they were imperfect. Under the new covenant all people could receive complete forgiveness and have the Holy Spirit live in them by repentance and faith in Christ.

Grace

For Christians the new covenant means that they no longer are saved by their own works or by obedience to the law, but through the grace of God. God's grace means that humans have His blessing even if they are imperfect and sinful as long as they have faith in Christ. This is summed up in Ephesians:

'For it is by grace you have been saved, through faith – and this is not from yourselves, it is the gift of God – not by works, so that no one can boast.'

(Ephesians 2:8–9)

Sin

The Bible writer, Paul, explains that sin first entered the world through the disobedience of Eve, and then of Adam, in the Garden of Eden. This original sin brought with it death (Romans 6:23). Humans continue to sin and disobey God, as Paul explains in Romans 3:23 when he writes, 'for all have sinned and fall short of the glory of God.' God, however, offers humans the gift of an eternal life in heaven because of Christ's death. Paul sums it up by saying:

'For as in Adam all die, so in Christ all will be made alive.'

(1 Corinthians 15:22)

Jesus' crucifixion is the key to providing humans with the redemption they need in order to receive the gift of eternal life. Paul is very clear in his writings that humans can do nothing to earn their salvation. Doing good deeds or following the laws of God in themselves are not sufficient to achieve eternal life in heaven. It is, according to Paul, only through God's grace to His people that they can be saved (Ephesians 2:8–9). It is because salvation is a gift that everyone stands before God equal; no one can boast that it was because of their righteous behaviour that they earned their way into heaven. This message reflects Jesus' own teachings on meekness and righteousness in his Sermon on the Mount (see p.28).

Redemption

Christians use the word 'redemption' to describe what they believe God has done for them. Redemption is the process of buying something back or paying off a debt. So Christians believe the salvation that God offers is actually Him offering to pay their debt of sin.

Repentance and forgiveness

Christians believe that in order to be saved, they need to say sorry to God for their sins (to repent) and to ask for forgiveness for them. They accept God's help to live a good life. God's help is brought to them by His Holy Spirit, which now lives within them.

Different Christian views about salvation

While all Christians believe in the concept of salvation and the need for humans to be redeemed from their sins, there are different understandings of how Jesus' death achieved salvation:

- As described on page 37 many Christians believe that Jesus was a sacrifice that paid for human sin. Unlike the animals that the Jews had sacrificed before, the sacrifice of Jesus paid for human sin once and for all.
- An alternate view (though similar) is that Jesus' death was a ransom, which paid for the release of human sinners.
- Another understanding is that by becoming human, as Jesus was, God also enabled this to work the other way, so that humans could achieve a union with God and this allows them to be saved.

There are also different views about how individuals receive salvation:

- Some Christians, for example Roman Catholics, believe themselves to be saved by being baptised and belonging to the Church. Their ongoing participation in the sacraments, for example the Eucharist, is key in ensuring their salvation.
- Some Christians, for example evangelical Christians, believe that it is faith in Jesus that will allow them to be saved.
- Some Christians believe that it is the way they act that is key to salvation and that by doing good deeds they will be able to enter heaven.

Tasks

1 Define sin, atonement and grace.
2 Describe the link between these three ideas.
3 Explain the way in which the new covenant is different from the old covenant.
4 What impact do you think the new covenant may have on the lives of believers?
5 'If faith is required for salvation, then Christians may not worry about how they behave.' Discuss this statement. Consider Christian responses as well as including your own perspective.

Bible bitz

'Now the serpent was more crafty than any of the wild animals the Lord God had made. He said to the woman, "Did God really say, 'You must not eat from any tree in the garden'?" The woman said to the serpent, "We may eat fruit from the trees in the garden, but God did say, 'You must not eat fruit from the tree that is in the middle of the garden, and you must not touch it, or you will die.'" "You will not certainly die," the serpent said to the woman. "For God knows that when you eat from it your eyes will be opened, and you will be like God, knowing good and evil." When the woman saw that the fruit of the tree was good for food and pleasing to the eye, and also desirable for gaining wisdom, she took some and ate it. She also gave some to her husband, who was with her, and he ate it. Then the eyes of both of them were opened, and they realised they were naked; so they sewed fig leaves together and made coverings for themselves.' (Genesis 3:1–7)

'For it is by grace you have been saved, through faith – and this is not from yourselves, it is the gift of God – not by works, so that no one can boast.' (Ephesians 2:8–9)

Link it up

a Describe the way that temptation influenced the choice that both Adam and Eve made.
b Temptation is in itself not bad. What is the sin that occurs in this Genesis account?
c Consider the Ephesians quote. If salvation was by works, what might humans become tempted to think or do? How might this result in sin?

Eschatological beliefs and teachings

Apocalyptic ideas in the Early Church

The first Christians believed that although Jesus had left Earth and ascended to heaven, he would return and establish a new world order to replace the sinful and evil world they lived in. They believed they were living in the end time, the last days of the world. The word used for this is the 'eschaton'. One of the eschatological beliefs was that of the Second Coming of Jesus Christ. This event is known as the Parousia.

As Christians at this time believed the end of the world was coming, their lives were lived with this expectation in mind. The end time was often imagined and described in dramatic and frightening ways, such as in the biblical book of Revelation. These ideas about the end of the world are usually called apocalyptic.

Some Christians today still live in expectation of the Second Coming and the end of the world happening at any moment. Others try to calculate when the world will end from what they believe are signs given in the text of the Bible. Most Christians believe that the teaching about the Second Coming and the end time is a different way of expressing the belief that God has a plan that is yet to be completed. For these Christians, living a Christian life is more important than speculating about when Jesus Christ might return and the world might end.

Resurrection and life after death

Christians believe that human beings possess an immortal soul that is distinct from their physical body. Unlike the physical body, the soul cannot be seen. It is the possession of a soul that makes human beings unique and sets us apart from all other creatures.

Christians believe that humans were made in the likeness of God, who is Himself eternal. In Genesis 2:7, it says that God breathed life into Adam. This means that humans received life in a different way from the animals, and animals and humans are therefore distinct.

For Christians, human life is sacred because people possess a soul. The Bible refers to the human physical body as being a temple for God, in which His spirit can live (1 Corinthians 3:16). Paul, the writer of the letter to the Corinthians, also explains that humans' imperfect and mortal bodies will die but that their spiritual bodies will be resurrected (1 Corinthians 15:42–44). Christians believe that Jesus' resurrection and ascension to heaven showed that there is life after physical death.

The belief in the resurrection is also an eschatological belief because many Christians believe that at the end of time all the dead will be raised to be judged by God.

Bible bitz

'The Lord God formed the man from the dust of the ground and breathed into his nostrils the breath of life, and the man became a living being.'

(Genesis 2:7)

'So it will be with the resurrection of the dead. … The body that is sown is perishable, it is raised imperishable … it is sown a natural body, it is raised a spiritual body.'

(1 Corinthians 15:42,44)

Hell

Hell is hardly mentioned in the Bible. In the Old Testament the word used is 'sheol', which is a place of departed spirits, but not necessarily a place of punishment. In the New Testament, Jesus refers to Gehennah, which is translated as hell. He also spoke of a place of punishment in some of his parables. The idea of hell developed after biblical times and for a long time Christianity concentrated on hell as being a place of indescribable, eternal torture for non-believers. The Church often used the fear of hell as a way of getting people to follow its religion. Clearly, a better scientific understanding of our world means we now know that a physical hell on Earth does not exist. There are some Christians today who do believe that hell is a place of eternal punishment, but they also believe God to be loving and forgiving. So they may try to encourage non-believers to seek out God's love, rather than trying to scare them into belief with fear of hell.

Some Christians have a completely different interpretation of the concept of hell. Their view is one of annihilation, meaning complete destruction so as to no longer exist. In this view hell is when the body and the soul both cease to exist at the point of physical death.

Other Christians believe that hell is a way of expressing an eternal existence without God's presence and blessing. These Christians see the biblical descriptions of hell as being symbolic – an aid to help people grasp a very difficult idea.

Heaven

In complete contrast to hell, Christians believe heaven means being in the eternal presence of God. This is not necessarily a place but a state of mind, according to some Christians, although the use of descriptive language often gives it a physical character.

The Bible describes heaven using many images, including those of blinding light, singing and beauty. A good example is contained in the book of Revelation 4 in the New Testament. This chapter speaks of

'a rainbow, resembling an emerald' encircling the throne of God. From this throne come 'flashes of lightning, rumblings and peals of thunder.'

In front of the throne is what appears to be 'a sea of glass, clear as crystal'. Most Christians take these descriptions as an attempt to show, in a limited way, how perfect and awe-inspiring heaven will be.

Heaven is believed to be a place where suffering and evil no longer exist:

'There will be no more death or mourning or crying or pain.'

(Revelation 21:4)

A belief in heaven encourages Christians to serve God and obey Him. It may also be a comfort in times of suffering. Christians believe that after death this is where they will spend eternity.

To discuss

Read these two quotes.

'Because of his transcendence, God cannot be seen as he is, unless he himself opens up his mystery to man's immediate contemplation and gives him the capacity for it. The Church calls this contemplation of God in his heavenly glory "the beatific vision".'

(The Catechism of the Catholic Church, 1028)

'The poet only asks to get his head into the heavens. It is the logician who seeks to get the heavens into his head. And it is his head that splits.'

(G.K. Chesterton, writer, 1874–1936)

a What do you think Chesterton means when he says that a poet wants to get his head into heaven?

b If you were going to write a poem about the Christian idea of heaven, what adjectives would you use?

c How does the Catechism of the Catholic Church help us to understand what Chesterton meant when he said the logician's head splits when trying to get heaven into his head?

Purgatory

Purgatory is a Roman Catholic belief. Roman Catholics believe that if you die in good spiritual state, in friendship with God, you will go to heaven. Many people, however, are not pure enough to come into God's presence immediately, so they will undergo purification to achieve the holiness necessary to enter into heaven; Catholics call this purgatory. 'The final purification of the elect' (people who will go to heaven) is how it is described in the Catechism, which contains a summary of Roman Catholic beliefs. It is different from the eternal punishment of souls in hell because people in purgatory know that they will go to heaven when they have been purified. This belief also explains why Catholics pray for the dead. They do not believe that when you die, you are beyond help; they believe that prayers can help people in purgatory.

Bible bitz

'If your right eye causes you to stumble, gouge it out and throw it away. It is better for you to lose one part of your body than for your whole body to be thrown into hell. And if your right hand causes you to stumble, cut it off and throw it away. It is better for you to lose one part of your body than for your whole body to go into hell.'

(Matthew 5:29–30)

'Do not let your hearts be troubled. You believe in God; believe also in me. My Father's house has many rooms; if that were not so, would I have told you that I am going there to prepare a place for you? And if I go and prepare a place for you, I will come back and take you to be with me that you also may be where I am.'

(John 14:1–3)

Different Christian beliefs about life after death

Christians have different views about the eschaton and eschatological ideas. This is not surprising as they are matters that can only be known about fully when or if! they actually happen. What Christians believe depends to an extent on whether they wish to take a literal view of the teachings in the Bible and of the Church. All Christians, however, believe and have faith that the events in the world are not random and uncontrolled but are part of God's plan, which in the end will have a good outcome.

Although most Christians look forward to a life after death in heaven, many will put this at the back of their minds and concentrate on trying to make life better for others here and now. They may do this because of Jesus' teaching in the parable of the sheep and the goats in Matthew 25 and believe that, unless they help others, their salvation and eternal life in heaven might be at risk.

Link it up

a   How is heaven described in John 14:1–3?

b   How does Matthew 5:29–30 demonstrate that hell is not a desirable place to be sent?

c   Read the parable of the sheep and the goats in Matthew 25:31–46. Explain what this parable teaches us about how God separates people to send them to heaven or hell.

d   Read 1 Corinthians 15. What is the significance of Jesus' death and resurrection for a person's afterlife?

Tasks

1   Describe what Christians believe about the body and the soul and how this makes humans distinct from animals.

2   Create a world to describe Heaven and another one to describe hell. Include Bible quotes within each world.

3   Outline the understanding of purgatory that some Christians have.

4   Explain how these beliefs of Heaven and Hell may influence the lives of believers.

2 Practices

Topic checklist ✔

- ✔ Worship
- ✔ Sacraments
- ✔ Prayer
- ✔ The role and importance of pilgrimage and celebrations
- ✔ The role of the Church in the local community and living practices
- ✔ Mission
- ✔ The role of the Church in the wider world

Key concepts

Christian worship takes many forms, depending on the traditions of the particular denomination and an individual's preference. Christians can worship as part of a congregation or individually. Congregational worship can follow a set pattern (a liturgy) or can be more spontaneous and informal. Prayer will form part of worship and is a way for an individual to communicate with God. Particular rituals (sacraments) have particular importance for Christians because they believe that through them they receive the blessings of God. This section will look at two rituals in particular: baptism and the Eucharist.

Christians also show their faith by marking certain festivals and visiting holy places, as well as by holding Christian services at important times in their own lives. Following Jesus' example means that many Christians believe they have a duty to share their faith and to try and encourage others to share it, as well as to help those in need both locally and around the world.

To discuss

Complete the first three tasks on your own and in silence.

a List all the good things about your school.

b List the ways in which you contribute to the life of your school. These can include how you treat your school environment and your attitude to others, as well as the activities that you take part in.

c Consider what you could do to make a positive difference either to your school environment or to the life of the school.

Either in pairs or small groups, discuss your answers to the first three questions.

d Produce a set of answers in your group and feed them back to the whole class.

e Now, as a class, decide on the top three ideas that would make a positive difference to your school environment.

f As a class, list:
- the benefits of completing the tasks on your own
- the benefits gained from going over the task in small groups
- the benefits of coming together as a whole class to make decisions.

Christians believe that there is value in them coming together as a community of people with shared beliefs. This is done in various ways but usually includes a communal act of worship each Sunday.

Worship

Worship is a word used by religious people to describe how they feel about and act towards God. In worship they show their adoration, love, honour and respect for God. Christians believe that worship is two-way and that through worship, God also communicates in some way with the believer.

In Christianity there are different ways of worshipping God. Worship is an area of practice where there is considerable divergence, even within individual Christian groups or denominations. Each form of worship has particular benefits for the believer or for groups of believers.

The most obvious form of worship for Christians in Britain is weekly worship as a group or congregation in a building dedicated for that purpose. 'Congregation' is the word used to describe a group of Christians meeting for worship. Christians do not worship only as part of a large congregation at church on a Sunday or other special day, however; they also worship alone and they might meet for worship in small groups. Each type of worship helps Christians in a different way, just as there were different benefits to be gained from completing the above task in each of the three ways. Christians may feel they benefit from the experience of worshipping with others who share the same beliefs and attitudes. This is known as communal or congregational worship. They might also find individual or private worship enables them to focus on their own needs without the distraction of others around them. On other occasions they might worship with a group of close friends or relations at home.

🎧 Worship in church

Communal worship

Christians usually go to worship in church on a Sunday with other people who make up the congregation. Sunday services take on different formats at different churches. There are three basic forms of worship – liturgical, non-liturgical and charismatic – but there are many variations between these three forms depending on the denomination and also on the purpose of the service of worship.

Liturgical worship

Some Churches are more formal in organisation than others and use set patterns for their services. This is known as liturgical worship. In this form of service the congregation responds to the person or people leading the service by reading set words from a service sheet or book. The service and many of the things that are said and done are the same every time the congregation meets for worship. The Roman Catholic Church, the Orthodox and the Church of England use liturgical worship. For some Christians the familiarity of the service and the words can help them reflect more deeply on their meaning and significance. There is also the advantage that nothing will be said that is different from or not appropriate to what the congregation believes.

Liturgy is not just about the things that are said and done in a service. There are also set changes to the church environment that reflect the importance of organisation and liturgy. The symbolic use of colour is important in both the Church of England and the Catholic Church and it is tied in with the Church year, during which different parts of Jesus' life and work are remembered. The most obvious of these are Christmas to celebrate his birth and Easter-time to recall his death and resurrection. The special church services or liturgies celebrated during the different seasons of the liturgical year have distinctive music and specific readings, prayers and rituals. All of these work together to reflect the spirit of the particular occasion. The colours of the vestments (robes) that the priest wears during the service or liturgy also help express the character of what it is that is being celebrated or remembered. Colours might be used in the following way:

- **White** and **gold** are used for special celebrations, like Easter and Christmas.
- **Red** (the colour of blood) is used on days when Christians recall the suffering and death (passion) of Jesus. It also recalls the coming of the Holy Spirit and is used on Pentecost and for Confirmation.
- **Green** is used during Ordinary Time, when there are no special events. Green is thought to represent hope.
- **Violet** or **purple** are used in Advent to help remind Christians that it is a time of preparation for the coming of Christ. These colours are also used during Lent, the season of penance and renewal.

In liturgical worship there are two main types of service. One is the Eucharistic service and the other is the service of the Word.

To discuss

The use of colour in the liturgical year often reflects the feelings associated with those times of year, for example joy at Christmas.

a Do you associate colours with feelings? What examples can you give?

b How effective do you think the symbolic use of colours is in helping worshippers relate to specific times in the Christian calendar?

c In what way do you think the use of colours may help remind Christians of the significance of certain times in the year?

🎧 'Jesus took the bread, gave thanks and broke it, and gave it to his disciples, saying, "Take and eat; this is my body." Then he took the cup, gave thanks, and offered it to them, saying, "Drink from it, all of you. This is my blood of the covenant, which is poured out for many for the forgiveness of sins."'

(Matthew 26:26–29)

The Eucharistic service

The Eucharistic service focuses on the Eucharist, the celebration or remembrance of Jesus' suffering and death. This is explained more fully on page 34. At his last meal with his disciples before his crucifixion, Jesus broke a loaf of bread for them to eat and poured wine for them to drink. As he did this, Jesus explained how his body would be broken and his blood shed, and he commanded them to do the same with bread and wine whenever they met together. During the Eucharist service the congregation receive bread and wine, which they believe represent Jesus' body and blood; there may be readings from the Bible, hymns and a short sermon. A sermon is a talk given by the person leading the service. At the service Christians will participate in prayer, confession and thanksgiving as they receive the bread and the wine.

Link it up

How is Jesus' commandment to his disciples at the Last Supper followed by Christians today?

The service of the Word

The service of the Word does not include Eucharist (so no bread or wine is used). The service focuses on Bible readings and the sermon. The sermon will be longer and more developed than that of a Eucharistic service.

Services in different Christian denominations

Anglican worship

Anglican services generally use the Book of Common Prayer or Common Worship liturgy books for congregational worship. The Book of Common Prayer sets out the words of the service and gives directions to the worshipers and minister. During the service hymns will be sung along with canticles; people stand to sing these. They will also stand for the reading of the creed and the Gospel reading. People may choose to kneel during the prayers; others may prefer to remain seated.

Here is an example of what might happen at an Anglican Eucharistic service:

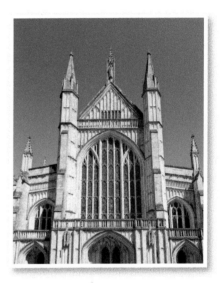

Part of the service	What happens
The gathering	The minister greets the people. The congregation might join in a Prayer of the Day.
The liturgy of the Word	There are Bible readings and a sermon. The Bible readings are taken from the Revised Common Lectionary, a three-year cycle of readings used by all the major denominations.
	The Nicene Creed: The Nicene Creed (p.11) is said. The Creed says that Christ is both human and God and the Church's belief in God as Father, Son and Holy Spirit.
	Prayers of intercession and confession: The congregation join in the Lord's Prayer, the prayer that Jesus taught. They might pray to God about their concerns about their lives and the wider world and ask for God's forgiveness for their sins.
	The Peace: Members of the congregation may shake or hold hands to show that they are one community.
The liturgy of the sacrament	**Preparation of the table:** Bread and wine are placed on the table and a collection might be taken. The money from the collection might be used to maintain Church buildings or support Church activities.
	The Eucharistic Prayer: The Eucharistic Prayer, gives thanks to God and recounts God's love for humanity.
	The breaking of the bread: The minister breaks the consecrated bread up ready for the congregation.
	Receiving communion: The congregation take the bread, which represents Jesus' body, and the wine, that represents Jesus' blood.
Sending out of God's people	The congregation leave the service. They will aim to follow Christ's example of love and peace in their everyday lives.

Roman Catholic worship

Roman Catholics also use an order of service, which is written in a book called a missal. Originally in Latin, these services are now said in the language of the local area. Catholic services have a similar structure to those of the Church of England. The main difference, however, is in the beliefs associated with the bread and the wine during the Eucharist. Whereas Catholics believe in transubstantiation (the transformation of the bread and wine into the body and blood of Christ), most Anglicans do not. Catholics believe that at each Eucharist service Jesus' sacrifice is truly recreated at the altar, but most Anglicans understand Jesus' death to have been a single event in time, never to be repeated, and yet effective throughout all time. This is seen in slight variations in the words used during the services. In the Church of England the minister will say 'Behold the Lamb of God. Behold him who takes away the sins of the world.' In contrast, the equivalent phrase in the Catholic Eucharist reads '*This* is the Lamb of God that takes away the sins of the world' as the priest raises the host and cup.

Quaker meeting

Quakers call their worship service a 'meeting for worship'. A meeting will last approximately an hour. People enter the meeting room and take a seat in silence. In this silence and stillness the worshippers are able to reflect, think and listen. There are no songs, set prayers, readings or talks. In this silence the Quakers believe that they are able to come closer to God. Quakers believe in the equality of all people so there are no ministers and anyone can contribute to the meeting.

During worship people may choose to speak, pray or read aloud. When someone does this it is called ministry. Ministry is listened to, in silence, by all who have gathered. In the meeting room there are Bibles available if people want to turn to them. There is also a small booklet called 'Advices and Queries', which contains insights and questions. Quakers will often read this. The meeting comes to an end when two Quakers shake hands. The rest of those gathered will then begin to shake hands with those around them.

Greek Orthodox

In Greek Orthodox churches, Eucharist is usually called the Divine Liturgy. The service lasts about an hour and a half and is separated into two major sections. Both parts of the liturgy involve a procession. At the Little Entrance the Book of the Gospels is carried into the sanctuary and at the Great Entrance the bread and wine are carried to the altar for the Prayer of Consecration and Holy Communion.

The first section of the service is called the 'Liturgy of the Word'. It contains hymns, prayers and a reading from the Bible set for that day. This is then followed by the 'Liturgy of the Faithful'. This is because, historically, only baptised believers were allowed to participate in this part of the worship. In this section the Nicene Creed is said by the whole congregation, and after further hymns and the reciting of the Lord's Prayer, the bread and the wine are consecrated.

The Orthodox Church emphasises the role of the Holy Spirit in the Divine Liturgy. During the 'Prayer of Consecration', God the Father is called upon to send down his Holy Spirit to bring about the change of the bread and wine into the body and blood of Christ.

The bread is soaked in the wine and distributed to the believers on a spoon. At the end of the liturgy bread that has been blessed is often given out to the congregation, and non-Orthodox believers are invited to share in this. This is a symbol of wider Christian fellowship.

Methodist worship

Methodist worship also follows a liturgy and the services are very similar to those of the Anglican Church. Some Methodist churches, however, may follow a less structured service. The Church publishes its own hymn book; the most recent one is called *Singing the Faith*. The Sunday Bible readings are usually taken from the *Revised Common Lectionary*. Eucharist is called the Service of the Table in the liturgy, but generally it is referred to as communion. Methodists practise open communion. This means that all people are welcome to participate in the communion. This is based on the belief that it is Christ's Table, not the Methodists' Table. The communion is led by the minister but he can be assisted by lay members of the Church. The wine is usually distributed in small individual glasses and small circular wafers may be used instead of bread. (Most Methodist churches serve grape juice rather than wine to show resistance against alcohol abuse.) Methodist churches tend to celebrate communion once a month.

Non-liturgical services

Other church services are non-liturgical, which means they may be more spontaneous and have little pre-organised structure. There will be a person known as the minister who leads the service, but anyone in the congregation might be invited to pray in their own way, choose a hymn or reading, or to preach the sermon. This form of worship is most common in Protestant and non-conformist Churches, for example Baptist, United Reformed, Presbyterian or Methodist Churches. For these Christians, a less formal kind of worship ensures they do not become stuck in a worship 'rut', always saying or doing the same things without thinking about what they really mean. The focus of these services helps to reinforce the importance of the Bible as the authoritative Word of God. The sermon will be the focus of the service and will help the congregation understand the message of the Bible, the Word of God and its application to their daily lives.

Charismatic worship

Some Christians today believe that it is possible to experience the same gifts of the Holy Spirit as the apostles did on the day of Pentecost, as recorded in the book of Acts (Acts 2:1–11). Before that day the apostles, Jesus' followers, had been frightened to speak openly about what they believed had happened to Jesus after his death. On the day of Pentecost (a Jewish feast day) they had powerful experiences of the power of God, the Holy Spirit,

which gave them the strength to go out and speak, in languages that they had not previously known, about what Jesus meant for them and how he had been raised from the dead. Charismatic Christians believe they receive similar gifts of the Spirit that can be used in worship, including speaking in tongues (glossolalia), prophecy and healing. Speaking in tongues takes different forms. A person may, for example, begin to talk in a different way and this may be believed to be a special communication with God.

This form of worship is known as charismatic worship. The word 'charismatic' originates from the Greek word for gifts and is a reference to the gifts of the Holy Spirit.

This type of worship does not follow a set pattern and often includes dancing, clapping and people raising their hands in the air as part of their worship to God. Worshippers seek to be open to the Holy Spirit and to be led by him during the service. This could mean that a person in the congregation feels it is the right moment for them to say a special prayer or for a hymn of praise or for a period of silent reflection. This form of worship can be found across all denominations but is most regularly found in its enthusiastic and lively form in Pentecostal Churches.

Individual worship

Often Christians will spend some time each day in their own private worship. This quiet time might include prayer and Bible reading with the help of a study book. Bible study books usually have a suggested reading for the day and then an explanation of the meaning of that particular biblical passage. They might also contain questions relating to the reading for people to think through on their own or within a group. Using another book alongside the Bible can help Christians to understand it or their faith better. Individual worship is important to believers because it is their way of developing their relationship with God. They are able to study the Bible and to seek God's specific guidance for them in their own lives.

To discuss

Explain the way in which personal prayer is an important part of the faith of Christians.

Bible bitz

'God is spirit, and his worshippers must worship in the Spirit and in truth.'

(John 4:24)

'For those who are led by the Spirit of God are the children of God.'

(Romans 8:14)

Link it up

Explain why the belief of the presence of the Holy Spirit leading their worship, is so important to some Christians.

Sacraments

A sacrament is a ritual through which the grace (or blessings) of God can be received. In the Anglican Book of Common Prayer, the meaning of the word 'sacrament' is explained as an outward and visible sign of an inward and spiritual grace given to Christians.

In the view of the Roman Catholic Church, as long as a sacrament is performed by a priest and according to the agreed practice of the Church, it gives the grace of God to the person, regardless of the faith of the person.

The Roman Catholic Church believes there to be seven sacraments:

● Baptism
● Eucharist (also known in some Churches as Holy Communion)
● Confirmation
● Reconciliation
● Marriage
● Holy Orders
● Anointing of the sick.

The Orthodox Church also regards these as sacraments, although they are sometimes called 'Holy Mysteries'. The Protestant Churches, including the Church of England, only recognise two sacraments. These are known as the Sacraments of the Gospel: baptism and the Eucharist. It is because these two sacraments have a direct link to Jesus that they are the only two recognised by some Churches. Not all denominations, for example Baptists, use the term sacrament to describe these two rituals – they prefer to call them ordinances, as they were ordained (established) by Jesus.

The Eucharist

In the previous section you read about the Eucharist. This began when Jesus, at the last meal with his disciples before his crucifixion, told them that when they met together they should share bread and wine in memory of his body being broken and blood spilled on the cross. It is because these two sacraments have a direct link to Jesus that they are the only two recognised by some Churches. Now in Eucharistic services, congregations share bread and wine in memory of Jesus' sacrifice.

There are differences between Christian denominations as to the way in which Jesus is believed to be present in the Eucharist.

The Catholic Church believes in transubstantiation. This means that Catholics believe that the bread and the wine are actually transformed into Jesus' body and blood, even though their appearance and taste do not change. Catholics refer to this as Jesus having 'a real presence' during mass.

A range of attitudes towards the Eucharist is found within the Church of England. For many Anglicans, Jesus is believed to be *spiritually* present in the bread and the wine, as his sacrifice is celebrated. This belief is known as consubstantiation. Others take the same view as the Roman Catholics.

The importance of the Eucharist

The sacrament of Eucharist is important in the life of Christians partly because it reminds them of the sacrifice of Jesus and the salvation they have received. It also brings them closer to the other members of the Christian community to which they belong and is symbolic of their connection with all Christians. As it is a ritual established by Jesus, it means the believer is obeying his command and is sharing in something that crosses the centuries between them and the time of the Last Supper. Having taken the Eucharist and reflected on their faith, a Christian may feel better prepared to deal with the things that happen in their life.

Baptism

The meaning of baptism

The sacrament of baptism symbolises a person's admission into the Christian Church. Water might be sprinkled over a person's head or they might be immersed in water, both of which symbolise purification and being washed clean from sin.

Infant baptism

⋔ Parents make spiritual promises for their children at an infant baptism service compared to adult baptism in which the person makes promises for themselves

In many denominations – like the Roman Catholic Church, the Orthodox Church and the Church of England – infant baptism often takes place. An infant baptism ceremony is called a christening. For these Christians it is the ritual of baptising the baby that allows it to receive God's blessing, and the baby's parents will make promises to raise the child as a Christian. Infant baptism was practised in the first year of Christian history and there is an account of whole families being baptised in the book of Acts, which probably included children.

In the Churches that practise infant baptism, this is often followed by the ritual of confirmation. Confirmation frequently happens in a person's teens, when they can make a public statement of faith and reaffirm the promises their parents made on their behalf when they were a baby.

Believer's baptism

In other denominations, such as non-conformist denominations like the Baptist or Pentecostal Churches, the emphasis is placed on the person making a conscious decision to be baptised. Obviously a baby cannot choose to be baptised, so people in these Churches must be baptised as adults. They believe that the grace of God is received as the result of their expression of faith rather than because of the performance of a ritual. In support of their view, these Christians point to the adult baptism of Jesus and others in the New Testament and to their belief that a person needs to be 'believer' before being baptised.

By being baptised, either as an adult or as a child, the way is opened up for the person to be a full member of the Christian community. In most denominations a person needs to be baptised before they can share in the Eucharist or **communion**.

However, for most Christians baptism is much more significant than simply signifying their entry in to the church community. There are some different views on the meaning of baptism between Christian denominations. However, most Christian denominations believe that baptism isn't just a symbolical removal of sin, but that it causes a real transformation by washing away sin. In Roman Catholicism baptism is believed to wash away original sin (see page 18), and is seen as necessary for salvation.

Some denominations such as the Quakers and the Salvation Army, do not practise baptism as they feel they receive God's grace inwardly and there is no need for the outward ceremony.

Bible bitz

'While they were eating, Jesus took bread, and when he had given thanks, he broke it and gave it to his disciples, saying, "Take and eat; this is my body." Then he took a cup, and when he had given thanks, he gave it to them, saying, "Drink from it, all of you. This is my blood of the covenant, which is poured out for many for the forgiveness of sins."'

(Matthew 26:26–28)

'Then Jesus came from Galilee to the Jordan to be baptised by John. But John tried to deter him, saying, "I need to be baptised by you, and do you come to me?"

Jesus replied, "Let it be so now; it is proper for us to do this to fulfil all righteousness." Then John consented. As soon as Jesus was baptised, he went up out of the water. At that moment heaven was opened, and he saw the Spirit of God descending like a dove and alighting on him. And a voice from heaven said, "This is my Son, whom I love; with him I am well pleased."'

(Matthew 3:13–17)

'"For I received from the Lord what I also passed on to you: The Lord Jesus, on the night he was betrayed, took bread, and when he had given thanks, he broke it and said, "This is my body, which is for you; do this in remembrance of me." In the same way, after supper he took the cup, saying, "This cup is the new covenant in my blood; do this, whenever you drink it, in remembrance of me." For whenever you eat this bread and drink this cup, you proclaim the Lord's death until he comes.'

(1 Corinthians 11:23–26)

'Therefore go and make disciples of all nations, baptising them in the name of the Father and the Son and the Holy Spirit.'

(Matthew 28:19)

Link it up

a Look at the quotes above. When Paul explains the celebration of the Last Supper to the Corinthians, what additional instructions or teaching does he give them that Jesus does not give to his disciples?

b In what way do you think Christians are 'proclaiming the Lord's death' when they celebrate the Eucharist together?

c Jesus was sinless and yet he was baptised. Explain why you think Jesus did this.

d What do the words of God, heard from heaven, show you about Jesus' decision to be baptised?

e How does the example of Jesus' baptism influence Christian practice today?

Prayer

Prayer is a way in which Christians believe they can communicate with God. For Christians, God is a personal God, not just an invisible force or power. So, just as it is important to talk to people in order to develop a relationship with them, Christians believe that prayer helps them to develop their relationship with God as a person.

Prayer in congregational worship

Sometimes, prayers in church services are led by one person – or by several people – and the congregation is invited to take part through set responses, such as 'Lord, hear our prayer.' At other times, the congregation may simply listen to the prayers and then confirm their agreement with all that has been said by saying 'Amen' at the end. In some church services any member of the congregation who wishes to stand and pray aloud is free to do so. Services can also include times for silent prayer, which allow people a period for reflection. In these times of silent reflection Christians believe that God may speak to them in some way, for example by helping them understand the answer to what they have prayed about.

Set prayers

Set prayers, or liturgical prayers, may help worshippers to express their thankfulness, confession and requests to God. It may be hard for believers to find the words they want to express themselves to God, and set prayers help with this. The words may take on more meaning and depth as they are regularly used and reflected upon.

Informal prayers

For others, more informal and spontaneous prayer gives them the freedom to relate to God in a uniquely individual way. This type of prayer is known as extempore prayer. For some believers this is a more intimate way of engaging in 'conversation' with God. Praying together as a congregation, whether using set or informal prayers, unites the congregation and fits with the pattern of the meeting of the first Christians, who according to the book of Acts, 'devoted themselves to … prayer' (Acts 2:42).

The Lord's Prayer

Prayer was very important to Jesus. He is recorded as going to pray on several occasions. He also taught his followers how to pray by giving them what is now known as the Lord's Prayer. The prayer includes key things that Christians need to remember when praying. It includes confession of things the Christian has done wrong, thanksgiving for all God has given them, adoration of God, concern for others, and supplication, which is asking for something special for themselves or others. In church services the words of the Lord's Prayer are often said aloud by everyone.

Bible bitz

'One day Jesus was praying in a certain place. When he finished, one of his disciples said to him, "Lord, teach us to pray, just as John taught his disciples."

He said to them, "When you pray, say:

'Father,

hallowed be your name,

your kingdom come.

Give us each day our daily bread.

Forgive us our sins,

for we also forgive everyone who sins against us.

And lead us not into temptation.""

(Luke 11:1–4)

Our Father in heaven,
Hallowed be your name,
your kingdom come,
your will be done
on earth as it is in heaven.
Give us today our daily bread.
Forgive us our sins,
As we forgive those who sin against us
And lead us not into temptation,
But deliver us from the evil one.

(Matthew 6:9–13)

To discuss

What does kneeling in prayer suggest about a person's attitude to God?

Tasks

One way to remember the pattern of prayer that is used by Christians and is seen in the Lord's Prayer, is to use the acronym STOP.

- **S**orry
- **T**hanks (and adoration)
- **O**thers
- **P**lease

Just think 'Christians STOP to pray'.

1 Copy out the STOP acronym above. Use each of the four words as headings and underneath each one either:
 - write the parts from the Lord's Prayer that fit that heading
 - or, create your own example of a prayer that follows the STOP pattern.

2 Divide your page into two columns, as shown.

Benefits of set prayer	Problems of set prayer

Place each of the ideas below into the column you think it belongs in:

- Gives a sense of unity to the congregation.
- Does not allow individuals to express themselves in their own way.
- May not relate to current issues in the life of the church or individuals.
- Gives people the words to say if they find praying aloud difficult.

Add other ideas to each column if you can.

3 Using the ideas from the task above, explain whether you think it is helpful for Christians to have set words to say for prayer.

Individual prayer and private worship

Christians will often spend time alone in silent reflection, being still and calm and considering what they believe God is saying to them. This period of quiet reflection gives Christians the opportunity to feel at peace. Some might describe it as an opportunity to listen to the voice of God. Private worship is therefore important to many Christians because it helps them develop a close and personal relationship with God.

Christians will often use their individual or private prayers to pray for people whom they know, or for charitable work in which they have a particular interest. Christians may also be aware of how God is working in their own lives day by day so they can respond to Him with personal thanks and praise. They might seek God's help, guidance or encouragement for particular challenges in their own lives, too – issues that are not relevant to everyone involved in public worship at a church service. For example, a person considering a change of career might seek God's help in guiding them to the right decision. By regularly praying to God and meditating on His Word, Christians' reliance on Him will increase, and their faith will be deepened as they seek His will in all aspects of their life.

As Christians pray to God, they believe He hears and responds to their prayers. In the Bible God commands His people to pray, and He promises to hear and answer their prayers. There are powerful examples in the Bible that illustrate the Christian belief that prayer brings about changes. It was with prayer that Jesus brought Lazarus back from the dead in John 11:42, and in Jesus' name that Peter and John healed a crippled beggar. Many Christians today can give examples of how prayer has powerfully affected situations or helped people that they have prayed for. This belief in the power of prayer is clearly displayed in the 24-7 Prayer movement (see p.58).

Stretch what you know

Catholics may choose to use a rosary in their private worship. The rosary is a string of beads with a crucifix. The beads are divided into five sets of one large bead and ten smaller-sized ones. Each set of ten beads is called a decade.

a Find out how Catholics use the rosary beads, including what is said during a 'Hail Mary'.

b Explain the link between the Apostles' Creed and the rosary.

c In what way do you think it may be helpful to use a rosary during prayer?

Types of prayer

Adoration

Prayers of adoration are literally prayers that focus on God's character and adore Him for who He is. As Christians turn to God in adoration, they are better able to keep their own lives in perspective. A recognition of His might and power in contrast with His care for each individual human can help a Christian grow in their sense of security in His safe-keeping. The Bible repeatedly speaks of God being worthy of praise in this way. For example in Psalm 48:1 'Great is the Lord, and most worthy of praise.' Prayers of adoration are a recognition of this.

Confession

So in prayers of confession people will bring before God anything that they believe they have done wrong, or things they have failed to do that they ought to have done. In these prayers Christians are seeking God's forgiveness. The prayers are also a time when the believer can consider how they need to change so that they don't continue doing these wrong things. This commitment to change, having asked for God's forgiveness, is an example of repentance.

Supplications and intercession

Supplications means asking for help. This may mean seeking God's help in a challenging situation, asking for God's healing or His intervention in a struggling relationship to bring peace. Christians will pray for God's will to be done and for people's needs to be met. A prayer of supplication is not meant to be a wish list. Prayers of intercession are like prayers of supplication, but they involve praying on behalf of others in the hope that God will help them.

Thanksgiving

The Bible provides examples of thankfulness in prayer.

Christians believe that God has plans for their good and so, even in hard situations, they are able to thank God. Prayers of thanks help Christians remain grateful for God's provision in their lives. These prayers also allow Christians to recognise God in all aspects of their lives, from recovering from an illness to having good times with their friends or family.

Tasks

1 Read the next two pages and outline the different types of prayer.

2 Explain the way in which meditation is different to other types of prayer.

3 How do different Christians understand what it means to pray in the Spirit.

4 Evaluate whether a Christian faith without prayer is possible.

Bible bitz

'If we confess our sins, he is faithful and just and will forgive us our sins and purify us from all unrighteousness.'

(1 John 1:9)

Bible bitz

'give thanks in all circumstances; for this is God's will for you in Christ Jesus.'

(1 Thessalonians 5:18)

Grace

Saying 'grace' is normally associated with the Christian practice of thanking God before eating a meal. Jesus gave thanks in the account of the feeding of the five thousand (Matthew 15:36). Acts records that Paul 'gave thanks to God' before eating bread during a sea journey (Acts 27:35). In the same way, Christians recognise that all they have received, especially the food they are about to consume, is part of God's goodness to them.

In some church services the congregation are invited to say The Grace. The Grace is a prayer that is based on 2 Corinthians 13:14.

Methodist Church services are often closed with the saying of the grace. The prayer acknowledges God's love and generosity to his people. Everything from God comes as the result of his grace and Christians are reminded that their relationship with him has not been earned by their behaviour.

Bible bitz

May the grace of our Lord Jesus Christ,
And the love of God,
And the fellowship of the Holy Spirit
Be with us all, now and evermore.
Amen.

(2 Corinthians 13:14)

Praying in the Spirit

For some people, praying in the Spirit means to pray an inspired prayer, one led by God's Holy Spirit within the believer. Praying in the Spirit is also, however, often understood as praying in tongues. This prayer is usually part of private prayer, although it may be practised out loud in some more charismatic forms of worship. Praying in tongues is understood by many Christians to be a unique language given to the believer by God, through which they are enabled to praise God in a way that human language cannot. Such prayers make no sense in terms of human language, but they are believed to have been strengthened by the Spirit and to bring the believer closer to God.

Bible bitz

'So what shall I do? I will pray with my spirit, but I will also pray with my understanding; I will sing with my spirit, but I will also sing with my understanding.'

(1 Corinthians 14:15)

Case study: www.24-7prayer.com

24-7 Prayer is an 'international, interdenominational movement of prayer, mission and justice'. It started as a student prayer vigil in 1999; from there it went on to co-ordinate the establishment of prayer rooms around the world and has had people praying 24/7 ever since.

It particularly aims its message at students and young people, helping them access prayer rooms to join the round-the-clock prayers as well as to establish their own.

It also sets up 'Boiler rooms', where prayer is combined with outreach work to help the poor and needy. The idea has spread around the globe.

Find out more about 24-7 Prayer from its website www.24-7prayer.com and answer the following questions:

1   What culture is 24-7 Prayer aimed at and whom does it say it is reaching?

2   Why does 24-7 Prayer aim to pray in a persistent and focused way?

3   Give two examples from history that show the Christian commitment to prayer.

4   24-7 Prayer says that prayer first changes the individual and then the world. How do you think Christians believe prayer changes them and how may this affect the world?

Meditational prayers

'Meditational prayer' is the term used to describe time when a believer focuses in stillness upon God. During Christian meditational prayer a Bible passage may be used to help the person concentrate upon God. Jesus spent nights alone in prayer, and over the centuries many Christians have followed this example. These times of contemplation may bring Christians a sense of particular closeness to God, or in the stillness they will hope to hear Him speak to them. Meditation is a time when Christians are expectant that God will reveal Himself directly to them.

Stretch what you know

St Teresa of Avila entered into 'devotions of silence'. During these times she claimed to receive tremendous closeness to God, a deep sense of sin as well as a 'blessing of tears'.

a Find out more about St Teresa and her experience of God achieved through meditation.

b Create a presentation on your findings.

To discuss

Why pray?

Because we need miracles more than we need strategies

Because the world is a vacuum waiting to be filled

Because the 'selfie generation' is lost in space

Because we've seen the end of the movie

Because this is not the dress rehearsal

Because the poor are getting poorer

Because we're aliens in the world

Because we're too sensible

Because boredom is sin

Because he's

worth it

(www.24-7prayer.com/cm/resources/1)

a What do you think is meant by each line in this quote about prayer?

b To what extent do you agree that prayer has the power to make a difference in all these areas?

c If prayer is not communication with God, what else could it be? Can this also explain the changes that are said to occur as a result of prayer?

Link it up

a What reasons do the Bible quotes give for Christians to pray?

b According to the Bible, who is it that hears and answers prayers?

c What reasons may Christians give to explain the power of prayer based on these verses?

Bible bitz

'You who call on the Lord,

give yourselves no rest,

and give him no rest till he establishes Jerusalem

and makes her the praise of the earth.'

(Isaiah 62:6–7)

'Do not be anxious about anything, but in everything, by prayer and petition, with thanksgiving, present your requests to God.'

(Philippians 4:5–7)

'Be joyful always; pray continually; give thanks in all circumstances, for this is God's will for you in Christ Jesus.'

(1 Thessalonians 5)

'The prayer offered in faith will make the sick person well; the Lord will raise him up. If he has sinned, he will be forgiven. Therefore confess your sins to each other and pray for each other so that you may be healed. The prayer of a righteous man is powerful and effective.'

(James 5:15–16)

'the eyes of the Lord are on the righteous and his ears are attentive to their prayer'

(1 Peter 3:12)

The role and importance of pilgrimage

A pilgrimage is part of a person's spiritual journey. It is often a physical journey that will take a person to a place of religious significance. Going on pilgrimage is an opportunity for a believer to step outside of the daily pattern of their life, allowing them to set aside significant time wholly devoting their time to God. By going on pilgrimage many Christians find that their own spiritual life benefits. It may be that experience helps to bring them closer to God as the other distractions in life are stripped away. A pilgrimage may also be a physically demanding challenge and some people come to a better understanding of themselves and their need for God as a result of this. Some places of pilgrimage have links with significant events within the Christian faith, or Christians from the past. Travelling to these places can be an intensely spiritual experience, believers may experience a real sense of awe and wonder or a fresh revelation of God.

Lourdes

In 1858 in France, a fourteen-year-old girl named Bernadette Soubirous claimed to have visions of the Virgin Mary near Lourdes, in a sheltered area of a cliff known as the Grotto of Massabielle. In these visions the Virgin predicted that a water spring would appear in the grotto, and it did. The spring was soon reported to have healing powers and a Roman Catholic church, called the Basilica of Our Lady of the Rosary, was built at Lourdes.

Lourdes has since become a place of pilgrimage, with many millions of people visiting every year. Many pilgrims travel to Lourdes praying for healing. Over 7,000 healings have been registered with the Catholic Medical Bureau at Lourdes, and 69 have been confirmed by the Church as miracles. Pilgrims may not always be seeking physical healing; spiritual healing is as important as physical healing to Christians. Pilgrims who spend time at Lourdes may feel their faith and relationship with God is strengthened and restored.

Jerusalem

Many Christians choose to go on pilgrimage to Jerusalem. Jerusalem is where Jesus lived towards the end of his life and it is where he died, was buried and was seen alive after his resurrection. It therefore has very special significance to Christians. For many, pilgrimage to Jerusalem helps the Bible come to life and enables them to reflect more deeply on their faith.

Some Christians will time their pilgrimage to coincide with the celebration of Easter. On Good Friday they may walk along the Via Dolorosa, 'the way of sorrows'. This route is believed to be the way that Jesus himself travelled to his crucifixion. Another focal point for pilgrims in Jerusalem is the Church of the Holy Sepulchre. This has been built over the spot where the tomb of Jesus is believed to have been. Many pilgrims pour oil on the Stone of Unction and then rub this off on a handkerchief to take home as a relic. The Stone of Unction is the stone on which Jesus' body is believed to have been laid and washed after his crucifixion.

Walsingham

Walsingham is a small village in Norfolk and it was here that, in the eleventh century, the Lady of the Manor in Walsingham had a vision of the Virgin Mary's home in Nazareth. The Lady of the Manor, Richeldis de Faverches, was told in her vision to have the Virgin's home built according to how she saw it in her vision.

In 1169 Augustinian monks became responsible for the care of this site. It became a shrine – a special place for pilgrims to visit. The statue of the Virgin Mary that was created for the shrine, known as Our Lady of Walsingham, and a bottle that was said to contain milk from Mary's breasts became focal points for many pilgrims. Many miracles were claimed to have taken place at the shrine. The site became known as 'England's Nazareth'. The original shrine was destroyed in 1538 but was restored by the Church in 1897. Today there is a carving of the Virgin within the house of Mary at Walsingham. Every day there are Eucharist services and evening prayers. In 1991 Richeldis House opened to provide increased accommodation for those coming on pilgrimage to the site.

Rome

Vatican City, in Rome, is the headquarters of the Roman Catholic Church. Vatican City itself is the smallest state in the world. St Peter's, the largest Christian Church in the world, is built above what is believed to be the remains of St Peter, a disciple of Jesus who became one of the most important leaders of the first Christians.

There is a myth that says that while fleeing persecution in Rome, Peter had a vision of Jesus. In this vision Peter asked Jesus where he was going, and Jesus told him that he was 'going to be crucified again'. Peter was ashamed and realised he should not flee the persecution in Rome. He therefore returned to Rome and requested to be crucified upside down, not wanting to have the same death as Jesus. St Paul, another influential early Christian, is also believed to have been executed by the Romans in Rome. Another reason Rome is important as a place of pilgrimage is because it is the home of the Pope, the head of the Roman Catholic Church. Pilgrims to Vatican City may visit holy sites and take part in a mass led by the Pope.

Tasks

1 What factors do you think a person may consider when deciding where to go on pilgrimage?

2 Explain the ways in which a pilgrimage may help a person's spiritual development. Use examples from the pilgrimages above to demonstrate the points that you make.

3 Do you think that it is necessary to go on a physical journey in order to complete a pilgrimage?

Celebrations

Advent and Christmas

Christians celebrate Jesus' birth at Christmas. The accounts of his birth are given in the Gospels of Matthew and Luke. In these accounts Jesus' conception is miraculous, because Mary was a virgin. Matthew records the coming of wise men, known as Magi, to visit Jesus. They were guided to the place of Jesus' birth by a star and they brought with them gifts of gold, frankincense and myrrh. These gifts have symbolic meanings and reveal some beliefs about Jesus. The gold suggests kingship, frankincense is used in worship and so suggests the presence of God, and myrrh was a herb used in burials, which seems to refer to and predict Jesus death. Luke's account does not include the visit of the Magi; instead he tells of angels appearing to ordinary shepherds in the fields and declaring Jesus' birth to them. They come to worship the baby Jesus.

How Christians celebrate Christmas

Many Christians consider the celebration of the season of Advent as a part of the Christmas celebrations, or at least as the run up to them. Advent begins on the fourth Sunday before 25 December, and it marks the start of the liturgical Church year in Roman Catholic and Anglican churches. The word 'Advent' means the arrival of that which has been awaited. Advent in the Church marks the period of waiting for the celebration of Jesus' birth, but also for his Second Coming (Parousia) at the end of time.

Churches may have Advent wreaths with four candles on them, and each Sunday in the Advent period one of the candles will be lit. Christians may use this time to get ready spiritually for Christmas, giving time to prayer and seeking God's forgiveness.

At midnight on Christmas Eve, many Christians go to a special service of Eucharist sometimes known as midnight mass. This is a tradition in Roman Catholic and some Anglican churches.

On Christmas Day churches will hold services that celebrate Jesus' birth. These services will include carols (hymns about his birth), readings from the Gospels and Nativity plays.

In the Orthodox Church, Christmas is celebrated on or near 7 January due to historical differences in the way calendars were calculated. Many Orthodox Christians fast before this day. Many people identify the Fast (doing without food) as the period of preparation to celebrate Jesus Christ's birth. It is believed that fasting helps people shift their focus from them and on to others, as they spend less time worrying about food and use more time in increased prayer and caring for the poor. Fasting before the Nativity enables Orthodox Christians to enjoy, appreciate and celebrate the birth of Christ.

To discuss

Christmas Day was originally the date in the Roman calendar that celebrated the sun god's triumph over winter.

Why do you think the Early Church used this date to celebrate Jesus' birth?

Children are often given Christingles. Research what each part of the Christingle represents

Many Orthodox Christians attend a special church liturgy on Christmas Day on 7th January. Orthodox Churches celebrate Christmas Day with various traditions. For example, many churches light a small fire of blessed palms and burn frankincense to commemorate the three gifts the Magi brought to the baby Jesus.

Why Christmas is important to Christians

Christmas is important to Christians because it is the celebration of Jesus' incarnation (see p.34). By being born as a human, God made the way for humans to be reconciled to Him. His birth is the point in history that Christians believe gives humanity hope for a new beginning, the possibility of a restored personal relationship with God and the hope of eternal life with Him after death. Christmas is a reminder to Christians of this.

Christians also believe that Jesus will return once more to Earth (the word for Jesus' return is 'Parousia', which means the presence). As Christians have this Parousia hope, they believe that they must live as Jesus commanded them to. They encourage others to share in this faith and have this hope for themselves. Christians believe that Jesus' Second Coming will be in glory, not as a humble man, and he will judge all people at this time.

Christmas is not just a time for celebration for many Christians; it is a time to reflect on the need for peace in the world and is also a time for remembering and helping those less fortunate. The Salvation Army is very active at Christmas trying to make sure everyone has shelter, remembering that Jesus' family struggled to find shelter when he was born.

Bible bitz

'The people living in darkness will see a great light.

On those who live in the dark land of death the light will shine.'

(Matthew 4:16)

'Do not be afraid to take Mary to be your wife. For it is by the Holy Spirit that she has conceived. She will have a son, and you will name him Jesus because he will save his people from their sins.'

(Matthew 1:18–21)

Link it up

a Christmas is a time of hope for Christians. How can this hope be understood from Matthew 4:16?

b Why is Jesus' conception by the Holy Spirit (Matthew 1:18–21) significant to Christians?

c In what way does the quote from Matthew 1:18–21 link together Christmas and Easter?

To discuss

a What do you think was Botticelli's purpose in having so many angels present in his painting?

b If you were to create your own piece of art based on the Nativity accounts what meaning would you want to convey through your own artwork?

Lent, Holy Week and Easter

Easter is a significant time for reflection and celebration for all Christian denominations. It recalls how, through his death and resurrection, Jesus brought about human salvation and gave Christians hope of eternal life with God. In doing this Christians hope to grow in their relationship with God, serving Him effectively in their daily lives. As they recall the sacrifice of Jesus on the cross and his resurrection, Christians are reminded of the grace and mercy of God (see p.34) towards them and of their need to act in the same way in their relationships with others.

The celebration of Easter takes place at the end of what is known as Holy Week. This week follows the main events in the last week of Jesus' life. In the lead up to this week many Christians, including those in the Orthodox Church, the Roman Catholic Church and the Church of England, observe a period of forty days known as Lent. Today Christians often use the period of Lent as a time of fasting, when they might do without food for a time or at least give up something they usually enjoy. In doing this they are recalling the Gospel accounts of when, after his baptism, Jesus spent forty days fasting in the wilderness (desert). According to the Gospels, Jesus was tempted by Satan during this time to give up his fast, but resisted all temptations. By doing without something or by fasting, Christians are showing that they too will try to resist temptation.

Churches have special Eucharist services on Ash Wednesday to mark the start of Lent. In these services worshippers will have the sign of the cross marked on their forehead with ashes. The ashes come from the palm crosses burnt during the previous year's Easter celebration. The ash on the forehead is a visual reminder to focus once again on the passion (suffering), death and resurrection of Jesus. As the priest or other church leader places the ash on a person's forehead, he or she will say words to remind the believer of the significance of the forty days of Lent for Jesus and for Christians. For example, 'Turn away from sin and be faithful to the Gospel.' During the next forty days Christians will make simple sacrifices in their own lives to help keep God as their focus for worship, and to seek His blessing in their spiritual lives.

This period of forty days is preparation for the celebration of Easter and all that it represents in a Christian's life.

Palm Sunday

This is the start of Holy Week and is the Sunday before the Easter weekend.

What it remembers

Palm Sunday recalls Jesus riding into Jerusalem on a donkey (John 12:12–13). Although Jesus entered the city on a donkey rather than a horse – which would have been symbolic of him being like a king – the crowds welcomed him, shouting, 'Hosanna' (meaning 'save now') and waving palm branches symbolising victory. They may have been hoping that he would be the military Messiah, ready to take on the powers that ruled Jerusalem at this time. Their welcome fits with a passage in Psalm 118:25–26 that describes the welcome of the Messiah (Messiah can be translated as 'king'). According to the Gospel writers, this welcome upset many of the Jewish leaders as they did not believe Jesus to be the Messiah, and they would also have been concerned about his popularity with the people.

How it is celebrated by Christians today

In churches, small crosses made of palm leaves are given out. These are used as reminders both of the palms that the people waved as Jesus entered Jerusalem and of his death on the cross at the end of the same week.

In some churches large palm branches are carried in processions to start the service.

Why it is important

Palm Sunday is a time for Christians to reflect upon their own faithfulness to Jesus. The crowds on Palm Sunday turned out to be hypocrites: they welcomed him into Jerusalem but days later they were calling for his death. Christians may consider how they have responded when remaining true to their faith has been hard.

Link it up

a Look up and read each of these passages:
- Luke 2:1–20
- Matthew 2:1–12
- Matthew 26:17–29
- Matthew 28:1–10.

b Divide an A3 page into four sections.

c Summarise one of these accounts in each of the sections of your A3 page.

d Explain the Christian significance of each account within the same box.

Maundy Thursday

What it remembers

This is a time for Christians to remember Jesus' Last Supper with his disciples, the twelve men who had been with him during his time of teaching and healing known as his ministry. It was at this meal that Jesus washed his disciples' feet, established the Eucharist and predicted that he would be betrayed by one of his disciples. The word 'maundy' comes from a Latin word 'mandatum', meaning commandment. It is given this name to recall the commandment that Jesus gives his disciples at this meal, to love one another just as Christ had loved them (John 13:12–15).

How it is marked by Christians today

In many churches a service is held that includes the washing of people's feet by the minister. In the Roman Catholic Church the priest will wash the feet of twelve people, just as Jesus washed his twelve disciples' feet. In other churches ministers will also follow this pattern of washing the feet of the congregation. In many Churches it will be a Communion service where bread and wine are shared to celebrate Jesus establishing the Eucharist at the Last Supper and to remember his death.

In Britain, the monarch takes part in the Ceremony of the Royal Maundy. This celebration happens at a cathedral and involves the distribution of Maundy money by the monarch to senior citizens. The people who receive the money are usually chosen because of their service to their community.

Why it is important

Marking the day when Jesus had a Last Supper with his disciples is important to Christians as it is a reminder that Jesus came to serve, and that they should follow his example. By washing his disciples' feet Jesus was taking on the role of a servant, in the same way that Christians are reminded to be humble and willing to serve others. Jesus' prediction of his own betrayal and death are significant points of reflection for Christians. Jesus' death was necessary for human salvation; this is a cause of great thankfulness by Christians to God at this time.

Tasks

1 What is Holy Week?

2 What days are Jesus' death and his resurrection celebrated on?

3 Explain why these two days of celebrations are important to Christians.

4 Explain how you think celebrating Easter will impact upon a Christian's relationship with God.

5 If a Christian's relationship with God is impacted by celebrating Easter, how might this enable them to better live out Jesus' command to 'love others as I have loved you'?

Good Friday

What it remembers

Jesus' crucifixion is remembered on Good Friday. It is a time of serious reflection.

How it is marked by Christians today

Special services are held to give people the opportunity to meditate on Jesus' death and on the sin of humanity that made it necessary for him to die. In many churches the main service will begin at midday and will last for three hours, reflecting Jesus' time on the cross. This service is called a service at the cross, as though the congregation were at the foot of the cross watching and waiting for Jesus to die. This service will include reading the accounts from the Gospels of Jesus' crucifixion, singing hymns and taking part in guided meditations. In many denominations, including the Roman Catholic Church, worshippers will move around the church, stopping at each of the fourteen Stations of the Cross and taking time to pray at each one. Jesus was made to carry his own cross, and the Stations of the Cross are points at which something happened or was said on his way to be crucified. Often there will be plays about his suffering and death, called passion plays. There may also be marches through the streets with someone carrying a cross to retell the events of Jesus' passion. Many churches remove all decorations and signs of colour for this day so banners will be taken down and candles removed.

Why it is important

All Christians believe that Jesus' death was God's redemptive act. Without Jesus' death the debt of sin owed by humans to God would still be unpaid and no relationship with God would be possible. Jesus' death is God's greatest act of mercy to humanity because He buys back or redeems the human race by the sacrifice of His own son on the cross (John 3:16). Christians are able to consider the depth of God's love for humans as they recall this part of the Easter story. They will also reflect on their own life and sinfulness, seeking God's forgiveness and strength. Jesus' death is also an important reminder that God understands human suffering because He suffered on the cross as Jesus. This is important to Christians as it means that God understands the suffering they may be going through in their own lives and that He can comfort them as they pray to Him.

Holy Saturday and Easter Sunday

What they remember

While Good Friday is solemn, this next part of Holy Week is a time for joy as Jesus' resurrection and victory over sin are celebrated.

How are they marked and celebrated by Christians today?

The Church of England, the Roman Catholic Church and others keep an Easter Vigil on the Saturday evening. For the Saturday vigil and Easter Sunday churches will be fully decorated. Often the congregation meets outside the church and a bonfire is lit. A special candle, known as the Paschal candle, is brought out and the minister puts five pieces of incense on it, each piece representing one of the five wounds that Jesus received on the cross. According to tradition, nails were driven through each of Jesus' feet and hands to fix him to the cross. The Gospel of John also records that his side was pierced by a lance to ensure he was truly dead before he was removed from the cross. The candle is lit and the minister leads the congregation into the church. The minister will say, 'Christ our Light' and the people will answer, 'Thanks be to God.' Each member of the congregation will then have a small candle lit from the Paschal candle to hold this during the Eucharist. The Easter vigil is also important because baptisms happen, the whole story of salvation history is read.

On Easter Sunday candles and banners will be put back up, often there are floral displays and, in Catholic and Anglican churches, the minister will wear white. The service will be full of praise as hymns are sung celebrating Jesus' triumph over death. Often a baptism will happen during this service as another symbol of new life.

Why are these days important?

This time of celebration is the most important in the whole of the Christian calendar as for all Christians Jesus' resurrection is what enables them to say they have been saved by God. It also confirms the truth of their hope of an eternal life in heaven after they have died. Through his resurrection Jesus demonstrated that he was God. Christians are thankful to God for all He has done for them. The gap between God and humans made by Adam and Eve can now be overcome and paradise is again open to humans.

To discuss

Alpha and Omega are the first and last letters in the Greek alphabet.

a Why do you think these symbols are on this candle?

b This candle will be lit throughout the year whenever there is a baptism. Why do you think this is?

c What design would you create to symbolise Jesus' victory over death?

The role of the Church in the local community and living practices

Rites of passage

Marking or celebrating important stages in life is something that happens in many societies and cultures. For Christians these rituals or rites have religious as well as social significance. Some of the rites are also sacraments for some Christians, meaning they have a special importance as they are a way of receiving the grace of God as well as being a celebration of a stage in life's journey. The rituals and ceremonies that mark a stage in life are important to the Church community, but also to the local community. Many people who are not very active believers still want to mark their child's birth with baptism and, of course, marriage in church is still very popular.

Infant baptism

As you discovered when you looked at sacraments (see p.51), baptism is a way of bringing a person into the Christian Church. In the Roman Catholic Church, the Church of England and Orthodox Churches, parents will have their babies baptised.

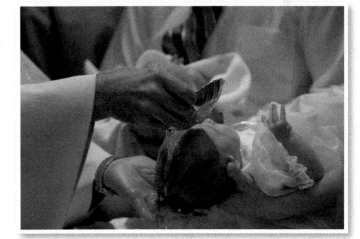

During infant baptism there is a significant amount of symbolism used in order to reinforce the meaning of what is happening. In the Roman Catholic Church and the Church of England, infant baptism involves the child having water from the font poured or sprinkled over their head. In the Orthodox Church, the child is immersed in the water in the baptismal bowl or font. This is to represent leaving behind the life of sin and entering a new Christian life. The priest says the baby's name and baptises the child in the name of the Father, the Son and the Holy Spirit. The use of water symbolises being cleansed of original sin and the beginning of new life.

Roman Catholics then rub blessed oil, called chrism, onto the child's forehead to symbolise the coming of the Holy Spirit, which will begin quietly working in the child's life. The priest may light a candle from the Paschal candle that was lit at Easter and hand it to the parents to represent moving from spiritual darkness to light. The congregation usually then welcomes the child into the family of God, reading from the liturgy. The parents are then expected to bring the child up in the Christian faith until he or she is able to accept the faith for themselves. As a sacrament, infant baptism is understood to have an inward effect upon the child, with God's spirit beginning to work in their life.

Confirmation

Children who have been baptised as babies may choose to make their own decision about belonging to the Christian faith when they are old enough. This is done through a ritual known as confirmation. Usually a person will be confirmed when they are

eleven or twelve years old, but there is no age limit. Confirmation happens in the Roman Catholic Church, the Orthodox Church, the Church of England and the Methodist Church. Confirmation is an opportunity for a young person to confirm their own personal faith and belief. Candidates for confirmation take part in a series of classes run by their church. Through these classes the young person will learn more about the Christian faith and understand what happens at a service of confirmation. In this way the young person is clear on the decision that they are making.

During the service of confirmation the candidates will answer for themselves the same questions that their parents answered on their behalf at their infant baptism. In the Church of England's confirmation service, which is conducted by the bishop, these questions will include:

'Do you turn to Christ?'

'Do you repent of your sins?'

The candidates then individually come to the front of the church and kneel at the altar rail, which separates the congregation from the more special or sacred area arund the altar. The bishop places his hand upon the candidate's head and prays for God's Holy Spirit in them. In a Roman Catholic service the bishop will also place some chrism oil on their forehead, a symbol of the richness of the Holy Spirit. The act of confirmation fulfils the promises made by the candidate's parents when they were first born. Once confirmed the young person is consciously setting out to live a Christian life.

Dedication

Some non-conformist Churches, for example Baptist Churches, do not believe in infant baptism. They believe that in the Bible baptism was a choice made by adults and so that is the pattern that they seek to follow. Parents in these Churches, however, may choose to have a service of dedication for their newborn baby. A dedication service gives thanks to God for the birth of the baby. The parents and the congregation make promises to commit to bring the child up in the Christian faith until such time as the child can make their own declaration of faith. Prayers are said for the parents of the child during this service, asking God to help them be good parents, and for his guidance and wisdom in their parenthood.

To discuss

a In what ways is a personal confirmation of faith seen as important in many churches?

b Do you think confirmation of faith needs to be done publicly?

Believer's baptism

In some non-conformist Churches, such as the Baptist Church, when a person comes to a personal faith in Christ they may choose to have a **believer's baptism**. This is symbolic of an individual's free will choice to become a Christian. The adult asks God for forgiveness of their sins and publicly commits him- or herself to following the Christian faith.

They may give a short account of how they have become a Christian, known as a testimony. The believer stands about waist deep in a pool of water in a church, although sometimes it may even be the sea or a river. Often the believer will wear white to symbolise purity and the forgiveness from sin that they have received from God because of their faith in Christ. They are asked by the minister leading the service to proclaim their repentance of sin and their commitment to the Christian faith. The minister then lays the believer fully back under the water, saying, 'I baptise you in the name of the Father, the Son and the Holy Spirit,' before lifting them back up to standing. By being taken under the water the believer is symbolising the removal of their sin. The believer being raised back up represents them being brought into a new life with faith in God and the presence of the Holy Spirit. As with infant baptism, the water itself symbolises the cleansing work of God.

Christian marriage ceremonies

Description

Teaching

At the start of a Christian wedding ceremony, the minister explains the purpose of marriage. Usually this introduction will acknowledge that marriage is a gift from God, through which a man and a woman can grow together in love and trust. The minister will also explain that the couple will come together in sexual unity and that children may be born and looked after through the marriage union.

The minister then checks that there is no lawful reason why the couple may not be married.

This explanation of the purpose of marriage ensures that the couple and the witnesses understand the meaning of the ceremony. The service is not simply an act that the couple make before family and friends, they also make it in front of God. This reminds the bride and groom of the lifelong, binding commitment that they are about to make to one another.

When someone is married to more than one person at a time it is known as bigamy. In the UK, this is illegal. Marriage relationships in the UK have to be monogamous: this means a person can be married to only one person at any one time. Christianity teaches that people should aim to have one monogamous relationship for life.

The couple exchange their vows in front of God and all the witnesses in the church. Wedding vows are promises to love and support one another in all circumstances until death.

'...from this day forward;

for better, for worse,

for richer, for poorer,

in sickness and in health,

to love and to cherish, (...and worship)

till death us do part;

according to God's holy law.

In the presence of God I make this vow.'

(Anglican Book of Common Prayer, 2000)

The vows, including those made during the exchange of the rings, break down the commitment that the couple are making to each other. They are important because they also can be referred back to during the course of a couple's married life. The vows provide:

- encouragement to stick to their original commitment to one another, whatever situation they are in
- reassurance that their partner is committed to them and has promised to be there for them until they die
- guidance on how to relate to their spouse – with love, respect and generosity.

The couple then exchange rings and the minister asks that God bless the vows they have made to one another. When the rings are exchanged the couple may make further promises to one another, for example:

'[Name], I give you this ring

as a sign of our marriage.

With my body I honour you,

all that I am I give to you,

and all that I have I share with you,

within the love of God,

Father, Son and Holy Spirit.'

The rings are a symbol of the commitment that the couple have made to one another. They act as an outward sign to others that a person is married and unavailable for a sexual or marital relationship with anyone else.

Description

Prayers are said for the couple to ask for God's blessing on their marriage and their life together in all situations. The prayers often ask God to help the couple to be kind to others and to be faithful to God, and that God will bless them with children to nurture. Hymns are usually sung during this part of the service.

Teaching

Through prayers, the couple are encouraged to rely on God and to seek Him for support during their married life. God is involved in the relationship right from the very start. Christian couples believe that by keeping God at the centre of their lives and their marriage, He strengthens their relationship with each other and guides them.

The hymns are often chosen to reflect the belief that love and marriage are from God, for example a hymn called 'Love Divine'.

The couple sign the marriage register.

Two witnesses also sign the register.

In some weddings there will be a Eucharist after the marriage service; this may happen in Anglican, Roman Catholic and Orthodox churches.

The couple are then given their marriage certificate.

This is a civic, legal requirement in the UK.

To discuss

1 How can the vows made between the bride and groom be useful to them in their married life?

2 Can you think of examples of situations when a couple may need encouragement, reassurance or guidance?

Orthodox wedding services

In Orthodox wedding services the couple exchange rings at an engagement before the wedding. This is called the betrothal ceremony. During this ceremony most rituals are repeated three times to represent the Trinity. The priest will hold the rings in his hands while pressing the bride's and groom's foreheads three times each. The rings are then exchanged between the bride's and the groom's hands three times, signifying how they will complement each other in their marriage. The rings are then placed on the third finger of the right hand. The couple are given candles to hold in their left hand to symbolise their willingness to receive God's blessing. The priest will pray for their future life together.

In the wedding service, silver crowns called stefanas, are held over the heads of the bride and groom. The crowns are then placed upon their heads as the priest joins their hands and prays for blessings on their married life together. The crowns represent the royalty of marriage. The best man may also present the couple with two crowns joined by white ribbon, symbolising the unity of the couple.

As part of the service the couple will take three sips of wine from a shared cup. This recalls the time recorded in the Bible when Jesus turned water into wine at a wedding in Cana. The cup is also a symbol of the shared life that the couple are about to begin together, with both its joys and its hard times.

They then follow the priest as he circles the altar three times, taking their first steps as a married couple. Traditionally the wedding service ends with a blessing; the priest may say to the groom:

'Be thou magnified, O Bridegroom, as Abraham, and blessed as Isaac and multiply as Jacob. Walk in peace and work in righteousness, as the commandments of God.'

Then to the bride he may say:

'And thou, O Bride, be thou magnified as Sarah, glad as Rebecca and multiply like unto Rachel, rejoicing in thine own husband, fulfilling the conditions of the law, for so it is well pleasing unto God.'

The service finishes with the exclamation 'May you live!'

To discuss

What do you think is meant by 'the royalty in marriage' as represented by the wearing of crowns in an Orthodox wedding service?

Christian funeral rites

To discuss

TOP TEN

1	**Always Look on the Bright Side of Life** Eric Idle/Monty Python	**6**	**All Things Bright and Beautiful**
2	**The Lord Is My Shepherd** Psalm 23	**7**	**Angels** Robbie Williams
3	**Abide With Me**	**8**	**Nimrod** Elgar
4	**Match of the Day theme**	**9**	**You'll Never Walk Alone** Gerry and the Pacemakers
5	**My Way** Frank Sinatra	**10**	**Soul Limbo** Booker T & the MG's

a Look at the titles of the ten most popular songs to be played at funerals. You may already be familiar with the lyrics to some of them. What reasons do you think people may have for choosing these songs for their funerals?

b Which on the left songs would you place in a top ten list for funerals? Why?

Many people will, at some point in their life, consider their own death and how they would like to be remembered. Some people even plan their own funerals, including the music, to ensure that their life is celebrated in the way they want. A funeral marks the close of a human life on Earth, but for Christians it also serves as a reminder of the hope of an afterlife with God. A Christian funeral service thanks God for the dead person's life on Earth. The mourners might benefit in several ways from attending the funeral service and taking part in the funeral rites:

- It is an acknowledgement that the person is no longer part of this world but is safe in God's care.
- They can draw comfort from other mourners, and in the reassurance that the dead person lives on with God.
- They might feel happiness as the dead person's life is celebrated.
- It is an opportunity to express publicly their love or admiration for the dead person.
- It marks the beginning of life without the person who has died, in which the loved one is remembered.

The Body of
B. FRANKLIN,
Printer
Like the cover of an old Book
Its contents torn out
And stripped of its lettering and gilding
Lies here. Food for worms
For, it will as he believed
Appear once more
In a new and more elegant edition
Corrected and improved
By the author.

🎧 Benjamin Franklin, a Founding Father of the United States of America, wrote this epitaph for himself as a young man

To discuss

An epitaph gives honour to someone who has died and is usually inscribed on their tombstone.

a Explain what Franklin's epitaph means and how it reflects the Christian understanding of death.

b What do you think would be the best epitaph that anyone could hope for? Explain your answer.

c Do you think epitaphs are worth having? Why or why not?

A Christian funeral service

Funeral services vary slightly between denominations, but there are some common features.

Bible reading – The reading focuses on the prospect of eternal life with God after death. For example, 'I am the resurrection and the life. He who believes in me will live, even though he dies' (John 11:25).

Eulogy – This is a talk or speech in which the person's life is remembered and their achievements are acknowledged, often through the sharing of memories. Close friends or relatives usually contribute to this aspect of the service. The minister will also remind the congregation of the Christian beliefs about life and death.

Prayers – Prayers are said for the friends and relatives of the dead person, asking that God support them in their time of grief and that they may have strength to move on. The dead person is entrusted to the care of God. In a Catholic service prayers will also be said for the dead person.

Hymns – One or more hymns might be sung. As with the Bible reading the focus is likely to be upon the hope of an afterlife with God. Sometimes the hymns are those chosen before their death by the person who has died, or they may be favourites of the dead person, chosen by relatives and friends.

Requiem Mass – In Catholic funerals a Requiem Mass is almost always performed. This is a mass for the dead. The liturgy begins with the request to God to 'Grant them [the deceased] eternal rest, O Lord.' In the Eastern Orthodox and Greek Orthodox Churches the requiem is the fullest form of a memorial service. It contains readings, hymns and liturgy. A full requiem can last up to three and a half hours. The Church of England does not have a Requiem Mass, but some High Anglican services will include a Requiem Mass as part of a funeral service.

Burial/cremation – The dead person might then be buried in the ground or they might be cremated. At a burial, it is usual for further prayers to be said at the graveside before the final committal statement by the minister. The committal statement is also said at a cremation as the curtain shuts around the coffin. The committal statement is so-called because Christians believe they are committing the dead person to God's care. The wording of the committal statement varies between denominations; the Church of England says: 'We therefore commit his [or her] body to the ground; earth to earth, ashes to ashes, dust to dust; in sure and certain hope of the Resurrection to eternal life.'

Stretch what you know

Some people consider the impact on the environment when planning a funeral. It is now possible to have environmentally friendly funerals, where the coffin is biodegradable and the burial takes place in an area of woodland.

Go to http://woodlandburialtrust.com and find out about:

a green or eco coffins

b woodland or green burials

c tree planting.

Tasks

1 Outline a Christian funeral.
2 Why is it important to many Christians to have a funeral?
3 Explain whether you think that a Christian funeral service is helpful to mourners.
4 How is the Christian belief about eternal life after death reflected in their funeral services?

How Church communities support families

The Church plays a major role in supporting and nurturing families. Church services mark significant life events for example welcoming new life (baptism) and celebrating people's desire to share their lives (marriage). The Church also supports families during difficult times, for example supporting families when they lose a loved one (funerals). The role of the priest or minister involves much more than taking services. They might provide support to families by visiting the sick in home or in hospital, or they might offer counselling to couples experiencing marital difficulties.

Church communities, in the sense of the people in the community who worship at the church, might also provide services to help families. They may run volunteer services to help groups such as young mothers or the elderly, providing them with help and advice and allowing them to socialise. The church may be involved with local charities and other organisations, such as providing respite care for families who are looking after ill or dependent relatives.

In the same way the Church might provide services for young people. Sunday School helps teach children about their faith and youth groups provide the opportunity for young people to socialise with others in the church community.

These are examples of Christian love (agape) in action and show how the Church is the body of Christ on Earth, acting as he would have done.

Link it up

a Explain what Jesus meant when he said that those who believe in him will 'live, even though they die'.

b How is this belief reflected in a Christian funeral service?

c In Ephesians 5, in what way is Paul talking about Christ and the Church when he describes a man and woman becoming one flesh through marriage?

Bible bitz

'"For this reason a man will leave his father and mother and be united to his wife, and the two will become one flesh." This is a profound mystery – but I am talking about Christ and the church. However, each one of you also must love his wife as he loves himself, and the wife must respect her husband.'

(Ephesians 5:31–33)

'Jesus said to her, "I am the resurrection and the life. The one who believes in me will live, even though they die."'

(John 11:25)

'Listen, I tell you a mystery: We will not all sleep, but we will all be changed – in a flash, in the twinkling of an eye, at the last trumpet. For the trumpet will sound, the dead will be raised imperishable, and we will be changed.'

(1 Corinthians 15:51)

⮑ These are some of the ways the Church might be involved in the local community. Can you identify what they are?

Mission

A **mission** is a task or a job that a person or organisation is given to do. Many organisations today have mission statements, which explain their purpose and what they would like to achieve.

Many Christians believed their mission was to take the Christian faith to everywhere in the world and convert all people to Christianity, believing all other religions to be wrong. This is known as evangelism and, while it does still take place, the Church is now much more aware of cultural sensitivities than in the past. Many missionaries, however, did a great deal of good work bringing scientific knowledge and education to less developed people. Today mission work is much wider in what it does.

> 'Let God have your life, He can do more with it than you can.'
> (Dwight L. Moody)

The World Council of Churches

The World Council of Churches (WCC) is an organisation that includes almost all the Churches in the world, apart from the Roman Catholic Church. In 1991 it said that 'a reconciled and renewed creation is the goal of the church's mission'. This gives Christian mission a two-part aim:

1 The goal of conversion. This means continuing the work of evangelism by helping people come to a personal faith in God and all that that means for their lives.
2 The goal of reconciliation. This means working to see the Christian message playing a part in all aspects of society, worldwide, in order to bring about communication between people (dialogue), peace and a world where humans can live in balance with the environment (ecological sustainability).

This approach to mission centres around the idea of Missio Dei. Missio Dei is understood to mean 'God's activity' or 'God's mission', which involves both the Church and the world, and which the Church is privileged to take part in.

The mission of the Church

So the mission of the Church will include a broad range of activities quite apart from evangelism. It has something to say and contribute to all parts of human activity. These activities may include starting up new churches in areas where there are none or where the Church seems to be failing; this is known as church planting. Meeting, talking and sharing views and having a dialogue with people from other religions is another activity. Examining each other's faith and beliefs increases understanding and helps to secure peace. The mission also includes action for justice, which can mean that the Church finds itself in conflict with organisations or governments that do not treat people fairly. The Church seeks to follow its mission because of the Great Commission that Jesus gave to his followers before his ascension. He said to them,

> **To discuss**
>
> In what way may a Christian believe that God can use their life through mission work?

'Go into all the world and preach the gospel to all creation.'

(Mark 16:15)

a What are the Salvation Army doing in each of these images?

b How is this work fulfilling the purpose of the Church as identified by the Archbishop of Canterbury?

The meaning and significance of evangelism in the modern Church

The Archbishop of Canterbury identified two purposes of the existence of the Church in his lecture on 'Evangelism and Witness' in March 2015. One of these is to worship God and the other is to make new disciples. Evangelism was one of the priorities that the Archbishop identified. Evangelism is the Christian action of sharing the good news about Jesus coming to this world and bringing the opportunity of salvation for all who believe.

The Salvation Army has a strong tradition of evangelism. The Salvation Army says that it exists to 'save souls, grow saints and serve a suffering humanity', and this is its understanding of what it means to be a disciple of Jesus in the modern world. It seeks to make Jesus known through both its actions and its message, with the intention of persuading people to become Christians. Evangelism is therefore at the centre of its work.

For many Christians, evangelism starts from the point of genuine relationships with people who themselves are not part of Church culture. It is through these relationships that many Christians seek to lead people to a shared faith in God. Many Christians look to the example of Jesus, who himself provided the perfect example for evangelism. Jesus met people where they were, met their immediate needs – such as of healing, thirst or hunger – and then called them to follow him.

Bible bitz

'And it happened that He was reclining at the table in his house, and many tax collectors and sinners were dining with Jesus and His disciples; for there were many of them, and they were following Him. When the scribes of the Pharisees saw that He was eating with the sinners and tax collectors, they said to His disciples, "Why is He eating and drinking with tax collectors and sinners?" And hearing this, Jesus said to them, "It is not those who are healthy who need a physician, but those who are sick; I did not come to call the righteous, but sinners."

(Mark 2:15–17)

'When a Samaritan woman came to draw water, Jesus said to her, "Will you give me a drink?" (His disciples had gone into the town to buy food.) The Samaritan woman said to him, "You are a Jew and I am a Samaritan woman. How can you ask me for a drink?"'

(John 4:7–8)

Link it up

a Investigate the way Jesus engaged with non-believers by reading the accounts quoted in the box above.

b What pattern of behaviour by Jesus can you identify in these two accounts?

c How can this relate to Christian evangelism?

Stretch what you know

The Church of England released a pastoral letter called 'Who Is My Neighbour?' for local churches in parishes in the lead-up to the General Election in 2015.

In the letter the bishops encouraged Christians to consider how they can 'build the kind of society which many people say they want but which is not yet being expressed in the vision of any of the parties'. The letter defends the Church's right to get involved in politics, explaining that its beliefs about its place in creation are bound to influence it and cause it to engage in politics.

Find out more about the message of the letter. This link may be useful: www.churchofengland.org/media/2170230/whoismyneighbour-pages.pdf

a How do you think this letter is advocating evangelism?

b In what way is this letter part of the modern Church's Missio Dei?

c Do you agree that it is acceptable and necessary for the Church to get involved in politics?

The growth of new forms of Church

The Christian Church is not about the building where Christians meet, but rather is about the gathering together of God's people, the congregation. This has many forms, and new forms of Church now exist. In these new forms of Church, community is often understood to be at the heart of Church life. Church has come to mean much more than simply gathering together on a Sunday morning in a church building. The word 'Church' has come to describe what Christian people are, and how they behave and act throughout the week, rather than simply being an event on Sunday morning. In this view, fellowship, sharing meals, witnessing (telling people about the Christian faith) and acts of service are as much a part of the Church as is the traditional element of worship. This approach to the Church reflects the religion of the first Christians, as described in Acts 2:42:

'They devoted themselves to the apostles' teaching and to fellowship, to the breaking of bread and to prayer.'

The first Christians were noted for their love and care for each other. This idea is shared in Paul's call to sacrificial living in Romans 12:1:

'Therefore, I urge you, brothers and sisters, in view of God's mercy, to offer your bodies as a living sacrifice, holy and pleasing to God – this is your true and proper worship.'

which calls for the giving up of things for the benefit of others by the people of the Church.

These new forms of Church may not meet in a specially designed church building; often they may meet in theatres, cafes or even in people's homes. Church sizes will vary and usually there will be small group meetings throughout the week, with friends and members often eating together as part of their fellowship. The leaders in these Churches may well not be 'ordained clergy' who have been trained and approved by a traditional Church. They are likely to be Christians devoted to living out their faith and serving God in the place where they live and in the work they do.

Stretch what you know

Messy Church began in 2004 and uses creative activities to encourage adults and children to learn about Christianity and become closer to God.

a Research Messy Church online.

b Do you think Messy Church is a better way for people to experience God than more traditional Churches?

To discuss

In what way might a house church in a café be more accessible for some people?

> 'Why can't we think of churching together as a web of relationships? Why are we obsessed with the singular event rather than seeking the rhythm of a community churching together?'
>
> (Michael Frost, Australian writer)

🎧 In what way could Church be understood as a 'web of relationships'?

Lots of the new forms of Church emerged out of the House Church movement in the late 1960s, led by ministers such as Gerald Coates. Believers started to meet and worship in their homes, led by the Holy Spirit and not controlled by the formal liturgies and ways of worship of the existing Churches. As these Churches grew and began to worship in larger congregations, they retained the importance of meeting in small groups in one another's homes during the week. In these home groups Christians may pray, study the Bible together and invite their friends to join them. Often these new forms of Church are charismatic in nature, with all members being able to take part when they feel the spirit of God leads them to speak or to lead the meeting in some other way.

Bible bitz

'Then the eleven disciples went to Galilee, to the mountain where Jesus had told them to go. When they saw him, they worshiped him; but some doubted. Then Jesus came to them and said, "All authority in heaven and on earth has been given to me. Therefore go and make disciples of all nations, baptising them in the name of the Father and of the Son and of the Holy Spirit, and teaching them to obey everything I have commanded you. And surely I am with you always, to the very end of the age."'

(Matthew 28:16–20)

'He said to them, "Go into all the world and preach the gospel to all creation."'

(Mark 16:15)

'For I am not ashamed of the gospel, because it is the power of God that brings salvation to everyone who believes: first to the Jew, then to the Gentile.'

(Romans 1:16)

'In the presence of God and of Christ Jesus, who will judge the living and the dead, and in view of his appearing and his kingdom, I give you this charge: Preach the word; be prepared in season and out of season; correct, rebuke and encourage – with great patience and careful instruction.'

(2 Timothy 4:1–2)

'But you will receive power when the Holy Spirit comes on you; and you will be my witnesses in Jerusalem, and in all Judea and Samaria, and to the ends of the earth.'

(Acts 1:8)

Tasks

1. Describe what Christians believe about mission.
2. Explain what Christians understand by the idea of Missio Dei.
3. Explain the significance of evangelism in the modern church.
4. The growth in churches in the UK is most seen in the new forms of church. Explain these new forms of church and why many Christians may choose to join these types of churches.

Link it up

a. The passage from Matthew is known as 'The Great Commission'. Why do you think it is given this title?
b. According to Acts, how does God equip His followers to share the Christian faith?
c. Using the quotes from Romans and 2 Timothy, explain why Jesus wants his disciples to go and share their faith to all nations.

The role of the Church in the wider world

Ecumenicalism and the World Council of Churches

Ecumenicalism is the idea of creating Christian unity, as it seeks to reconcile Christians from different denominations. Ecumenicalism recognises differences between the denominations but aims to bring Christians together in shared worship and service. Through ecumenicalism the aim is that Christians will have an increasing understanding of each other.

In 1948 the World Council of Churches (WCC) was set up by members from both Orthodox and Protestant Churches, including the Church of England. The Roman Catholic Church is not a member but it takes part in the key group – the Commission on Faith and Order. The WCC has over 345 member Churches from over a hundred countries, representing more than half a billion Christians around the world. Members of The WCC all believe that Jesus is their saviour, in line with the teaching of the Bible, and together they want to bring glory to his name. It is this shared foundation that enables them to work together, despite their other differences. The WCC has a worldwide vision and focuses on three areas:

1 To seek visible unity (between Churches) in one faith and one Eucharistic fellowship.
2 To promote common witness (telling people about their Christian faith) in work for mission and evangelism.
3 To engage in Christian service by meeting human needs, breaking down barriers between people, seeking justice and peace, and upholding the integrity of Creation.

In all of these areas the WCC aims to increase the strength of relationships between the member Churches. Together the WCC campaigns on key issues, including HIV and AIDS, food security and sustainable agriculture, and climate change.

> The WCC says that it seeks to: 'renew the true vocation of the Church through collaborative engagement with the most important issues of justice and peace, healing a world filled with conflict, injustice and pain.'
> (World Council of Churches)

The meaning of 'Church'

The word church actually comes from the Greek word 'ekklesia'. It is present in Acts 19:32, 39 and 41. 'Ek' means 'out' and the 'klesia' means 'call'. The church is therefore a reference to Christians, the 'called out people'. When Jesus tells Peter that he will 'build his church' (Matthew 16:18) he's not talking about a physical building but a growing body of believers. Jesus builds his church through his own sacrificial death and resurrection that creates a means of salvation.

Christians believe that the church, the body of believers, are the bride of Christ (Ephesians 5:25). Every believer, wherever they live, whatever denomination they belong to forms this one body. Jesus himself is head of his people, the church (Colossians 1:18). Baptism brings a person into this body of believers (1 Corinthians 12:12–13).

To discuss

a Do you agree with the WCC that justice and peace are 'most important issues'?

b How do you think the work of the Churches Together Movement could bring healing in our world?

85

The word church in the Bible is therefore not referring to a building or denominations. The ecumenical movement is thus working hard to bring greater unity in the church, which is the whole body of Christ.

Churches Together Movement

The Churches Together Movement encourages Churches to work together. The movement in England, for example, describes itself as:

'a visible sign of the Churches' commitment as they seek a deepening of their communion with Christ and with one another, and proclaim the Gospel together by common witness and service. Its strength comes from people from different traditions finding new ways to work and worship together.'

It aims to strengthen the relationship between the different denominations, as well as to nurture new believers. It also helps those in need and fights injustice.

Ecumenical communities

Some Christians have chosen to put ecumenicalism into practice by creating what are known as ecumenical communities, where Christians from all denominations share worship and life together. Three communities are particularly well known:

- Taizé in France
- Iona in Scotland
- Corrymeela in Ireland.

Although set up for different reasons, each encourages and enables Christians to share what they have in common and to show that differences do not mean that they cannot work together.

Taizé in France

Set up by Brother Roger Schütz in 1940 to give refuge to Jews escaping Nazi persecution, Taizé became a place where wartime enemies could put aside their differences. It is also a community where dialogue and friendship between Protestant and Roman Catholic Christians can be encouraged.

Iona in Scotland

This is a holy island that has been a place of Christian pilgrimage since 563CE. A non-denominational community was founded in 1938 by George McCleod. It works for peace and social justice, rebuilding of community and the renewal of worship.

Corrymeela at Ballycastle in Northern Ireland

This was founded in 1965 to encourage good relations between Protestant and Roman Catholic Christians ('Corrymeela'). It was founded by Ray Davey, a military chaplain who experienced being a prisoner of war during the Second World War. It is Northern Ireland's oldest peace and reconciliation organisation.

Tasks

Find out more about two of these ecumenical communities. Explain what they do and how they are helping build good relations between Christians.

♫ Iona

♫ Prince Charles and the Duchess of Cornwall visiting the Corrymeela centre

The persecuted Church

To be persecuted is to be subjected to hostility and ill-treatment, especially because of race or political or religious beliefs. Persecution can take many forms:

ISIS video shows brutal execution of 3 Assyrian Christians in ethno-religious cleansing (*Christian Post*)

More Christians shot for their faith, this time in Oregon (Christian Post)

Bangladeshi pastor survives knife attack in his home (*Barnabas Fund*)

Indian Evangelists arrested and accused under anti-conversion law (*Barnabas Fund*)

Pakistani headteacher beaten in violent attack (Barnabas Fund)

More Christians have been murdered for their faith in the past century than at any other time in human history. Christians may be persecuted through physical assault, including beatings, torture and rape, their children may not be allowed an education unless they turn away from their faith, and others may lose their lives. Open Doors, an organisation that helps people have access to Bibles, estimates that 100 million Christians face persecution for their faith in the world today. As members of the largest religion in the world, Christians are a visible target for persecution. Christians also seek to evangelise and convert those who perhaps have a different religion or no religion. This often causes offence to people of other religions and Christians' claim to the truth causes further conflict. Despite persecution, some Christians continue to live missionary-driven lives and many people are converting to Christianity in regions where persecution is at its greatest. For example Open Doors reports a significant increase in the number of Christians in Iran. Often these Christians meet in small house churches with no more than five or six members. Encouraging the spread of Christianity is banned in Iran and so believers have to be very careful about how they live out their faith in that country.

There are many organisations that exist to support the persecuted Church. The Barnabas Fund is a charity that works to bring hope to those Christians under persecution. It directs aid to Christians largely through existing churches or Christian organisations in the countries where the persecution is happening. The Fund publicises the cases of persecuted Christians through its website and magazine, providing them with a voice. It also lets governments and international groups know about the persecution. Its work includes public petitions, letter writing campaigns and constant prayer for the Persecuted Church worldwide.

To discuss

a From these news headlines, what conclusion can you reach about the safety of Christians around the world?

b What do you think are some of the causes of the persecution of Christians in the world today?

Tasks

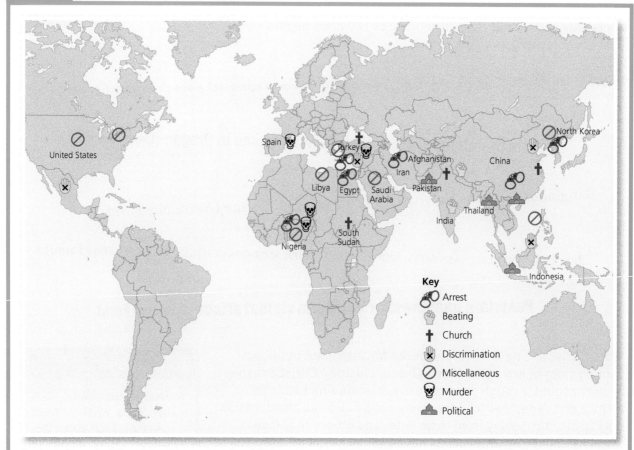

Key
- Arrest
- Beating
- Church
- Discrimination
- Miscellaneous
- Murder
- Political

1 Describe what the map shows you about the persecution of Christians around the world today.

2 Christianity is an evangelical religion. In what way may this increase the persecution that Christians face?

3 Jesus said, 'Blessed are those who are persecuted for the sake of righteousness, for theirs is the kingdom of heaven' (Matthew 5:10). Explain what he meant by this.

4 In what way may Jesus' teaching be a comfort to those who are being persecuted?

5 Choose one place from the map where Christians are being persecuted and find out more about Christians in that location. Put together a presentation for your class on what you find out.

Stretch what you know

Persecution.org is another organisation that works to support the Persecuted Church. It aims to create a bridge between the free church, which means Christians who are able to practise their faith openly, and the Persecuted Church. Providing aid, encouragement and prayer support, it helps the free church hear about what is happening to those in the Church who are being persecuted. It has three aims: to provide Assistance, Advocacy (another word for legal advice and support) and Awareness.

a Use the **www.persecution.org** website to find out one thing that it is doing for each of its three aims: Assistance, Advocacy and Awareness.

b Create your own presentation to raise awareness about one case of Christian persecution.

The work of Christian aid agencies

Christian aid agencies work to meet the needs of people in practical ways as an act of service. This reflects the command that Jesus gave to 'love your neighbour as yourself' (Mark 12:30–31). Christians believe that Jesus showed the extent of this love when he gave his own life in sacrifice on the cross. Christian aid agencies continue to love others in this sacrificial way as they meet the needs of people of all cultures, races and religions around the world. Christian aid agencies include:

- **Cafod**, a Catholic agency that works in the developing world to bring hope to those in poor communities.
- **Christian Aid**, a Christian development charity that works to get rid of poverty in around fifty countries.
- **Tearfund**, which has similar aims to Christian Aid.

All Christian aid agencies aim to put Jesus' message of love and compassion into action. They are also aware that, according to Jesus' words in Matthew 25, they will be judged according to how well they have responded to the needs of other people. Being a Christian is about belief and practice!

Bible bitz

'A new command I give you: Love one another. As I have loved you, so you must love one another. By this everyone will know that you are my disciples, if you love one another.'

(John 13:34–35)

Link it up

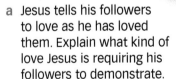

a Jesus tells his followers to love as he has loved them. Explain what kind of love Jesus is requiring his followers to demonstrate.

b In what way does a person's behaviour reveal whom they worship?

Tasks

Work in pairs for this task. One person needs to complete the tasks below by researching Cafod and the other person needs to focus their research on Christian Aid.

1 For the organisation that you are researching, you must find out and record:
   - who it is
   - the aims of the organisation
   - one project it is currently involved in.

   You must present your work in the form of a mind map, using colour-coded sections and images/sketches.

2 Once you have each completed your mind map, share your findings with your partner.

3 Complete this task by providing a written response that explains what you think of the impact of these Christian organisations have on our wider world.

Case study: Tearfund

tearfund

Tearfund works to help alleviate poverty around the world by helping local communities to help themselves. It does this by working through partner churches in the country or local area in which it is working. This support enables the partner church to help change and improve life for whole communities.

One example of this is the work it has done in Cajamarca, Peru. The work there started in 1999, when the local church partnered with Tearfund and began to teach women and children from the surrounding countryside to read and write. It also helped the local people to develop handicraft skills so that they could make and sell items. The church, through the support of Tearfund, has helped farmers cope with climate change, and has provided the farmers with seeds and ways to protect their crops. The farmers are also being taught new methods for irrigation so that they become less dependent upon rainfall. Through this work many people in the local area have grown in their Christian faith.

Tearfund also responds when disasters strike. Disasters all too often seem to affect the poor most, as they destroy what little they have and leave them with no means of re-establishing themselves. Tearfund has disaster response teams to react to disaster situations where there are no local partners. For example, a response team has worked in Sudan since 2004 because of war, drought and famine, and the disorder that has resulted. The team helps provide food aid for children, pregnant women and nursing mothers. It continues to teach about the importance of clean water and hygiene to help reduce disease. Tearfund is also involved in building schools there and helping people grow food.

Let's Revise

a Describe what is meant by the term Trinity. (3 marks)

- This question requires you to give a brief description of the Christian teaching about The Trinity.

- You can answer by making three clear statements about this belief or by developing one or more statements about this belief.

b What do Christians mean when they describe God as transcendent? (3 marks)

- This question is asking you to show your understanding of this characteristic of God.

- Write your answer in three clear sentences.

- You can include examples or develop a point in order to achieve the full three marks.

c Describe the Christian concept of God as creator. (3 marks)

- This question also requires three clear sentences, this time you must show an understanding of God as the creator.

- Your answer may include a description of how God is recorded as creating the world in Genesis 1 as well as the Christian belief of creation occurring ex nihilo.

d Explain why Jesus' teachings and life are important to Christians. (6 marks)

- In this question you must explain why Jesus' teachings and life are important to Christians.

- You might make reference to Jesus' teachings for example The Sermon on The Mount, his miraculous acts and his sacrificial death.

- Your answer must analyse the importance of this to Christians. For example you could develop the following points; Jesus provides Christians with a role model for their own lives, his teaching helps them to work out how to make moral decisions and his life was a practical demonstration of God's love for humanity.

- Take care to write in clear paragraphs making reference to appropriate Bible material.

e *'Jesus' incarnation is the most important teaching in the Christian faith.'*

Discuss this statement. In your answer, you should:

- analyse and evaluate the importance of points of view of common and divergent views within Christianity

- refer to sources of wisdom and authority. (15 marks)

Spelling, punctuation and grammar (3 marks)

- You must demonstrate an understanding of the importance of Jesus' incarnation, especially in relation to salvation.

Let's Revise contd.

- In this answer you must show that there are different Christian responses to this statement.

- Some Christians will believe the incarnation to be the most important teaching because it is unique to the Christian religion. The incarnation is God reaching out to humanity and providing the means of reconciliation, and ultimately an eternal life in Heaven for all believers. You may point to the significant celebrations associated with Christmas in the Christian year as evidence of the importance associated with Jesus' incarnation. You might refer to the story of Jesus Birth and to the references in the Creeds as sources of wisdom and authority.

- However, other Christians may argue that the teaching of the Trinity is the most important Christian belief as this makes sense of the incarnation. You might refer to the Creeds and to John 1 as sources of wisdom and authority.

- Others may say that God's benevolence, mercy and grace are the most important teachings as it is these aspects of his nature which cause the incarnation of Jesus. You might refer to the Creeds or to John 3:16 for example as sources of wisdom and authority.

- Make sure you offer a judgement on this issue in order to get the highest marks.

BELIEFS, TEACHINGS
AND PRACTICES

ISLAM

Introduction

Who are Muslims?

Islam is the world's second-largest religion, with 1.6 billion followers worldwide. It is the main religion of many countries in the Middle East, North Africa and Asia.

In England and Wales there are about 2.7 million Muslims, forming about 4.8 per cent of the population.

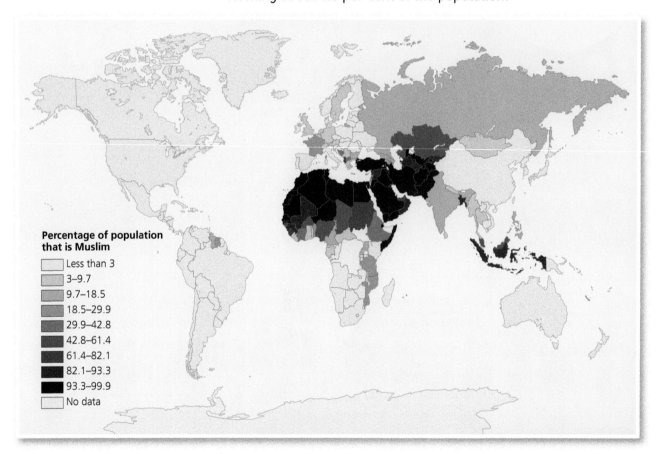

Percentage of population that is Muslim

- Less than 3
- 3–9.7
- 9.7–18.5
- 18.5–29.9
- 29.9–42.8
- 42.8–61.4
- 61.4–82.1
- 82.1–93.3
- 93.3–99.9
- No data

Muslim beliefs

Muslims believe in one god, Allah. They believe He created the world and is all-powerful. They believe that He communicates with humans through angels, who pass His message on to the prophets. Some of these prophets have written books of God's Word.

Muslims believe that God knows everything that will happen (predestination), that everything they do is recorded and that they will be judged by God on the Day of Judgement at the end of the world.

Muhammad ﷺ

The final prophet of Islam is Muhammad ﷺ. Unlike in Christianity, where Jesus is believed to be divine, Muhammad ﷺ was just a normal human. When Allah gave him His message this was recorded in the Qur'an.

◖ Pages from the Qur'an

In order to show respect when talking about Muhammad ﷺ, when his name is written it is often followed by the letters 'pbuh' or this symbol: ﷺ. These both stand for 'peace be upon him'.

Sources of authority

The Qur'an is the holy book of Islam – Muslims believe it is the true Word of God exactly as it was given to Muhammad ﷺ. The Qur'an is made up of verses called ayahs. The Qur'an has been translated into many languages, but it is only considered to be the true Word of God in its original Arabic. It is the first source of wisdom for Muslims looking for guidance.

As well as the Qur'an, Muslims also look to the example set by the prophet Muhammad ﷺ in order to determine how to live their lives. The Sunna records the actions of Muhammad ﷺ, while the Hadith record his sayings.

With reference to the Qur'an, the Sunna and the Hadith, Muslim lawyers have put together a set of laws for Muslims to follow, this is known as Shari'a.

Muslims are also guided by their religious leaders, who are known as Imams in Sunni tradition of Islam or Mujtahid in Shi'ah tradition of Islam.

To discuss

a The Qur'an is only considered to be its true form in Arabic. Why is this?

b What is the link between Shari'ah, the Qur'an, Sunna and Hadith?

Beliefs and practices

There are many practices that are important to the Muslim way of life:

- Muslims are required to pray five times a day. As well as these set prayers they can also make personal prayers.
- Giving to people in need is also important in Islam and all Muslims give alms to help the poor.
- Fasting during the Muslim month of Ramadan helps Muslims remember when God revealed the Qur'an to Muhammad ﷺ, as well as helping them focus on Allah and come together as a community.
- The most holy place for Muslims is the Grand Mosque in Makkah; Muslims should visit there, at least once in their lifetime, on pilgrimage (Hajj) if they are able.
- Festivals and holy days are important events in the Muslim calendar to help commemorate key events in the development of Islam.

Denominations

The main denominations of Islam are Sunni and Shi'a. Sunnis form approximately 85 per cent of Muslims worldwide and Shi'a about 15 per cent. The division between the two branches of Islam arose because of different beliefs about who should lead the Muslims after Muhammad ﷺ died. Shi'a Muslims believe that Muhammad ﷺ identified Ali as his successor and that he was the first of Twelve Imams who led the faith. Sunni Muslims believe that Abu Bakr, Muhammad's ﷺ friend and father-in-law, was the rightful successor to Muhammad ﷺ.

These disagreements about leadership have led to some differences in belief and practice between Sunni and Shi'a Muslims, though they share many elements in common.

3 Beliefs and teachings

Topic checklist

✔ Core beliefs
✔ Nature of Allah
✔ Prophethood (Risalah)
✔ Books (Kutub)
✔ Angels (Malaikah)
✔ Eschatological beliefs

Key concepts

Both Sunni and Shi'a Muslims believe that there is one God, in Arabic known as Allah, who is all-powerful. The key beliefs in Sunni tradition of Islam are called the Six Articles of Faith, whereas Shi'a Muslims have the five roots of Usul ad-Din or Principles of Faith. Both believe in the oneness of God and in prophets, and both have beliefs about life after death, but there are significant differences between Sunni and Shi'a traditions of Islam when it comes to beliefs about Imamate (leadership) and justice.

Link it up

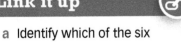

a Identify which of the six articles is supported by each of the Qur'an quotes shown opposite.
b Explain the links that you have made.

Core beliefs

The Six Articles of Faith in Sunni tradition of Islam

In Sunni tradition of Islam, Muslim beliefs can be summarised in the Six Articles of Faith. The belief in these six articles is called Iman. These articles are believed to have been revealed by Allah and are recorded in the Qur'an.

The six beliefs are as follows:

1 **Tawhid** (oneness of Allah): this includes Muslim beliefs about Allah and the supremacy of Allah's will.

Risalah (prophethood): to include the ways in which Allah communicates with humans:

2 Beliefs about angels of Allah.
3 Beliefs about the books of Allah.
4 Beliefs about the messengers of Allah – the prophets (rasuul).
5 **Akhirah** afterlife: Muslims believe that this life is only a test for what happens after death. They believe in a Last Day, when Allah will judge people on their deeds and will either reward or punish them.
6 **Al-Qad'r** (predestination): Muslims believe that everything in the universe follows a masterplan set by Allah.

These beliefs will be discussed in detail in this chapter.

Qur'an quotes

"The Messenger has believed in what was revealed to him from his Lord, and [so have] the believers. All of them have believed in Allah and His angels and His books and His messengers, [saying], "We make no distinction between any of His messengers." And they say, "We hear and we obey. [We seek] Your forgiveness, our Lord, and to You is the [final] destination."'

(2:285)

'...Righteous is he who believes in Allah and the Last Day and the Angels and the Scriptures and the Prophets....'

(2:177)

'Say: He is Allah, the One and Only; Allah, the Eternal, Absolute; He did not give birth nor was He born; and there is none like Him.'

(Surah 112)

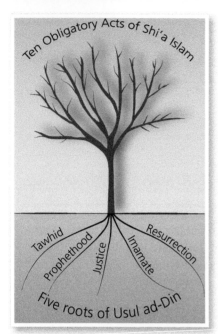

Ten Obligatory Acts of Shi'a Islam

Tawhid · Prophethood · Justice · Imamate · Resurrection

Five roots of Usul ad-Din

To discuss

Do you think any one of the five roots is more important than the others?

Five roots of religion in Shi'a tradition

Shi'a tradition of Islam rests on the five roots of religion. These five principles are:

- Belief in Oneness and Unity of God: Al-Tawhid.
- Belief in Divine Justice: Al-Adl.
- Belief in Prophethood: Al-Nubuwwah.
- Belief in Imams: Al-Imamah.
- Belief in the Day of Resurrection: Al-Ma'ad.

While there is a shared belief in the oneness of Allah, prophethood and the Day of Judgement, there is a significant difference between Sunni and Shi'a belief in relation to the leadership of the faith (Al-Imamah) and belief in Divine Justice (Al-Adl).

Belief in Imams

The historical divide between Sunni and Shi'a traditions of Islam was based on disagreements about who should have succeeded Muhammad 🕊 as leader of the Muslim community.

After Muhammad's 🕊 death the majority of Muslims at the time declared Abu Bakr his successor, and he was known as the first Caliph. Abu Bakr was from the Quraysh tribe, the same as Muhammad 🕊, and Muhammad 🕊 had married his daughter. After Abu Bakr died other leaders (caliphs) were appointed, the fourth caliph to be elected was Ali. Ali was the son of Muhammad's 🕊 uncle and he was the second person to believe in Muhammad's 🕊 prophethood, after Muhammad's 🕊 wife, Khadijah.

Shi'a Muslims, however, regard Ali as Muhammad's 🕊 true successor; they refuse to acknowledge the three caliphs before him because they believe that Muhammad 🕊 identified Ali as the rightful leader.

In the Shi'a tradition the Imam is completely different from the imam in the Sunni tradition. In Sunni tradition of Islam the Imam leads prayers in the mosque, but in Shi'a tradition of Islam Imams are the successors of Muhammad 🕊. Al-Imamah is the Shi'a belief in the twelve Imams chosen by Allah, who were the direct descendants of the Prophet Muhammad 🕊. The Imams are believed to be infallible and inspired by Allah. Ali was the first of these leaders, appointed – according to Shi'a belief – by Muhammad 🕊. Every Imam after this has had to confirm their successor as determined through divine inspiration. The Imams were appointed to preserve the religion after Muhammad's 🕊 death. Shi'a Muslims believe that the Imamah is protected by Allah from committing any sin in order to keep the religion true and pure. The role of the Imams is to interpret the Muslim (Shari'ah) law that was told to Muhammad 🕊 by Allah and to explain any issues arising from it.

The first eleven Imams were martyred. The twelfth Imam is believed to be in occultation waiting to reappear at God's appointed time. Shi'as believe the twelfth Imam is still a living, breathing human. Shi'a Muslims believe their Imam is in occultation (hiding) by the order of God. His reappearance is awaited by his followers and that is also on the order of God. God will send him back as a Messiah to bring justice, peace and coexistence at the end of the world.

Shi'a Muslims believe that there are many signs that will precede the reappearance of the twelfth Imam. The first of these will be the Second Coming of Jesus. After this, the twelfth Imam will appear in Makkah (the holy city of Islam) at the Kaaba.

🎧 There are jubilant celebrations by Shi'a Muslims of the Twelfth Imam's birthday

Qur'an quotes

`And We made them leaders (Imams) who guide (people) by Our command, and We revealed to them the doing of good and the establishing of salah (prayer) and giving of zakah (charity) and they were worshippers of Us (alone).'

(21:73)

Belief in Divine Justice (Al-Adl)

All Muslims believe that Allah is just, but for Shi'a Muslims Divine Justice is one of the five roots of religion. Shi'a Muslims believe that:

- God possesses foreknowledge of human actions, but does not force them to act in any particular way.
- There are many parts of life which are within our power, while some others are not within our power. Those things for which we can be advised, praised or blamed are within our power.
- Therefore, it is wrong to say that Allah is responsible for our sins and good deeds, whether we are obedient or disobedient to Allah or whether we hold true or incorrect beliefs.

Sunni Muslims question these beliefs, arguing that there is no objective right and wrong, but that everything Allah does is right simply because he does it. They do believe in pre-destination, where Allah determines all human action.

Tasks

1 State the difference between the Six Articles of Faith in Sunni tradition of Islam and the Usul ad-Din in Shi'a tradition of Islam.

2 Explain the significance of Al-Imamah to Shi'a Muslims.

3 Why do Sunni Muslims have a different view from this?

Nature of Allah

Tawhid (oneness)

Tawhid is the most important of all Islamic beliefs. It is the belief that Allah is The One God, that He alone created the Earth and sustains it. Tawhid encompasses all beliefs about the nature of Allah. Key Muslim beliefs about Allah are:

- that He is infinite – as The One God He is without beginning or end; He was not created and nor can He be destroyed
- that He is omnipotent and omniscient – Allah created the whole universe, controls everything in it and will one day bring the world to an end; He sees all creation
- that He is merciful and benevolent – He helps humans by sending messengers in the form of the prophets to help people understand how to live a life following His will; every chapter of the Qur'an, apart from 9, begins with 'In the name of God the merciful, the Compassionate' (which is known as the Bismalah)
- that He is transcendent but also immanent – Muslims believe that God is much greater than humans and beyond human understanding (transcendent); they also believe, however, that He is close to them and involved in their lives (immanent); 'closer than (their own) jugular vein.'
- that He is fair and just – Muslims believe that this life is a test for what will happen to them after death. On the Day of Judgement they believe Allah will judge their actions in life and either reward or punish them.

⮑ Piece of Islamic art expressing Tawhid

What Tawhid means for Muslims

Belief in Tawhid has a significant effect upon Muslim believers because they give their whole lives completely to the will of Allah, seeking to become a servant of Him. This means that a Muslim will live his/her life in obedience to the commands of Allah. Muslims believe that Allah has knowledge of everything and so they will try not to sin, as even a sin that is not visible to others will be seen by Allah. Tawhid enables the believer to understand that everything they have is by the will of Allah, and that they are completely dependent upon Him. This should mean that Muslims demonstrate a humble attitude as there is nothing that they can do without the kindness of Allah. There is no reason to be boastful; to do so would be sinful. Placing anything above Allah is idolatry: this is the sin of shirk and is considered the worst of all sins. Knowing that Allah is the ultimate provider can enable a Muslim to be content with their life. Muslims believe that even the time of their death is set by Allah, and so they have nothing to fear, as whatever happens is His will.

The belief in Tawhid means that Muslims think the Christian understanding of God as the Trinity (Father, Son and Holy Spirit) is completely wrong, as it sees God as three persons rather than one. Similarly, polytheistic religions that worship more than one god are completely condemned in the Qur'an. Muslims would consider followers of polytheistic religions to be committing shirk by placing other things equal with God.

To discuss

How might the attitudes represented in these images be impacted by a Muslim belief in Tawhid?

- **a** Pop or film stars as role models **b** Gambling in the pursuit of wealth **c** Caring for the natural world and animals

Stretch what you know

Muslims are forbidden to create images of Allah because this may lead to idolatry and an inaccurate representation of Allah. One of the highest forms of art in Islam is calligraphy, however, and, as Allah has 99 names, the names of Allah are often shown in beautiful calligraphy.

a Investigate some of Allah's names and explain what else they reveal to you about His nature.

b Create your own piece of calligraphy for one or more of Allah's names to help you to remember it.

■ One of the 99 names of Allah

Link it up

a Create two columns to write in.

b In the left-hand column write the quotes from the Qur'an.

c In the right-hand column explain what these quotes teach about Allah.

Qur'an quotes

'In the name of Allah, the Entirely Merciful, the Especially Merciful.'
(Surah 1)

'God has not taken to Himself any son, nor is there any god with Him: For then each god would have taken of that which he created and some of them would have tried to overcome others....'
(23:91)

'Say: He is Allah, the One and Only; Allah, the Eternal, Absolute; He did not give birth nor was He born; and there is none like Him.'
(Surah 112)

'God is the Creator of everything. He is the guardian over everything. To Him belong the keys of the heavens and the earth....'
(39:62,63)

'He is God; there is no god but He, He is the Knower of the unseen and the seen; He is the All-Merciful and the All-Compassionate. He is God, there is no god but He. He is the King, Holy, Peace, Giver of security, the All-Preserver, the All-Mighty, the All-Compeller, the Supreme... He is God the Creator, the Inventor of all things, the Shaper of all forms ...'
(59:22–23)

'To every people [was sent] a Messenger: when their messenger comes [before them], the matter will be judged between them with justice, and they will not be wronged.'
(10:47)

'And indeed We have created man and We know what his soul whispers to him, and We are closer to him than [his] jugular vein'
(Surah 50:16)

Prophethood (Risalah)

Risalah, or prophethood, is the means of communication between Allah and humans. A prophet is a messenger, chosen by Allah to teach, guide and train people to follow Him. Risalah is therefore immensely significant to Muslims. The messengers of Allah are themselves human and they are not to be worshipped. Through them Allah calls all people to worship Him alone. They give guidance on how to follow Allah and live in a way that pleases Him. Every prophet is of equal status, none is more significant or important than any other. Each is a messenger chosen by Allah to deliver His guidance, and that is what is important to Muslims.

Humans are limited in their knowledge and are imperfect; this is why Islam teaches that humans need Allah's guidance. The last and most important book of Allah's guidance is the Qur'an, which was revealed through the prophet Muhammad ﷺ.
The Qur'an is clear that messengers and prophets have been sent to every nation at various times so that people can be brought back to follow Allah's will (Qur'an 10:47). The Qur'an mentions 25 of these Prophets beginning with Adam. Muslims believe that Muhammad ﷺ was the final prophet; he is referred to in the Qur'an as the 'Seal of the Prophets' (33:41).

The Qur'an refers to other books that were revealed to other prophets. These are:

- the Tawrat (Torah) of Musa, revealed to Moses
- the Zabur (Psalms) of Dawud, revealed to David
- the Injil (Gospel) of Isa, revealed to Jesus
- Suhuf Ibrahim (Scrolls of Abraham), revealed to Abraham.

The Qur'an, however, is the only book that exists in its original form, written in Arabic and entirely unchanged. The other books were written down after the death of the prophets and so the contents are believed to be distorted; they are thought to be no longer the literal words of Allah but to be mixed with those of humans.

To discuss

a Why do you think Muslims learn and study the Qur'an in Arabic rather than using translations?

b How is the Qur'an different to all other revealed books in Islam?

◖ Qur'an placed on a kursi to keep it off the ground

To discuss

What is the link between Adam, Iblis and the forbidden fruit?

Adam

The name 'Adam' in Arabic means man. Adam was the first man created by Allah and also the first prophet of Islam. Allah created Adam in His own image and as His 'vicegerent' or 'khalifa', which means He wanted Adam to act for Him on Earth. When Allah told the angels that He was going to create Adam, they questioned Him, asking:

'Will you place therein such as will cause disorder in it or shed blood?'

But in His omniscience Allah created Adam using the dust off the ground, which He combined with water to form clay, breathing life into him by His spirit. Allah gave Adam knowledge of the created world, as well as the ability to reason and make choices. He tested him on his knowledge in front of His angels. Adam was able to answer all Allah's questions and the angels bowed in respect to him, all except Iblis (Satan). Iblis believed himself better than Adam because he was made from fire, whereas Adam was made from dust. Allah expelled Iblis from His presence. For this reason Iblis seeks to misguide Adam and all his descendants.

For Adam, Allah made Hawwa (Eve) to live with him in Jannah (Paradise). Allah gave them one rule: not to eat from one specific tree. Iblis succeeded in tempting them to eat from the forbidden tree. Feeling guilty at their disobedience and unable to hide from Allah, they asked for His forgiveness, which He gave to them. Allah sent them out of al-Jannah, however, to live on Earth. On Earth Allah was merciful and kind to them: He promised to give them His guidance so that they could be obedient to Him. All humans are descended from Adam and Hawwa.

Ibrahim

Ibrahim (Abraham) is a prophet described in the Qur'an as 'a man of truth' (19:41). The Qur'an describes him as a man who believed in one true God and was an example for others to follow. Ibrahim was born into a polytheistic (believing in many gods) family in Babylon (modern-day Iraq) and his father was an idol maker, but even as a young boy Ibrahim realised that these idols were not worthy of worship.

Allah chose him as His prophet, and Ibrahim told his father and the people of Babylon that they were wrong to worship the carved idols, but they rejected his message and sent him out of Babylon. On the command of Allah, Ibrahim and his wife Sarah travelled through Syria, Palestine and on into Egypt. Ibrahim had his first son Isma'il (Ishmail) with his second wife Hajar (Hagar), and then another son, named Ishaq (Isaac), with his wife Sarah. Through his descendants Ibrahim, through Isma'il, became known as the father of the Arab people. Both his sons also became prophets of Allah.

Allah tested Ibrahim's faith, for example He told Ibrahim to sacrifice his son Isma'il. Despite being told three times by Iblis (the devil) not to do it, Ibrahim resisted by throwing stones at Iblis. Ibrahim was prepared to follow Allah's instructions, but to reward his faith Allah provided a ram as an alternative sacrifice. Ibrahim's journey and life are commemorated as part of many of the rites undertaken during the pilgrimage of Hajj.

Ibrahim's life of commitment to the faith is honoured in Islam. He is considered to be the father of monotheism as he was a hanif (believer in one God). Speaking of his relationship with Allah, the Qur'an says, 'Allah did take Ibrahim for a friend' (4:125). At the end of every salah (prayer) Muslims recite a special prayer (du'a') asking Allah to bless Ibrahim and his family.

Isma'il

Isma'il was born as the son of Ibrahim as a blessing from Allah (37:100). Allah required Ibrahim to leave his son with his mother, Hajar, at the place where the Kaaba now stands in Makkah, Saudi Arabia. It was a deserted place, absent of any other life or even water. Ibrahim left them there with some dates and a flask of water. Ibrahim remained obedient to Allah's command even though his wife repeatedly asked him why he was leaving them there. Ibrahim prayed to Allah that they would receive kindness so that they could be thankful. As the flask of water ran out Hajar ran seven times between two hills (Safa and Marwa) in search of water. As she was about to leave for the eighth time, Isma'il began to kick the ground with his heel and from this spot water miraculously began to spurt up from the ground. He and his mother settled down to live in this region.

Later, after Hajar's death, Ibrahim is believed to have visited Isma'il, and together they rebuilt the Kaaba, the building at the centre of the Grand Mosque in Makkah. Makkah today is the centre of Islam and Muslims visit the site on pilgrimage and always pray facing it wherever they are in the world.

From Isma'il came the Ishmaelite tribe, the family Muhammad ﷺ belonged to.

Musa

Musa (Moses) was from the Banu Isra'il – Children of Israel or Israelites (an Israelite is a descendant of the Jewish patriarch Jacob). The Pharaoh of the time ordered the killing of all male Israelite children so that they would not grow to become a powerful nation and conquer Egypt. Musa's mother, following Allah's guidance, managed to place Musa in a basket in the River Nile to keep him safe. Maryam, Musa's sister, watched the basket as it floated down the Nile to see where it stopped. It came to rest in the reeds and was picked up by the Pharaoh's family. The Pharaoh's wife adopted Musa as her own son and hired a nanny to care for him – this nanny was Musa's own mother! Muslims believe that this demonstrates Allah's care over Musa and Allah's power to protect whom He chooses.

To discuss

In what way did Allah's request of a sacrifice test Ibrahim's faith?

♩ The place where the water sprang up in Makkah is known as the ZamZam well and pilgrims are encouraged to drink the water as much as possible which is readily available in water coolers and from taps around the Holy Mosque

When he had grown up, one day Musa saw an Egyptian beating an Israelite slave and when he tried to stop him he accidentally killed the Egyptian. Musa had to flee Egypt. He was called by Allah, however, to be His messenger, and Allah told him to return to Egypt. Allah told him to go to the Pharaoh and to call for the release of the Israelite people. After many displays of power by Allah, including the sending of ten plagues upon the Egyptian people, the Pharaoh eventually released the Israelite people. As they left Egypt and reached the shore of the Nile, however, the Pharaoh changed his mind and sent his army after them. Allah caused the Nile to separate to create a dry path for the Israelites to walk through to safety. As the Egyptian army began to travel through the Nile, Allah brought the river back down, thus drowning the Egyptians. This shows Muslims how God oversees His servants and punishes those who try to oppose Him.

Musa led the Israelites, under Allah's guidance. Allah revealed the Tawrat (Torah) to Moses and gave him the Ten Commandments. The Qur'an records Musa as a grateful servant of Allah. Despite the Israelites not always obeying Allah's Word, Musa is given honour by Allah:

'Believers, do not be like those who annoyed Moses. God proved him to be innocent of what they had said about him. And he was an honourable person in the sight of God.'

(33:69)

Dawud

Dawud (David) was both a prophet and eventually King of the Israelites, a position given to him by Allah. Dawud did many heroic things, including killing the giant Goliath. Goliath was part of the Philistine army (whom the Israelites were at war with), and Dawud killed him when the rest of the Israelite army was too scared to fight the giant. The Philistines ran from the Israelites

⊃ Dawud slays Goliath

after this defeat. Talut (Saul), king at the time, rewarded Dawud and made him commander of the army. Talut soon became jealous of Dawud, however, despite Dawud's efforts to be at peace with him. When Talut was killed by his enemies, the Israelites all agreed that Dawud should become king. Under the reign of King David, the nation of Israel prospered and they lived with a fear and respect for Allah. They worshipped Allah as the one true God. The Zabur (book of Psalms) was revealed to Dawud by Allah; the book contains lessons of guidance for the Israelites to cause praise to Allah.

Isa

Isa (Jesus), like all the prophets before him, was a law-giver; he received the revelations from Allah as recorded in the Injil (Gospel). Sunni Muslims believe that Isa is the Messiah, who will return on the Day of Resurrection at the end of the world and bring together true Muslims. According to the Hadith (the sayings of Muhammad ﷺ), Isa will establish Islam in the end times and will make war until all religions except Islam are destroyed. Isa was born to the virgin Mary (Maryam) and had no father.

Isa spoke while still in the cradle and performed many miracles in his life, including healing people and raising the dead. In the Qur'an Isa also foretold the coming of the prophet Muhammad ﷺ, saying

'…O Children of Israel! I am the messenger of Allah [sent] to you, confirming the Law [which came] before me, and giving Glad Tidings of a Messenger to come after me, whose name shall be Ahmad'…' (Ahmad is another name for Muhammad ﷺ).

[61:6]

Muslims believe that Isa did not die; instead, Allah took him into His presence.

Unlike Christians, who believe Jesus was divine, Muslims believe that Isa was a human who had been chosen by Allah to deliver His message, like the other prophets.

Stretch what you know

a Create two columns and compare what you know about the Christian teaching about Jesus with the Muslim teaching on him.

b Investigate more of what the Qur'an says about Isa; you may find this a helpful link: **www.islam-guide. com/ch3-10.htm**

Tasks

1 What is Risalah?
2 State five prophets of Islam.
3 Describe the life of two of those prophets.
4 Explain the significance of Muhammad ﷺ to Muslims.

Muhammad ﷺ

Muhammad's ﷺ life

Muhammad ﷺ is the last prophet of Allah and his life is an example that Muslims today follow because he demonstrated how to obey Allah. This is seen in the Qur'an, as it says:

'Certainly you have in the Messenger of God an excellent example ....'

[33:21]

Muhammad ﷺ was sent by Allah to declare the truth of Islam as opposed to all other religions:

'It is He who has sent His Messenger with the guidance and the religion of truth, that he may uplift it above every religion, though the unbelievers may hate it.'

(61:9)

Muhammad ﷺ was born in Makkah, Arabia in around 570CE. Muhammad's ﷺ parents had both died by the time he was six, and after the death of his grandfather when he was only eight years old he was brought up by his uncle, Abu Talib, a leader of the Quraish tribe. On a trip to Syria a Christian monk, Bahira, identified Muhammad ﷺ as one who would later become a prophet. As Muhammad ﷺ grew up he gained a reputation for justice and honesty, gaining the names 'Al-Amin', meaning the Trustworthy, and 'As-Sadiq', meaning the Truthful. Whilst working for a wealthy woman named Khadijah, she proposed to him. He was twenty-five and she was forty and a widow. Together they had several children, though both Muhammad's ﷺ sons died before Allah made him a prophet.

Makkah was a holy city, and once a year Arab tribesmen came there on pilgrimage. In Makkah was a cube-shaped building called the Kaaba, which contained 360 idols. One year the Kaaba needed rebuilding after bad floods. The work was carried out by a number of tribes of the Quraysh. Muhammad ﷺ was involved in this work. The final part of the rebuild was to place the Hajar al-Aswad, a sacred black stone from Jannah, on the East wall of the Kaaba. A dispute broke out as each tribal chief wanted to have the great honour of placing the stone. In order to avoid bloodshed it was decided that whoever would turn up first in the morning would decide who should place the stone. In the morning everyone was delighted that it was Muhammad ﷺ who was there first as they respected him for his honesty and trustworthiness. He asked for a large sheet of cloth to be brought and he placed the stone in the centre. He then asked all the tribal chiefs to get hold of the sheet from all around and lift together. He then placed the stone into the wall. Every one was happy that they had participated in the proves and there was no bloodshed. Muhammad ﷺ was not yet a Prophet by this time. Muhammad's ﷺ role in bringing about peace in such situations is significant to Muslim believers. Importantly, he also became a monotheist, rejecting all idols and worshipping only Allah. This belief in one God is the central belief of Islam today, Tawhid.

⋒ The Kaaba

To discuss

a What does Muhammad's ﷺ solution for placing the Black Stone reveal about him as a leader?

b Imagine you had been one of the people holding a corner of that cloth. What would you have felt about your participation in that event?

The revelation of the Qur'an and prophethood

It was during a time of meditation in a cave outside Makkah that an angel appeared to Muhammad ﷺ. The angel commanded him to read, but Muhammad ﷺ replied, 'I am not a reader.' The angel then squeezed him so tightly he thought he would die. Once the angel released him, he again commanded Muhammad ﷺ to read. This happened three times, with the angel finally saying:

'Read in the name of your Lord who created.

Created man from a clot of blood.
Read, And your Lord is most generous.
Who taught by the pen.
Taught man what he did not know.'

(96:1–5)

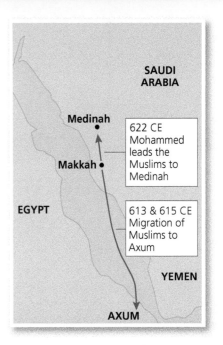

In response Muhammad ﷺ recited the verses as though they had been written on his heart. These were the first revealed verses of the Qur'an. Muhammad ﷺ saw the angel Jibril flying away from him, declaring him as the messenger of Allah. Muhammad ﷺ received many more revelations and these make up the complete Qur'an. The word 'Qur'an' itself means recitation. Khadijah, Muhammad's ﷺ wife, was the first to accept Muhammad ﷺ as a prophet and to commit to following Islam.

The Night of Power

The night when Muhammad ﷺ received the first verses of the Qur'an is known as Laylat al-Qad'r, meaning the Night of Power. It is believed to have occurred during the last of the ten nights of Ramadan (the ninth Muslim month). The Night of Power is still commemorated during Ramadan today. It is a time when many Muslims devote themselves to prayer and to the reading of the Qur'an. As the start of Allah's final revelation, this is important to Muslims.

Prophethood

Over time Muhammad ﷺ began to preach publicly, sharing the words he believed Allah had revealed to him. The followers of Muhammad ﷺ increased but so did the opposition to him. In 622CE Muhammad ﷺ left Makkah and travelled to the city of Yathrib on the invitation of its leaders. This journey is now known as the Hijrah, meaning emigration. Meeting him there were many Muslim families that Muhammad ﷺ had already sent on ahead. The community at Yathrib became the first to be run according to Islamic principles and this migration marked the beginning of the Islamic calendar: Islamic calendars are dated from AH, meaning 'in the year of the Hijrah'.

Muhammad ﷺ ruled the community of Yathrib (which became known as Madinah – 'City of the Prophet') for over half of his prophethood. It was during this time that Islam became more organised, with Muhammad ﷺ giving instructions on prayer, fasting, charity and pilgrimage. Much of the guidance that Muhammad ﷺ gave quoted the words of Allah as revealed in the Qur'an.

🎧 The Plain of Arafat, where Muhammad ﷺ delivered his farewell speech

Stretch what you know

Read a copy of Muhammad's ﷺ farewell speech; you may find this link helpful:
http://islam.about.com/od/muhammad/a/Prophet-Muhammad-Farewell-Sermon.htm

a Summarise the key teachings delivered through this speech.

b To what extent do you agree with his teachings on harming others and the treatment of women?

Between 624CE and 630CE there was a series of battles between the people of Makkah and the Muslims of Medinah. Eventually, in 630CE, the Muslims of Medinah won victory over the people of Makkah. All the idols of Makkah were destroyed and the city was reclaimed as the Muslim holy city. Only two years later Muhammad ﷺ died of a fever and was buried in Medinah. He left behind a community of about a hundred thousand Muslims.

In his farewell speech on his last pilgrimage to Makkah in 632CE Muhammad ﷺ said:

'O people, no prophet or apostle will come after me and no new faith will be born … I leave behind me two things, the Qur'an and my example the Sunnah, and if you follow these you will never go astray.'

(The Prophet Muhammad's ﷺ Last Sermon)

Muhammad ﷺ as the Seal of the Prophets

Muhammad ﷺ is known as the Seal of the Prophets because he provided the final revelation of Allah to his people in the form of the Qur'an. The words of the Qur'an remain unchanged and as such are the direct words of Allah to Muslims today. Muhammad's ﷺ faithful and trustworthy character ensured the establishment of Islam at a time when monotheism was not the general practice. He is considered to be a wise prophet, as shown in the way he responded to many events in his lifetime.

Shi'a Muslims also believe that Muhammad ﷺ is the 'Seal of the Prophets' to whom the Qur'an was revealed as God's final revelation. They also believe in the twelve Imams and that God communicates new messages, not like the Qur'an, to them through inspirations.

After Muhammad's ﷺ death there was division in the Muslim community over who should succeed him as leader. The majority of Muslims, the Sunni, chose Muhammad's ﷺ companion and father-in-law, Abu Bakr, as the next leader (Khalifah). A minority group, however, known as the Shi'a, believed that his successor should be his son-in-law and cousin, Ali ibn Abi Talib. The Shi'a believe Ali to have been divinely appointed and to be the first Imam.

Qur'an quotes

'Muhammad ﷺ is no more than a Messenger. Indeed many Messengers have passed away before him. So if he was to die or be killed, would you turn back on your heels [to unbelief]? And he who turns back on his heels will never harm Allah at all; but Allah will reward the grateful.'

(Surah 3:144)

'Cursed were those who disbelieved among the Children of Israel by the tongue of David and of Jesus, the son of Mary. That was because they disobeyed and [habitually] transgressed.'

(Surah 5:78)

'And We have already written in the Zabur (Book of Psalms) after the (previous) mention that the land (of Paradise) shall be inherited by My righteous servants.'

(Surah 21:105)

'Say, "I am not something new among the messengers, nor do I know what will be done with me or with you. I only follow that which is revealed to me, and I am not but a clear warner."'

(Surah 46:9)

Tasks

1 Produce a leaflet that could be used to inform people about the key events in the life of the prophet Muhammad ﷺ.

2 Describe why Muhammad ﷺ is unique amongst all the other prophets in Islam.

3 Explain the difference between Sunni and Shi'a belief in relation to Muhammad ﷺ as the seal of the prophet's.

Link it up

a Explain the way in which these Qur'an quotes help you to understand the role of the prophets.

b In what way does Surah 5:78 demonstrate the importance of obedience to Allah's commands through His prophets?

Books (Kutub)

When Allah created Adam as His 'vicegerent' to live on Earth and act for Him, He needed to provide him with advice and guidance to help him act in the correct way.

Allah provided Adam and the prophets who came after him with instructions on how they should live. The Word of God as given to certain prophets was recorded in written form:

- The Tawrat (Torah) of Musa: contains God's revelation to Moses.
- The Zabur (Psalms) of Dawud: contains God's revelation to David.
- The Injil (Gospel) of Isa: contains God's revelation to Jesus.
- Suhuf Ibrahim (Scrolls of Abraham): contain God's revelation to Abraham.

To discuss

What is the difference between Shi'a and Sunni understandings of the Qur'an?

Over time, however, Allah's message and the written texts became distorted so that they were no longer, entirely or accurately, the true Word of God. In order that humans had a record of His Word that could not be distorted, Allah gave His final revelation. Muhammad ﷺ simply recited the words of Allah's final revelation exactly as they were given to him by God – and these became the Qur'an. Muslims believe that this is a record of Allah's words exactly as they were said and that they haven't been changed by humans. The Qur'an is only the true Word of God when it is in Arabic, however – the language in which it was given to Muhammad ﷺ; any translation of the Qur'an is seen as a meaning or interpretation of the original text.

Because Muslims believe that the Qur'an is the true Word of God, it is the most important thing in Islam. Copies of the Qur'an are treated with the utmost respect. The Qur'an contains guidance on what Muslims should believe and how they should live their lives, and to be a good Muslim they must live by these rules.

Muslims believe that the Qur'an has always been in existence, though not in its written form, and it is eternal like God. Muslims believe that the Qur'an is the eternal miracle and the living proof of the truth of Islam.

Other sources of authority

The Qur'an as the final and undistorted Word of God forms the basis of Islamic law – Shari'ah – which governs how Muslims should behave. Sometimes the Qur'an is difficult to interpret, and there are some issues that it doesn't cover, particularly those arising in the modern world.

Therefore, the Muslim scholars who develop Shari'ah law sometimes look to other sources of wisdom to tell them how Muslims should behave. Two of these sources come from examples from the life of Muhammad ﷺ, as Muhammad ﷺ is seen as the 'perfect example' for Muslims on how to live their lives. The Sunna of the Prophet contains records on what Muhammad ﷺ did, and the Hadith of the Prophet contains information on what he said. Looking at these can help Muslims lead their life like Muhammad ﷺ.

The Sunna and Hadith also don't cover all areas of behaviour, however, and are at times contradictory, so sometimes Muslims need to take the instructions that are set out in the Qur'an, Hadith and Sunna and try to work out from these what the right thing to do would be in a given situation. Muslims might also refer to the opinions of Muslim lawyers and scholars.

Shi'a Muslims may also refer to the Ahadith of the 12 Imams (who they believe to be the successors of the Prophet Muhammad) ﷺ to help their decision-making.

🎧 Muslim lawyers practise Shari'ah law based on the Qur'an and what we know of Muhammad's ﷺ life

> **To discuss**
>
> Do you think holy books should be translated to make them more accessible?

Qur'an quotes

'Recite in the name of your Lord who created'

(Surah 96)

'And We sent, following in their footsteps, Jesus, the son of Mary, confirming that which came before him in the Torah; and We gave him the Gospel, in which was guidance and light and confirming that which preceded it of the Torah as guidance and instruction for the righteous.'

(Surah 5:46)

'Indeed, We have revealed to you, [O Muhammad ﷺ], as We revealed to Noah and the prophets after him. And we revealed to Abraham, Ishmael, Isaac, Jacob, the Descendants, Jesus, Job, Jonah, Aaron, and Solomon, and to David We gave the book [of Psalms].'

(Surah 4:163)

To discuss

a What does retaining the original language of the Qur'an suggest about the value that Muslims place upon it?

b How does a commitment to learning Arabic demonstrate a Muslim's love for Allah?

c How do the Qur'an quotes help Muslim's to understand Allah's revelation and guidance for them?

Angels (Malaikah)

Before He created humans, the first thing Allah created was the angels. The angels were created from Nur, meaning divine light. Unlike humans, they are not free beings: they exist to carry out the will of Allah and as such do not have free will. They praise Allah and are completely obedient to Him so are free from sin. They are immortal and don't have the physical needs that humans have, such as the need for sleep, so they are constantly able to serve Allah. Muslims believe that the angels are there to help them and that it is through them that Allah communicates with His human messengers on Earth. The angels also record all that each human does and says, ready for the Day of Judgement. On this day the angels will welcome into heaven all those who have been obedient to Allah, but will throw into hell all those who have been disobedient. In order to do the will of Allah the angels sometimes take on human forms, for example the angel Jibril appeared in human form to Maryam (Mary), the mother of Isa (Jesus).

Jibril

The Qur'an mentions several angels by name, and the chief angel is Jibril (Jibra'il). Jibril brought God's message to Muhammad ﷺ and all the other prophets. Jibril would sometimes take the shape of a man when he appeared. The Prophet Muhammad ﷺ, however, is the only one who saw Jibril in his natural form. He described Jibril as having six hundred wings, which covered the sky from the Earth to the horizon.

Izra'il

Izra'il is known as the angel of death and is responsible for the ending of each person's life by taking their final breath. This angel has the role of separating a human's soul from his or her body at the time appointed for death by Allah. Izra'il's appearance to the non-believer brings with it a sense of dread, as he brings news of punishment for unbelief. For the obedient believer, however, Izra'il is a pleasant angel as he is taking them on to Paradise with Allah.

Mika'il

The angel Mika'il is named once in the Qur'an, when it says:

'Say: Whoever is an enemy to Allah and His angels and prophets, to Jibril and Mika'il … Allah is an enemy to those who reject faith.'

(2:98)

Mika'il is seen as the guardian of heaven who also, according to Muhammad ﷺ, sends rain, thunder and lightning to Earth by the command of God.

Israfil

Israfil is the angel of the Last Judgement and he will blow the trumpet to announce the Day of Resurrection. He keeps the trumpet constantly ready by his lips to sound it at Allah's command. On the Day of Resurrection the first blast of the trumpet will destroy everything and then on its second blast every human who has died will be brought back to life.

There are also angels that are responsible for recording the deeds of humans, both the good and the bad. These angels are known as the honourable scribes. Each person has been assigned two recording angels,

'When the two receivers receive [each human being after he or she has attained the age of puberty], one sitting on the right and one on the left. Not a word does he utter, but there is a watcher by him ready (to record).'

(50:17–18)

The angels record the person's every word and action. Muhammad ﷺ explained that the intention (niyyah) behind a good deed means that it is recorded as a good deed even if the consequences of the deed are not good. If the person actually performs the good deed then it is written as ten or more good deeds. Furthermore, if a person intends a bad deed but does not carry it through, then that is recorded as a good deed. A single evil deed is recorded if someone thinks of a bad deed and then acts upon it.

𝍖 Angel Israfil

Tasks

1 What are the angels made from?
2 In what other way are angels different to humans?
3 Describe some of the roles of the named angels.
4 Explain the link between angels and humans.
5 'It is right that deeds in this life should affect our next life.' Discuss this statement; include possible Islamic responses as well as you own, supported, opinion.

Qur'an quotes

'[All] praise is [due] to Allah, Creator of the heavens and the earth, [who] made the angels messengers having wings, two or three or four. He increases in creation what He wills. Indeed, Allah is competent over all things.'

(35:1)

'And We have not made the keepers of the Fire except angels. And We have not made their number except as a trial for those who disbelieve – that those who were given the Scripture will be convinced and those who have believed will increase in faith and those who were given the Scripture and the believers will not doubt and that those in whose hearts is hypocrisy and the disbelievers will say, "What does Allah intend by this as an example?" Thus does Allah lead astray whom He wills and guides whom He wills. And none knows the soldiers of your Lord except Him. And this is not but a reminder to humanity.'

(74:31)

'And to Allah prostrates whatever is in the heavens and whatever is on the earth of creatures, and the angels [as well], and they are not arrogant.'

(16:49)

Link it up

a Explain what each of these Qur'an quotes reveals about Muslim beliefs in angels.
b How may these beliefs about angels, especially the recording angels, influence a believer in their thinking and actions?

Eschatological beliefs

Predestination (al-Qad'r)

Muslims believe that everything that happens in this world is planned by Allah; this belief is known as al-Qad'r (predestination). Allah is believed to have foreknowledge (`Ilm) of all things, including those things that have not yet happened. Muslims believe that Allah wrote this in Al-Lawh al-Mahfooz (Preserved Tablet) before the creation of anything else. No change can take place to what is written unless Allah wills it (Qur'an 13:39). Muslims believe that nothing happens unless it is the will of Allah. Whatever happens in this world, a Muslim need not be disheartened or and can pray for Allah to change it; a Muslim is taught to accept all things as the will of Allah. Equally, if something happens that brings success into a Muslim's life, he or she must not boast about it since it is happening only because of the will of Allah.

There have been disagreements within Islam over the correct understanding of human free will, predestination and Allah's foreknowledge of all things. Some Muslim schools of thought, for example the Jabariyyah, believed that all human actions are determined by Allah and that humans have no free will at all. This raises some issues, however. If God is responsible for all human actions then this means He is also responsible for evil and suffering, so how can He be merciful and benevolent? Furthermore, Muslims believe that on the Day of Resurrection at the end of the world Allah will judge humans on their actions. Humans can only be judged fairly on their actions if they have responsibility for them; but how does this tie in with the idea that everything is planned by Allah?

⟳ If Allah plans everything, is He then responsible for suffering or is it caused by humans' free will?

Different Islamic understandings of predestination and free will

One school of Islamic thought, that of the Mu`tazilah, which originated in the eighth century CE, was that human free will meant that there could be no predestination, because through their free will, it is humans that determine what happens in the world rather than Allah. The Mu'tazilites believed that on the Day of Judgement each person would be judged on the actions they had taken with their free will. The fate of each person would be determined by Allah's Divine Justice.

Some Muslims believe in Divine Intercession, where Allah could show mercy to sinners and free them from the fires of hell. The Mu'tazilites believed, however, that Allah's Divine Justice was absolute and so there could be no mercy for those who were sent to hell, as this would contradict His Justice.

Shi`a Muslims believe in partial freewill although Allah has knowledge of all. They believe that Allah is always in possession of the full and complete knowledge of all things, but believe that He may choose to change anything He wills at any time. For example, in the Qur'an (7:142) Allah changes the period that Musa worships, from thirty nights to forty, before he receives the Tawrat. This was a change from Musa's perspective, but had been known by Allah all along. Shi'a also believe that human choices and actions can cause changes, as suggested by the Qur'an:

'… Indeed, Allah will not change the condition of a people until they change what is in themselves'…

(13:11)

A separate school of thought within Islam is the Ash`ari School (based on the teachings of the ninth century CE Muslim thinker Imam Al-Ash`ari). He tried to find a middle way between believing in free will and believing in predestination. Al-Ashari argued that while God created everything, including human actions, humans could 'acquire' the act and make a choice between the right course of action and the wrong one. This allowed them to believe both in free will and in predestination. They also believed that Allah could use Divine Intercession and show mercy to remove sinners from hell.

This belief in both predestination and free will is largely reflected in Islam under the teachings on al-Qadr. The common teaching is that Allah gives, and requires people to use, their free will. Allah allows humans to do what they choose, even if they choose evil, but Allah knows what choices they will make. For their choices there will come a final judgement after death – a judgement already known by Allah.

Sunni teaching says that 120 days after conception each baby in the womb receives its soul. An angel then records their sex, their lifetime earnings, and whether they will enter Paradise or be sent to hell. The angels will continue to record everything a

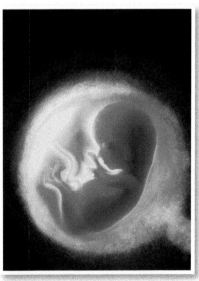

◑ Sunni Muslims believe that a baby receives its soul 120 days after conception

person ever does and on the Day of Judgement the book of their life will be read out. Those who have been good Muslims will be sent to Paradise, and those who have not will be sent to hell. Decisions humans make with their free will affect the rewards or punishments from Allah in the afterlife, but Allah already knows what decisions humans will make.

Qur'an quotes

'There is no compulsion in the religion [Islam]. The right direction is distinctly clear from error.'

(2:256)

'As for those who believed and carried out good deeds they will be delighted in paradise. But as for those who disbelieved and rejected Our signs and the meeting of the Hereafter, then those will be brought forth in the punishment.'

(30:14–16)

'And for every person We have tied their fate to their neck and on the Day of Judgement We shall bring forth a book which they will find wide open.'

(17:13)

'There is not to be any discomfort upon the Prophet concerning that which Allah has ordained upon him. (This was) God's practice with those (Prophets) who went before. And God's command must be fulfilled.'

(33:38)

'And he said to the one whom he knew would go free, "Mention me before your master." But Satan made him forget the mention [to] his master, and Joseph remained in prison several years.'

(12:42)

Link it up

a Explain which quotes support the Sunni teaching that all things are predestined by Allah.

b How would you support the Shi'a rejection of predestination?

c Which of these two perspectives do you think fits best with the character of Allah? You may find it helpful to refer to some of the names of Allah in response to this task.

Tasks

1 What is al-Qad'r?
2 Describe the Mu'tazilites' understanding of free will.
3 Explain the way in which the Asharis' beliefs are different to this.
4 'Free will and predestination are compatible.'

Discuss this statement. In your answer you should:

● analyse and evaluate the importance of common and divergent points of view in Islam

● refer to sources of wisdom and authority.

Life after death (Akhirah)

Muslims believe that this life is just preparation for the next. This belief in life after death is known as 'Akhirah', meaning afterlife or hereafter.

Humans were put on Earth as representatives of Allah and are expected to act as stewards of His creation and to make the world as God wills it. The guidance on how they should do this is in the Qur'an and in the example of the Prophet Muhammad ﷺ. How well they follow this guidance will decide how they are judged in the afterlife.

Muslims believe that after death will come the Day of Judgement, also known as Yawm al-Qiyamah. At a time of Allah's choosing the dead will be resurrected to life. Each person will be judged by Allah, starting with the Prophet Muhammad ﷺ.

Barzakh

In between an individual's actual death and the Day of Judgement there is believed to be a period of waiting called Barzakh. Muslim belief on what happens to the soul during its time in Barzakh varies. Some believe that the soul's experience in Barzakh will be affected by the life the person has led, either good or bad, leading to either punishment or reward. Others believe that the soul is given a temporary body during this time. The temporary body will be light or dark, to reflect the good or bad in their life, so the soul will know what its final judgement will be because of the temporary body that it has been given.

The Day of Judgement

There will be signs that the end of the world and the Day of Judgement are approaching. Sunni Muslims believe that Isa (Jesus) as the Messiah will reappear. Some believe he will bring together true Muslims; others believe he will lead a battle until Islam is left as the one true religion. Shi'a Muslims believe that the Twelfth Imam, who is in occultation (hidden), will reappear and Isa will also join him to bring the religion of Islam in its true form.

On the Day of Judgement Allah, as The All-seeing and The All-knowing, is The Bringer of Judgement. His judgement on this day will display perfect justice. This life is therefore seen as a test for people; their belief in and obedience to Allah in this life, or not, is what they will be judged upon. Those who die while believing that 'there is no true god but God, and Muhammad ﷺ is the Messenger [prophet] of God', and who are Muslim, will be rewarded on that day and will be admitted to Paradise forever. But those who are not Muslim will lose Paradise forever and will be sent to the fires of hell, known as Jahannam. Allah is merciful, however, and even a bad person may enter Paradise eventually, after being punished. Only the sin of shirk permanently excludes Allah's forgiveness. The resurrection that will take place on the Last Day is physical, and the Qur'an indicates that Allah will re-create the decayed body:

'Could they not see that God who created the heavens and the earth is able to create the likes of them...'

(17:99)

The Day of Judgement is described as passing over hell on a narrow bridge, the Siraat, to reach Paradise. Those who fall, due to the weight of their bad deeds, will remain in hell forever. The Qur'an provides two exceptions to this:

1 Warriors who die fighting in the cause of God are sent immediately into the presence of Allah.
2 Enemies of Islam are sentenced immediately to hell upon death.

Heaven

In the Qur'an al-Jannah (heaven) and Jahannam (hell) are described as physical places. Al-Jannah is described as a beautiful garden ('jannah' means garden), where people are young again, and where they are happy and enjoy the garden. On the other hand, Jahannam is described as an unquenchable fire. According to the Qur'an both these places will appear and be seen only on the Day of Judgement, and they are eternal.

Upon entry into al-Jannah the Qur'an says that believers will be welcomed by angels delivering a message of peace into their 'final home' (13:24). Once in heaven there will be no nastiness or sin: instead there will be a constant state of peace (56:25–26). The gardens will contain 'beautiful mansions in gardens of everlasting bliss' (9:72). According to Muslim tradition al-Jannah has eight gates, which Muhammad ﷺ named. They include Baab As-Sadaqah for those who have often given to charity, Baab Al-Hajj for those who have completed the Hajj pilgrimage, and Baab Al-Iman for those who constantly work hard to be obedient to Allah. Muhammad ﷺ was asked if anyone will be called to enter through all eight gates: Muhammad ﷺ replied yes, and that he hoped to be one of them.

Hell

In contrast, Jahannam is believed to be a place of punishment and eternal suffering. The Qur'an says that those who are sent there will be in constant pain. The fire is described as 'almost bursting with fury' (67:7). Jahannam is presented as a place of darkness and fear. For sinful believers it is a place of purification, and when Allah chooses He will move these believers on to al-Jannah. For unbelievers, though, Jahannam is a place of eternal punishment.

Some Muslims believe that these physical descriptions of heaven as a garden and hell as a fiery pit are just metaphorical and intended to help humans understand what they may be like, whereas in reality heaven and hell are beyond human understanding. Only a minority of Muslims hold this view, however; most believe the descriptions of heaven and hell in the Qur'an are literally what they will be like.

Martyrdom in Islam

For some Muslims, standing for and defending their faith may lead to martyrdom. This means the person being killed in defence of or struggle for (jihad) their faith. Dying in this way will cause the person to enter into the presence of Allah immediately. Some people have misunderstood this teaching and also the nature of jihad. As a result some violent extremists have used the teaching on martyrdom as a way of justifying suicide bombing and violent acts of aggression against non-Muslims in order to try to establish some form of Islamic rule.

This is contrary to the teaching in the Qur'an, made especially clear when it says: 'Let there be no compulsion in the religion [Islam]. The right direction is distinctly clear from error' (2:256). This quote shows that the religion of Islam is not to be forced on anyone; rather, people should choose it freely.

Stretch what you know

Research Muslim beliefs about the end times. (There is an excellent BBC Radio 4 *Beyond Belief, End Time Beliefs in Islam* podcast that you could listen to: www.bbc.co.uk/ programmes/b054pq21.)

a Summarise what you find out about Muslim beliefs about signs of the end times.

b Explain the role of Isa (Jesus) in the end times and how this differs from the role of Mahdi (the divine guide).

The impact of these teachings upon Muslims

The Muslim belief in life after death effects the lives of believers. Obviously, because Allah will reward or punish them based on this life, Muslims will aim to do good and be obedient to Allah, holding back from doing evil. It also teaches believers not to be obsessed with possessions or outward appearances because they know that all they have is given by Allah, and it is their inner-self that will survive after death. Belief in the reality of eternal punishment for unbelievers also causes many Muslims to seek to share their faith so that others may convert to Islam and eventually share in al-Jannah (Paradise) after death.

To discuss

● In December 2015 heavy rain caused flooding across large parts of northern Britain, including Hebden Bridge (above) and Rochdale, and many people had to leave their homes and businesses. Al-Khair Foundation supported residents of Rochdale with food and blankets, and ensured they had access to gas and electricity (www.alkhair.org). In what way may their belief in the Day of Judgement and Akhirah (life after death) have influenced the actions of the Muslims who helped as they worked to support flooded communities in England during the floods of 2015?

Qur'an quotes

'Except for those who repent and correct themselves and make evident [what they concealed]. Those – I will accept their repentance, and I am the One who accepts repentance, the Most Merciful.'

(2:160)

'And do not think of those who have been killed in the way of Allah as dead. Rather, they are alive with their Lord, (and) provided for ...'
(3:169)

'And they say, "What? When we are turned to bones and dust, will we be resurrected as a new creation?" Say, "Be you stones or iron Or [any] creation of that which is great within your breasts." And they will say, "Who will restore us?" Say, "He who brought you forth the first time." Then they will nod their heads toward you and say, "When is that?" Say, "Perhaps it will be soon – On the Day He will call you and you will respond with praise of Him and think that you had not remained [in the world] except for a little."'
(17:49–52)

'There is no compulsion in the religion [Islam]. The right direction is distinctly clear from error.'
(2:256)

Tasks

1 Create a flow diagram to present the Muslim beliefs about The Day of Judgement, al-Jannah and Jahannam.

2 Add Qur'an quotes to your diagram to support these beliefs.

3 'Akhirah is the main belief that will affect the way a Muslim chooses to live.'

Discuss this statement. In your answer, you should:

- analyse and evaluate the importance of points of view of common and divergent views within Christianity.
- refer to sources of wisdom and authority.

4 Practices

Topic checklist

- ✔ The importance of practices
- ✔ Public acts of worship
- ✔ Private acts of worship
- ✔ Zakah
- ✔ Sawm
- ✔ Hajj
- ✔ Festivals and special days
- ✔ Jihad

Key concepts

Islam means submission, and all Muslims seek to submit fully to the will of Allah. They believe that in every moment of their lives they should be following Allah's will; as such Islam is a complete way of life. There are certain practices in Islam that are compulsory for believers to do as part of their submission to Allah. Sunni and Shi'a Muslims have different ways of categorising these compulsory actions. Sunni Muslims describe them as five pillars whilst Shi'a Muslims categorise them as ten obligatory acts which include four of the five pillars also – salah, sawm, zakah and hajj.

The importance of practices

Muhammad ﷺ called on Muslims to worship Allah and to observe what are known as the Five Pillars of Islam. These Five Pillars are the essentials of Islam. They are:

- **Shahadah**: declaration of faith.
- **Salah**: five daily prayers.
- **Zakah**: giving of wealth as a tax to the poor and needy.
- **Sawm**: fasting during the month of Ramadan.
- **Hajj**: pilgrimage.

These pillars are often depicted as a house, with each one supporting the house of Islam. If any of them were removed, the house would fall down.

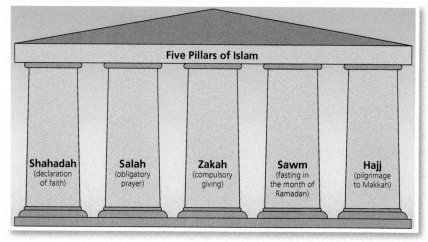

Five Pillars of Islam

| **Shahadah** (declaration of faith) | **Salah** (obligatory prayer) | **Zakah** (compulsory giving) | **Sawm** (fasting in the month of Ramadan) | **Hajj** (pilgrimage to Makkah) |

♬ The Five Pillars of Islam

Shi'a Muslims have a total of ten obligatory acts known as furu'al-din. These ten acts include salah, sawm, zakah and hajj contained in the five pillars plus:

- **Khums**: an annual taxation of one-fifth (20 per cent) of savings. Khums is paid to religious leaders and used to help poor and needy people.
- **Jihad**: struggle to live in the way God wants.
- **Amr-bil-Maroof**: commanding what is right. Maroof means something that is right and just.
- **Nahi Anil Munkar**: forbidding what is wrong. Munkar is something that is evil.
- **Tawalla**: Holding love for the Prophet Muhammad ﷺ and his Ahlul-Bayt (descendants) and all they stood for and strived to achieve.
- **Tabarra**: Holding disdain for the enemies of Prophet Muhammad ﷺ and his Ahlul-Bayt (descendants) and all the negative things they stood for and tried to achieve.

Qur'an quotes

'O believers! When the call is made for prayer on Friday, hurry toward the remembrance of Allāh, and leave all business. That is better for you, should you know.'

(62:9)

'Oh you who believe! Fasting has been prescribed for you as it was prescribed for those before you, so that you may be mindful of God.'

(2:183)

'A kind word and forgiveness is better than charity followed by hurtful (words). Allah is Self Sufficient, forbearing.'

(2:263)

'And We made them leaders guiding others by Our command, and We inspired them to do good works and to keep up salah and the giving of zakah, and they were Our worshippers.'

(21:73)

'O you who believe! When you rise up to prayer, wash your faces and your hands as far as the elbows, and wipe your heads and your feet to the ankles'

(5:6)

'There is no god except Him, the Almighty, the All Wise.'

(3:18)

Link it up

a Create a Venn diagram as shown.

b List the quotes and number them.

c Place the number of each quote into the appropriate part of the diagram.

d To do this you will need to identify what Islamic practice each quote can be linked to and whether it is part of the Obligatory Acts as well as the Five Pillars.

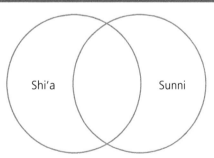

Public acts of worship

Shahadah

The first of the Five Pillars is the only one that is not an action. Instead, this pillar is the declaration of faith. It contains two statements: 'There is no god but Allah, and Muhammad ﷺ is the Messenger of Allah.' This declaration of two statements is known as kalimat al-tawhid. It embodies the Muslim belief in Tawhid (the oneness of Allah) and reflects the monotheistic nature of Islam as established through the prophet Muhammad ﷺ.

It makes clear that only Allah is worthy of worship because He alone is God and supreme over all things, and that to place anything above Him would be to commit the sin of shirk. The second part of the declaration is a reminder to believers that Allah has chosen to reveal Himself to people through Muhammad ﷺ and the prophets who came before him.

It is through declaring the Shahadah that a person professes the Muslim faith. The Shahadah is whispered to a newborn baby so that it is the first words they hear, and it should be the last words on a Muslim's lips before they die. Saying this declaration of faith is also the way for non-believers to convert to Islam. Saying the words, however, must be accompanied by an understanding of the meaning and importance of them. It is the intention to live by the will of Allah that is important. The Shahadah has to be professed until death; anyone who abandons this belief commits the sin of apostasy.

◯ La ilaha illallahu Muhammad Rasulullah

Salah

Salah (prayer) is the ritual Muslim prayer that is carried out five times every day. It is the first duty believed to have been given by Allah and is one of the Five Pillars for Sunni Muslims and one of the Ten Obligatory Acts for Shi'a. One of the 99 names of Allah is The Hearer and Muslims believe that when they pray they are in direct communication with God. They believe he will listen and respond to everything they say. In carrying out this prayer Muslims regularly and without hesitation declare their faith in Allah. By offering Salah Muslims also seek to gain Allah's favour. In the Hadith (the sayings of Muhammad ﷺ) Muhammad ﷺ provided Muslims with the timings for each of the five daily prayers:

- Fajr – morning prayer, between dawn and sunset.
- Zuhr – midday prayer in the early afternoon.
- Asr – late afternoon prayer.
- Maghrib – prayer just after sunset.
- Isha – night-time prayer.

The exact times for each prayer will vary depending on the time of the year. Muslims are individually responsible for praying at these times. Prayer is preferably done in the mosque; if a Muslim is not praying in the mosque they must find a suitably clean place for prayer.

Call to prayer

Before every salah a call to prayer known as the adhan is made by the mu'adhdhin (caller to prayer) in Arabic whilst facing the qiblah in the direction of Makkah. In some Muslim countries he climbs up the tall minaret (tower) to do this. Nowadays, in most countries loudspeakers are used. In some British towns and cities the adhan can sometimes be heard from the loudspeakers in the mosques. The meaning of the adhan is:

> Allah is the Greatest (repeated four times)
> I bear witness that there is no god but Allah
> (repeated twice)
> I bear witness that Muhammad ﷺ is the Messenger
> of Allah (repeated twice)
> Come to prayer (repeated twice)
> Come to success (repeated twice)
> Prayer is better than sleep (only said for morning
> prayer and repeated twice)
> Allah is the Greatest (repeated twice)
> There is no god but Allah

The muezzin gives a second call to prayer in the main worship hall of the mosque for those who have come to the mosque to pray, this is called the 'iqamah' and it lets worshippers know that prayer is about to begin.

Wudu

An important part of preparing for prayer is **wudu**; this is the ritual washing that a Muslim must do before Salah prayer. Wudu is done as a symbolic action to reinforce the niyyah declaration that the believer makes as they begin. The niyyah is the believer's intention to worship Allah with a pure heart; this may be said out loud or it may just be declared within the believer's heart. Wudu always follows the same set pattern and includes the washing of arms, hands, feet and mouth. The Qur'an states:

'Allah loves those who turn to him and who care for cleanliness.'

(2:222)

∩ 1 Hands are washed

∩ 2 The mouth is rinsed out three times

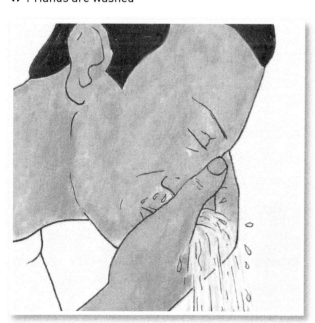

∩ 3 The nose is washed as water is blown out three times

∩ 4 Using both hands the whole face is washed three times

This underlines the importance of wudu before Salah. After completing wudu a Muslim will recite the phrase:

'I bear witness that there is no god but Allah and He is one and has no partner and I bear witness that Muhammad ﷺ is His servant and messenger.'

🎧 5 Both arms, starting with the right arm, are washed including the elbow three times

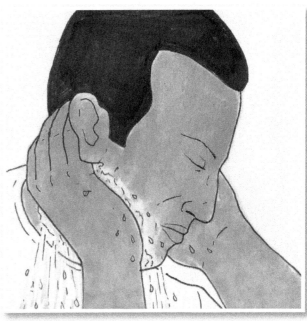

🎧 6 Wet fingers are moved backwards over the top of the head and palms over the sides in a forward direction. Then the index fingers are passed inside the ears and the thumbs outside the ears. Lastly the back of the fingers are passed over the nape

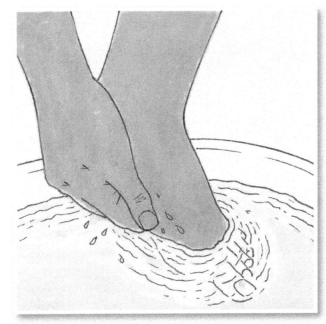

🎧 7 Both feet, starting with the right foot, are washed thoroughly including the ankle. Shi'a Muslims do not wash feet instead they simply wipe over them with wet hands.

To discuss

a How may a day at school be affected by a Muslims duty to salah?

b In what way does wudu reinforce the niyyah declaration?

Rak'ahs

Salah involves the recitation of parts of the Qur'an and some phrases in Arabic whilst carrying out a sequence of movements. There are eight movements in each prayer sequence and each one has a religious significance. A complete sequence of prayer is called a **rak'ah**, and the number of rak'ahs can be two, three or four depending on which prayer it is.

🎧 1 Hands are raised to the ears and the words 'Allahu Akbar', meaning 'Allah is the Greatest', are said. This symbolises the intention to focus only on Allah and to leave every thought or concern behind

🎧 2 Whilst in the standing position, the opening chapter and other parts of the Qur'an are recited.

🎧 3 Bowing to demonstrate respect and saying the words: 'Allahu Akbar', and then, three times, 'Glory to my Lord the great.'

🎧 4 Standing upright, arms straight down to the side, the words said are: 'Allah has heard all who praise him. Our Lord: Praise be to you.'

🎧 5 Prostrate on the ground using the words 'Allahu Akbar', followed three times by the saying: 'Glory to my Lord, the most high.' Then sitting back on the heels for a moment before prostrating again. This position demonstrates complete submission to the will of Allah. This completes the first rak'ah

🎧 6 After the second rak'ah they sit back with hands placed on knees. Remaining in this position further prayers are recited, especially asking for Allah's blessing upon Muhammad ﷺ and Ibrahim

🎧 7 Once the rak'ahs are complete, while sitting on their knees, they turn their head to the right and then to the left, blessing their fellow Muslims each time and saying the words: 'Peace be on you.' This is called 'salam', which means peace

Jumu'ah prayer

Every Friday, instead of Zuhr prayer the Jumu'ah prayer is offered at mosques. This is known as **Jumu'ah** prayer and male Muslims must make every effort to attend; women may also attend, although they will pray in a separate room from the men. Surah 62:9 says,

'O believers! When the call is made for prayer on Friday, hurry toward the remembrance of Allah, and leave all business. That is better for you, should you know.'

Gathering together in this way is a reminder of the wider Muslim **Ummah** (community). During Jumu'ah prayers, Muslims will line up in rows, shoulder to shoulder, to perform the rak'ahs. It is very important that Muslims have the correct **qibla** when they pray: this means that they must face in the right direction – towards Makkah. In the mosque Muslims will face the **mihrab**, a semi-circular niche in the wall of the main prayer hall, which indicates the direction of Makkah. When praying alone, or away from the mosque, Muslims will use prayer mats. During Jumu'ah, the imam delivers a sermon called a **khutba** and therafter leads the congregation in two rak'ahs of prayer. Joining together at this time helps the Muslim community to be cohesive as a sense of unity is developed. It also provides a time to discuss any community issues and resolve any problems.

Qur'an quotes

'In the name of Allah, the Entirely Merciful, the Especially Merciful. [All] praise is [due] to Allah, Lord of the worlds – The Entirely Merciful, the Especially Merciful, Sovereign of the Day of Recompense. It is You we worship and You we ask for help. Guide us to the straight path – The path of those upon whom You have bestowed favour, not of those who have evoked [Your] anger or of those who are astray.'

(Surah 1)

'And when you have completed the prayer, remember Allah standing, sitting, or [lying] on your sides. But when you become secure, re-establish [regular] prayer. Indeed, prayer has been decreed upon the believers a decree of specified times.'

(4:103)

'And when the prayer has been concluded, disperse within the land and seek from the bounty of Allah, and remember Allah often that you may succeed.'

(62:10)

'And establish salah at the two ends of the day and during parts of the night. Indeed, good deeds do away with bad deeds. That is a reminder for those who remember.'

(11:114)

Tasks

1 State the meaning of the word 'rak'ah'.
2 Describe the movements associated with a rak'ah.
3 Explain the religious significance of these movements.
4 Explain the effect that you think praying in this way, five times a day, may have on a believer.
5 Discuss whether self-discipline in religious life is as valuable as more spontaneous worship.

'Verily between man and between polytheism and unbelief is the negligence of prayer'
(Sahih Muslim).

To discuss

Why do you think neglecting prayer was linked with such significant consequences by the Prophet Muhammad ﷺ?

Link it up

Use the quotes above to explain the way that Salah should continue to influence a Muslim during the rest of their day.

To discuss

Why do you think Shi'a Muslims place such importance on prostrating onto something of the ground rather than on to something human-made?

Shi'a prayer

Shi'a Muslims also pray five times a day, but they are allowed to join the midday (Zuhr) Salah and the afternoon (Asr) prayers together, as well as the evening (Maghrib) and night-time (Isha) prayers. So it may appear that they pray only three times a day. Shi'a Muslims prostrate themselves on things that are counted as part of the Earth; often they may use a piece of wood or a slab made of clay from Kerbala (a city in Iraq they believe is sacred) but can be from anywhere, to place their heads on during prostration. This is different to the Sunni Muslims, who touch their heads directly on the mosque's carpeted floor. For Shi'as the ground is considered a pure material and fulfils the need for the place of prayer to be clean. Shi'a Muslims believe that it is wrong to prostrate to Allah on something human-made and artificial. The fact that Muhammad ﷺ used a mat made of natural fibres supports this Shi'a belief.

Tasks

1 Describe why it may seem like Shi'a Muslims only pray three times a day instead of five.
2 Outline the difference between Shi'a and Sunni prayer practices
3 What makes Friday Zuhr prayer unique compared to prayer at other times? Explain the benefit this can have on a Muslim community.

Private acts of worship

Du'a' (Supplication)

In Islam, apart from the obligatory Salah prayer, there is also du'a prayer, which is private. The word 'du'a' simply means asking. It is in du'a prayers that a Muslim will bring their own special concerns to Allah. Du'a prayers may include thanksgiving to Allah, or requests for his forgiveness or help. In the Qur'an it says:

'And when My servants ask you, [O Muhammad ﷺ], concerning Me – indeed I am near. I respond to the invocation of the supplicant when he calls upon Me. So let them respond to Me and believe in Me that they may be [rightly] guided.'

(2:186)

By carrying out du'a prayer a Muslim is seeking Allah's guidance as he tells them to; they are showing faith in Allah's closeness and immediacy to them (his **immanence**). A Muslim may choose to say du'a prayers in his or her own language directly after finishing Salah, or they may choose to recite other Arabic prayers. Some Muslims may choose to offer additional rak'ahs of salah. Du'a prayers can be said at any time of the day and this may include the use of prayer beads. In this way du'a is different from the structured form of Salah; it is individual and demonstrates further dependence by the believer upon Allah.

Prayer beads

Prayer beads are passed between the thumb and the forefinger of the believer. Each set of prayer beads has either 33 or 99 beads, which are used to recite the 99 names of Allah or to repeat phrases. The phrases most commonly used are: 'Subhan Allah' (Glory to Allah), 'Alhamdulillah' (Praise be to Allah) and 'Allahu Akbar' (Allah is Great), each is repeated 33 times. The Prophet Muhammad ﷺ is recorded in a hadith as telling his daughter, Fatima, to remember Allah by using these phrases. Abu Hurairah reported that Muhammad ﷺ said that whoever completes the recitation with the phrase:

'There is no true god except Allah. He is One and He has no partner with Him. His is the sovereignty and His is the praise, and He is Omnipotent'

will have all his sins pardoned even if they may be as large as 'the foam on the surface of the sea.'

Some Muslims do not agree with the use of prayer beads because the Prophet Muhammad ﷺ did not use them. Some Muslims will instead use their fingers to count recitations.

Tasks

1 List the benefits of du'a prayer.
2 Explain what is achieved through Salah prayer that cannot be gained from du'a prayer.
3 Discuss whether a religion without congregational prayers is likely to foster a stronger or weaker community.

To discuss

a How do you think repetition of phrases while using prayer beads might be of value to a Muslim?
b In what way might having something physical to use during prayer be of help to a believer?
c Why do you think many Muslims choose to not use the beads?

Zakah

As Muhammad ﷺ was orphaned at a young age, he had a real concern for the needs of the poor and disadvantaged. One of the Five Pillars of Sunni tradition of Islam is obligatory almsgiving, for all those who can financially afford it. Whether or not a Muslim can afford to pay Zakah is determined by whether their net worth is more than a certain amount; this minimum amount is known as the Nisab. Zakah isn't just paid on monetary savings but on a range of possessions, for example on money, livestock and produce. Muslims give 2.5 per cent of their wealth above the nisab as Zakah. Each Muslim is individually accountable for paying the correct amount.

In Muslim countries the government collects it in much the same way as a tax. In other countries, including in the UK, Zakah is collected by local mosques and charitable organisations. This money is then distributed to help the needy within the Muslim community as well as being used for religious purposes.

The word 'Zakah' literally means purification, because Zakah is believed to purify a person's heart of greed. Ultimately a Muslim knows that they will be accountable to Allah on the Day of Judgement, and this should cause them to be honest in their giving. Muslims believe that what they possess is only with them because Allah has provided it; they therefore seek to share their wealth and use it to support others in need. It is not considered charity-giving because Muslims believe that it is simply the sharing of the wealth given by Allah, and that all Muslims have a right to share in this wealth. In the same way, a Muslim who receives money from Zakah should feel not lessened by it, but instead should feel blessed by Allah. In the Qur'an it states what money given through Zakah can be used for. It is to be used to support the poor and the needy, to free slaves (in the olden days) and those in debt (9:60). Zakah is a way of making society fairer and of showing practical concern for those in need.

⮑ Zakah can be used for helping individuals in need or for benefiting the whole community, for example by investing in education or maintaining religious buildings

Sadaqah

In addition to Zakah, Muslims may choose to make further voluntary donations, known as Sadaqah. This comes from the word 'sidq', meaning sincerity. Giving Sadaqah is a sign of a Muslim's sincerity to their faith. Unlike with Zakah, there are no limits or guidelines for Sadaqah; any amount may be given at any time and to anyone. Giving in charity extends beyond just money, as Muhammad ﷺ is recorded to have said that:

'Every act of goodness is charity.'

(Sahih Muslim, Hadith 496)

Furthermore, Muhammad ﷺ linked charitable giving to being saved from hell itself when he is recorded to have said:

'Save yourself from hellfire by giving even half a date-fruit in charity.'

(Sahih Al-Bukhari, Volume 2, Hadith 498)

Most importantly, while such giving should be done in secret so that no pride is present, Allah is aware of what is done (2:215).

Khums

Shi'a Muslims give khums as one of the ten obligatory acts. It is an annual tax. It becomes compulsory at the beginning of the new financial year on the profit or surplus of the past year's income. During the time of Prophet Muhammad ﷺ and his successors (the Imams), it was paid directly to them or their appointed agents. As the Twelfth Imam is in hiding, it is paid to religious scholars. It is used to help the poor and needy as well as to support religious establishments, religious schools, teachers and students. Shi'a Muslims are reminded to pay the Khums, as not paying is the same as disobeying God.

Stretch what you know

Visit the website of the Khums Bank at
http://khumsbank.com/kb/mstate.asp

a Investigate what the mission statement of the bank is and also the projects that it funds.

b Find out how Khums are distributed and write up a summary or produce a diagram to illustrate your findings.

Tasks

1 State what Zakah is.
2 Describe what Zakah donations are used for.
3 Explain why a Muslim may choose also to give Sadaqah.
4 Explain the difference between Zakah and Khums.
5 To what extent do you agree that keeping money that should be given as Khums is like keeping stolen money?

🎧 You are exempt from fasting during Ramadan if it will harm your health

To discuss 💬

a What are the benefits of sawm for a Muslim community?

b When Muslims exchange Id Mubarak greetings and reflect upon their fasting for the previous month, why do you think they are thankful to Allah?

c How might their thankfulness impact upon their lives over the year before the next period of obligatory fasting?

Sawm

Sawm is fasting in Ramadan, the ninth month of the Islamic year. This is the month when it is believed the Qur'an was revealed to Muhammad ﷺ. Muslims go without food, drink and sex during the daylight hours for the whole of this month. Sawm is the fourth pillar of Sunni tradition of Islam and also one of the Ten Obligatory Acts for Shi'a Muslims. It is commanded by Allah in the Qur'an:

'O you who believe, fasting has been prescribed for you just as it was prescribed for people before you so that you may become mindful of God.'

(2:183)

Exemptions from fasting

It is a practice that Muhammad ﷺ also followed. Every Muslim who is able to should fast during Ramadan. If fasting is going to seriously endanger a person's health, however, they are exempt from it, for example the sick, people who are making long journeys and pregnant women or women who are menstruating. Children usually begin to participate in sawm from the age of twelve.

The benefits of fasting to individuals and the ummah

By participating in sawm with an attitude of repentance, Muslims believe that their sins will be forgiven by Allah. Muslims develop their self-discipline in obedience to Allah. They are able to overcome selfishness as their own physical needs are not driving what they do during this month. During this month Muslims will have times of feeling hungry and thirsty, which helps them to appreciate the needs of others, leading them to develop a greater sense of empathy and ideally a greater willingness to help. Through this experience Muslims are thankful to Allah for all that He has given them and their dependence on Him should increase. Sawm helps a Muslim to be completely obedient to Allah; this is known as being a Muttaqi. The development of obedience to Allah and also be mindful of His presence. This is known as being a Muttaqi. The development of an awareness of God's presence is known as Taqwa, and this is what helps to keep a Muslim away from sin. By becoming more self-controlled a Muslim increasingly does good deeds as they are pleasing to Allah. Many Muslims will spend extra time studying the Qur'an and praying during the month of Ramadan, which increases their sense of closeness to Allah. It heightens their awareness and understanding of their faith and draws them together as a united community.

Duties during Ramadan

Muslims get up early during the month of Ramadan so that they can eat and drink before the fasting for that day begins. In the Qur'an it says that fasting should be:

'…until the white thread of dawn becomes distinct from the black. Then complete the fasts till nightfall …'

(2:187)

Often mosques will give Muslims timetables for the fasting period. In Islamic countries a canon may be fired or a drum beaten in order to wake Muslims up in time to eat each day before the start of fasting; this pre-dawn meal is known as suhur. Apart from not eating or drinking, a Muslim must not allow anything to enter their body through the nose or mouth, meaning smoking is also forbidden. During sawm a Muslim is also expected to stay away from bad or negative actions such as lying or breaking promises. They must also work hard to control their thinking, avoiding bad thoughts and anger.

In the evening the fast is broken with a meal known as Iftar. Muslims start this meal by consuming a small amount along with a glass of water. The Maghrib (evening) prayer is then performed before the main meal is eaten. The poor are often invited to share in a meal with a family or are given food. Some mosques put on a meal every evening during the month of Ramadan so that the Muslim community breaks fast together each night. Every night during Ramadan special prayers known as Taraweeh are said at the mosque. They include the recitation of large portions of the Qur'an. Taraweeh can last for up to an hour or more and involves many cycles of movements, prostration and standing to read the Qur'an. After every four cycles of movement Muslims will sit to rest briefly before continuing in prayer. The word 'taraweeh' means rest. By the end of Ramadan the whole of the Qur'an will have been read during Taraweeh.

Last ten days of Ramadan and the Night of Power

The final ten days of Ramadan are especially important; the Hadith says that it was during this time that the Night of Power occurred, which was when Muhammad ﷺ received the first pages of the Qur'an (see page 106). During these ten days many Muslims will aim to worship Allah as much as possible. Some Muslims will make a point of taking these ten days as holiday from their work so that they can focus on worship. It is believed that it was the practice of Muhammad ﷺ to spend these last ten days of Ramadan at the mosque in study of the Qur'an and prayer. Some Muslims seek to follow this example, remaining in the mosque, if not for all ten days, for at least some of that time. Many Muslims who have not attended previous Taraweeh prayers will aim to go to these during these final ten days. Men and women can go to these prayers and, while they are not obligatory, Muslims are encouraged to go as they are considered a blessing. Taraweeh prayers are broadcast live from Makkah on television and they are also accompanied by an English translation.

The end of Ramadan

The new moon indicating the start of the month of Shawwal brings an end to Ramadan and to sawm. This is marked with the celebration of Id-ul-Fitr, which simply means Festival of Fast Breaking. During this festival children are given presents, sweets and new clothes. In preparation for Id-ul-Fitr homes are decorated, food is prepared and Muslims may send one another cards wishing one another 'Id Mubarak', meaning happy festival. On the morning of Id Muslims will usually go to the mosque for special prayers. It is a day for thanksgiving to Allah and for celebration.

Sawm in Islamic and non-Islamic countries

In Islamic countries quite often the pace of everyday life slows a little during Ramadan; carrying out everyday work is obviously made harder during fasting, especially in hot weather. In non-Muslim countries, however, where fewer people observe Ramadan, it can be even more challenging. Young people who are participating and who are still at school may need to be excused from doing PE.

Tasks

1 State the month in which sawm occurs.

2 Describe the significant event that occurred to Muhammad ﷺ during this month.

3 Explain how this event affects the practice of sawm for many Muslims.

4 In what way does this have a spiritual impact upon Muslims?

5 'Without sawm Muslims would be less aware of Allah's goodness to them.' Discuss this statement, include Muslim perspectives as well as your own opinion.

Link it up

a What does the Qur'an say someone who is ill or on a long journey should do if they have to miss fasting?

b What reason is given for this?

Qur'an quotes

'It was in the month of Ramadan that the Qur'an was revealed as guidance for people, clear messages giving guidance and distinguishing between right and wrong. So any one of you who is present that month should fast, and anyone who is ill or on a journey should make up for the lost days by fasting on other days later. God wants ease for you, and does not want hardship for you. He wants you to complete the prescribed period and to glorify Him for having guided you, so that you may be thankful.'

(2:185)

Hajj

Hajj is both one of the Five Pillars of Sunni tradition of Islam and one of the Ten Obligatory Acts for Shi'a Muslims. The word 'Hajj' means to set out for a definite purpose, and for Muslims Hajj is the pilgrimage to the holy city of Makkah in Saudi Arabia and to the Kaaba. It can only be performed between the eighth and twelfth and in some circumstances between the eight and thirteenth of Dhul-Hijjah, the last month of the Islamic calendar. Hajj is the only one of the Five Pillars that Muslims are not obliged to perform; if they are physically unable or don't have the financial resources to go then they are exempt. Men who have completed the Hajj are given the title hajji and women are given the title hajja. Only Muslims can enter Makkah – it is a city set apart for the sacred purpose of Hajj. It is haram, which in this case means it is sacred. On approaching the city everyone has to have their passes checked to confirm that they are Muslim and are arriving for pilgrimage.

The Origins of Hajj

The origins of the Hajj date back to 2000BCE when Ibrahim's wife Hager and his young son, Ishmael were stranded in the desert. Ishmael was close to death from thirst, so Hager ran between the hills of Safa and Marwa looking for water. Then the angel Jibril came and created a spring of fresh water for Ishmael, this is known as the Well of Zamzam.

Ibrahim is then told by Allah is to build a monument at the site of the spring. This monument was called the Kabba. Worshipers from all different faiths travelled to see this site, placing idols in the Kabba to be worshipped. However in 630AD, the Prophet Mohammed led a group of Muslims there in the first official Hajj. They destroyed the idols placed there by the polytheistic worshippers and re-dedicated the Kabba in the name of Allah. The path that Muhammed and his followers travelled is retraced as part of the Hajj rituals every year.

Ihram

Ihram is a state of holiness that Muslims are required to be in before beginning on Hajj. This means that Muslims must wash their bodies fully or perform wudu before they arrive at Makkah. As part of this Muslims will wear special clothing, also known as ihram. For men ihram is two pieces of unsewn white cloth worn instead of their everyday clothes. One piece is tied around their waist the other placed over their left shoulder. Men wear sandals on their feet and leave their heads uncovered. Women have no set dress code but often they will choose to wear a simple white dress and headscarf. Women will be fully covered, showing only their hands and face. White is a symbol of purity and it serves as a reminder to Muslims not to sin. Some pilgrims save the ihram

cloth and hope it will be used to wrap their body to be buried after they die. It is a reminder that they are there to focus entirely on their worship of Allah, disconnected from the things of their everyday lives. This simple dress is also symbolic of their humility before Allah. Every Muslim on Hajj takes on an equal status: they are all dressed the same and their personal appearance should be of no concern during this time; their focus ought to remain solely on Allah. Once on Hajj many men and women choose to stay in separate accommodation from their spouses. They are not allowed to have sex during Hajj because it would take their focus away from Allah. In other expressions of self-control during this time, Muslims show no violence nor do they cut their nails, shave, wear perfume, swear, argue, lie, damage plants or marry. In this state of Ihram Muslims will recite the Talbiyah prayer, which says:

'Here I am at Thy service O Lord, here I am. Here I am at Thy service and Thou hast no partners. Thine alone is All Praise and All Bounty, and Thine alone is The Sovereignty. Thou hast no partners.'

This prayer is said often during Hajj and it is a repeated submission to Allah and a commitment to ongoing service to Him. This commitment to service is also an indication of a Muslim's love for Allah and their desire to become closer and closer to Him.

The Kaaba

In the courtyard of the Sacred Mosque in Makkah is the Kaaba. The Kaaba is a large, cube-shaped structure, measuring approximately 13 metres in height. It is believed that it was originally built by Adam and then later rebuilt by the Prophet Ibrahim. In the courtyard of the Sacred Mosque is the Station of Ibrahim, believed to be the spot from which he began the process of rebuilding it. Just as Ibrahim prayed here, so pilgrims are required to do the same.

> ### To discuss
>
> a To what extent does what you wear affect your attitude and thinking?
>
> b How can putting on ihram be understood as a spiritual act?

In the south-east corner of the Kaaba is a black stone. Some Muslims believe that the stone was given to Ibrahim by the Angel Jibril; others think it is a meteorite sent down from heaven. One tradition teaches that the stone was originally white, shining like a light, but that human sin caused it to go black. Muslims try to kiss the Black Stone as they circle the Kaaba, which has caused an indentation in the centre of the stone where the kisses have worn it down.

It was Muhammad ﷺ who in 630CE removed all the idols from the Kaaba and dedicated it to the worship of Allah alone. The Kaaba is covered with a black cloth made of silk and wool, this covering is called the **al-Kiswah**. Sections from the Qur'an are incorporated into it with gold embroidery. On the ninth of Dhul-Hijjah the cloth is replaced with a new one. The old cloth is then cut into sections and sold to pilgrims.

Tawaf

It is in the Holy Mosque that Muslims begin their pilgrimage. On his final visit to Makkah, Muhammad ﷺ visited the Kaaba and this is copied by the pilgrims. In an act of drawing closer to Allah, pilgrims circle around the Kaaba seven times in an anti-clockwise direction. Before beginning this circling, known as 'tawaf', each Muslim says the niyyah, a prayer of intent:

'O Allah, I perform Tawaf of Umrah to please You. Make it easy for me and accept it from me.'

They start from the corner of the Black Stone, men walk very briskly for the first three circuits and walking at normal pace for the remaining four. On each circuit Muslims will try to touch or kiss the Black Stone just like Muhammad ﷺ did. The number

Task

Sketch your own map of the route of hajj using the map here. Read through the following pages to add detail on what happens at each of the places on the map.

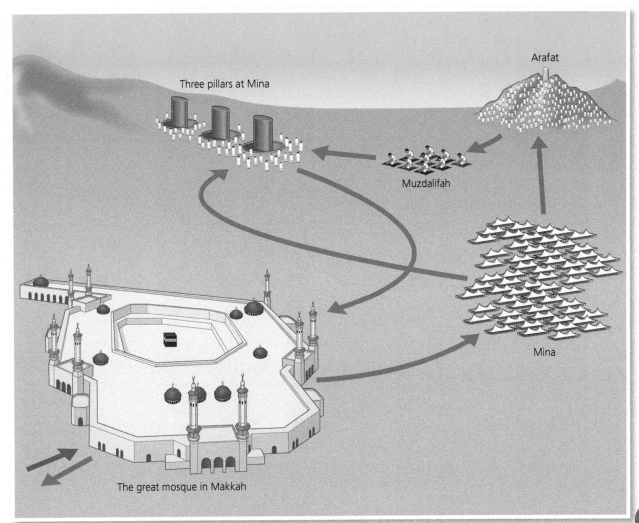

Three pillars at Mina

Arafat

Muzdalifah

Mina

The great mosque in Makkah

of Muslims participating in Hajj often makes this impossible, however, and many Muslims will simply salute the Black Stone as they pass it. During the tawaf each Muslim will be reciting verses from the Qur'an or other prayers. Tawaf is a powerful demonstration of Muslim unity and of their desire to worship their one true god, Allah. Having completed the seven circuits Muslims will then move to the Station of Ibrahim to pray and to complete two rak'ahs.

Sa'y

Sa'y is the running, or hurrying, between two hills known as As-Safa and Al-Marwa. The hills are about 420 metres apart and nowadays are linked by a covered walkway. Muslims will move seven times between the two hills in re-enactment of Hagar's search for water when she was left alone in the desert with her son Isma'il. It was only when her son dug his heel into the ground that a spring of water rose up. This spring can be visited today at the Well of Zamzam. Some pilgrims take home water from the well.

∩ There is now a covered walkway between As-Safa and Al-Marwa for pilgrims to walk through

Arafat

After Fajr (dawn prayer) at Mina the pilgrims travel approximately 24 km to the Mount of Mercy at the Plain of Arafat in the east. The pilgrims have to be there from midday to dusk on the ninth of Dhul-Hijjah. They face towards the Kaaba, just as it is believed the Prophet Muhammad ﷺ did. Many will hold umbrellas to keep off the scorching heat of the sun. It is here that the pilgrims stand before Allah and plead for the forgiveness of their sins. It is one of the most important rituals during the Hajj. Even Muslims who are not on Hajj may set this day aside for prayer and fasting.

From here Muslims move on to Muzdalifah; here they will complete their sunset and night prayers and camp in the open. They will collect 49 stones ready for use at Mina over the next three days.

To discuss

How can symbolic acts impact upon a person's faith?

🎧 Plain of Arafat

Mina

On the tenth of Dhul-Hijjah pilgrims travel to Mina and it is here that the 'Stoning of Iblis' takes place. There are three very wide and high walls which symbolize Iblis (Satan) and pilgrims. Pilgrims throw seven pebbles at the pillar known as 'jamrah', meaning great devil. This ritual is repeated on the eleventh and twelfth of Dhul-Hijjah, when they throw seven pebbles at each of three pillars.

It recalls the time when Allah told Ibrahim to sacrifice his son, Isma'il, as a test of Ibrahim's faith. Three times Iblis told Ibrahim not to do it and encouraged Isma'il to run away; both resisted Iblis' temptations, driving him away by throwing stones at him. Allah was testing Ibrahim's and Isma'il's faith, and instead of sacrificing Isma'il, Allah provided Ibrahim with a ram as an alternative sacrifice. By throwing the stones the pilgrims are demonstrating their own rejection of evil and Iblis. It is an action that symbolises their desire to withstand any temptations and to remain faithful to Allah.

🎧 Pillars at Mina

At Mina pilgrims who can afford to are required to offer an animal sacrifice. The meat is eaten by the pilgrims, with at least one-third being given away to pilgrims who cannot afford to make their own sacrifice. This sacrifice is a further reminder of Allah's provision to Ibrahim of a sacrificial ram in place of sacrificing Ishma'il. Muslims recognise what Allah has provided them and that everything they possess is because of Allah's goodness to them; this can encourage an even-greater sense of humility in the pilgrims. Muslims around the world also participate in this animal sacrifice as they celebrate Id-ul-Adha.

Male pilgrims will then have their heads shaved and women will cut a small lock of hair. This symbolises coming out of the state of ihram.

Most Muslims return to the Great Mosque when Hajj is complete to perform final tawaf around the Kaaba.

What does Hajj mean for Muslims?

Having completed Hajj the pilgrims will have memories of all that they have done. There may well be a greater sense of ummah (community) as they have worshipped together with more than two million other Muslims, standing shoulder to shoulder in ihram. The closeness to Allah that they have felt during this time, especially from their experience at Arafat, will encourage them and probably leave them with a lasting sense of awe. Many pilgrims will feel relieved of their weight of sin as they have pleaded with Allah for His forgiveness, and this may drive them on to being more obedient Muslims in their everyday life. They will be joyous at completing Hajj as commanded by Allah and more certain of their place in Paradise after death.

Festivals and special days

Id-ul-Adha

Id-ul-Adha is the 'Festival of Sacrifice' and it is the major Muslim festival. As the pilgrims on Hajj sacrifice an animal near to Makkah, Muslims all over the world also make an animal sacrifice. The festival can last up to three days, depending on the country in which it is being celebrated. In Muslim countries Id-ul-Adha is a national holiday, unlike in countries such as the UK. The festival remembers the time when Allah provided a lamb for Ibrahim to sacrifice instead of his son, Ishma'il.

How the festival is celebrated

Muslims do several things in preparation for the festival, following the traditions of the Prophet Muhammad ﷺ. Obviously an animal is selected for sacrifice. In Islamic countries an animal will be slaughtered in the backyard of each Muslim family. In other countries, such as the UK, a licence is required to slaughter an animal, so instead Muslim families in these countries are likely to go to a slaughterhouse and have the animal slaughtered in the traditional Muslim way. This means the animal is slaughtered in the traditional humane Muslim way as the following words:

'In the name of God, God is the greatest.'

are said in Arabic. At the start of the festival Muslims dress up, often putting on new clothes ready for the celebration.

The festival begins with prayers usually at the mosque, and the delivery of a khutbah (sermon) by the imam. Id prayers may also be offered in an open air gathering place known as an Musalla. Men, women and children go to the Id prayers although significant numbers of women choose not to as it is not compulsory upon them. Thereafter Muslims greet each other saying "Id Mubarak". Many children receive presents and some Muslims also send cards to their families and friends.

Once the animal has been sacrificed the meat is divided into three portions. One-third is kept by the family, one-third is given to friends and relatives, and the final portion is given to the poor and needy.

The meaning of the festival

This festival is a demonstration of Muslims' willingness to make sacrifices for Allah. It is also an opportunity for them to be thankful to Allah for His provision, especially in the food that they eat. It helps to develop the sense of ummah, both in the gathering together for prayers but also through the distribution of the meat. This is also a sign of support for those who are on Hajj and who are completing their animal sacrifice near Makkah.

To discuss

a What personal characteristics do you think are developed through sacrificial giving?

b To what extent do you think sacrificial giving is necessary as a demonstration of genuine faith?

c Explain what an Eidgah is?

Id-ul-Fitr

Id ul-Fitr is the festival of ending the fasting of Ramadan when the crescent moon is sighted. Before the Id prayers Muslims give sadaqat ul-fitr, a special charity to atone for any mistakes they might have made whilst fasting. This is sometimes also known as **zakah** ul-fitr. Id-ul-Fitr is a three-day festival, beginning on the first day of Shawwal, the tenth month of the Islamic calendar. Many Muslims try to spot the new moon. In Muslim countries the sight of the new moon is often announced through the firing of a canon; in other countries it is broadcast via TV or radio. In the morning families attend the mosque for Id prayers – these gatherings are often so large that the prayers spread outside the mosque as well! As in Id-ul-Adha, the imam will deliver a khutbah (sermon), which often focuses on the duty to care for the needy.

After this, families return to their homes and gather with their friends for celebratory parties. Muhammad ﷺ called this festival 'The Day of Reward' as it comes after the hardships of Sawm during Ramadan. This celebration is also a national holiday in many Muslim countries and marks three days off work and school. Muslims will enjoy specially prepared food, exchange gifts, buy new clothes and enjoy one another's company, forgetting past disagreements and being thankful to Allah for all He does for them. Their thankfulness includes the success that Allah has given them in the completion of their fasting, enabling them to look forward to their reward on the Day of Judgement. Some Muslims will also visit the cemetery to remember those who have been separated from them by death.

To discuss

a Why do you think Muslims give one another Id Mubarak cards?

b How can the spiritual meaning of a celebration be reinforced with physical objects or actions?

Id-ul-Ghadeer

The meaning of the festival

Id-ul-Ghadeer is a Shi'a festival on the eighteenth of the Islamic month of Dhul-Hijjah, to celebrate the day on which the Prophet Muhammad ﷺ delivered his last sermon. It is believed by Shi'a Muslims that on this day Muhammad ﷺ appointed Ali ibn Abi Talib as his successor. Muhammad ﷺ was travelling to Medinah when part of the Qur'an, now known as the 'verse of announcement', was revealed to him:

'O Messenger! Proclaim everything that has been sent down to you from your Lord; if you do not, then you will not have communicated His message. And God will protect you from the people. God does not guide those who reject Him.'

(5:67)

The verse of announcement is saying that Muhammad ﷺ has an important message to proclaim in order to fulfil his mission as the prophet of Allah. After this revelation Muhammad ﷺ stopped his journey back to Medinah at a place called Ghadir Khumm, and it is here that he made a speech. For Shi'a Muslims one of the most significant parts of this speech is when he held up Ali's hand and said:

'Of whomsoever I had been Master [Mawla], Ali here is to be his Master. O Allah, be a supporter of whoever supports him [Ali] and an enemy of whoever opposes him...'

(Hadith of the pond of Khumm)

Following this, Muhammad ﷺ ordered a tent to be set up for Ali to sit in while Muslims came to him to pledge their allegiance to him as Muhammad's ﷺ successor. Sunni Muslims do not accept the Shi'a interpretation of these events at Ghadir Khumm; instead, they say that Muhammad ﷺ was calling for Ali to be respected but not to be seen as his successor. Thus Sunni Muslims do not celebrate this event.

How the festival is celebrated

In celebration of this event Shi'a Muslims are recommended to perform rituals during the day. They are also recommended to read specific prayers as part of this celebration. Shi'a Muslims gather on the eve or the day of Ghadeer where, as a part of celebration, the event is narrated and poems of praise are recited. There are great celebrations and in Shi'a Muslim countries, such as Iran, there are often festivities in the streets as Muslims greet one another. Presents are given between Muslims and celebratory meals are had.

Tasks

1 Pair up with another student.
2 One of you needs to create a presentation on Id-ul-Adha and one of you needs to create a presentation on Id-ul-Fitr.
3 Make sure you include what is being celebrated as well as how it is celebrated.
4 At the end of your presentation write five questions about what you have learned.
5 Once completed take it in turns to go through your presentation then each of you must complete the questions written by your partner on their topic.

Ashura

Ashura is celebrated by Sunni and Shi'a Muslims for different reasons. It takes place on the tenth of Muharram, the first month of the Islamic year. It is a day that the Prophet Muhammad ﷺ dedicated to fasting. It celebrates two events: the first is the day that Nuh (Noah) left the Ark, and the second is the day that Musa (Moses) was saved from the Egyptians by Allah. Muhammad ﷺ made this fast voluntary but for Shi'a Muslims it has remained a major festival. At this time Shi'a Muslims remember the martydom of Hussayn on the tenth of Muharram 680ce. He was the son of Ali and the grandson of Muhammad ﷺ, and was the third Imam of the Shi'as. Hussayn, along with his family and a small group of his companions, was massacred by forces at a battle in Karbala, in present-day Iraq. Hussayn's death is generally understood by both Sunni and Shi'a Muslims as a symbol of the struggle against injustice and oppression.

During this sad day many Shi'a Muslims participate in public expressions of mourning and grief. Despite prohibitions from

Ayatollahs some Shi'as whip and beat themselves to express their grief. They do this as a way to link themselves with Hussayn's suffering and death. Many Shi'as believe that this will help them on the Day of Judgement.

In London, around 3,000 Shi'a Muslims gather at Marble Arch on Ashura for a mourning procession and speeches.

Many Shi'a make visits on Ashura to the Mashhad al-Husayn, the shrine in Karbala that is believed to be Hussayn's tomb.

🔊 Ashura celebration in London

Celebrating Islamic festivals in non-Muslim countries

 Shi'a celebrations of Ashura around the world

Celebrating Islamic festivals in a non-Muslim country can raise certain issues. The significance of the festival to Muslims may not be understood as well as it is in an Islamic country. This may make it difficult for Muslims to have the time off work or out of school in order to celebrate their festivals as fully as they would like to. Depending on the community that a Muslim is in they may feel isolated at times of key celebrations, or they may have to travel in order to join in the celebrations with other Muslims.

Tasks

1 Describe what is being celebrated by Shi'a Muslims during Ashura.

2 Explain why Sunni Muslims reject this focus for the celebration.

3 Explain one other festival that is celebrated by Shi'a but not by Sunni Muslims.

To discuss

a What can you learn about Ashura from these images?

b What differences do you notice between the celebrations in London and those in Muslim countries?

149

Jihad

'Jihad' is an Arabic word that means striving; it is important for all Muslims and one of the Ten Obligatory Acts of Shi'a tradition of Islam. This striving takes two forms in Islam: Greater Jihad and Lesser Jihad. Greater Jihad is the inner struggle that a Muslim strives with in order to control bad desires and intentions. Lesser Jihad is an outer struggle and is often linked with a military struggle. Islam, however, is a religion that teaches peace. Muhammad ﷺ himself spent his first thirteen years as Allah's prophet in Makkah spreading the faith of Islam using only peaceful means. Later, when his opponents sought to wage war against him, he migrated to Medinah. Despite further attempts by his opponents to fight against him and his early followers, Muhammad ﷺ agreed a ten-year peace treaty, known as the Sulh al-Hudaybiya, on his enemies' terms.

Greater Jihad

Greater Jihad is a continuous process as each Muslim strives to follow 'the straight path' and to please Allah. So in all Islamic duties Muslims are learning to be obedient to Allah, to control their own desires and to lead a disciplined life that will bring pleasure to Allah. These duties help a Muslim increasingly to live a faithful life, possibly even being prepared to die for their faith one day if it becomes necessary. Their reward will be to enter Paradise after death. Achieving this requires Muslims to overcome many negative qualities, such as greed and anger; overcoming these is the Greater Jihad. When the Qur'an calls Muslims to:

'do great jihad with the help of the Qur'an.'

(25:52)

this is a call to holiness through better understanding of the words of Allah. Greater Jihad requires Muslims to conquer their hearts and minds with the words of the Qur'an, not with the use of a sword or a gun. Striving against doing what is wrong (Munkar) and seeking to do what is good (Maroof) is called Nahi 'Anil-Munkar and Amr-bil-Maroof. This is built upon the teaching of the Qur'an (3:110). This section of the Qur'an sets the Muslim ummah (community) up as the best model for all societies. Greater Jihad is essential for all Muslims and it takes precedence over Lesser Jihad, as without overcoming badness within themselves it is hard for Muslims to deal with the Lesser Jihad.

Qur'an quotes

'Fight in the way of Allah against those who fight you and do not go beyond the limits. Indeed God does not love those who go beyond the limits.'

(2:190)

'But if the enemy incline towards peace, do thou also incline towards peace, and trust in Allah; for He is One that hears and knows all things.'

(8.61)

'Do great jihad with the help of the Qur'an.'

(25:52)

'And when he goes away, he strives throughout the land to cause corruption therein and destroy crops and animals. And Allah does not like corruption.'

(2:205)

'Let there be no compulsion in the religion [Islam].'

(2:256)

'You are the best nation produced [as an example] for mankind. You order what is right and forbid what is wrong and believe in Allah.'

(3:110)

Link it up

a Explain which of these quotes encourage believers to take part in Greater Jihad.

b Describe what you can learn about Lesser Jihad from these quotes.

c In what way do these quotes help to show that Islam is a religion of peace?

Lesser Jihad

The Lesser Jihad is an outward jihad that is about creating a good and fair Muslim society. Some also believe it to include War. When speaking specifically about war, however, the Qur'an uses the word 'qital' rather than 'jihad'. If Lesser Jihad is in the form of a war then it should either be defensive or be a war against an unjust regime. Such a war should be fought against the leaders of that regime in order to liberate the people so that they are free from tyranny and oppression.

Islamic law has very strict guidelines for when a Lesser Jihad is led by a religious leader as a military action. These are:

1 The opponent must always have started the fighting.
2 It must not be fought to gain land.
3 It must be started by a religious leader.
4 It must be fought to bring about good (something that Allah will approve of).
5 It must be the last resort.
6 Innocent people should not be killed or harmed.
7 Enemies must be treated with justice.
8 Wounded enemy soldiers must be treated in exactly the same way as one's own soldiers.
9 The war must stop as soon as the enemy asks for peace.
10 Property must not be damaged.
11 Poisoning wells is forbidden: or in modern terms, chemical or biological warfare is not allowed.

The Muslim sect of the Kharijites added Jihad to the Five Pillars of Islam, making it Six Pillars. This kind of belief is seen within extremist Muslim groups, including Daesh and al-Qaeda. They use jihad as a justification for killing or using violence against anyone who isn't a Muslim, also known as 'kafir'. Some extremists are driven to use violence in this way out of a belief that Christian and Jewish society are trying to destroy Islam. Most Muslims disagree with this extremist position.

Let's Revise

a Name three Prophets in Islam. (3 marks)

- List three different prophets from Islam to gain the three marks.

b Describe the role of Risalah within Islam. (3 marks)

- The question is asking you to show your knowledge about prophethood in Islam.

- Write your answer in three clear sentences.

- You can include examples or develop a point in order to achieve the full three marks.

- Consider including who the prophets were, how Allah used them and what they gave to Islam.

c Why is the Qur'an important to Muslims? (3 marks)

- This question also requires three clear sentences, this time you must show an understanding of the importance of the Qur'an.

- Your answer may include a description of how the Qur'an was revealed, what it contains that has an impact on the lives of Muslims.

d Explain the significance of the Day of Judgement for Muslims. (6 marks)

- In this question you must explain why the Day of Judgment is significant to Muslims.

- You may refer to The Day of Judgement being when the dead will be resurrected to life, and starting with the prophet Muhammad, each person will be judged.

- Link this judgement to the Muslim belief in Jahannam and al-Jannah.

- Make sure you analyse why these beliefs about the eternal effect of the Day of Judgement are significant to Muslims.

e 'Sincerely reciting the Shahadah is the most important religious practice for a Muslim.'

Discuss this statement. In your answer, you should:

- analyse and evaluate the importance of points of view of common and divergent views within Islam

- refer to sources of wisdom and authority. (15 marks)

Spelling, punctuation and grammar (3 marks)

- You must demonstrate an understanding of the importance of Shahadah for Muslims. You may start by mentioning that it is the first of the five pillars and what that is and how they are a source of wisdom and authority for Muslims.

- In this answer you must show that there are different Islamic responses to this statement.

- Some Muslims may consider the recitation of the Shahadah the most important as it is the declaration of the faith, it means that the person making the declaration is a Muslim. It embodies the belief in Tawhid, the central to the teaching of Islam, as established by the prophet Muhammad. You could explain that it is because of this declaration that a person will then be caused to follow the remaining pillars of Islam (Sunni) or the ten obligatory acts of Shi'a tradition of Islam which are a source of wisdom and authority for Shi'a Muslims. Rejecting this belief is known as apostasy and this is a terrible sin in Islam.

- However, other Muslims may argue that the declaration once made must then be followed with the acts of submission to Allah. The sincerity of the words is in fact revealed in the acts. Salah prayer which incorporates the declaration is a practical outworking that the rest of the Muslim day is built around, so you could perhaps argue for example, that salah is more important.

- Make sure you offer a judgement on this issue in order to get the highest marks.

RELIGION, PHILOSOPHY AND ETHICS IN THE MODERN WORLD FROM A CHRISTIAN PERSPECTIVE

5 Relationships and families

a What are the different types of family that you are aware of in our society?

b In what way could it be said that families are the building blocks of society?

c What type of family do you think Christianity believes is the pattern set by God?

Topic checklist

In this topic you will learn about:

✔ **Relationships** and families, including attitudes towards the role and purpose of the Christian family, marriage and different attitudes to sexual relationships.

✔ Christian beliefs, teachings and attitudes about the roles of **men and women**, in both the family context and the wider Christian community.

✔ **Christian understandings of equality** and the influence of culture on these views. Also, Christian attitudes towards prejudice and discrimination.

Key concepts

Christians believe the family is the key building block of society where relationships are formed and children brought up. They believe that marriage is the basis of stable families.

Christianity teaches that marriage was given by God to unite two people and is the relationship in which sex should occur, as an expression of love and a means of reproduction. Ideally marriage should be a lifelong commitment, however sometimes divorce breaks up this relationship. Divorce is not desirable but some Christians recognise that it is sometimes necessary.

Christians disagree about whether same-sex marriage is acceptable. Some argue that it provides a loving and stable union, while others believe it goes against biblical teaching.

There are also different Christian beliefs about the roles men and women should play in families and relationships as well as the wider community.

Different Christian understandings of equality relate not just to their beliefs about sexuality but also to their beliefs about gender prejudice and discrimination. These beliefs affect the way that the Christian teachings are applied for individuals, in communities and society.

Relationships

The Christian family

Christianity teaches that the family unit is where loving and respectful relationships can be formed. The Bible shows the model family consisting of a mother, a father and children. Moreover, the Bible teaches that the family should provide a place for the nurture and disciplining of children. Parents are required to respect their children, and children to honour their parents.

The family also provides a place where children can be brought up with Christian values and an understanding of the faith until they may commit to this faith themselves. This is demonstrated through the Christian practice of infant baptism and confirmation in some denominations of Christianity such as the Catholic Church and Church of England.

The Christian Churches teach the importance of marriage. In order that men and women are prepared for the responsibilities of family life, many Churches support couples to understand the importance and significance of marriage. For example, the Church of England recommends that every diocese should encourage its parishes to run courses in marriage preparation and in parenting to help strengthen family life.

Christianity teaches the value of fidelity in a marriage relationship. Fidelity means that a married couple are faithful and committed to one another. They should not have affairs, which would damage their marriage and also break the seventh commandment, which instructs married couples not to commit adultery. Fidelity helps to protect the stability of the family.

Strengthening family life is seen as part of the mission of the Church. The *Catechism of the Catholic Church* reminds believers of the central importance of families in society, saying:

'The family is the original cell of social life.'

(Paragraph 2207)

Stretch what you know

'Fix the Family' is a Catholic website that offers material to support Catholic marriage and family life. It promotes a Catholic lifestyle and develops discussion and study materials for men, women and children. It does this through blogs, videos and articles.

- Go to **www.fixthefamily.com** to research more about the Catholic teaching on family life.

To discuss

a In what way do you think supporting families can impact on the stability of the wider society?

b How does the work of the Mothers' Union reflect the Christian attitude towards the role of the family?

Case study: Mothers' Union

Mothers' Union is a Christian voluntary organisation that works to do 'all they can to support stable family life in their own communities.' It considers this an important part of putting its Christian faith into action. The organisation works in more than eighty countries. All of its work is supported by prayer, and guidance on what to pray for can be found on its website: www.mothersunion.org

The Union campaigns in countries where family life is affected by social injustice. A recent campaign focused on challenging gender-based violence, for example, providing counselling and support for women who have been sexually abused in the civil war in the Congo. The Mothers' Union also offers practical support to the victims of such violence.

One of the largest elements of its work is the Parenting Programme, which operates in more than twenty-five countries. The Mothers' Union trains community-based women to lead groups for parents. These groups aim to 'help each person to develop their parenting skills, build relationships and contribute to the stability of family life in society.'

The Mothers' Union believes that as it works to support couples and families it is helping to strengthen society as a whole.

Link it up

a Look at the Bible bitz quote from St Mark's Gospel. What does the Bible mean when it talks about a man and a woman marrying and becoming 'one flesh'?

b Read each Bible bitz quote. What does each say about the role of the family?

Bible bitz

'Be fruitful and multiply, and fill the earth and subdue it'
(Genesis 1:26–28)

'Fathers, do not provoke your children to anger, but bring them up in the discipline and instruction of the Lord.'
(Ephesians 6:4)

'Listen to your father, who gave you life, and do not despise your mother when she is old.'
(Proverbs 23:22)

'Honour your father and your mother, so that you may live long in the land the Lord your God is giving you.'
(Exodus 20:12)

'The Lord God said, "It is not good for the man to be alone. I will make a helper suitable for him."'
(Genesis 2:18)

'Man will leave his father and mother and be united to his wife, and the two will be become one flesh ... Therefore what God has joined together, let man not separate.'
(Mark 10:7–9)

Attitudes towards the importance and purpose of marriage

The majority of Churches – including the Anglican Church, the Catholic Church and the Methodist Church – teach that marriage should take place only between a man and a woman. As such, a Christian marriage in these Churches excludes same-sex marriage. Christianity teaches that the outward act of marriage is evidence of the spiritual unity that occurs as a couple become united. This uniting of the couple is described in the Bible:

'…a man leaves his father and mother and is united with his wife, and they become one flesh.'

(Genesis 2:23–24)

Christians believe that the promises the couple make to one another in the wedding service are for life and that they shouldn't be broken. The binding nature of marriage is reinforced by Jesus, as he teaches that once a couple are joined together in marriage:

'…man must not separate what God has joined together.'

(Mark 10:9)

The vows made during a Christian marriage service are not just between the man and the woman getting married; they are believed to be between the couple and God as well. God's blessing is asked for through prayer and His presence in the marriage relationship is believed to make it stronger.

The writer of the book of Ecclesiastes in the Bible states that:

'…a cord of three strands is not quickly broken.'

(4:12)

The three strands of the cord are the two people getting married and God. Marriage is believed to have been put in place by God and to be very important in establishing strong, lifelong human relationships between a man and a woman.

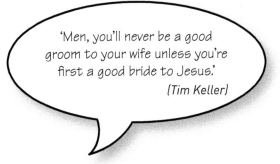

'Men, you'll never be a good groom to your wife unless you're first a good bride to Jesus.'
(Tim Keller)

To discuss

What do you think Tim Keller means by his quote?

The Church of England

The Church of England teaches that through marriage, a couple learn to love one another over the course of their lives together. In *Marriage: A Teaching Document* the Church states that marriage is a commitment to 'live and grow in love' as shown in the Bible. The Church of England teaches that a Christian marriage should reflect Christ's love for the Church. Christ is committed to his people and to the Church, just like the married couple have promised to remain committed to one another. Christ also showed his love through his death on the cross. In the same way, a married couple should be prepared to love one another by not being selfish, and by considering each other's needs.

Marriage offers three blessings:

- The creation (procreation) and the nurture of children.
- The correct place for sexual relations.
- Help and comfort during all aspects of life.

The Church teaches that marriage is important because other relationships are developed from it and love is extended. Through marriage each person is able to learn patience and forgiveness, which they can offer to others in the wider society.

♩ Christians believe that marriage binds not only the couple, but also God; like a rope with three strands

The Catholic Church

The Catholic Church teaches that the act of marriage creates a unique and unbreakable bond between the couple and it can't be dissolved. Catholics believe that the couple's permanent and faithful commitment to one another expresses Christ's love and commitment to his people. In this way marriage in a Catholic Church reveals God's unconditional love. As a sacrament, marriage brings God's grace to the couple in a unique way. God's grace through this sacrament helps each spouse to be faithful to one another and to be good parents when they have children.

The Catholic Church teaches that couples who marry should place themselves in God's care as they set out on their married life together. This means following the teachings in the Bible that relate to marriage. In a document called *The Call, The Journey, The Mission*, the Church tells those who marry to 'not pay attention to this makeshift culture which can shatter our lives.' This is a reference to the Church's understanding of marriage as permanent, despite the increasing rate of divorce in wider society.

↻ Pope Francis became Pope in 2013

The Catholic Church teaches that the constant presence of Christ in a Christian marriage helps to sustain and strengthen the promises that the couple have made. It is through times of difficulty that the couple may experience growth in love for both God and each other. Pope Francis teaches that it is the presence of God's love in a marriage that ensures harmony between the couple:

'With trust in God's faithfulness, everything can be faced responsibly and without fear. Christian spouses are not naïve; they know life's problems and temptations. But they are not afraid to be responsible before God and before society. They do not run away, they do not hide, they do not shirk the mission of forming a family and bringing children into the world.'

(Pope Francis, 26 October 2013)

To discuss

a What does the Pope say about Christian spouses?

b Why do you think Pope Francis says that for Catholics everything can be faced 'without fear'?

c What are some of the 'problems and temptations' that husbands and wives may face?

d How may the sacrament of marriage help a couple cope with these situations?

The Christian marriage service and differences in practice

Catholic and Orthodox Churches

In the Catholic Church and Orthodox Churches marriage is a sacrament. During the service the couple become spiritually joined together, reflecting the teaching in Genesis that explains that:

'...a man leaves his father and mother and is united with his wife and they become one.'

(Genesis 2:22–23)

The Catholic Church requires the couple to both be baptised in order for the marriage to be considered sacramental. If one person in seeking to get married has not been baptised then special permission for the marriage to go ahead is required from the bishop. Such a marriage is known as a disparity of cult. It is not possible for a non-Christian to receive the sacraments in a Catholic Church. If a Catholic wants to marry a non-Christian the marriage will not be a sacrament, but permission may be gained from the bishop for a priest to witness the marriage.

Weddings in a Catholic Church often include a special 'nuptial' mass. It is usually included when both the bride and groom are both Catholics, so that they can each take part in receiving the sacrament. The couple may bring the bread and wine to the altar. This active role in the sacrament, the saying of the vows and the following of the liturgy all help to direct the couple's thoughts to God during the marriage ceremony. A personal blessing will often be said for the bride and the groom by the priest as part of the mass.

The Church of England

In contrast to the Catholic Church, the Church of England welcomes any heterosexual couple to marry in the Church, whether or not they are Christian or baptised. The Church is also prepared to carry out mixed-faith marriages.

The vicar is likely to offer any couple wanting to marry in the Church a course in marriage preparation, which explores all aspects of married life, including the spiritual side.

The significance of the institution of marriage is also reflected through the structure of a wedding in the Church of England. The Church of England believes that a church wedding adds a spiritual dimension to the marriage, as God is included. They believe that the vows made to God and the prayers said during the service all bring blessings into the married life of the couple.

The couple are able to make choices about the Bible readings and hymns in their wedding service and their involvement in this planning is important.

Most weddings in the Church of England use the words from *The Marriage Service from Common Worship* (2000). These words include the vows that the couple will say to one another. The Church of England considers these vows (see p.74) to cover all that is good and to be hoped for in a healthy marriage. A Church of England wedding may also include a Eucharist after the service (see p.51).

The Church of England as the official religion in England performs state weddings, for example the marriage of Prince William to Kate Middleton.

Non-conformist Churches

In non-conformist churches there may be much more freedom for the bride and the groom as they plan their wedding service. The bride and groom can write their own vows, rather than following vows set down by the church. This gives more emphasis on the couple saying things to God.

Quakers

In a Quaker wedding the belief that only God can join the couple together means that they have no minister to lead the proceedings. The couple will sit in silent worship with the congregation until they feel it is the right time to say their vows. They will stand together and say:

'In the presence of God and before these our families and friends, I take thee (bride's/groom's name) to be my wife/husband, promising with Divine assistance to be unto thee a loving and faithful husband/wife so long as we both shall live.'

After this they sign the Quaker marriage certificate and return to their seats. A friend or relative will then read the certificate out. After this silent worship is returned to. During this time anyone may stand and speak as they feel led to do so by God. At the end of the service everyone present will sign the marriage certificate as a witness to it. This approach to marriage stresses the belief that the union is being made between the couple and God.

Mark

I got married at 22. Many of my friends thought this was too young to get married, and that I should be carefree and party. They felt that marriage at this age was taking on too much responsibility. I knew it was right to marry Clare. We had been seeing each other for over two years. As we are both committed Christians, we knew that marriage would be the next step in our relationship.

We both believe that sex is the most intimate you can get with anyone, and that it should be saved for and enjoyed in a married relationship. That doesn't mean it was easy, but waiting until we were married was an act of love to each other and to God.

We chose to marry in church; our promises in the wedding were to one another and to God. I was happy and proud to declare my love for Clare in front of all our friends and family.

Love in our marriage is not just the passionate and romantic feeling you get when you first fancy someone – it is about considering the other person's needs as well as your own. At times this is hard.

Even though I am sure there will be challenging situations in our marriage, I am committed to Clare for life. My wedding vows help me focus on the promises I have made to Clare. A successful marriage is based on not taking the other person for granted – it is a relationship in which husband and wife learn to develop and mature in their love for each other throughout their lives together.

Reverend Jonathan Willans

Most Churches offer support or classes before a couple marry. This is to help them understand fully the commitment that they are making and to explore any potential disagreements they may have before they actually marry. How one vicar supports couples is outlined below.

As a vicar in the Church of England, I spend a lot of my time preparing couples for marriage, as well as helping already-married couples who may be facing difficult times.

Every couple planning to get married is encouraged to attend the marriage-preparation course run by the church. It provides useful advice on a wide range of issues, such as the importance of mutual trust, spending time together, sorting finances, resolving disagreements, coping with the in-laws, sex, parenting, etc.

The course is run over several evenings, the number of sessions depending on the time made available by the couple. At least three couples attend any one session. Evenings consist of watching a DVD on a particular topic and then discussing it over a glass of wine. Couples who attend say they find the course to be of real benefit.

Married couples often turn to the clergy if they are experiencing difficulty in their marriage. This is a common pastoral situation, which works almost as a "counselling service". Everything said and done is strictly confidential.

Tasks

1 Describe why Christian couples may choose to get married.

2 State why Christians believe that marriage is important to society.

3 For Christians, marriage is all about LOVE. Marriage is about:

L a lifelong commitment

O obedience to God

V vows made to one another

E extending the family

Copy out the LOVE acrostic. Use the four statements as headings. Write a paragraph under each one, explaining how it is important in a Christian marriage.

4 'The love demonstrated in Christian marriages is a helpful picture of Christ's love for his Church.' Discuss this statement. In your answer, you should:

● draw on your learning from across your course of study, including reference to beliefs, teachings and practices within Christianity

● explain and evaluate the importance of points of view from the perspective of Christianity.

Sexual relationships

In the media we frequently hear stories or see images related to human relationships, such as those shown on the next page. The media, and society as a whole, recognise and accept many different types of relationships – such as marriage, co-habitation, same-sex relationships – as well as the end of these relationships, sometimes meaning divorce.

Tasks

◯ (a) Fathers 4 Justice: divorced fathers fighting for their rights to see their children. Why do you think some men are driven to take this kind of action?

◯ (b) A newly wed couple as shown in brides' magazines

◖ (c) The front covers of women's glossy magazines

1 Look at the images above.

- For each image, make a list of words to describe how it relates to human relationships.

- Imagine if you were an alien visiting Earth. What would you think British society's views on sexual relationships, marriage and divorce were? Use your list of words to imagine what you would think.

- Give reasons for your answer.

2 What do you think a Christian might think about each of the images? Would they describe any of the aspects of human relationships shown as unacceptable? Explain your answer.

Christian responses to civil partnerships

On 21 December 2005 it became legal in the UK for same-sex couples to have their union recognised in civil partnerships.

By law, couples who want a civil partnership have to register their intention with local councils. Unlike in a marriage, the signing of the legal documents does not need to happen in public but the couple may still choose to have a ceremony. The partnership can be registered in a registry office or in any approved premises, and the couple receive a certificate of their partnership. Civil partnerships are different to marriage though they give the couple largely the same legal rights. Christians have different responses to civil partnerships.

The Catholic Church and the Church of England

The Catholic Church and the Church of England are against civil partnerships and do not perform them. This is because of their teachings about sexual relationships. Both Churches teach that marriage is the proper place in which sexual relationships should occur, the main role of sex being to create new life. Therefore, performing a civil partnership would suggest that homosexual sex is as acceptable as married heterosexual sex, which is completely against their teaching. They also think that making civil partnerships the same as heterosexual marriages in the eyes of the Church would undermine their teaching that it is best that children be raised by their biological mother and father.

The House of Bishops has told the clergy of the Church of England not to carry out services of blessing for civil partnerships. A service of blessing is a service performed in the Church of England to give thanks, before God, for a marriage. Often it is done when a couple who have been married for some time want to reaffirm their wedding vows. The House of Bishops has ruled that such a service must not happen for homosexual partnerships because it does not accept that such partnerships are in keeping with the biblical teaching on sexual relationships.

Church of England vicars are allowed to have civil partnerships, but they are required to remain celibate. In June 2008, however, the Reverend Martin Dudley carried out a blessing ceremony after the gay civil partnership of Reverend Peter Cowell and the Reverend Dr David Lord. (Reverend Martin Dudley received a strongly worded letter from the Bishop of London condemning the blessing and requesting an investigation in to it.)

Other homosexual clergy in the Church of England believe that gay civil partnerships should be recognised and blessed by the Church. The Reverend Paul Collier, an openly gay Church of England vicar, believes that by not doing so the Church is 'failing to respond to an opportunity to celebrate and affirm love, fidelity and commitment'.

Other Christian responses

There are some Christians who believe that civil partnerships should be acceptable to the Church since civil partnerships provide companionship, unity and stability in the same way that heterosexual marriage does. Christians who believe this think civil partnerships reflect the biblical value of equality and God's desire to bless faithful lifelong marriages, regardless of the sex of the couple. At the 1996 Unitarian Universalist General Assembly, delegates voted overwhelmingly that because of 'the inherent worth and dignity of every person', same-sex couples should have the same freedom to marry that other couples have.

Bible bitz

'But for Adam no suitable helper was found. So the Lord God caused the man to fall into a deep sleep; and while he was sleeping, he took one of the man's ribs and closed up the place with flesh. Then the Lord God made a woman from the rib he had taken out of the man, and he brought her to the man.

The man said,

"This is now bone of my bones
and flesh of my flesh;
she shall be called 'woman,'
for she was taken out of man."

For this reason a man will leave his father and mother and be united to his wife, and they will become one flesh.'

(Genesis 2:20–24)

'If a man lies with a man as one lies with a woman, both of them have done what is detestable.'

(Leviticus 20:13)

'Do you not know that the wicked will not inherit the kingdom of God? Do not be deceived: Neither the sexually immoral nor idolaters nor adulterers nor male prostitutes nor homosexual offenders nor thieves nor the greedy nor drunkards nor slanderers nor swindlers will inherit the kingdom of God.'

(1 Corinthians 6:8–10)

To discuss

'The fact of the matter is that God does not endorse this [civil partnerships], shall never endorse this and we are standing for the word of God and for the protection of our children.'

(The Reverend Dr Ian Brown, of the Free Presbyterian Church; source: 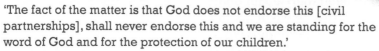 www.religioustolerance.org/hom_maruk1.htm*)*

Read the quote above.

a What do you think Reverend Brown meant when he said that by opposing civil partnerships he was standing for 'the protection of our children'?

b Do you think civil partnerships are a necessary part of society today?

Link it up

a Using the Church teachings and the Bible quotes above, explain why many Christians oppose civil partnerships.

b How do some Christians support the view that civil partnerships are acceptable?

Christian responses to same-sex marriage

Same-sex marriage became legal in England and Wales in March 2014. This means same-sex couples can either choose to marry or have a civil partnership and those that have already had a civil partnership are able to convert it into a marriage. Same-sex couples can marry in either civil ceremonies or religious ceremonies, where a religious organisation – such as the Quakers – has opted in to conduct such ceremonies. Religious organisations that do not wish to conduct such ceremonies, however, are protected by law. This means they do not have to agree to carry out a service for a same-sex marriage. For example, both the Catholic Church and the Church of England do not carry out same-sex marriages. For many people this change in the law was a significant event, signalling an end to discrimination against people who were in same-sex relationships but not allowed to marry.

Marriages are very similar to civil partnerships, but there are some differences. For example, by law, a marriage requires set words to be said to agree the marriage. In contrast the registering of a civil partnership simply requires a legal document to be signed by the couple.

To end a marriage requires a divorce, but to end a civil partnership a dissolution order is required.

The main argument for most people who campaigned for the legalisation of same-sex marriage was that a same-sex couple ought to have their relationship recognised in a completely equal way to a heterosexual couple. By not doing this many people felt the law was discriminatory.

The Church of England

The law does not allow ministers of the Church of England to carry out same-sex marriages. The Church of England's House of Bishops also ruled out special services of blessing for married same-sex couples and vicars are not allowed to enter into same-sex marriages themselves. Members of the Church of England may enter into same-sex marriages without facing any punishment from the Church; however such weddings cannot be conducted by the Church. This is because the Church teaches that marriage should be between a man and a woman, with one of its purposes being procreation.

> ### Task
>
> Imagine you are writing to your local MP on the issue of civil partnerships.
>
> a Write a letter from the point of view of a Christian who is against same-sex partnerships.
>
> b Write a letter from the point of view of a Christian who is for same-sex partnerships.
>
> Make sure that in both responses you give clear reasons for the viewpoint that you are expressing.

🎧 Neither the Church of England or the Catholic Church allow same-sex marriage

To discuss

Pope John Paul II noted in 2004 that attempts to re-define marriage to include homosexual couples 'contradict right reason' and create 'a false understanding of the nature of marriage'.

a What do you think caused the Pope to argue that same-sex marriage was 'a false understanding of the nature of marriage'?

b Do you agree with this argument? Explain your reasons.

The Catholic Church

The *Catechism of the Catholic Church* states:

'Men and women who have deep-seated homosexual tendencies … must be accepted with respect, compassion, and sensitivity. Every sign of unjust discrimination in their regard should be avoided.'

(Paragraph 2358)

The Catholic Church also teaches, however, that homosexual acts are against the natural law since they cannot result in children. It is opposed to same-sex marriage and is concerned that it will have harmful effects on society by undermining the value of heterosexual marriage.

Other Christian responses

In contrast to the Catholic and Church of England responses to same-sex marriage is that of the Episcopal Church, a member of the Anglican Communion found largely in the United States. In June 2015 the Episcopal Church voted to change its Church law and to allow same-sex marriage, changing its marriage rites so that they can be used by all marrying couples. In 1976, the General Convention of the Episcopal Church declared that:

'homosexual persons are children of God who have a full and equal claim with all other persons upon the love, acceptance, and pastoral concern and care of the Church.'

This underlying teaching has led to acceptance of same-sex marriages within the Church. The Church's approach supports same-sex marriage as a committed relationship through which love can be securely expressed. The Episcopal Church of Scotland is similarly considering allowing same-sex marriage. This is based on a belief that 'love transcends sexuality and gender' (General Synod of the Scottish Episcopal Church).

Tasks

1 State the position of the Church of England and Catholic Church on same-sex marriage.
2 List the reasons that these Churches may give for their position.
3 Describe the opposing view of the Episcopal Church in America.
4 Explain the response of the Anglican Church to this.
5 Discuss whether you think it is possible for the Anglican Church to respond in this way and at the same time 'affirm again that God's love for every human being is the same, regardless of their sexuality'.

⚲ Archbishop of Canterbury Justin Welby with LGBT protestors

ARCHBISHOP OF CANTERBURY APOLOGISES TO THE LGBT COMMUNITY

On 15 January 2016, the Archbishop of Canterbury issued a statement that apologised to the Lesbian, Gay, Bisexual and Transgender (LBGT) community for the 'hurt and pain' that the Anglican Church has caused them. The reason he made this statement is because the Anglican Church decided to take action against the US Episcopal Church for accepting same-sex marriage. The Anglican Church maintains that marriage within the Church should be for heterosexual couples only. The Archbishop was acknowledging that the persecution of people because of their sexuality was wrong and unloving. The Anglican Church condemns homophobia and acts of violence against people because of their sexuality. The Archbishop was also clear that he and the Church were opposed to the discrimination of people because of their sexuality. The Anglican Church stated that they affirmed '…that God's love for every human being is the same, regardless of their sexuality, and that the Church should never by its actions give any other impression'.

Christian responses to pre-marital sex and cohabitation

Cohabitation is when a couple live together without being married. Christians agree that one of the main roles of sex is to create new life and that it is a God-given expression of love between two people. In Genesis 1:28 (see p.173) the Bible specifically links the act of sex with reproduction. For this reason, many Christians believe that a sexual relationship should be unique and happen only within marriage, so they believe pre-marital sex is wrong. In contemporary society, however, some Christians accept that couples may live together and have sex as part of a committed relationship, even if they are not married.

Nevertheless, all Christians would agree that casual sex is wrong. Casual sex takes place outside of a loving relationship. An example of this would be when a person has a one-night stand, where they have sex with a person whom they have only just met and whom they have no intention of forming a more permanent relationship with. This is known as fornication. One of the reasons many Christians believe this is wrong is that the Bible teaches that having sex with someone to whom a person is not married is sinful.

◉ Although Church of England and the Catholic Church think that sex should happen within marriage, many Christians do accept cohabitation as a step towards marriage

The Catholic Church

The Catholic Church talks about sex as being the body's language. By this it means that sex is one way in which a married couple communicate their absolute, committed and exclusive love to one another.

The Catholic Church teaches that every time the act of sex occurs there should be the possibility for a new life to be created. This is because Catholics believe that God gave humans the gift of sex in order to reproduce and populate the Earth. Sex outside a married relationship is considered wrong by the Catholic Church.

The Church of England

The Church of England teaches that the proper place in which sexual relationships should occur is within a marriage, because sex is an act of love and loyalty reflecting total commitment, as expressed in the Christian wedding vows. While it teaches that sex outside marriage falls short of God's purposes for human beings, the 1995 report *Something to Celebrate* recommended that Christians accept that for many people cohabitation, including a sexual relationship, is a step towards the commitment of marriage.

Celibacy

Some Christians choose to remain unmarried and to abstain permanently from sexual relationships. This is known as celibacy. For many Christians the reason they choose this way of life is so that they can fully focus on serving God. Paul, the apostle, was celibate and he encouraged his followers to follow his example. He recommends this lifestyle as the best way to live in service to God. Paul tells believers, however, that if they cannot control their sexual desires, then they should marry (1 Corinthians 7:8–9). Those choosing the celibate way of life are seeking to keep God as their primary focus and first love.

In the Catholic Church priests are required to be celibate, as are monks and nuns. The Church teaches that celibacy is a gift rather than a restriction for those who are called into the priesthood. The priest is better enabled to share the love of God with all, rather than being distracted by the love he would otherwise have for a wife and children.

To discuss

What is the purpose of sex within a relationship?

Tasks

1 Describe what is meant by 'celibacy'.

2 Explain different Christian attitudes to sexual relationships.

3 Write a letter to a newspaper to explain the benefits of celibacy for Christians.

4 Discuss whether allowing a Christian minister to have a sexual relationship within marriage is a help or a hindrance to his work.

⋂ The Catholic Church requires priests, nuns and monks to remain celibate

∩ Artificial forms of contraception aren't allowed by the Catholic Church though other Christian Churches think they are acceptable

Contraception

Contraception is sometimes known as 'birth control' and is used to help prevent pregnancy resulting from sex. It can be divided into two broad types – artificial and natural.

1 **Artificial contraception:** the use of a device such as a condom, an operation such as a vasectomy, or a form of medication such as the mini pill, to try to prevent unwanted pregnancy.
2 **Natural contraception:** also aimed at reducing the chances of a woman becoming pregnant. This type of contraception includes a couple choosing to have sex during the least fertile time in a woman's menstrual cycle and the withdrawal method. The withdrawal method is when the man withdraws from the woman before he ejaculates, thus reducing the likelihood of pregnancy occurring.

Some kinds of contraception, such as condoms, are not only used to reduce the likelihood of a woman getting pregnant, but also as a way of minimising the risk of passing on sexually transmitted diseases.

Christian beliefs about contraception

The Catholic Church teaches that the use of artificial contraception is sinful. This is because it teaches that God gave sex to humans for reproduction. It does, however, accept the use of some natural forms of contraception – this usually means only having sex at certain times during a woman's monthly cycle, when she is at her least fertile. This allows a couple some control over when they have children. Some individual Catholics choose not to follow the Church's teaching and use contraception.

Traditionally the Catholic Church has taught that condoms should never be used, even to help stop the spread of sexually transmitted diseases, and that abstinence (see below) should be used instead. Recently, however, one of the Church's Cardinals has accepted the use of condoms as the lesser of two evils in married couples where one has HIV/Aids and could pass it on to the other. The Vatican, however, has made no official comment on this.

Other Christian responses

Most other Christian denominations teach that artificial contraception is acceptable. For example, the Church of England teaches that it is responsible to use contraception in order to ensure that children are planned and wanted.

Abstinence

There are campaigns and organisations that promote not having sex until marriage, this is known as abstinence. The work of these organisations is mainly directed at young people and reflects the beliefs of some Christians. One such organisation is Teen-Aid, which promotes the advantages of abstinence through poster campaigns, videos and training. Young people can indicate their commitment to sexual abstinence by filling in a commitment card like the one shown below.

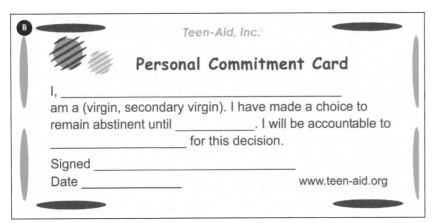

A Advantages of Abstinence

Freedom From
- pregnancy
- abortion
- pressures to marry before I am ready
- doubt, disappointment, worry, guilt or rejection
- sexually transmitted diseases
- trauma of relinquishing a baby
- exploitation by others
- bother or dangers of contraceptives

Freedom To
- be in control of my life
- develop self respect
- focus my energy on establishing and realizing life goals
- experience fuller communication in dating
- develop unselfish sensitivity
- enjoy being a teenager

Teen-Aid, Inc. • 723 E. Jackson • Spokane, WA 99207
1.800.357.2868 • www.teen-aid.org

B Teen-Aid, Inc.

Personal Commitment Card

I, _____
am a (virgin, secondary virgin). I have made a choice to remain abstinent until _____. I will be accountable to _____ for this decision.

Signed _____
Date _____   www.teen-aid.org

🎧 The front and back of Teen-Aid's commitment card

Other organisations that promote similar messages include Love Waits and Silver Ring Thing. These organisations emphasise the Christian belief that sex was created by God as an expression of love within marriage, and that abstinence reflects a sense of self-worth and value.

Link it up

Using the Church teachings and the Bible quotes above, explain in what order many Christians would say love, sex and marriage should occur in a relationship.

To discuss

a Explain to the people you are sitting with what order you think it is right for sex, love and marriage to happen in. Remember to say why you hold this view.

b How does your view compare with those of others in your class?

c How do your ideas on love, sex and marriage compare to the Catholic and Anglican views?

Tasks

1 List the benefits and weaknesses of artificial and natural contraception.

2 Read through the advantages of abstinence on the commitment card above. Do you agree with them? Explain your answer.

3 Design your own poster to promote the Christian belief in abstinence until marriage. Use the commitment card to help you.

4 What is your view on organisations such as Teen-Aid promoting abstinence?

Christian beliefs about divorce, annulment and remarriage

Stretch what you know

a There were 13 divorces an hour in England and Wales in 2012.

b Women were granted 65 per cent of all divorces.

c 9,703 men and 6,026 women aged over 60 got divorced.

d One in seven divorces was granted as a result of adultery.

e 719 divorces (less than 1 per cent) were granted because of desertion.

f The average age at divorce was 45 for men and 42 for women.

g Nine per cent of couples divorcing had both been divorced before.

h 48 per cent of couples divorcing had at least one child aged under 16 living with the family.

i It is expected that 42 per cent of marriages will end in divorce.

(Office for National Statistics, data from 2012)

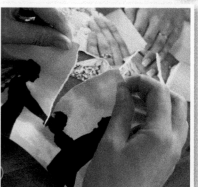

To discuss

a What conclusions can you reach about divorce based on the data given here?

b What do you think are some of the reasons for divorce?

Tasks

■ Hey presto, one flesh becomes two!'

1 Why do people find the idea of a magician actually sawing a person in two so unbelievable?

2 Can you make a link between the cartoon and the Christian attitude to divorce? Consider the Bible quote that teaches that in marriage two people become 'one flesh' (Mark 10:7–9).

Divorce is necessary in our society because marriages don't always work out.

Divorce is wrong if a couple have children. They should stay together for their sake.

Sometimes people think they'll be able to get along but then discover that they disagree on so many things that it is better for them to split up.

Sometimes divorce is used as a quick fix – instead of working at a relationship and getting help for their problems, people just get divorced. I don't think this is right. Marriage needs to be worked at.

If a married person has an affair then I think divorce is okay. After all, the trust in the relationship has already been broken.

When a person is being abused in any way in a relationship, then I think divorce is right. No one has the right to hurt someone else.

If people have promised to stay together for life then that is what they should do.

175

Task

Divide your page into two columns, headed 'Views for divorce' and 'Views against divorce'.

● Read the different views about divorce given in the speech bubbles on the previous page. Identify the reason each 'talking head' gives, either for or against divorce, and record it in the correct column in your table.

● Add any other reasons for and against divorce that you can think of. Leave space to add more views after you've read about the Christian views on page 177.

● Explain which views on divorce you agree with.

Support for couples thinking about divorcing

Most churches offer support or classes before a couple marry. This is in order to help the couple understand fully the commitment they are making and to explore any potential disagreements they may have before they actually marry. When marriages do get into difficulty, churches usually offer some kind of support or counselling, or they may refer a couple on to a specific relationship counselling service. An example of such a service is Relate.

Stretch what you know

Using the 'About us' link on Relate's website (**www. relate.org.uk**), find out the following information:

1 Who are the peer listening schemes for and what are their objectives?

2 When did Relate start its work in prisons and how does it support prisoners and their families?

3 What service does Relate offer to local authorities in targeting homelessness?

Case study: Relate

Relate is the largest relationship counselling service in the UK. A major part of its work is to help couples understand what is happening in their relationship and to change it for the better. Relate offers support to individuals, couples and families. It does this through counselling, workshops, mediation and face-to-face meetings. In 2008, 73 per cent of people who had gone through relationship counselling with Relate said that their relationship had improved.

Relate also works in communities in four main ways:

■ **School work** – providing relationship courses and developing peer listening schemes with the aim of helping young people develop positive relationships with others.

■ **Prison work** – establishing programmes to help prisoners develop and sustain relationships with their families.

■ **Tackling relationship problems** – one of the major causes of homelessness is relationship breakdown. Relate works with local authorities to tackle relationship problems within families that may lead to homelessness.

■ **Supporting professionals and volunteers** – Relate provides courses and workshops for people who work in communities in order to develop their communication skills as well as their ability to deal with relationship issues.

(Based on information from **www.relate.org.uk**)

Christian teachings about divorce

Christians believe that a marriage relationship is entered into as a lifelong commitment. Divorce, however, causes disagreement among Christians.

The Catholic Church

The Catholic Church in England is aware of the high rate of divorces and knows that many people believe divorce is often the best option when a relationship has broken down. The Catholic Church, however, believes that marriage is permanent. This means that Catholics do not believe a marriage can be broken by humans, and for this reason they do not accept divorce. The Catholic Church teaches that while a divorce breaks the legal agreement made in marriage, it does *not* break the holy agreement made with God.

The Church understands that the divorce process is painful. As such, Catholics believe advice and support should be given to anyone who has gone through the process, even though they do not agree with divorce.

When a couple are experiencing difficulties in their marriage, the Catholic Church teaches that they may separate. While a couple are separated they should work on trying to restore their marriage and not enter into any other sexual relationships.

The Catholic Church does, however, annul marriages. This means agreeing that the promises made in marriage were not valid and so neither is the marriage. One reason for an annulment would be if either person had been forced into the marriage without their consent. Once a marriage has been annulled, individuals are free to marry someone else.

'A divorce is like an amputation; you survive, but there's less of you.'
(Margaret Atwood, novelist)

The Church of England

The Church of England believes that couples should work hard to keep their vow of a lifelong commitment to each other in marriage. It does, however, recognise that sometimes it may be impossible for a couple to remain together and that divorce is inevitable, for example when abuse is occurring in the marriage, or in the case of adultery.

If divorce does occur, the Church of England sees it as a priority to care for the couple. Divorcees are free to remarry someone else, and if a divorcee wants to remarry in church, then it is up to the parish priest whether to allow this. The priest will take into consideration why the person got divorced in the first place and what efforts they made to keep their first marriage together.

'Getting divorced just because you don't love a man is almost as silly as getting married just because you do.'
(Zsa Zsa Gabor, actress)

To discuss

a Identify what is happening in each of the illustrations. Do you think Anglicans would find divorce an acceptable option in any of these situations?

b What do you think the two quotes on the previous page, from Margaret Atwood and Zsa Zsa Gabor, mean?

c Discuss whether you think either of the quotes reflects Church teaching on divorce.

Hazel

When a marriage breaks up, the ripples spread far and wide. Divorce is not a private matter between two individuals. It involves everyone in the family, friends, colleagues at work and, above all, any children.

In my work as a teacher I often meet children who are struggling to maintain good relationships with both their divorced parents, or who have to live with one parent when they need and love both.

Marriage is meant to be a lifelong commitment to one person. It is life-enhancing, and brings a unique sense of fulfilment and an opportunity to mature as an individual. This ideal is, sadly, not always achieved. The relationship can instead become destructive, bringing misery to all.

Jesus himself recognised the existence of divorce, but he did not condone remarriage.

The Catholic Church, to which I belong, teaches that when two people are no longer able to live together they may separate but may not divorce, because marriage is for life. Catholics may therefore not marry again while their partner lives. I sometimes think this teaching is very harsh, but I also believe it is a way of demonstrating how very seriously marriage is regarded.

Bibble bitz

'It has been said, "Anyone who divorces his wife must give her a certificate of divorce." But I tell you that anyone who divorces his wife, except for marital unfaithfulness, causes her to become an adulteress, and anyone who marries the divorced woman commits adultery.'

(Matthew 5:31–32)

'Anyone who divorces his wife and marries another woman commits adultery against her. And if she divorces her husband and marries another man, she commits adultery.'

(Mark 10:11–12)

'The two will become one flesh. So they are no longer two but one. Therefore what God has joined together, let man not separate.'

(Mark 10:8–9)

'A wife must not separate from her husband. But if she does, she must remain unmarried or else be reconciled with her husband. And a husband must not divorce his wife.'

(1 Corinthians 7:10–11)

Link It Up

1 Add Christian views for and against divorce to the table you produced in the Task on page 176. Use the Church teachings, the 'Bible bitz' box and Hazel's views to help you to do this.

2 Can you link the Bible quotes to the Church teachings? Draw two columns. In one column list the different Church teachings on page 177, in the other column list the Bible quotes. Then draw lines from one to the other to show where the links are.

Tasks

Dear Sarah,

I really don't know who to talk to. I feel I am trapped and unable to do anything about it. I married my husband Paul five years ago when I was just 20. Paul is a genuinely loving man but this is part of the problem. I feel smothered. Whatever I do, wherever I go, he wants to know all about it, or he comes out with me. He says he just can't bear being apart from me. I need space and time to be myself and to do my own thing. I have tried to explain this to him but he just gets all defensive and makes stupid suggestions about me having secret affairs. What should I do?

From Ann

Ann,

You must take control of your life and your relationship. Paul is manipulating you, using your love for him to stop you living your life. If he loved you, he would trust you. If you want your relationship with this man to work then you must sit down together and explain how you feel and what needs to change. If he won't listen, I suggest you get yourself out of the relationship and move on with your life. You say he won't listen and that he suggests you are being unfaithful – clearly he is insecure and not as certain of your love as you are of his. Marriage is a two-way commitment of love and trust. If that commitment isn't there from both of you, then perhaps the marriage is already over.

Sarah

1 Select and write down any of the advice Sarah gives that a Christian would not agree with.

2 Write an alternative Christian response to the problem page letter, explaining what a Christian would think Ann should do in her situation.

Men and women

The roles of men and women in a Christian family

◑ Man as leader of the family

◑ Man as provider

◑ Woman as wife and mother

◑ Role equality

Christianity teaches that all people are equal. This includes equality between men and women. Christians tend to have differing views of the roles of men and women within the family, but all agree that all people, whatever role they take, are valuable to God.

Traditional views

Some Christians interpret teachings in the Bible to mean that women are literally men's helpers, and that men are the leaders in a marriage relationship. For this reason, some women still choose to promise obedience to their husband during their wedding ceremony. Moreover, some Christians consider women to be weaker than men; this is because in Genesis the woman, Eve, gave in to temptation before the man, Adam.

Christians who hold these more traditional views see the woman's role as primarily being in the home, caring for the children. They see the man's role as the main wage-earner and provider for his family. The role of the woman in the home has equal value to the work of the man, but each role is unique to the person's gender.

Should men and women be equal?

In the picture on the right, balance on the scales is achieved. Even though the weights are made up in different ways, the two sides of the scales are of equal value. In the same way, some people believe that equality between people does not necessarily mean being identical to one another in every way. In fact, it is about being valued equally while perhaps having different roles in life. This approach to equality is reflected to some extent in the Church teachings. The role a man or woman takes within a Christian family will depend upon their own understanding of the Bible teachings.

Pope John Paul II (Pope between 1978 and 2005) spoke of men and women having equal dignity and responsibility in the family as well as in society. In his speech 'Familiaris Consortio' in 1981, he said:

⌒ The weights are made up in different ways, but the two sides of the scales are of equal value

'In creating the human race "male and female", God gives man and woman an equal personal dignity with the rights and responsibilities proper to the human person.'

The Catholic Church recognises the equal right of opportunity for women as for men to work outside the home, but it values the role of a woman in the home as highly as any career she may choose to have. The Catholic Church, alongside many other Christians, believes that a woman should not feel under social pressure to have a career if she would rather be a full-time housewife and mother. For example, Pope John Paul II also said that:

'men should truly esteem and love women with total respect for their personal dignity, and society should create and develop conditions favouring work in the home.'

Many Christians believe men should be as involved in family life as women. These beliefs focus on the equality of all people and on the shared needs of a couple for one another. St Ambrose (a bishop in the fourth century CE) wrote of husbands:

'You are not her master but her husband; she was not given to you to be your slave, but your wife … Return her attentiveness to you and be grateful to her for her love.'

Jesus and the role of women

Jesus himself challenged many cultural stereotypes by the way he treated women. In biblical times women were certainly treated with less respect and value than men, but Jesus gave them respect. For example in John 4:9 Jesus speaks with a Samaritan woman at the well, which was not usual practice at the time – even the disciples are surprised by this. In the same way that Jesus accepted this woman as worth taking the time to talk to, Christians believe God has time for men and women alike and therefore so should we.

Stretch what you know

a Explain what you think the Catholic Church means when it refers to both sexes being 'an image of the power and tenderness of God'.

b Explain how, in a marriage relationship, one can observe the equal dignity of men and women in different ways.

Task

1 Divide your page into three columns, like in the example below.

In the left-hand column, write down in bullet points each of the different Christian beliefs about the roles of men and women.

In the middle column, match each of the pictures from the start of this topic (p.180) with these beliefs. Use the picture captions to do this.

In the right-hand column match up the Bible quotes with the Christian beliefs and pictures. Some quotes below and captions may be used more than once.

Christian belief	Picture caption	Bible quote
Men and women are of equal value to God.	Role equality	'There is neither Jew nor Greek, slave nor free, male nor female, for you are all one in Christ.'

Bible bitz

'Wives submit to your husbands as to the Lord. For the husband is the head of the wife as Christ is the head of the church … Now as the church submits to Christ, so also wives should submit to their husbands in everything.'

(Ephesians 5:22–24)

'There is neither Jew nor Greek, slave nor free, male nor female, for you are all one in Christ.'

(Galatians 3:28)

'The Lord God said: "It is not good for the man to be alone. I will make a helper suitable for him."'

(Genesis 2:18)

'Wives, in the same way be submissive to your husbands … Husbands in the same way be considerate as you live with your wives, and treat them with respect as the weaker partner.'

(1 Peter 3:1–7)

To discuss

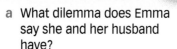

a What dilemma does Emma say she and her husband have?

b What may affect a couple's decisions about the roles that they have within their family?

c Do you think that the traditional Christian beliefs about the roles of men and women in the family are practical today?

Emma

People always seem to get worked up about the role of men and women in a marriage relationship. I've been married for seven years and when I made my vows to my husband I promised to obey him. Peter promised to love me. After the wedding some of my friends joked that I'd have to jump to Peter's every order! You know the sort of thing: cooking, washing and so on. But to us it was so different from that idea. As a Christian Peter believes that as head of our family he has to work towards the kind of love Christ has for us. This type of love is completely sacrificial, it's not a demanding and selfish love. So if Pete really does keep his promise to love me, he won't make any unfair or completely selfish demands on me. His love will put me first.

We both work at the moment. We need both our incomes to pay our mortgage. I like working, it helps me feel challenged and stimulated; I couldn't stay at home all the time. If we ever have children, however, I believe it would be right for one of us to stay at home. God has given parents the huge responsibility of bringing up children. My only worry is whether we could actually afford to do this. For us this is a real dilemma.

The role of men and women in Christian communities

When people are treated differently and unfairly because of their sex, this is discrimination in relation to gender. Sex discrimination is against the law in the UK. It is, for example, illegal for an employer to advertise a job and state that it would be better suited to female applicants. Sexual discrimination laws do not apply in religious organisations, however, including Christian Churches. The Churches are free to specify the sex of the ministers they wish to appoint.

The Roman Catholic Church teaches Christian complementarianism. This means that they believe that men and women were created as different by God and so have different roles to play. They will not permit women to become priests or bishops. It teaches that this is God's law:

- Jesus chose men to be his disciples. The Early Church leaders were all men.
- Priests represent Jesus (who was of course a man) when celebrating the mass – a church service based on Jesus' Last Supper. Women therefore cannot do this.
- The authority of the Church has been passed on through men, a tradition that cannot be broken.

Christians would approve of the appointment of women as priests. They would say that:

- Jesus came to break down barriers between people, not to reinforce them.
- Jesus was following the tradition of his time. If he were alive today, he would include women among his chosen disciples.
- God created women in his image as well as men.

To discuss

a Which view on the roles of men and women in Christian communities do you think is more reasonable?

b How do you support your view?

⮑ The Church of England allows women to be ordained as priests and deacons, and Libby Lane became the first female bishop in 2014

The religious upbringing of children

The Bible teaches that parents have a responsibility towards their children. They are required to discipline their children to help bring them up as obedient and well-behaved young people. They should not be too hard on their children, however:

'Children, obey your parents in everything, for this pleases the Lord. Fathers, do not embitter your children, or they will become discouraged.'

(Colossians 3:20–21)

Christians also aim to bring their children up with a knowledge and understanding of the Christian faith.

The religious upbringing of children is often shared between the adults caring for the children. Cultural differences and the variety of family types in Britain today make it difficult to say whether a man or a woman has a particular role in the religious upbringing of children. If a family follows the traditional roles for husband and wife for example, then the father would be responsible for family worship and the mother would ensure the children followed his instructions. Religious upbringing happens both in the home and in the Christian community. The adults caring for children will ensure they encounter the faith in both the home and the church community.

The Catholic Church and the Church of England

In the Catholic Church and the Church of England, a child is baptised, usually within the first year after their birth. As a result of the promises made at the baptismal service the parents, godparents and members of the Church try to help bring the child up within the Christian faith. They also commit to praying for the child and incorporating their faith into their daily routines. This will often include saying grace before the start of a meal. Grace is a simple prayer of thanks to God for the food that they are about to eat. Often parents will take time each day to read a section of the Bible with their child and discuss its application in their own lives.

A child who grows up within the Catholic Church or the Church of England is likely to attend Sunday School each week. Sunday School is a class run in part of the church building while the adults are in the main church service. During their time at Sunday School children will be taught stories from the Bible and the teachings of the Church. Some children may also attend mid-week church youth groups and as they get older be involved in greater study of the Bible. Christian parents will encourage their children to attend these groups as part of their religious upbringing, praying that they will take on the Christian faith for themselves as they get older.

Children in the Catholic Church and the Church of England may choose to get confirmed. Confirmation is a special church service that signifies a young person's desire to commit themselves to following the Christian faith. Once a person has been confirmed

⋒ Children brought up within Christianity may attend Sunday School or church youth groups

they are then allowed to take Eucharist in the church. In the Church of England any person over the age of 10 may be considered for confirmation and in the Catholic Church a young person may receive confirmation from the age of seven. This is a decision that each young person would be expected to discuss and explore with their parents and their minister.

The Amish community

In other Christian communities, the religious upbringing of children can be far more structured. For example, in the Amish community (a Christian denomination based largely in North America) they use Ordnung, which is a list of rules that outlines the way they should live. The Ordnung, however, varies between different Amish communities. Amish people are instructed to marry only other Amish. They keep themselves separate from the world and live in their own communities.

These communities provide schooling for the children, which ends at fourteen. At this age children are taught practical skills on the job. For example, this may be in farming for the boys and work in the home for the girls. In an Amish family women are under the authority of men: the man is in charge both of the spiritual life of his family and of provision for the needs of the family by going out to work. Women take on the domestic role and the primary care of the children.

The children are brought up to respect their parents and those older than them. From a young age children are given small jobs to do, such as feeding the chickens, so that they contribute to the family and community life. The children are taught not to be selfish and to be humble and they are encouraged to get along with others. This reflects the Amish belief that God is pleased with harmony.

At the age of 16 Amish children are allowed to live outside the community for a few years, this is known as Rumspringa. In this time they have to decide if they want to become fully baptised members of the Amish community. Often during this stage many Amish disobey the rules of their own community: they may get drunk, drive cars and investigate the latest fashions. The Amish community tolerates this as a way of allowing the young people to investigate the outside world before they commit to the strict rules of the Amish community. Most Amish children choose to return to the Amish community and are baptised.

Tasks

1 Describe the ways that different Christian families will bring up their children.
2 Explain why the Amish community give their children Rumspringa.
3 Explain the effects that a religious upbringing may have on a child.

To discuss

a How does the upbringing of Amish children compare to your own upbringing?
b What may be some of the benefits of the way the Amish raise their children?

Christian understandings of equality

Equality is the fair and level treatment of all human beings, regardless of ethnic background, nationality, gender, disability, religion or belief, sexual orientation or age. It is based on the belief that all individuals have equal worth, simply because they are human. It is expressed through the idea that we should treat others as we ourselves would want to be treated.

In order to show respect to and value others it can help if a person is first able to see their own value and have a good sense of self-esteem. Self-esteem is about valuing yourself as a person. A person's self-esteem may be affected by the words or actions of those around them.

Task

1 Consider how these words or actions may affect self-esteem:
- Being called names
- Being ignored
- Being invited to join in
- Being thanked
- Being treated differently to others
- Hearing thoughtless comments
- Being valued.

2 Draw a thermometer.
- Position each of the phrases on the thermometer, based on how positive (hot) or how negative (cold) they may make you feel about yourself.
- Think of two other phrases you would like to add that also affect your self-esteem.

To discuss

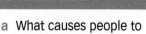

a What causes people to value themselves?
b Is it important that individuals value themselves? Explain your thoughts.
c How may the way a person values him- or herself affect their own view on equality?

Tasks

Who's Who

I used to think nurses

Were women,

I used to think police

Were men,

I used to think poets

Were boring,

Until I became one of them.

(Benjamin Zephaniah)

1 What do you think this poem is about?
2 How do you think our judgement of others can affect their self-esteem and sense of value?

Equality

Equality is not sameness. It is impossible to deny that people have different talents, different levels of intelligence or different abilities. Equality means that no one should be advantaged or privileged because of these differences. People should not be treated the same, but should be treated fairly because of differences.

Yet the world is a place of inequality. There are examples of inequality or unfairness in the treatment of different ethnic groups, between the sexes, between the able-bodied and disabled people, and between the old and young.

In addition, there are 'embedded inequalities'. These occur when the set-up of structures or organisations provides advantages for some while marginalising or producing disadvantages for others. For example, an institution where the premises have stairs but no lifts is likely to disadvantage some disabled people as they will not have access to all of its facilities.

Equality is not just a Christian idea. It is one that is shared between religious and non-religious ways of thinking.

Christian teachings and beliefs about equality

Christians believe in the value and equality of all people. They believe that humans are created in God's image. This means that the perfect characteristics of God are reflected in all human beings, and for this reason they believe each individual has worth and value. This value is not dependent upon how others see us, or even on what we think of ourselves. Christians do believe, however, that each person should recognise their value as being equal to all others as God's unique creation, and also respect all other human beings regardless of ethnicity, sex, age or religion.

The basis of Christian teaching is the Bible. The Christian Churches base their teachings on their interpretations of what the Bible has to say, and individuals base their beliefs on the teachings of the Bible and of their Church.

🎧 Christians believe that all humans should be respected regardless of age, sexuality, gender or disability

Bible bitz

'For it is improper for a woman to speak in an assembly, no matter what she says, even if she says admirable things, or even saintly things, that is of little consequence, since they come from the mouth of a woman.'

(Origen (d. 258ce): Fragments on 1 Corinthians 74)

'What is the difference whether it is in a wife or a mother, it is still Eve the temptress that we must beware of in any woman … I fail to see what use woman can be to man, if one excludes the function of bearing children.'

(Saint Augustine (354–430ce): De Genesi ad Litteram, 9, 5–9)

Bible bitz

'So God created mankind in his own image; in his own image God created them; he created them male and female.'

(Genesis 1:27)

'Then Peter began to speak: "Now I understand that God shows no partiality. Indeed, whoever fears him and does what is right is acceptable to him in any nation."'

(Acts 10:34–35)

'From one man he made every nation of humanity to live all over the earth, fixing the seasons of the year and the national boundaries within which they live.'

(Acts 17:26)

'I'm giving you a new commandment … to love one another. Just as I have loved you, you also should love one another.'

(John 13:24)

'Therefore, whatever you want people to do for you, do the same for them, because this summarises the Law and the Prophets.'

(Matthew 7:12)

'Because all of you are one in the Messiah Jesus, a person is no longer a Jew or a Greek, a slave or a free person, a male or a female.'

(Galatians 3:28)

'Nevertheless, you are doing the right thing if you obey the royal Law in keeping with the Scripture, "You must love your neighbour as yourself." But if you show partiality, you are committing sin and will be convicted by the Law as violators.'

(John 2:8–9)

'Sin began with a woman and thanks to her we all must die.'

(Ecclesiasticus, 25.33)

'For the man is not of the woman; but the woman of the man.'

(I Corinthians 11.8)

'Wives, submit yourselves unto your own husbands, as unto the Lord.'

(Ephesians 5.22)

Link It Up

a The Bible clearly teaches that human beings are equal. Identify which Bible quote could be used to support each of the bullet points below:
   - God created men and women to be equal.
   - God accepts everyone, regardless of ethnic or national background.
   - All people are connected and interrelated.
   - Jesus expects people to respect all others, following his example.
   - People should not expect more of others than they are prepared to do themselves.
   - Religious, social and gender difference have no meaning in Christian communities.
   - Showing favouritism is wrong.

b What do the Bible quotes that you have not used seem to suggest about equality between men and women?

c How does this link up with the quotes from the Early Church from Origen and Saint Augustine?

Slavery

Other biblical teaching was also used to promote inequality in the form of slavery. In the past, although some Christians argued that slavery went against the principles of Christianity, some Catholic clergy, and even Popes, owned slaves. Even in the second half of the nineteenth century, the Catholic Church seemed to support slavery:

'Slavery, considered as such in its essential nature, is not at all contrary to the natural and divine law. There can be several just titles of slavery and these are referred to by approved theologians and commentators of the sacred canons [of the Catholic Church]. It is not contrary to the natural and divine law for a slave to be sold, bought, exchanged or given.'

(Holy Office of the Roman Catholic Church, Instruction 20, 1866)

Bible bitz

'At that time I also noticed that Jews had married women from Ashdod, Ammon, and Moab. Furthermore, their children spoke half of the time in the language of Ashdod, and could not speak in the language of Judah. Instead, they spoke in the languages of various peoples. So I rebuked them, cursed them, struck some of their men, tore out their hair.'

(Nehemiah 13:23–24)

'You may buy male and female slaves from the nations all around you. Also you may buy slaves from the children of the foreigners who reside with you, and from their families that are with you, whom they have fathered in your land, they may become your property.'

(Leviticus 25:44–45)

'Slaves are to submit to their masters in everything, aiming to please them and not argue with them or steal from them. Instead, they are to show complete and perfect loyalty.'

(Titus 2:9–10)

Link It Up

a Explain what these three Bible quotes say about slavery.

b How does this teaching fit with the broader Bible teaching on equality?

Tasks

1 What is equality?

2 What reasons are given in the Bible to say that all people are equal?

3 Does the Bible express clear teachings about equality? Give some examples to explain your answer.

4 If the Christian Churches seem to act against what the Bible teaches, does this make the message of the Bible weaker? Explain your answer.

5 Is it possible to use twenty-first century European standards to judge those of biblical times? Try to present reasons to both agree and disagree.

> 'If there is equality it is in His [God's] love, not in us.'
>
> (C.S. Lewis)

To discuss

a Why may some Christians agree with C.S. Lewis?

b Do you think humans have the capacity to achieve equality within societies?

The influence of culture on attitudes and views about equality

In spite of the fact that there are clear teachings in the Bible that all human beings are equal because God created them to be equal, the Christian Churches have been slow to ensure that all people are treated equally.

For example, in the Bible Jesus teaches that wealth can be built up through greed, that wealthy people have a duty to share their wealth with people less fortunate, and that spiritual riches are more important than financial riches.

'It is easier for a camel to squeeze through the eye of a needle than for a rich person to get into the kingdom of God.'

(Matthew 19:24)

Yet today the Catholic Church is the wealthiest organisation in the world. One of the most famous hymns ever written seems to support the view that God created social inequality:

'The rich man in his castle,
The poor man at his gate,
God made them high and lowly,
And ordered their estate.'

(Cecil Frances Alexander, 'All Things Bright And Beautiful', 1848)

One of the reasons the Christian Church did not historically support or champion equality was because various members and institutions of the Church benefited from inequality. So they had no reason to challenge cultural views that were held at the time. Christian views were instead used to justify the *status quo*. For example in the nineteenth and early twentieth centuries Christian teachings were used to justify the unequal distribution of wealth.

The way these teachings are applied for individuals, in communities and society

While Christianity gives equal value to all humans, Christians may not agree with the beliefs that others choose to hold, including the religions they may follow. Many Christians believe that when Jesus was crucified he took God's punishment for all human sin, providing a way for humans to be forgiven by God (see p.34). God is able to forgive anyone who believes that Jesus' death happened as a way for them to have a connection with God. In this view, accepting Jesus as saviour is the only way that God can be known. For this reason some Christians consider all other religions to be wrong.

Some Christians believe in evangelism (see p.331). They see it as their mission to share their faith with others. Sometimes these Christians become missionaries and decide to spend their lives encouraging others to become Christians. Missionaries may work in their own country or they may travel abroad to work as part of overseas mission teams.

Prejudice and discrimination on the basis of gender

The word 'prejudice' is in two parts. 'Pre-' means before and '-judice' means judgement. So 'prejudice' means making a judgement about a person or a situation before knowing all the facts. This is not necessarily a bad thing. There are many occasions when it is important to have an idea about a person before you meet them so you can know what to expect.

The trouble with prejudices, however, is that they are often wrong. They are wrong because they are often based on stereotypes. A stereotype is a view or image of a group of people based on the characteristics of a few members of that group. It does not follow that every member of the group is the same.

The other trouble with prejudices is that they can lead to discrimination. People tend to act on their judgements about individuals. If the judgement is wrong, though, then the action is likely to be wrong, too.

It has been argued that gender stereotypes start very early in life – think of the kinds of clothes or toys given to babies of different sexes. Boys wear blue; girls wear pink. Girls play with dolls; boys play with cars. The argument goes on to say that this affects career opportunities later in life: engineers tend to be male; nursery nurses tend to be female. And, since the caring professions tend to pay less than technical jobs, women tend to earn less money than men.

On the other hand, some would argue that these are not examples of gender stereotypes, but of gender roles. They would say that males and females are biologically different, and it is this that accounts for social differences. For example, women are child bearers; therefore, it is natural for women to want to care for children. It is natural for them to want to bring up their own children and stay at home to do so, while men go out to work and provide for their family.

Christian attitudes

Christian attitudes and beliefs are divided between these two positions.

- **Christian egalitarianism:** egalitarians believe that men and women are created by God as equals. They may have different biological and psychological make-ups, different temperaments, different skills, but they are equal in every respect. They should have equal opportunities to succeed and should treat each other fairly.
- **Christian complementarianism:** complementarians say that men and women have been created by God to be different and to have different roles in life, including in Christian life.

🎧 Are the differences between boys and girls gender stereotypes or the result of biological differences?

Tasks

1 What is prejudice?
2 Explain the links between stereotypes, prejudice and discrimination.
3 Explain the differences between egalitarianism and complementarianism. Give examples of both positions.
4 Whether you are a Christian or not, do you think that men and women are exactly equal (egalitarian) or complementary (complementarian)? Give reasons for your views, and argue against the opposing view.
5 'Christian egalitarianism is unbiblical.' Do you agree with this? Support your answer with evidence from this chapter and other evidence you find from your own research.

To discuss

a How is the Christian Feminist Network responding to prejudice and discrimination in society on the basis of gender?

b What Christian beliefs and teachings does it refer to in its response to this prejudice and discrimination?

c What biblical evidence could you use to support the work of the Christian Feminist Network?

Case study: The Christian Feminist Network – connecting faith and feminism

■ The Christian Feminist Network logo

The Christian Feminist Network is an ecumenical Christian organisation based in the UK. It is made up of people who are interested in looking at faith and feminism. Any person is welcome to join the network, regardless of their gender, ethnicity, background, age or sexuality. The organisation believes in the equal value of men and women, while working for the improved status of women across all areas of society. It believes that the message of the Bible is one of equality, including gender equality. For this reason the Christian Feminist Network opposes, and will campaign against, any such discrimination.

Its aims are:

● to promote gender equality and challenge oppression in society, church and home

● to provide a safe space for Christian feminists to support each other

● to contribute a Christian voice within the feminist community.

The Christian Feminist Network puts on alternative acts of worship and study days that focus on feminist theology, and it also offers conferences.

(Source: http://christianfeministnetwork.com/about)

Stretch what you know

Find out more about the Dwell Project, which is supported by the Christian Feminist Network. You may find this link useful: http://dwelldomesticviolence.com

a Summarise what the Dwell Project is trying to achieve.

b Explain the way in which it is working to achieve this.

Let's Revise

a Describe one Christian belief about the roles of men and women in Christian family relationships. (3 marks)

- In this answer you must identify one Christian belief about the roles of man and women in Christian family relationships. For example the role of the wife to support her husband by taking responsibility for the home and the care of the children.

- You must then describe this role in a further two sentences. You may make a link to a Bible source.

b Outline different Christian attitudes towards the religious upbringing of children. (6 marks)

- Answer this question in clearly written paragraphs.

- Include at least two different Christian attitudes towards the religious upbringing of children. For example you could write about the Quaker upbringing of children and the religious upbringing in the Church of England.

- You could consider the choice of faith schools by some Christian parents as part of their child's religious upbringing.

c Explain why marriage is important to Christians. (6 marks)
You should refer to sources of wisdom and authority in your answer.

- Answer this question in clearly written paragraphs. Include links to relevant Bible passages. For example you may refer to Genesis 2:23–24 and the unity that marriage brings between a husband and a wife.

- You could make specific reference to differences between Christian wedding services and how these variations in practice emphasise the importance of marriage. For example the crowns used in an Orthodox marriage service compared to the leaderless marriage service in a Quaker wedding.

- You should explain the belief that marriage is a sacrament and why this is important.

- In your answer include an explanation of how Christians believe that God is involved in the vows that are made and through the prayers. The text of the marriage service could be considered a source of wisdom and authority for Christians of that denomination.

- You may also refer to the purpose of marriage as part of the reason for it's importance to Christians.

e 'It is better to divorce than to stay in a unhappy marriage.'
Discuss this statement. In your answer, you should:

- draw on your learning from across your course of study, including reference to beliefs, teachings and practices within Christianity

- explain and evaluate the importance of points of view from the perspective of Christianity. (15 marks)

Let's Revise contd.

Spelling, punctuation and grammar   (3 marks)

- You must evaluate this statement from different Christian perspectives.

- The Roman Catholic Church teaches that divorce is never acceptable. Make sure you explain the Catholic response to this statement, refer to biblical evidence as you do this. You could also refer back to the content of the marriage ceremony in Part 1 and the importance of the vows. (The role of the church in the local community and living practices.)

- However, other Christians may argue that divorce can be acceptable depending on the degree and cause of the unhappiness. You may contrast the Catholic perspective with the Church of England teaching. For example you may include some discussion on the Church of England's view on divorce in the event of adultery.

- Make sure you offer a balanced judgement on this issue in order to get the highest marks.

6 The existence of God

The question of God

Christian beliefs about what God is like

Christians do not believe in a God who is limited by the laws of nature or by having a physical body. They believe God has certain unique characteristics that make Him holy. To Christians, God is:

- **Omnipotent** – all-powerful. They believe He had the power to create the whole universe (as described in Genesis), to perform miracles and to become a human being as Jesus.
- **Omniscient** – all-knowing.
- **Omnipresent** – able to be everywhere at once because He is not limited by having a physical body.
- **Eternal** – without beginning or end, outside time and space. They believe He is **transcendent** and not limited by our world.
- **Immanent and personal** – despite being all-powerful, Christians believe that God is 'immanent', which means He is involved with our lives on a personal level.
- **Perfectly good** – God is the source of all goodness.
- Our **judge** – Christians believe God will judge us on they way we have lived our lives and that His judgement will determine what happens to us after death. They also believe, however, that He is forgiving and kind (benevolent) to people who ask for His forgiveness.

The Trinity

Christians believe that there is only one God; they believe, however, that He is a trinity with three parts:

- **The Father** – God is seen as the protector and creator. Some Christians see their relationship with God as being like that between father and child.
- **The Son** – Christians believe Jesus was God in human form (incarnated). He came to Earth to die on the cross to pay the price of human sin. Jesus rose from the dead to show God's power over death and to provide an example of how Christians should live.
- **The Holy Spirit** – Christians believe the Holy Spirit is the presence of God that is with them all the time and helps them live in the way that He wants.

The Father, the Son and the Holy Spirit are known as the three persons of the Trinity. Each element of the Trinity is equal, but distinct. The Trinity is understood to have been fully present at Jesus' baptism:

'Just as Jesus was coming up out of the water, he saw heaven being torn open and the Spirit descending on him like a dove. And a voice came from heaven: "You are my Son, whom I love; with you I am well pleased."'

(Mark 1:10–11)

The importance of this belief is also seen in Christian practices. For example, during confirmation in the Anglican Church candidates are asked if they believe and trust in the Father, His Son and His Holy Spirit.

Belief in God as three persons means that He can relate to Himself as well as to humanity. Belief in the Trinity is unique to Christianity.

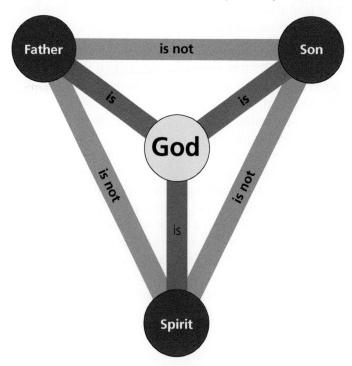

Reasons for different Christian views on what God is like

There are some differences of opinion within Christianity about various parts of God's nature. The majority of Christians accept the teaching of the Trinity. Unitarianism, however, is a Christian belief that states God is one being. The Unitarian belief is that Jesus was in some way a 'son' of God, but not that he was literally God. They still believe Jesus was sent to Earth as a saviour and see him as a human who was inspired by God in all he did.

Jehovah's Witnesses, a Christian-based religious group, also reject the teaching of the Trinity. They believe that God is a single being and that His personal name is Jehovah. According to the Jehovah's Witnesses there is no one equal to God and they see Jesus as, in some way, the son of God. They argue that Jesus was created by Jehovah and because – unlike Jehovah – he had a beginning: he is not eternal. They also do not believe that the Holy Spirit is a separate person from God. The Holy Spirit is understood to be Jehovah's force, through which He acts.

Tasks

○ The Holy Spirit with a Model of Ptolemy's World by Hermann Han, 1610

Look at Han's painting, which portrays all three members of the Trinity.

1 State who is represented by:
- the dove
- the white-bearded man
- the second bearded man.

2 Explain, using evidence from the Bible, what makes you identify each figure in this way.

3 Using your knowledge of Christian beliefs and teachings, explain what you think the Trinity are doing in this painting.

4 Explain what a Jehovah's Witness may say about the beliefs represented by this painting.

5 Explain how a Christian who believes in the Trinity may respond to the views of the Jehovah's Witness. Include Bible quotes in your response.

Disagreement between the Western and Eastern Churches

Historically, disagreements over the nature of the Trinity have caused splits in the Church. The Nicene Creed of the Western Church includes a phrase meaning '…and from the Son' to describe the existence of the Holy Spirit. This suggests that the Spirit comes from both God the Father and God the Son. In support of this teaching, John 1:3 does explain that all things are made through the Son, Jesus. In contrast, the Eastern Orthodox Church teaches that the Holy Spirit comes only from the Father. Their creed instead states belief 'in the Holy Spirit who proceeds from the Father'. The Orthodox Church maintains that God the Father is the source of all things and, therefore, rejects the teaching of the Western Church. The Orthodox Church points to John 15:26, which clearly states that the Holy Spirit '…proceeds from the Father'

Bible bitz

'…the Lord … Is he not your Father, your Creator, who made you and formed you?'
(Deuteronomy 32:6)

'…let your light shine before men, that they may see your good deeds and praise your Father in heaven.'
(Matthew 5:16)

'Grace and peace from God the Father and Christ Jesus our Saviour.'
(Titus 1:4)

'In the presence of God and of Christ Jesus, who will judge the living and the dead…'
(2 Timothy 4:1)

'Jesus Christ … is the atoning sacrifice for our sins … for the sins of the whole world.'
(1 John 2:2)

'Your attitude should be the same as that of Christ Jesus: Who, being in very nature God … Taking

the very nature of a servant, being made in human likeness…'
(Philippians 2:6)

'…the Counsellor, the Holy Spirit, whom the Father will send in my name, will teach you all things and will remind you of everything I [Jesus] have said to you.'
(John 14:25)

'…the Spirit of him who raised Jesus from the dead is living in you…'
(Romans 8:11)

'Do not worship any other god, for the Lord, whose name is Jealous, is a jealous God'
(Exodus 34:14)

'Whoever does not love does not know God, because God is love'
(1 John 4:8)

Link it up

a Based on the information in the 'Bible bitz' box, list all you can about the nature of the Father, Son and Holy Spirit under three headings in a table like the one below.

The Father	The Son	The Holy Spirit

b Read the section on Christian beliefs in Chapter 1 and add any additional information about the nature of the Father, Son and Holy Spirit to your lists.

God's relationship with the world

Christian understandings of God's relationship with the world come from the account of how the world was created given in the biblical book of Genesis. According to this account, God speaks and causes things to come into existence (see Chapter 1).

The world is dependent on the command of God. According to the account, He causes all things to exist and ensures that everything is provided for the Earth. For example, He supplies water and sunlight for plants and vegetation for animals to eat. The language of the Bible often presents God's work as that of a craftsman, with the writer of the book of Job asking:

'can you beat out the vault of the skies, as he [God] does hard as a mirror of cast metal?'

Whether the account in Genesis is taken literally, or as a myth, it still illustrates the Christian belief that the world is dependent on God for its existence.

God's involvement with the world continued after Creation. Christians believe the seasons are controlled by God, for example, in Ecclesiastes it says,

'There is a time for everything, and a season for every activity under the heavens.'

(Ecclesiastes 3:1)

In Psalms God's sustaining work in nature is shown:

'He covers the sky with clouds; he supplies the earth with rain and makes grass grow on the hills.'

(Psalm 147:8)

In this way God brings order to the world, unlike the 'formless' emptiness (Genesis 1:1) before Creation. Some Christians disagree about whether God formed the world *ex nihilo* (from nothing), or whether He created the world from pre-existent matter. The wording of Genesis 1 is not clear. Most Christians, however, believe God created the world *ex nihilo* since He is all-powerful and the only eternal being. If He created the world from existing material, this may suggest that He is not unique in being eternal; because this would require other matter to have existed prior to Creation.

The Bible also explains that the natural world itself is a witness to God's existence when in Romans 1:20 it says:

'For since the creation of the world God's invisible qualities – his eternal power and divine nature – have been clearly seen, being understood from what has been made, so that people are without excuse.'

This teaches Christians that everything God has created in some way reveals His existence. Ultimately the world has been created to be able to sustain not just animal life, but human life and it is God's relationship with humanity that is at the centre of the Christian faith.

⋒ Christians believe the complexity and beauty of nature reveals something about God

God's relationship with humanity

God's relationship with humanity is seen in Genesis 1 when God says:

'Let us make man in our image, in our likeness...'

(Genesis 1:26)

This sets humans apart from the rest of creation and means there is a unique link between humans and God, because humans were made in His image. In the Creation story, God also gives humans a role of stewardship over His creation. This means that He gives them power over it, but also responsibility for looking after it. No other creature is given this role. When God creates Adam He uses the dust from the ground to make him. He then breathes into his nostrils to give him life (Genesis 2:7). For many Christians, this demonstrates God's unique relationship with humans right from the point of Creation.

➲ The Creation of Adam, by Michelangelo. What does this art suggest about God's creation of humans?

In the Garden of Eden God ensures Adam and Eve are provided for and that they are blessed with children (Genesis 1:29). God's ongoing care for humanity is shown throughout the Bible. For example:

- His provision of the Promised Land of Canaan for the Israelites. God chooses the Israelites as His people, called to serve Him and be obedient to Him. As His chosen people, God promises them a land of their own. The Old Testament describes how God leads the Israelites and sends them to war and how eventually they come to inhabit the land of Israel.
- His provision of laws and commands, for example, the Ten Commandments recorded in Exodus 20, which help humans understand how to live a good life.
- His provision of a means for salvation through animal sacrifice in the Old Testament. When God's people sin in the Old Testament, He requires them to repent and to make an atonement for their sin. In the Old Testament God therefore allows His people to sacrifice animals in atonement.

God's love as shown by the life and death of Jesus

God's care for, and relationship with, humanity are most clearly seen in His incarnation, when He became human as Jesus. Christians believe that Jesus came to Earth to teach people about God's love and to show people how to live in obedience to God – and that ultimately he died as a sacrifice for human sin. Jesus' sacrifice on the cross repaired the relationship between humans and God, which had been broken when Adam and Eve disobeyed God in the Garden of Eden (see p.17). His death provides humanity with the opportunity for forgiveness and salvation, if they seek forgiveness for their sins and put their faith in God (see p.37–39). Christians seek to worship and serve God in thanks for the gift of this restored relationship. This reflects the teaching about God's relationship with humanity that is found in Philippians 2:5–10:

'In your relationships with one another, have the same mindset as Christ Jesus:

Who, being in very nature God,
  did not consider equality with God something to be used to his own advantage;
rather, he made himself nothing
  by taking the very nature of a servant,
  being made in human likeness.
And being found in appearance as a man,
  he humbled himself
  by becoming obedient to death—
even death on a cross!

Therefore God exalted him to the highest place
  and gave him the name that is above every name,
that at the name of Jesus every knee should bow,
  in heaven and on earth and under the earth.'

This quote demonstrates the sacrificial nature of God's relationship with humanity. As Jesus, God lowered Himself to the level of a human, even though God is eternal and omnipotent. Jesus served people in his time on Earth. The end of the quote, however, is a reminder to Christians that one day Jesus will come again and that this time he will not be limited and everyone will worship him.

Jesus describes God's relationship with Christians, saying that God the Father loves those who are obedient to His teaching (John 14:23). God maintains this relationship with Christians through the presence of His Holy Spirit in their lives. The Holy Spirit acts to remind believers of their faith (John 14:26), intercedes as they pray to God (Romans 8:26) and helps believers develop lives that reflect God's characteristics (Galatians 5:22–23). Through His Holy Spirit, God comforts Christians in times of suffering. Christians therefore believe that they have a close, personal relationship with God. They believe that this is a relationship God offers to all humans if they have faith in Him.

Tasks

1 Describe the relationship between God and the world.

2 Explain what aspects of God's nature this relationship most clearly reflects.

3 Compare God's relationship with the world to His relationship with humanity – how are they different?

4 Explain what God's relationship with humanity reveals about His benevolence.

Reasons for different Christian views on God's relationship with the world and with humanity

Is God outside time or active in the world?

There are differences of Christian belief about God's relationship with the world and with humanity. Traditionally, God has been understood to be timeless. This means that He is outside time and not limited by it. God created all things, including time. This view of God describes Him as atemporal. If God is understood to be atemporal, then He can see and know all things: the past, the present and even the future. This view supports the Christian belief that God is not limited, nor does He change. From this perspective God's plans for the world are bound to happen since He can see all time. In Jeremiah it says:

> '"For I know the plans I have for you," declares the Lord, "plans to prosper you and not to harm you."'
>
> *(Jeremiah 29:11)*

This teaching fits with the view that God is atemporal.

Some Christians, however, believe that if God were outside time and unchanging, then He would not be able to relate to His creation. In order to answer prayers, for instance, many Christians say that He has to be able to respond and change. In the book of 2 Kings in the Bible, for example, a king called Hezekiah is sick and about to die. He prays that God will grant him more life and God responds, saying 'I will add fifteen years to your life' (2 Kings 20:6). In this example, God is shown to interact with His people in response to their prayers. At other times in the Bible God is also shown to interact with the physical world – for example the Flood in Exodus and the destruction of the city of Sodom and Gomorrah – because of the sinfulness of the people living there.

From this perspective, God is seen as active in time and as changing in response to events in the world and the requests of His people. Christians who hold this view argue that God is everlasting. This means that instead of being outside time He is in time, without beginning or end, but with humans each and every moment. This is a belief that sees God as personal and engaged with His creation and with humanity. This is different from the atemporal understanding, which presents God as far less proactive. According to the atemporal understanding, God has a set plan and He simply allows it to unfold exactly as He knew it would.

Can humans communicate with God directly?

The Catholic Church has another understanding of the relationship between humans and God. In the Catholic Church, priests believe that they have been called into their ministry by God. When a priest is ordained, the Church teaches that he is acting in the power of Christ, not in his own power. This is linked to the teaching in Galatians in which Paul says:

> 'It is no longer I who live, but Christ who lives in me.'
>
> *(Galatians 2:20)*

This is an intimate relationship created through God in the priest. Therefore, in the Catholic Church, as well as an individual having a relationship with God, the priest can also act as a link between humans and God. For this reason Catholics may go to their priest to confess their sins and it is through him that forgiveness can be offered. The priest has a responsibility to work to become more Christ-like with the help of the Holy Spirit.

Christians in Protestant Churches, however, do not believe that they need a mediator between themselves and God. They believe that Jesus enabled all people who truly believe in God to pray directly to Him and have a personal relationship with Him. Hebrews 7 explains that the need for priests as mediators is no longer needed.

Christian beliefs and views on God as good

Christians believe that God is perfectly good; in fact that He is the source of all goodness. Thomas Aquinas, a philosopher from the thirteenth century, wrote about how God's nature is entirely good; this means that everything God commands and does is also good. His goodness is demonstrated throughout the Bible and revealed by His actions in several ways, as discussed below.

God's goodness revealed through creation

In the accounts in Genesis, God creates the world and all that is in it, and everything that He creates is described as 'good'. On the final day of Creation, when everything has been made, the whole of creation of is described as 'very good'. In His creation God provides all that is needed to sustain the world and its inhabitants. For example, in Psalms it says:

He covers the sky with clouds;
he supplies the earth with rain
and makes grass grow on the hills

(Psalm 147:8)

God's goodness revealed through His provision of law

According to the Bible, God desires that people should choose to do what is right. Straight after the creation of Adam and Eve, God gives them the responsibility of caring for creation and also gives them a rule: not to eat from one particular tree.

God continues to give humanity rules about how to live a good life, for example, He gives Moses the Ten Commandments. These laws demonstrate that God wants people to act in a way that is morally good and caring. It is because God is good that His rules are good and show the best way for humans to live.

God allows humans free will. He does not force goodness upon anyone. God, because He is perfectly good, cannot tolerate sin and evil and punishes people who do not follow the rules He has given.

⚭ God gave Moses Ten Commandments as laws for the Israelites. In what ways do these laws demonstrate God's goodness?

God's goodness revealed through judgement

Christianity teaches that God will judge all humans when they die and that this will determine what happens to them after death. Unlike any human judge, God knows and sees everything, He is therefore able to judge fairly, ensuring justice. This is seen in Psalm 9:8, which says:

'He rules the world in righteousness and judges the peoples with equity.'

To discuss

'Sir, my concern is not whether God is on our side; my greatest concern is to be on God's side, for God is always right.'

(Abraham Lincoln)

a What do you think Abraham Lincoln meant when he said this?

b What is it about God's nature that would cause a Christian to agree with Abraham Lincoln?

c Why is this aspect of His nature important to Christian understandings of God as being good?

God's goodness revealed through salvation

As part of His goodness God chooses to offer humans forgiveness. Before Jesus, the Old Testament tells us that humans showed they were sorry for their sins and asked for forgiveness by sacrificing animals. These sacrifices, however, had to be repeated regularly to cover the sins committed each year. John 3:16 explains that out of His love for humanity God sent His son, Jesus, to die to cover all human sin, once and for all. Christians believe that if people have faith in Jesus and repent (turn away from their sins), then God will forgive them and they will be able to spend eternity in heaven with Him when they die. By sending His son, God made the ultimate sacrifice for humanity and this reveals His goodness.

Stretch what you know

The Euthyphro dilemma is a philosophical problem that concerns the goodness of God. Many attribute the problem to the Ancient Greek philosopher Plato (428–348BCE). From a Christian perspective, the dilemma is whether something is morally good because God has commanded it, or if God has commanded it because it is good. If something is good simply because God commands it then in theory God could command anything, even something we currently consider to be bad, and it would be good simply because He commands it. Alternatively, if God commands things because they are good, then this suggests that goodness exists separately from God and that He too is dependent on this external goodness and can be subject to judgement.

a Investigate Christian responses to the Euthyphro dilemma.

b Explain how Christians may resolve this dilemma.

c Do you think the Christian solution is reasonable?

To discuss

⋒ Jesus as the Lamb of God

a What is the relationship between this piece of art and the Christian teaching on salvation?

b Why might this image help some Christians to reflect upon the goodness of God?

Challenges to God's goodness

Some people outside the Christian faith do not accept the claims of Christianity about God's goodness. They point to events, especially in the Old Testament, that appear to demonstrate a lack of goodness. Such events include the flooding of the world during the time of Noah, or God's request to Abraham to sacrifice his son Isaac, only to provide a replacement sacrifice of a ram at the last moment.

Some argue that the actions of God in the Old Testament show his anger, jealousy and lack of justice. They point to times when God enables His own people to destroy other nations in order to take land for themselves. For example, God told Joshua:

'Three days from now you will cross the Jordan here to go in and take possession of the land the Lord your God is giving you for your own.'

(Joshua 1:11)

Richard Dawkins, the author and scientist, goes as far as describing such a God as immoral.

As mentioned above, in the New Testament, however, God made the ultimate sacrifice for humanity by sending His son to Earth to die to cover human sin and this reveals His goodness.

Tasks

1 Cut out four hexagons and on each one write one way that God's goodness is said to be revealed. For example, 'Through salvation'.

2 Cut out ten hexagons and write one Bible verse on each, using the quotes in the 'Bible bitz' box on page 198.

3 Now arrange the hexagons so that every time one side of a hexagon touches another, you are able to explain the link between the information on the hexagons. Stick these into your book once you have arranged them effectively. For example:

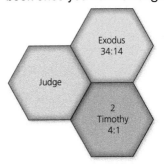

4 Now annotate your hexagons by drawing arrows to at least three different sides that touch and adding an explanation for the link you have created.

5 Use this work to explain how you think a Christian may respond to the challenges against God's goodness.

6 'God was not good when he gave humans free will.' Discuss this view. Include different perspectives, including Christian views, as well as your own opinion.

The Flood of the world by God, which only Noah's family survive (*Genesis* 6–9)

God's destruction of Sodom and Gomorrah in response to their sin (*Genesis* 19)

Abraham preparing to sacrifice his son Isaac at God's command (*Genesis* 22)

a What conclusions could you draw about the character of God from the three biblical events illustrated above?

b How do these conclusions compare to what you have already learned about the Christian teachings on the nature of God?

c How do you think Christians would explain these events to fit with their understanding of God's character?

Christian beliefs, teachings and views about the relationship between God and human suffering

To discuss

'POVERTY IS THE WORST FORM OF VIOLENCE'

This quote from Gandhi suggests that poverty is an intentional and violent act

a To what extent do you agree with the quote from Gandhi?

b If poverty is an act of violence, who would you say is to blame?

Tasks

'The fact of suffering undoubtedly constitutes the single greatest challenge to the Christian faith.'

(John Stott (1921–2011), Christian writer and Anglican minister)

1 Why do you think John Stott identifies suffering as the greatest challenge facing Christians?

2 What other problems do you think Christianity faces? Do you think any of these are greater than the problem of suffering? Use the ideas below to help you respond to this.

- Increased interest in other religions, including Islam and Buddhism.

- Declining church attendance.

- Negative attitudes towards Christianity.

- Changing attitudes in society – for example, about whether couples should get married before having children.

Christian approaches to why there is evil and suffering in the world

Evil as a result of human sin

Christians have different views on why there is suffering in the world. In the Genesis story of the Fall, Adam and Eve disobey God's instruction not to eat fruit from the tree of knowledge and thus they first bring evil into a perfect world. Adam and Eve both use the free will that God has given them to do something He has forbidden. Not only is the perfect world affected by this, but so is the perfect relationship that humans originally had with God. This account led St Augustine (354–430CE), a Christian bishop, to teach that human beings are responsible for evil as a result of making wrong choices. This view often leaves people asking why God chose to create Adam and Eve if He knew they were going to be disobedient.

HEY, DON'T LOOK AT ME – I WAS *AGAINST* FREE WILL!

🎧 What does this cartoon suggest about God's decision to give humans free will?

Evil as a lesson

Another Christian bishop, Irenaeus (130–202CE), however, proposed a different view of this story in Genesis. Irenaeus suggests that man was not created perfect, but immature, needing to grow and develop to perfection, as planned by God. So some Christians believe that evil is necessary for us to understand goodness. If there was no wrongdoing then we would be unaware of justice. It is because of the existence of evil that we can be aware of the goodness of God. From this perspective the existence of evil teaches us lessons.

This notion, however, does not explain suffering that cannot be learned from, for example, the suffering of a baby. Sometimes suffering does not help us develop God's perfect qualities and become more like Him, so it is hard to see why it is necessary. For example, when a person is diagnosed with a terminal illness they may feel that they do not deserve the illness. They may feel a sense of anger towards God for allowing them to be ill, especially if they believe that they have tried to live in a way that would please God.

Evil as a test

Other Christians think that suffering is a test of faith for believers and a punishment for the wicked. In the book of Job, God allows the Devil to bring evil and suffering on Job to see whether he will remain faithful to God. Job does remain faithful and God rewards him. Some Christians may believe that they too are being tested by God during difficult times in their lives and may trust that He will never allow them to be tested beyond what they can bear (1 Corinthians 10:13).

Tasks

1 In what way do St Augustine and Irenaeus differ in their views of the Genesis story of the Fall?

2 Explain the beliefs Christians have about the reason for suffering.

3 Explain what you think are the most convincing explanations for evil and suffering.

4 Recall from your work on Christian beliefs and teachings the difference between moral and natural evil. Write down a definition of each.

5 Do you think humans bear greatest responsibility for either of these types of evil, or do you think God or the Devil is to blame for all evil? Give reasons for your answer.

6 What could humans do to reduce suffering?

7 At times of disaster people often ask why innocent people must suffer. Explain different Christian responses to this question.

Stretch what you know

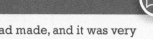
◑ Thomas Aquinas (1225–74)

Read the following extract from the New Advent Catholic website:

'St Thomas Aquinas, a thirteenth-century Christian monk, provides an explanation of why God chose to create anything at all. First, it is asked why God, foreseeing that His creatures would use the gift of free will for their own injury, did not either abstain from creating them, or in some way safeguard their free will from misuse, or else deny them the gift altogether?

St Thomas replies that God cannot change His mind, since the Divine will is free from the defect of weakness or mutability. Such mutability would, it should be remarked, be a defect in the Divine nature (and therefore impossible), because if God's purpose were made dependent on the foreseen free act of any creature, God would thereby sacrifice His own freedom, and would submit Himself to His creatures, thus abdicating His essential supremacy.'

(www.newadvent.org)

a According to this website, why does Aquinas say that God created Adam and Eve even though He knew they would disobey Him?

b Explain what you think would be the effect of a God who abdicated His supremacy.

Bible bitz

'God saw all that he had made, and it was very good. And there was evening, and there was morning – the sixth day.'

(Genesis 1:31)

'My God, my God, why have you forsaken me? Why are you so far from saving me, so far from my cries of anguish?'

(Psalm 22:1)

'And when the people ask, "Why has the Lord our God done all this to us?" you will tell them, "As you have forsaken me and served foreign gods in your own land, so now you will serve foreigners in a land not your own."'

(Jeremiah 5:19)

Link it up

a How may some Christians interpret Genesis 1:31 when considering whether God causes evil or suffering in the world?

b Using Jeremiah 5:19, explain how some Christians may suggest that God allows suffering to occur.

c Look up and read the parable of the Prodigal Son in Luke 15:11–32. Explain what the prodigal son goes through before returning to his father.

d What does this the parable of the Prodigal Son teach Christians about some forms of suffering?

e Explain the link between the parable, Psalm 22:1 and Jeremiah 5:19.

The nature of reality

For centuries philosophers have been coming up with reasoned arguments, based upon evidence, which try to prove the existence of God.

Four of the main arguments are:

- The design argument
- The anthropic principle
- The first cause argument, or the cosmological argument
- The moral argument.

The value and importance of arguments about the existence of God

Such arguments are important because they enable people to consider whether belief in God is reasonable. While Christianity requires faith on the part of the believer, this does not mean the belief is irrational. These philosophical arguments help demonstrate logical ways in which it is possible to accept that God may exist. Some of these arguments reflect aspects of the teaching found in the Bible, for example, the nature of God as creator. Other arguments focus on human behaviour as an indicator of God's existence, for example, the moral argument. These arguments enable people with or without a faith to enter into discussions and considerations about God's existence.

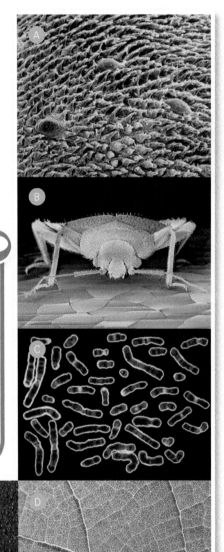

To discuss

a Try to identify what is shown by each of the images A–F.

b What conclusions might you draw about the natural world from this collection of images? For example, would any of the images lead you to agree with the following points?
- The natural world contains a great deal of beauty.
- The world is intricate.
- The world has been carefully designed.
- Every person is unique.

c What other images would you add to these six to reflect your conclusions?

The design argument

The six images on the previous page show different aspects of the natural world:

A Magnified image of a human tongue.
B Magnified image of a bed bug.
C Strands of DNA.
D Detail of a leaf.
E A human fingerprint.
F The centre of a flower.

Some philosophers have suggested that observation of the natural world reveals an order and complexity that could only have been achieved through intelligent design. This means that instead of coming into existence through a chain of natural events, the world is the result of design by an intelligent being – God. This argument for the existence of God is known as the **teleological argument**. It takes its name from the Greek word *telos*, meaning 'purpose', and suggests that because the world was designed, it has a purpose. This argument is also known as the design argument.

Experiences of awe and wonder

The fascination and awe created by observation of the natural world can, for some people, be a revelation. Recognising the intricacy and complexity of the natural world around them may move them to a belief in a designer God.

William Paley

William Paley (1743–1805), a philosopher, uses the example of a watch to explain the argument from design. He said that the way in which all the parts of a watch work together to meet a purpose suggests that the watch must have a designer. This is because such order and purpose could not be simply the result of an accident. He said that, in the same way, if you look at the world and the way nature appears to work to meet a purpose, it also suggests that the world must have a designer – God.

John Stuart Mill

John Stuart Mill (1806–73) disagreed with Paley's argument. His main line of reasoning was to examine the way nature operates. Mill pointed to the cruelty that is part of the natural order of things, for example, certain animals being efficient killers or certain creatures living on other animals. Other elements of nature occur as the result of faults in the Earth's structure, such as earthquakes, tsunamis or volcanic eruptions. This cruelty, and what he believed to be evidence of bad design in nature, led him to argue that if a designer God existed, He would in fact be a cruel God. After all, His creation brings about all kinds of pain and suffering. Mill argued that people surely cannot want to worship a God who would design such a world.

Task

Read Paley's accounts of the teleological argument and then:

● explain the argument in your own words
● list any problems that you can see with this argument.

Stretch what you know

🎧 The theory of evolution

Charles Darwin's theory of evolution was first published in 1859 in his work *On the Origin of Species*. Darwin suggested that species have developed ('evolved') over millions of years through a process he called natural selection. According to this process, individual members of a species might be born with a certain characteristic at random, for example, a distinctly – shaped beak for a bird. In certain circumstances this characteristic might prove useful, for instance the differently-shaped beak might help the bird access food more easily than could a normal beak. Thus, individuals with that characteristic would be more likely to survive and breed and pass that characteristic on to their offspring. This is called 'survival of the fittest'. In this way species change over time, and ultimately whole new species are created, leading to the complex world we see today. This is obviously very different from traditional Christian beliefs that God created the world and all the species in it exactly as they are today.

Darwin's work has been developed by much scientific research and is supported by the atheist Richard Dawkins. Dawkins argues that as science discovers and understands more about the natural world, the less need there is for a belief in God. He famously wrote in *River Out of Eden* that 'life is just bytes and bytes and bytes of digital information', meaning that DNA is the explanation for the cause of life.

a Describe the impact you think Darwin's theory of evolution has upon the design argument that was originally put forward by Paley.

b In what way could scientific discovery reduce the human need for God?

c Explain how you could counter Dawkins' view that there is less need for God as scientific discovery develops.

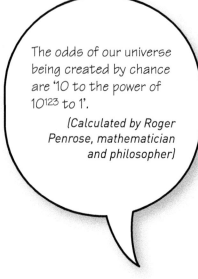

The odds of our universe being created by chance are '10 to the power of 10^{123} to 1'.

(Calculated by Roger Penrose, mathematician and philosopher)

🎧 What does this statistic make you think about your own existence?

The anthropic principle

The phrase 'anthropic principle' was first used by F.R. Tennant (1866–1957). He used it to refer to the way that the universe was so perfectly structured to ensure life would develop. Tennant saw evolution as further evidence for the existence of a designer God. He argued that the very process of evolution has a purpose, which is to develop increasingly complex life forms. These increasingly complex life forms become more intelligent and ultimately, in the form of humans, also come to possess moral awareness. Tennant believed this demonstrates that evolution was guided by God, rather than using evolution as an argument against a designer.

Professor John Polkinghorne is a theoretical physicist and an Anglican minister. He explains that in order for life to exist there has to have been a precise development of the universe. He writes:

'A fruitful universe has to have exactly the right sort of stars. A universe exactly the same as ours except that in it gravity was three times stronger, would have been boring and sterile in its history because its stars would have burnt themselves out in a few million years, long before any life could get going on an encircling planet.

The second role the stars have to perform is to produce the raw materials of life in their nuclear furnaces. The chemistry of life is the chemistry of carbon (since all life on earth depends on it) and there is only one place in the whole universe where carbon can be made, namely inside stars.'

(www.faradayschools.com)

For Polkinghorne, the need for such precision in the universe in order to allow our existence supports an anthropic principle. That means he believes God created the universe in this way so as to ensure human existence. He rejects the view that it is all simply luck, random chance or coincidence. This belief is supported by the biblical account of Creation in Genesis. In Genesis 1 and 2, God creates an environment that is suitable for human habitation. The stars are put in place, plants grow and in turn ensure food for the creatures that God creates. Once all this is in place God creates man and then woman, thus ensuring the possibility of human reproduction. Whether this story is taken literally or as a myth, it is clear that the writer is demonstrating the way God ensured human existence and survival.

The first cause argument

Another philosophical argument for the existence of God is the first cause argument, also known as the **cosmological argument**.

There is, in fact, no event in the natural world that doesn't have a cause. This idea was identified by the philosopher Aristotle (384–322BCE), who said that everything must be created by some cause. The cosmological argument suggests, therefore, that the universe too must have a cause. This is because something must have triggered the process that started the development of the universe – rather like someone pushing over the first domino in a line and then observing the rest falling down. In this argument, God is this 'prime mover', or first cause. God Himself doesn't have a cause. One philosopher who developed this argument was Thomas Aquinas (1225–74).

To discuss

a Look at the pictures. What is happening in each? Discuss what may be the cause(s) for each event.

b Is it possible for something to happen that has no cause?

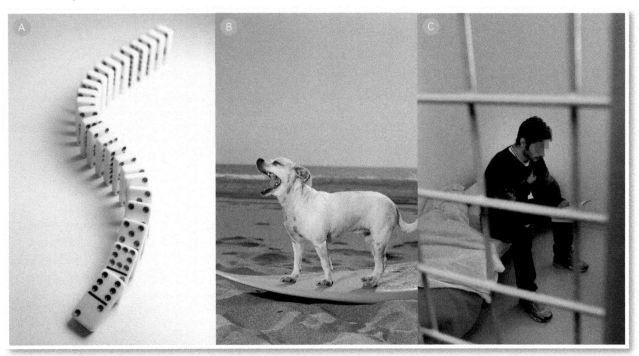

Both the teleological (see p.210) and the cosmological arguments for the existence of God rely on reasoning to try to prove their case.

Stretch what you know

Thomas Aquinas' arguments for the existence of God are often referred to as the Five Ways:

1 The unmoved mover
2 The uncaused causer
3 Possibility and necessity
4 Goodness, truth and nobility
5 Teleological.

a Find out what is meant by the second and third of Aquinas' arguments.

b Summarise these two arguments in two clear written paragraphs.

To discuss

Apart from the teleological and first cause arguments, what other reasons do you think Christians might give for their belief in the existence of God?

Conscience and moral consequence

⋂ What would you do if you saw a child stealing?

⋂ What would you do if you saw a person being bullied?

To discuss

Discuss what you think would be the right thing to do in each of the situations shown. Justify your answers.

⋂ What would you do if you saw an elderly lady had dropped her shopping?

⋂ What would you do if someone asked you if their clothes looked nice?

Some Christians may use the **moral argument** to explain their belief in God. Various forms of this argument have been put forward. One of these came from Cardinal John Newman (1801–90), who linked our sense of guilt when we do something wrong with the voice of God speaking through our conscience. He argued that it was God who enabled each person to know right from wrong. When people do something wrong, they become aware of it within themselves. Obviously people can choose to ignore their conscience because humans have been given free will, but Newman taught that God's voice within us was a reminder that we are responsible to Him. If there was no God then humans would not have this inner sense of right and wrong.

To discuss

a Apart from God, what other explanations could a person give for having a moral conscience?

b Whose argument do you think is stronger – Newman's or Kant's? How would you support this claim?

c How could a Christian use their beliefs about God to support the argument that humans' moral conscience comes from Him?

Soul-making and judgement

Philosopher and theologian John Hick (1922–2012) linked our behaviour in this life to our existence after death. Hick, much like Irenaeus (see p.23), argued that in this life humans have to make decisions about what is right to do in any given situation. He said that suffering and evil are opportunities for humans to learn and to act in a way that would best please God. Through this process Hick said that people could become more like God, who is absolutely good and perfect. Hick said that this process would continue after death, meaning that every person continues on their journey to goodness after death. This is often referred to as the **soul-making argument**, because through moral decisions a person's soul is able to develop.

Some Christians reject this argument because it does not fit with the belief that God judges people after death. They say it does not include the teaching that after death a person's soul will be sent to heaven or hell, which many Christians believe (see p.40). Christians do, however, believe that moral behaviour will have an impact on God's judgement of people. This is seen in the parable of the sheep and the goats in Matthew 25:31–46. In this parable, God judges people based on the love and compassion that they have shown to others. He identifies the way people have treated others as a reflection of their love for Jesus. Those who have acted kindly, for example, by visiting prisoners and giving food to the hungry, are rewarded with an afterlife in heaven. In contrast, those who have been less caring and failed to act in this way are sent away from God for eternity. For Christians, then, the choices that they make in this life are believed to have a direct impact on their afterlife and this belief should influence their behaviour.

𝅘 In the parable of the sheep and the goats Jesus taught that people will be judged on how they have treated others

The role of the human conscience in decision-making is apparent throughout the Bible. In 1 Timothy it says:

'The goal of this command is love, which comes from a pure heart and a good conscience and a sincere faith.'

(1 Timothy 1:5)

And in 2 Corinthians:

'Our conscience testifies that we have conducted ourselves in the world, and especially in our relations with you, with integrity and godly sincerity.'

(2 Corinthians 1:12)

Christians believe that by listening to their consciences and being guided by the Holy Spirit within them, they are better able to make good decisions and live lives that will be judged positively by God.

Ethical living

Belief in the existence of God, the possibility of Him speaking to humans through their conscience and the way a person lives impacting their afterlife, all affect the way a Christian may choose to live. Christians want to live in a way that shows obedience to God and that pleases Him. In doing so they demonstrate the authority and worth that they give to God in their lives. Christians will aim to live in way that is ethical. This can influence what they choose to buy, what moral decisions they make and what careers they have. Examples of ways Christians have tried to live ethically are:

- As stewards of the Earth many Christians will intentionally choose to buy products that demonstrate their concern for the world. For example, they may choose products that have been produced from recycled materials.
- Christians will also consider how the products they use have been made, whether the workforce is likely to have received fair pay and have good working conditions. As a result many Christians choose to buy Fair Trade products. Some churches have also become very involved in helping their local towns to become Fair Trade towns; for example, the town of Dorking.
- Many Christians also aim to use renewable sources of energy, such as solar power. The Methodist Church promotes the use of solar panels on its church buildings; for example, Bethesda Methodist Church, Cheltenham, Gloucestershire is a Grade II listed building and it had 32 solar panels installed in 2009.
- An organisation called Trees for Life works around the world to increase reforestation. They have worked alongside Christian groups, for example, in Mexico, reforesting and planting many different types of trees, including lemon trees.

◖ Bethesda Methodist Church has had solar panels installed on its roof to generate energy

Christians seek to follow Jesus' example as they work out how to live their lives in a way that pleases God. While on Earth Jesus regularly met the needs of people who came to him. Christians try to be aware of the needs of people in the world and to respond effectively. There are many different ways that Christians may achieve this, but supporting the work of Cafod or Christian Aid is one way.

In all the decisions Christians make they aim to act in accordance with God's Word. Obviously different interpretations of his Word lead to different moral decisions, for example, on abortion or euthanasia (see p.309). However, the intention of Christians when working through their decisions is to follow both their conscience, as they believe the Holy Spirit guides them, and the teachings of God in the Bible.

Case study: Toilet Twinning

Toilet Twinning provides people in the poorest communities on the planet with a toilet, clean water and all the information they need to stay healthy. People donate £60 and this pays for a toilet to be built in a country somewhere else in the world, for example, in Kenya. For £240 a block of toilets can be built in a school. The person who makes the donation then receives a personalised certificate, complete with a colour photo of their toilet's twin and GPS coordinates so they can look up the toilet that they have become twinned with.

The donation is used by Tearfund to provide clean water, basic sanitation and hygiene education. Through this work children are healthier and able to go to school, and parents are well enough to work their land and grow enough food to feed their family.

1 Go to the Toilet Twinning website **www.toilettwinning.org** and find out more about what this organisation does and the impact of its work.

2 Investigate whether there are any toilets twinned in your local community, including at the local churches.

3 Find out whether there are opportunities in your school to twin one or more toilets.

4 Why do many churches and individual Christians support toilet twinning?

Experiencing God

Christians believe that they are able to know God because He has chosen to reveal Himself to humans. All Christians believe that when they were converted they were filled with God's Holy Spirit and that they experience His impact in their lives.

As described previously, some Christians feel that God is revealed to them through their conscience. They believe that God gave them their sense of right and wrong and so by listening to their conscience they can better understand how God wants them to act in the world.

Some Christians believe that they have had experiences of God, for example, visions, through which He has revealed more of Himself to them personally. As creator, God is also believed to have revealed Himself in the natural world. God Himself is invisible, however, and so He came in the form of Jesus to meet directly with His people and to offer salvation through his death and resurrection. God has also revealed Himself through the writings of the Bible, which Christians consider to be sacred.

God revealed through scripture

'For the word of God is alive and active. Sharper than any double-edged sword, it penetrates even to dividing soul and spirit, joints and marrow; it judges the thoughts and attitudes of the heart.'

(Hebrews 4:12)

> ### To discuss
>
> This quote is from the Hebrews 4:12. What do you think it means?

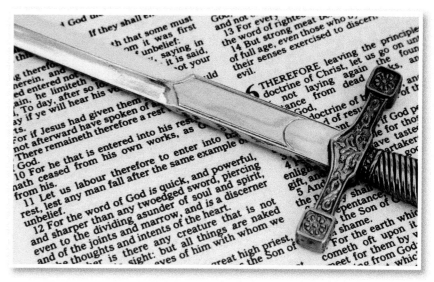

Christians believe that God reveals himself through the Bible. The Bible is a collection of writings written over a long period of time by many different authors. The Bible contains various styles of writing, including history, law, poetry, prophesy and letters. Before being translated into English it was written in Hebrew, Aramaic and Greek. To Christians the Bible is the Word of God. All Christians believe that in some way God reveals Himself through the Bible, but they don't necessarily agree on how He does this.

The Bible as the Word of God

For some Christians, the Bible is literally God's words recorded on the page. These Christians do not believe that there are any errors in the Bible and think that it is true in all that it says. For example, when science and the Bible seem to contradict each other, these Christians place the authority of the Bible over the claims of science. Such Christians are usually called fundamentalists or literalists?

Fundamentalists argue that God is infallible, unlike humans who are fallible. In order to get to the truth, it is therefore necessary to trust the Word of God rather than the words or ideas of humans. Many Protestant and charismatic Christians hold this view. This perspective came about in response to the rise in scientific discoveries during the period of time known as the Age of Enlightenment in the eighteenth century. The Age of Enlightenment focused on the importance of reason and on the truths discovered through the increasing amounts of scientific discovery. The literalist view was a defence against those who used the new scientific knowledge to challenge Christian beliefs and teachings.

This approach has led to some believers trying to live strictly according to the Bible. They do so to avoid the watering-down of the authority of the Bible. For example, the Amish community in the USA refuses to adopt modern culture or technology. They will not allow their photos to be taken because of the second commandment, which requires God's people not to make 'graven images' or idols. They seek to live peacefully and separate themselves from the rest of society as God instructs His people to do in the Old Testament.

The Amish people in America try to live as described in the Old Testament and don't use modern technology

Others, however, have used a literal interpretation of the Bible to support prejudices against others. For example, the Dutch Reformed Church in South Africa used the Bible to support apartheid, the racial segregation of people, during the twentieth century. They used Genesis 11, which is an account of God separating people of different nations, to justify apartheid. They claimed that people were spiritually, but not physically, equal before God. This allowed them to support the separation of people from different races under the apartheid regime.

Conservative interpretations of the Bible

Other Christians take a more conservative view of the Bible. These Christians believe the Bible writers were inspired by God, but that they were human and as such the Bible may have mistakes in it. Also, they were writing at a certain point in history and the Bible therefore needs to be interpreted so that it is relevant and applicable in the world today.

For example, teaching in the Bible relating to slaves being obedient is understood to be a cultural reference and not an attitude that should be promoted today. Equally, the accounts of Adam and Eve, Jonah and the Whale and David and Goliath may be interpreted as myth. The purpose of such stories is to teach us something, but the event described is unlikely to have actually occurred.

This conservative view still maintains, however, that the authority of scripture comes directly from God, not through the Church. All decisions on issues arising within the Christian community should be checked against what the Bible says. Those following a conservative approach to the Bible would say that if decisions conflict with biblical teaching then those decisions should be rejected.

Liberal views of the Bible

An alternative view of the Bible is a more liberal one, which sees the stories in the Bible as mythical and symbolic. Liberal Christians will usually accept that scientists have a far better understanding of the world than anything recorded in the Bible. For example, this more liberal view would result in Christians rejecting the belief that God actually created the world in six days, because science explains the existence of the universe as the result of the Big Bang. The Bible is understood as the account of the writers' own lives. Their encounters with God and His impact on their lives provide a source of guidance and inspiration for these believers. There is no claim in scripture to it being inerrant (without error).

With this approach, individuals seek to find meaning in the writings in the Bible and then apply them to their own lives. This liberal view may lead to different Christians taking different meanings from the same section of scripture. Within this view the authority of the Bible is lessened compared to the other two approaches, as from a liberal perspective it all comes down to each individual's personal response.

Tasks

1 Describe the differences between the fundamentalist, conservative and liberal views of the Bible.

2 List the advantages and disadvantages of each of these views of scripture.

3 Explain what you can conclude about scripture from the quotes in the 'Bible bitz' box.

4 Discuss whether it matters that Christians have different interpretations of scripture.

Bible bitz

'For the word of God is alive and active. Sharper than any double-edged sword, it penetrates even to dividing soul and spirit, joints and marrow; it judges the thoughts and attitudes of the heart.'
(Hebrews 4:12)

'The secret things belong to the Lord our God, but the things revealed belong to us and to our children forever, that we may follow all the words of this law.'
(Deuteronomy 29:29)

'All Scripture is God-breathed and is useful for teaching, rebuking, correcting and training in righteousness, so that the servant of God may be thoroughly equipped for every good work.'
(2 Timothy 3:16–17)

God revealed through Jesus Christ

For Christians, the most significant way in which God revealed Himself to humans was when He came to Earth as Jesus. In the Gospel of John it says:

'The Word [Jesus] became flesh and made his dwelling among us. We have seen his glory, the glory of the One and Only, who came from the Father.'

(John 1:14)

The quotation reflects the Christian belief that God Himself took human form by coming to Earth as Jesus. This was God's way of showing to humans what He was like. In coming as a human, God demonstrated His great love for humanity. He took on the limitations of a human body as Jesus in order to teach people, provide an example for godly living and show God's love through his miracles and, ultimately, through his sacrificial death on the cross.

Jesus was fully human and so was aware of the pressures, emotions and realities that all humans experience. At the same time that he was fully human, however, he was also fully God and so he remained perfect in all ways. Christians believe that by coming to Earth in this way God has shown His absolute love for humanity. This love was ultimately shown through Jesus' death and resurrection:

'God demonstrates his own love for us in this: While we were still sinners, Christ died for us.'

(Romans 5:8)

Christians come to know about Jesus through the Gospels. In Jesus, God showed Himself in a way that humans can understand. In this sense God has literally been seen in history and can still be seen today through the Biblical writings.

To discuss

⋒ Incarnation of Jesus by Piero di Cosimo (painted 1495–1505)

a What imagery is used in this artwork to show that Jesus was coming as God incarnate?

b Create your own piece of art to illustrate the Christian belief that God is revealed through Jesus.

God acting in the world: miracles

Christians believe that God intervened in the world when He sent His son Jesus to Earth. Christians believe that three days after his death, Jesus was resurrected. This miracle is central to Christian belief. The resurrection demonstrates the Christian belief that Jesus was God incarnate, possessing power over death. Many Christians believe that God still gets involved in the world today through miraculous works. A miracle may be defined as a supernatural event or act. Christians understand this to be when God intervenes and apparently breaks the laws of nature. For example, if Christians pray for a person who has been blind since birth and the person's sight returns, that could be regarded as a miracle.

Miracles can be divided into four main categories:

- **Healing miracles** – when someone who is unwell immediately returns to health, or when a person recovers after being told by doctors that they are dying from an incurable disease.
- **Miracles over nature** – when the natural elements are controlled, for example, when a storm suddenly ceases.
- **Raising the dead** – when someone who is declared dead returns to life.
- **Exorcisms** – when a person who is believed to be possessed by an evil spirit has that evil spirit sent out of their body.

Christians believe that God reveals His power through miracles and that He has the ability to intervene in this world and go against against the laws of nature. When Jesus performed miracles they were often acts of compassion that involved the healing of people or in some way meeting their needs. For example, Jesus fed a crowd of over 5,000 people who had been listening to him teach. For Christians the message that is demonstrated through miracles is God's love for humanity.

Link it up

a Identify which category each of the miracles on the next page falls into:
- Healing miracle
- Nature miracle
- Raising the dead miracle.

b What was shown by Jesus performing miracles, according to the writer of Acts (see artwork D)?

c What do you think God's intervention in the world through miracles leads Christians to believe about God?

➲ Pilgrims at Lourdes, where Catholics believe that God has healed the sick

Biblical miracles

'A man with leprosy came and knelt before him [Jesus] and said, "Lord, if you are willing, you can make me clean." Jesus reached out and touched the man … Immediately he was cured of his leprosy.'

(Matthew 8:2–3)

'Men of Israel, listen to this: Jesus of Nazareth was a man accredited by God to you by miracles … which God did among you through him.'

(Acts 2:22)

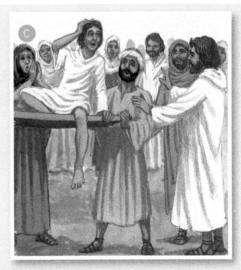

'As he [Jesus] approached the town gate, a dead person was being carried out – the only son of his mother, and she was a widow. And a large crowd from the town was with her. When the Lord saw her, his heart went out to her and he said, "Don't cry." Then he went up and touched the coffin … He said, "Young man, I say to you, get up!" The dead man sat up and began to talk, and Jesus gave him back to his mother.'

(Luke 7:12–15)

'A furious squall came up, and the waves broke over the boat, so that it was nearly swamped. Jesus was in the stern, sleeping … The disciples woke him and said to him, "Teacher, don't you care if we drown?" He got up, rebuked the wind and said to the waves, "Quiet! Be still!" Then the wind died down and it was completely calm.'

(Mark 4:37–39)

Modern-day miracles

Christians may disagree on the authenticity of individual or specific miracles, but they largely agree that God is able to perform miracles today, just as He did in the biblical accounts.

The Catholic and Anglican Churches both accept the ongoing work of God through miracles. Christianity teaches that believers have a personal relationship with God. This is shown in the Bible when God responds to the prayers of His people, including those of Habakuk, who pleads with God to extend his life and Hannah, who prays to fall pregnant. Many Christians today pray for God's intervention in their lives as part of their relationship with Him. The Bible calls believers to bring their 'prayers and petitions' to God (1 Timothy 2:1). Jesus himself tells his followers to ask from God in prayer and he says that God will reply, just as a good father gives good things to his child. This causes many Christians to pray for miracles and to claim miracles in their own lives today. These miracles help Christians reinforce their faith and personal relationship with God. They also reveal God's glorious perfection, which they believe is a revelation of heaven. Through miracles many Christians believe that they are able to demonstrate to others that God exists and that He cares.

There are Christians within the charismatic Church who believe that God is continuing to work through them to bring about miracles in the world today. For example, evangelist Benny Hinn holds healing services around the world and he claims to have held the largest ever healing service during a mission in India. He says,

'His [God's] ability to perform the miraculous is not and never has been restricted to a certain timeframe in church history… Miracles still happen! And they are available to you and me!'

Lourdes

For Catholics, Lourdes in the south of France is a special site of miraculous healing. Over 6,500 people have claimed to have been miraculously healed at Lourdes, although the Catholic Church has officially recognised only 67 healing miracles there. Lourdes became a place of Christian pilgrimage in 1858 after Bernadette Soubirous, a fourteen-year-old girl, claimed to experience eighteen separate visions of the Virgin Mary there.

On 9 November 2005 the Catholic Church declared Anna Santaniello, an Italian, to be the sixty-seventh person to be miraculously cured in Lourdes – 53 years after her healing experience there. On 19 August 1952, at the age of 41, she was cured after being bathed in the water of Lourdes while on pilgrimage. Prior to her healing she had several illnesses, including severe heart disease and excessive breathlessness (Bouillaud's disease), which made it impossible for her to walk and very difficult for her to speak. When the Medical Committee based at Lourdes and the Catholic Church reviewed her case in 2005, she was 93 years old and still in good health. The Catholic Church is always careful to authenticate miracle claims.

Tasks

1 Do you think the possibility that God performed miracles in biblical times makes it more or less likely that He performs miracles today? Consider what Benny Hinn says as you answer this question.

2 How credible do you believe the case of Anna Santaniello to be? You can read more about it on the Lourdes website.

3 Why do you think the Catholic Church is so careful about officially recognising miracles like those at Lourdes?

Some Christians, however, do not accept that God continues to perform miracles in the world today. They argue that God revealed Himself through Jesus and then through the Bible, so further revelation is unnecessary. These Christians may also be concerned that miracles can be seen as random and even immoral. For example, if God chooses to heal a broken arm of a Christian praying in England but does not miraculously stop the spread of Ebola or malaria, then doesn't this make Him cruel, or raise questions about His power? Equally, these Christians may say that God created the laws of nature and so has no reason to constantly intervene and break these laws.

Raj Persaud's account of his trip to Lourdes

Making a radio programme about one of the most remarkable places on Earth – Lourdes – was always going to be demanding and precarious. This is because Lourdes as a place where miracles occur and pilgrims are cured of serious diseases has a very special place in the hearts of the religious. Now, millions from all around the world visit this eerie place. I am primarily a scientist and a doctor, and of course science strives constantly to be objective, not subjective. So I wanted to make a scientific investigation of whether miracles really happen – or is there some other more mundane explanation for the mysterious phenomena of Lourdes? What I found, much to my surprise, is that it seems even hard-headed scientists can still be convinced in the twenty-first century that miracles, which violate the known laws of nature, still happen. But perhaps most intriguing of all was encountering, as we did in the programme, a man who appeared to have been cured of multiple sclerosis during an astonishing visit to Lourdes, and whose cure was ratified by doctors and scientists as scientifically inexplicable. This man, although largely serene, did seem a little troubled now by the ultimate question, which was: "Given many go to Lourdes and don't receive the blessing of a cure, why was he singled out for a miracle?" It seems that even for those who believe in miracle cures or have directly experienced them there remains this last disquieting question – why me?

(© Dr Raj Persaud, MSc MPhil MRCPsych, Consultant Psychiatrist, the Maudsley Hospital, London)

To discuss

Read the box about Raj Persaud's visit to Lourdes and discuss the following questions:

a Do you think the article proves that miracles happen today?

b What other explanations might there be for the man's recovery from multiple sclerosis?

c If the man's recovery was a miraculous event caused by God, what questions would this lead you to ask about God?

Stretch what you know

Use the internet to investigate miracle claims in the modern Church.

a Summarise one miracle account in your own words.

b Explain fully your own view of the apparent miracle. This might include further questions about the event to which you would like answers.

c Identify any similarities with the biblical miracles described on page 222 or any other accounts that of miracles in the Bible.

Meeting inspirational people

Meeting an inspirational Christian can have a significant effect on some people. As they hear the way God has worked in and through the life of that inspirational person they may feel a sense of God's presence.

Meeting Mother Teresa – a nun who worked in the slums of India, serving the poor – was like this for many people. She believed that through her work she was serving God in the way He had called her to. Journalist Malcolm Muggeridge wrote about Mother Teresa:

'I never met such enchanting, happy women, or such an atmosphere of joy.'

An article in *USA Today* shortly after her death said that 'to millions of people of all faiths and stations in life, Mother Teresa radiated pure, selfless goodness.' Those who met Mother Teresa speak of the peace that came from her and of a sense of her holiness. Inspirational people need not be famous or well-known like Mother Teresa, Nelson Mandela or the Pope, though. Christians may have a sense of God's presence and be inspired through the testimony of someone who comes to faith through the work of their church.

Many people gain a real sense of God's presence at work when someone is converted to Christianity from a life of drugs or alcohol abuse and their life changes completely. The transforming power of the Holy Spirit in a person's life is, for many, an inspiration and source of encouragement in their own faith.

Tasks

Find out more about the life of Mother Teresa and why she is an inspiration for many people.

Figures from Christian history

There are many examples of people in history who claim that their lives were completely changed by the power of God at work within them. Christians may look to these historical figures and study their lives in order to understand how God has worked through people in the past.

The lives of these people and the positive impact that they have had on the world is a source of revelation to many people. There are those in history whose faith has caused them to bring about social change. These include Elizabeth Fry, who was involved in prison reform in the early 1800s and was driven by a sense of the value of all people and by God's command to show love.

Others in history have led the way in improving living conditions for the lower classes. An example of this is George Cadbury, a Quaker who developed the Bournville Estate – a village that offered improved living conditions for the workers in his chocolate factories. Other figures from Christian history include those who led periods of revival as God worked through them. A revival is a time of increased numbers of people converting to Christianity. One such example is the revival seen in the Methodist Church in England in 1738, when John Wesley preached in open fields to thousands of people.

Many Christians are encouraged that God has worked in this way in the past and this causes them to pray that He will do so in the current world as well. Other figures from Christian history have given their lives sacrificially, following the example of Christ, in order to take God to people who may never have otherwise heard of Him.

Jom Elliott was a missionary who travelled to Ecuador in order to share the Christian message with an Indian tribe called the Auca. On his second meeting with the tribe, however, he and four other missionaries were massacred. Incredibly, after his death his wife Elisabeth, her daughter and Rachel, the sister of another of the missionaries, moved to work with the Auca Indians. The love of Christ shown through their forgiveness allowed them to have amazing success, with many of the Indians converting. For believers today the key thing about figures from Christian history is the way their lives reveal the power of God at work across the ages and around the world.

Case study: James Hudson Taylor

On 25 June 1865, James Hudson Taylor was in a church in Brighton. There were over a thousand people in that church 'all rejoicing in their own security', and Hudson Taylor was aware of the millions of people in China who were dying and perishing without knowing the gospel. He walked out of the church and wandered along Brighton beach, and was driven to his knees to pray that the Lord would raise up 24 willing missionaries to go to inland China. Later that year he founded the China Inland Mission (CIM), and then in the next year, 1866, he set sail for China with his family and sixteen workers. By the end of 1866 there were 24 missionaries active in four mission stations across inland China. By 1886 there were over 200 missionaries in inland China. Despite terrible times of persecution of Christians in China in the years that followed, the work of CIM continued to grow. Today the work started by Hudson Taylor continues, under the name of OMF International.

To discuss

a How did God reveal Himself to Hudson Taylor?
b What was the effect of Hudson Taylor's encounter with God?

Religious experiences

Religious experiences are when people claim to have had some kind of direct encounter with God. Those who experience such an encounter are left in no doubt that it was God who caused it. Encounters may take the form of seeing visions of God or the Virgin Mary, or they may be mystical experiences through which the believer has an overwhelming sense of awe and wonder. Conversions are also religious experiences, which cause a person to move from a state of non-belief or doubt about the existence of God, to a belief and faith in God. Such experiences frequently lead to a change in a person's life and behaviour. This change is often explained as the impact that meeting God has had on their life.

Conversions

Conversions happen in many different ways but they cause a person to adopt a belief in God. A convert will have a new sense of direction in their life, with God at the centre. This may cause the convert to change their behaviour and the choices they make.

Stretch what you know

The philosopher and psychologist William James gave a series of lectures at the beginning of the twentieth century about accounts of religious experience. He based his work on a series of studies that he had done on people who had had conversion experiences. James' intention was to look at the outcome of these conversions in order to gain some insight into such experiences. He argued:

"To say that a man is "converted" means, in these terms, that religious ideas, previously peripheral in his consciousness, now take a central place, and that religious aims form the ... centre of his energy."

From studying these conversion experiences, James concluded that it was reasonable to believe that there is a personal God who is interested in the lives of individuals. He argued that rejection of this as a reasonable view was not acceptable just because a person may, themselves, be a sceptic.

a Explain what effect James identifies as the result of a conversion experience.

b Use the internet to investigate some of the conversion accounts studied by James. What can you conclude about the nature of conversions?

c Do you agree with James that, in the light of conversion experiences, belief in a personal God is reasonable?

Ruth Bushyager

I grew up going to church every Sunday, so I knew some prayers, and I knew what Christians believed. But it did not make any difference to my life. I was a 'church-goer' but did not have a personal relationship with Jesus. When I was 19, that all changed. I went on a weekend away with some Christian friends from university. There was a speaker who took time to explain why Jesus died on the cross, and what it meant for me. I remember standing on the beach, thinking this is either nonsense, or this is the most important, life-changing thing I have ever heard. I wrestled with the evidence for Jesus' life, death and resurrection. There was no way I wanted to base my whole life on a fairy tale or on wishful thinking. Over the next few months, it all began to make sense, and I changed from being a 'church-goer' to becoming a follower of Jesus. The whole direction and purpose of my life changed completely; I discovered the reality of the living God, and the joy and freedom of His saving grace.

Paul's conversion

'Meanwhile, Saul was still breathing out murderous threats against the Lord's disciples. He went to the high priest and asked him for letters to the synagogues in Damascus, so that if he found any there who belonged to the Way, whether men or women, he might take them as prisoners to Jerusalem. As he neared Damascus on his journey, suddenly a light from heaven flashed around him. He fell to the ground and heard a voice say to him, "Saul, Saul, why do you persecute me?" "Who are you, Lord?" Saul asked. "I am Jesus, whom you are persecuting," he replied. "Now get up and go into the city, and you will be told what you must do." The men travelling with Saul stood there speechless; they heard the sound but did not see anyone. Saul got up from the ground, but when he opened his eyes he could see nothing. So they led him by the hand into Damascus. For three days he was blind, and did not eat or drink anything.'

(Acts 9:1–6)

🎧 Saul being blinded by a light from Heaven

In this account of Saul's conversion, God appears to him in a dramatic way, causing him to lose his sight. Saul is at first confused about who has cause this to happen to him, but God speaks directly to Saul so that he is in no doubt. Once in Damascus a disciple named Ananias is called by God to place his hands on Saul and cause his sight to return. The impact of this meeting with God is immediately apparent:

'At once he [Saul] began to preach in the synagogues that Jesus is the Son of God.'

(Acts 9:20)

Saul's name was changed to Paul and he dedicated the rest of his life to spreading the Christian faith.

Rachel Hopper

I was 27 with a huge hole in my heart that had developed over the years through being filled with lots of things this world had to offer; from the party lifestyle to fashion and everything in between. What I came to realise is that when I temporarily fixed the hole with the satisfaction of a moment or the newest 'thing', nothing actually changed. In fact I felt worse than before the event and the gaping burning on the inside was penetrating my soul. I knew deep down there must be another way to wholeness and life, I knew of God, I had heard about Jesus. As I had tried everything else there was on offer, I threw my hands in the air and said, "God, if you are real, come and change my life." From that moment on I gave God authority in my life, I saw immediate changes within my thinking. I asked Jesus into my heart and it was as if Jesus himself gave me heart surgery; I felt different. The outrageous love of God swept over me and I was changed from the inside out; there was no condemnation, just love that made me whole.

Tasks

1 Describe Paul's conversion account from Acts 9:1–6 in your own words.

2 Extend your account by looking up and reading Acts 9:7–20. Explain how Paul's conversion impacted his life.

3 Compare the account of Paul's conversion to the modern conversion accounts above. What are the similarities and the differences?

4 Explain what you could conclude about God as a result of what you have learned about conversion experiences.

Lucy Mason

I was brought up in a Christian family and at a young age attended a beach mission in Cornwall, where I decided to invite Jesus into my heart. As I hit my teenage years I became more distant from Jesus and my friends became my priority. God seemed to be someone who was full of discipline and was ultimately there to stop me having fun. Those years soon passed and I learnt about the grace of God, that He loves me for the person I am – irrespective of my mistakes.

At 23 years old I married, but life got pretty tough as my husband entered a six-year battle with heart disease. During the last 16 months of critical illness, he had a machine keeping him alive while he waited for a heart transplant, which he received in 2004. God was my strength and all I needed. I can only cope because Jesus walks next to me on the journey of life – such a different relationship from in my teens.

God is my best friend; He knows my weaknesses and is the foundation of my life. He is always there in the happy and dark times and I love Him.

Mystical experiences

Some believers claim to have had an overwhelming awareness of the presence of God, leading to feelings of awe and wonder. The name given to experiences like this is 'mystical' and they are unique to the person who is experiencing them. Such experiences may cause a sense of peace in the believer and a oneness with God. These experiences are so powerful and genuine for the person they happen to that they are left in no doubt that God is real. Mystical experiences are recorded in the Bible, for example, Paul writes:

'I know a man in Christ who fourteen years ago was caught up to the third heaven. Whether it was in the body or out of the body I do not know – God knows. And I know that this man was caught up to paradise and heard inexpressible things…'

(2 Corinthians 12:2–3)

Christians' claims of mystical experiences continue today and often occur during times when a person is meditating. Such experiences are highly significant to the individual but they cannot be observed or verified by other people. They provide a strengthening of faith for the person who has been subject to it, but reveal nothing more about God's existence to other people. Some Christians, however, downplay or dismiss these experiences, on the basis that mystical experiences seem to imply that God's revealed Word and Jesus' incarnation are not sufficient.

'God establishes himself in the interior of this soul in such a way that when I return to myself, it is wholly impossible for me to doubt that I have been in God and God in me.'

(St Teresa of Avila)

Case study: St Teresa of Avila (1515–82)

○ The Ecstasy of Saint Teresa by Bernini (created 1647–52)

At the age of 14, after the death of her mother, St Teresa devoted herself to the Virgin Mary as her spiritual mother. She was sent to study in a monastery and during this time she suffered several periods of illness. She spent much time in meditation and inner reflection. It was during this time she claimed that she rose through a series of stages of mystical experience, including to what she called devotions of ecstasy. She described this experience as one of perfect union with God. During this stage, she said she often experienced a 'blessing of tears'. She says she came to understand the awfulness of sin. She also became conscious of her own natural inability to deal with her own sin and of the necessity of giving in completely to God. On St Peter's Day 1559, Teresa became convinced that Jesus Christ presented himself to her in bodily form, though invisible. These visions lasted for more than two years.

Visions

During a vision, the person having the experience claims that they can see something supernatural. What they are 'seeing' is not visible to other people with or near them, although some people claim they see their vision in the same way as they see other things in the natural world. In the Bible, for example, Isaiah claims to see God on His throne, surrounded by angels (Isaiah 6:1–8). Some people claim that their visions are accompanied by the hearing of voices as a message is given to them. This was the case for Bernadette Soubirous' vision of the Virgin Mary at Lourdes. On her third vision of the Virgin Mary, St Bernadette heard the vision tell her to return to the grotto at Lourdes every day for a fortnight. She did this and experienced a total of eighteen visions of the Virgin Mary. As with mystical experiences, some Christians are concerned that such visions are adding to the Word of God and are not genuine revelations by God Himself. For some Christians, visions are like adding something new to what is revealed in the Bible, which is against its teaching, for instance, Revelation 22:18 warns against anyone adding to the words of the Bible.

Gerald Coates

Can God reveal Himself through visions today?

Well – Scripture says that "Jesus Christ is the same, yesterday, today and yes forever" (Hebrews 13:8). So whatever he did with visions, by the Holy Spirit in the Early Church – he can do today.

The Church in the west has been in slow decline throughout the whole of my lifetime. But the Evangelical parts of the Church, which have a high view of Scripture and a strong belief in the supernatural, have been slowly growing. Now they have overtaken the numbers lost by liberal/traditional Churches, and for the first time in my lifetime the Church is growing. In London alone there are churches with 8000 worshipers, an Anglican church of 4000 and numerous with 1000 members. And almost without exception, belief in the supernatural – including visions.

Years ago a friend of mine did a Walk of Reconciliation through the Middle East. Often he talked to Muslims about the Christian faith. He did this several times with a team, over a period of years. And he would come to my home quite often and tell me amazing stories. And many of those stories consisted of entire villages receiving a vision of Christ and an identical message. He often asked whom they prayed to – they would answer "Jesus" – entire villages! Recent reports tell me this is still happening.

Many non-religious people ask how it is possible to be certain that religious experiences in fact come from God. Also they argue that Christians are biased in their interpretation of any experience they have, in that they already believe God exists. Therefore, they say that these experiences could be the result of Christians' misinterpretation of a psychological experience, rather than a direct encounter with God.

In response some philosophers, including Richard Swinburne, argue that we ought to trust the testimony of the person who has had the religious experience. After all, he argues, we generally trust people when they give accounts of the things that have happened to them. This is especially true if we know that person. He suggests that we should accept religious experiences in the same way – it is less likely that someone is trying to trick a person than that they are telling the truth.

To discuss

a What reason does Gerald Coates give for believing that God continues to reveal Himself through visions today?

b What are some of the effects that he identifies in those Churches that share this view?

c Why may other Christians disagree with Gerald Coates' claim that visions continue to happen today?

Charismatic and ecstatic experiences

Religious ecstasy is a type of altered state of mind. People in religious ecstasy become less aware of the world around them and experience intense emotional and spiritual feelings about God. They may enter a trance-like state and may also see visions. Many people who have experienced religious ecstasy have done so while they were worshipping. Historically, large groups of individuals have experienced religious ecstasies during periods of Christian growth, known as revivals.

Charismatic Christian Churches use the term 'slain in the Spirit' to describe their experience of religious ecstasy. This is often experienced when a minister lays hands on people, usually on their foreheads, and they fall backwards. This falling is involuntary, as the believer feels that they are overcome by the Holy Spirit. One believer describes being slain in the Spirit as feeling 'like you are floating in the love of God. Peacefulness and tranquillity fills you and surrounds you. What do you think about while you're on the floor slain in the Spirit? Nothing. Are you unconscious? No.'
(www.prayingscriptures.com/slaininthespirit.shtml)

Ω People being slain in the Spirit during a church service

Baptism in the Holy Spirit

Pentecostal Churches believe in the baptism in the Holy Spirit. This is not the same as a baptism using water or oil. Baptism in the Spirit is an experience in which the believer gives control of themselves over to the Holy Spirit. It happens after conversion and often after immersion or adult baptism. Through the experience they come to know Christ in a more personal way and they have a sense of being filled with the Spirit's power to enable them boldly to share their faith with others and grow spiritually. It is believed to be an action of God's grace, but one that is available only to people who put themselves forward to receive it.

Glossolalia

Through their experience of God, Pentecostals believe that they are equipped with the gifts of the Spirit. These include prophecy (God-inspired predictions about future events), healing and speaking in tongues, also known as glossolalia. 'Speaking in tongues' means miraculously speaking in a language unknown to the speaker, as enabled by the Holy Spirit. This language is never not an existing human language, it is an ecstatic language – that is, a language given by the Holy Spirit and through which the believer is able to worship God.

Being filled with the Holy spirit

In Ephesians 5:18 Paul tells believers to be 'filled with the Holy Spirit', and Jesus tells his disciples in Luke 11:13 that God is ready to give his Holy Spirit to those who ask for it. Pentecostals therefore believe that being filled with the Holy Spirit is not a one-off experience but is a part of their regular relationship with God.

Other Christians say that at conversion God gives His Holy Spirit to be with the believer, just as Jesus promised. They reject the idea of a person being repeatedly 'topped up' by the Holy Spirit, however, because once the Spirit is present nothing more can be added. They would argue that the believer can allow God's Spirit to have more influence over their lives, but not that there is more of Him. These Christians understand the reference to the apostles speaking in tongues to mean that God enabled them to speak in other human languages. This was particular to the apostles because they were speaking to a large crowd who all spoke different languages. For example, Acts records that over three thousand people became Christians on one day after being spoken to by the apostles. Claims of being given the ability to speak to them all using glossolalia are rejected as not being in line with biblical teaching.

Pentecostalists and ecstatic experiences

Pentecostalism is largely based on the coming of the Holy Spirit to the twelve apostles during the first Festival of Pentecost after Jesus' ascension to heaven. During this time the apostles became more confident in their preaching of the Gospel. They went on to carry out healings and spoke in new languages (tongues). Pentecostalism seeks to return to these original roots of Christianity. Pentecostalism is not a denomination itself, it is a movement within Christianity. Churches that embrace the Pentecostal movement include Assemblies of God churches and Vineyard churches. It is one of the fastest-growing movements within Christianity.

Pentecostalism emphasises the work of the Holy Spirit and the direct experience of the presence of God by the believer. This direct sense of God's presence helps to drive Christians in their service of God. Pentecostalists believe that faith must be experienced and is not something found just through religious rituals or thinking.

Stretch what you know

On 20 January 1994 at the Toronto Airport Christian Fellowship, there was a supposed outpouring of the Holy Spirit, now commonly referred to as the Toronto Blessing. A Pentecostal pastor, Randy Clark, spoke at the church and gave his testimony of how he would get filled with the Spirit and laugh uncontrollably. In response to this testimony, the congregation started to laugh, growl, dance,

shake and some even became stuck in positions of paralysis. These experiences were attributed to the Holy Spirit entering people's bodies. The pastor of the church, John Arnott, referred to it as a 'big Holy Spirit party'. This phenomenon quickly spread to churches around the world. Many Christians were sceptical as the experience had no biblical basis and at times seemed to contradict the call for the church to be accessible and reasonable to everyone (Philippians 4:5). This is because the hysterical and irrational behaviour made it impossible for someone not affected to engage with.

a Find out more about the effects of the Toronto Blessing and the reasons for the variety of Christian reactions to it.

b Present your findings either as a presentation for your class or as a written discussion.

Are ecstatic experiences really acts of God?

Supporters of this particular experience point to times in the Bible when people are recorded as falling in the presence of God. For example, in John it is written that:

'Jesus said to them, "I am He." And Judas, who betrayed Him, also stood with them. Then when He said to them, "I am He," – they drew back and fell to the ground.'

(John 18:6)

Examples are also present in the Old Testament, for example:

'Then the Lord opened Balaam's eyes, and he saw the Angel of the Lord standing in the way with His drawn sword in His hand; and he bowed his head and fell flat on his face.'

(Numbers 22:31)

There is disagreement among Christians about whether religious ecstasies and experiences like being slain in the Spirit are genuine acts of God. Some Christians do not believe that they are. They argue that nowhere in the Bible do the prophets, the apostles or Jesus himself ever lay hands on someone, allowing the Holy Spirit to come through their hands and causing the person to fall over. Often they explain that the only time people fell in the presence of God was when God was giving some type of judgement and not as an ecstatic experience.

The theologian Jonathan Edwards (1703–58), however, argued that while a religious ecstasy may be caused by several things, it was the long-term effect it had on the believer that determined whether it had come from God. He believed a religious ecstasy that had come from God would change the believer so that they were more in line with the godly characteristics presented in the Bible.

To discuss

a What causes disagreement amongst Christians about religious ecstasies?

b How would a Christian support the validity of these experiences using biblical evidence?

Bible bitz

The Holy Spirit comes at Pentecost:

'When the day of Pentecost came, they were all together in one place. Suddenly a sound like the blowing of a violent wind came from heaven and filled the whole house where they were sitting. They saw what seemed to be tongues of fire that separated and came to rest on each of them. All of them were filled with the Holy Spirit and began to speak in other tongues as the Spirit enabled them. Now there were staying in Jerusalem God-fearing Jews from every nation under heaven. When they heard this sound, a crowd came together in bewilderment, because each one heard their own language being spoken. Utterly amazed, they asked: "Aren't all these who are speaking Galileans? Then how is it that each of us hears them in our native language? Parthians, Medes and Elamites; residents of Mesopotamia, Judea and Cappadocia, Pontus and Asia, Phrygia and Pamphylia, Egypt and the parts of Libya near Cyrene; visitors from Rome (both Jews and converts to Judaism); Cretans and Arabs – we hear them declaring the wonders of God in our own tongues!" Amazed and perplexed, they asked one another, "What does this mean?" Some, however, made fun of them and said, "They have had too much wine."'

(Acts 2:1–13)

Tasks

1 Define these terms:
- mystic religious experiences
- ecstatic religious experience
- pentecostalism
- glossolalia.

2 Create a concept map with a branch for each of the four terms you have just defined. For each term include links to Bible teaching, the effects on believers and the counter-arguments.

3 Explain why Pentecostalism has a significant focus on the gifts of the Spirit and direct religious experiences.

4 Why do you think Pentecostalism is the fastest-growing movement in Christianity? Can you predict any issues that this may cause?

5 'The Bible is God's final and complete revelation. It is through His Word that people can experience Him in the modern world.' Discuss this statement. Include different Christian views as well as your own reasoned opinion.

Worship and the sacraments

When Christians participate in worship they believe that they are giving praise to God and that He is able to communicate with them in some way. In 1 Kings 19 God speaks to the prophet Elijah in what is described as a 'still, small voice.' Many Christians believe that God speaks to them in their minds as they focus on Him. This is not necessarily an audible voice but an inner understanding, a peace or sometimes a fresh understanding. Some Christians will use meditation as a time for creating stillness and a conscious opportunity to listen to God.

Liturgical worship provides the structure through which some Christians encounter God. As they repeat the words and practices associated with liturgical worship they have an increased sense of His presence or direction. In contrast, Christians involved in more charismatic services find that the freedom of these services allows them greater personal expression and they feel better able to connect with God.

Sacraments are another way that many Christians, including those in the Catholic and Orthodox Churches, believe people experience God. A sacrament is an outward act and sign of an inner and invisible grace. 'Sacrament' comes from the Latin word *sacramentum*, which means to make holy. Baptism, confirmation and confession are all examples of sacraments. Through sacraments Christ acts in the believer and makes them holy. The Church teaches that sacraments help believers to worship God correctly.

Eucharist

Most denominations celebrate Eucharist in some form, but the way in which they believe they experience the presence of God in the service varies.

To discuss

'God is always speaking to us. Sometimes we are just too busy or preoccupied to listen.'

(Anon)

a In what way may some Christians say that God is always speaking to them?

b How does the way God speaks to Elijah link to the second part of this quote?

U The celebration of Mass

Catholic and Orthodox Churches

The Catholic Church teaches a belief in transubstantiation during Mass. Transubstantiation is the teaching that the bread and wine are transformed into the actual body and blood of Jesus; they are no longer bread and wine, although they keep the appearance of bread and wine. This is referred to as the 'real presence'. Paragraph 1376 of the *Catechism of the Catholic Church* states:

'that by the consecration of the bread and wine there takes place a change of the whole substance of the bread into the substance of the body of Christ our Lord and of the whole substance of the wine into the substance of his blood. This change the holy Catholic Church has fittingly and properly called transubstantiation.'

The Catholic Church believes that this teaching reflects what Jesus says:

'The Jews therefore began to argue with one another, saying, How can this man give us His flesh to eat? Jesus therefore said to them, "Truly, truly, I say to you, unless you eat the flesh of the Son of Man and drink His blood, you have no life in yourselves."'

(John 6:52–53)

Orthodox Churches are in agreement with this understanding of the real presence of Christ during the Eucharist.

Taking the bread and wine provides believers with a way of receiving God's grace. Through this practice Catholic and Orthodox believers feel that they become united with Christ. The bread and wine are the representation of Christ's sacrifice on the cross, through which they believe they receive eternal life with Christ after death.

The Church of England

In contrast, the Church of England teaches 'consubstantiation'. This belief accepts the real presence of Christ at Eucharist, but the substance of the bread and the wine remains unchanged.

Other Protestant Churches

Other Protestant non-conformist churches, such as the Baptist Church, however, believe that Eucharist is entirely symbolic. The taking of the bread and wine is an act of remembrance of Jesus' death and resurrection. The reason that these Christians reject the real presence is because in the Bible there is no suggestion that the apostles were aware of any change in the substance of the bread and wine. The first celebration of the taking of the bread and wine, at the Last Supper, occurred before Jesus' death and resurrection. Therefore they do not accept that the bread and wine were anything more than symbols used by Christ to help in this act of remembrance. Furthermore, Jesus commands his apostles to 'do this in remembrance of me' (Luke 22:19). Through this remembrance they believe Eucharist is a time to encounter God, through prayer and reflection.

To discuss

a How does consubstantiation differ from transubstantiation?

b What causes some Protestants to reject the belief in the real presence?

The Sacrament of Penance

The Sacrament of Penance in the Catholic Church involves the confession of sins to a priest. The priest provides absolution to the person so that their sins are forgiven. The person confessing their sin has to be remorseful and regret what they have done. This sacrament enables Catholics to draw close to God and relieves them of their guilt.

Non-conformist Churches and the Anglican Church do not teach that confession is a sacrament. They argue instead that the Bible teaches the priesthood of all believers. This means they believe that every individual Christian can come directly before God in prayer and can confess their sins. They do not believe a priest is necessary in this process. When they do confess their sins, however, they believe God does act to remove their sins and forgive them.

🎧 Confession in a Catholic church

To discuss

Why do some Christians disagree with priests providing absolution for other humans?

Tasks

1 Describe how Christians believe that they may experience God through worship.

2 Explain the significance of sacraments as a means of experiencing God. Use at least one specific sacrament as an example to develop your answer.

3 'Sacraments are essential for Christians to experience God in their lives.' Discuss this statement. In your answer, you should:

● draw on your learning from across your course of study, including reference to beliefs, teachings and practices within Christianity

● explain and evaluate the importance of points of view from the perspective of Christianity.

Stretch what you know

Eucharist and the Sacrament of Penance are two of seven forms of sacrament in the Catholic Church. The other five sacraments are: Anointing the Sick, Baptism, Confirmation, Holy Orders, and Marriage. Investigate one of these other sacraments and the way in which Catholics believe that they receive God's grace through it.

● Produce a presentation on the sacrament that you have researched, explaining the significance of the sacrament to the believer.

Let's Revise

a Describe one philosophical argument for the existence of God.
(3 marks)

- You could choose to explain any of the philosophical arguments for the existence of God for example the argument from design or the cosmological argument.

- Aim to describe the argument in three clear sentences.

b Outline different Christian teachings about God's relationship with the world. (6 marks)

- Answer this question in clear paragraphs.

- Make clear links between Christian beliefs and God as the creator, as described in Genesis 1 and Genesis 2.

- Outline Christian beliefs about God's ongoing sustaining of the world. You could make a link to Ecclesiastes 3:1

- You could extend yours answer by explaining the way that Christians believe that God reveals his existence through the created world. This could be linked to Romans 1:20.

c Explain why miracles are an important way that some Christians believe God reveals himself today. (6 marks)

You should refer to sources of wisdom and authority in your answer.

- Answer this question in clearly written paragraphs. Include links to relevant Bible passages. For example you may refer to 1 Timothy 2:1 that instructs believers to bring all their requests to God in prayer.

- You could explain the way that miracles are believed by some Christians to be ongoing revelation by God in the world today. They are important as evidence of his love and desire to bring good to his people when they call on him in prayer, for example for healing.

- You could explain that miracles today continue on from the miracles demonstrated in the Bible. They reinforce the belief of God's unchanging nature and his omnipotence.

- In contrast some Christians may be less accepting of the many miracle claims that are made in the world today, their concern that the Bible was God's final revelation.

d 'God is most closely experienced by believers through the sacraments.'

Discuss this statement. In your answer, you should:

- draw on your learning from across your course of study, including reference to beliefs, teachings and practices within Christianity

- explain and evaluate the importance of points of view from the perspective of Christianity. (15 marks)

Spelling, punctuation and grammar (3 marks)

- You must evaluate this statement from different Christian perspectives.

Let's Revise contd.

- The Roman Catholic Church and the Church of England both believe that certain practices in Christianity are sacramental. However remember that there are only two sacraments in the Church of England compared to seven in the Catholic Church.

- Explain what a sacrament is and possibly provide an example.

- Explain how some Christians would argue that through a sacrament a believer may experience God in a unique way. For example during Eucharist.

- However other Christians may argue that experience of God comes in many diverse ways including charismatic, religious or conversion experiences. Some Christians reject the belief that any practice in the church is a sacrament.

- Some Christians would argue that a conversion experience of God, is the closest and most powerful because it brings about a lifelong change and causes a person to then engage with sacramental aspects of worship, such as Eucharist.

- Make sure you offer a balanced judgement on this issue in order to get the highest marks.

7 Religion, peace and conflict

Topic checklist ✔

✔ Christian understandings of **violence and conflict**, including the roles Christians play in conflict and Christian attitudes to terrorism and warfare.

✔ The idea of pacifism and Christian attitudes towards **peace and peacemaking**, including whether it is acceptable to use violence to achieve peace and how Christian individuals and communities work for peace.

✔ The concepts of forgiveness, reconciliation and justice and Christian teachings about them, including social injustice and the ways Christians work to tackle it.

Key concepts 🔑

One of the key concepts in this topic is that Christians never consider violence as the first way of dealing with a situation. This is because they believe that God requires His people to love others. So although some Christians have resorted to the use of terror – believing that it is the only way to bring about change – most Christians are opposed to it.

However, at times, some Christians believe violence in the form of war may be necessary as a last resort although certain conditions must be met (a just war) and certain behaviour must be observed during the war.

Other Christians are completely opposed to violence in any situation, believing it goes against the command to love that is given to Christians in the Bible. They are pacifists and believe that Christians should work for peace and follow Jesus' teaching to forgive in order to achieve reconciliation.

Injustice is one of the reasons people turn to violence – Christianity teaches that God is just and that Christians should work to ensure justice within society. For this reason many Christian groups work to respond to injustice in society, for example, the Salvation Army.

Violence and conflict

Christian teachings about violence

The Old Testament

Violence is present in the Bible from the very beginning. The first person to die in the Bible is Abel, who is murdered by his brother, Cain, out of jealousy and anger. It is from Cain's own sinful heart that violence comes and God condemns Cain's sinful action and punishes him. Murder is forbidden in the Bible:

'Whoever sheds human blood, by humans shall their blood be shed; for in the image of God has God made mankind.'

(Genesis 9:6)

This message is reinforced in other parts of the Old Testament, including in Numbers 35:16 and in Exodus 20:13. In the latter, the sixth commandment is given: 'You shall not murder.' Furthermore, in Exodus 21:15–18 attacking, kidnapping and hitting with a fist or a stone are all condemned and punishments laid out for each offence.

In other parts of the Old Testament, however, God allows the use of violence within the context of wars. These wars, fought by the Israelites, are ordered by God. The wars are either to claim or to protect the land that God has promised to them. In the book of Joel, God commands His people to prepare for war, saying 'Prepare for war! Rouse the warriors! Let all fighting men draw near and attack.' (Joel 3:9). These calls to war, though, are set in the context of looking forward to a time of peace. The Bible teaches that one day God will bring absolute peace, although it is unclear when this will be. This is shown in Isaiah:

'He will judge between the nations and will settle disputes for many peoples. They will beat their swords into ploughshares and their spears into pruning hooks. Nation will not take up sword against nation, nor will they train for war anymore.'

(Isaiah 2:4)

Ⓝ Cain slaying Abel, by Rubens

Many Christians interpret these events in the Old Testament as giving justification for wars intended to defend peoples and nations. They argue that in such circumstances war may be the only way left to help establish a peaceful resolution.

Jesus' teachings

In the Sermon on the Mount in the New Testament, Jesus speaks of the peacemakers being blessed. In the same passage he teaches his followers to love their enemies, to pray for those who persecute them and to turn the other cheek in response to violence. Some Christians believe that Jesus' teaching makes it wrong to use violence in any context, therefore they always look for peaceful solutions. This belief is known as pacifism.

Tasks

1 What does the Archbishop suggest was the cause of some of the rioting?

2 How does the churches' response to the riots begin to address this cause?

3 What Christian teachings would support the Bishop of London's statement that the rioting should be condemned?

4 If you had had to issue a statement about the rioting on behalf of a local church what would you have said?

Jesus' teaching does not do away with righteous anger. Jesus himself reacted violently when he came across the traders and money changers in the temple at Jerusalem. He overturned their tables and drove them out, angered by their corrupt practices. Some Christians suggest that this means there are times when violent reactions to injustice and corruption may be necessary and acceptable.

Case study: Mark Duggan

On 4th August 2011 Mark Duggan was shot dead by police as they tried to arrest him. At the scene an illegal gun was found. This shooting was followed by public protests in Tottenham, but these escalated into violence with the police and a series of riots across London and other English cities. Reflecting on these events Richard Chartres, the Bishop of London, said: 'What has occurred should be condemned unequivocally'. During the riots many churches stayed open all night and helping local residents who lost their homes during the riots. Ongoing work by the churches in London focuses on youth groups, community events and work with local schools. All seeks to demonstrate God's love in a practical way, trying to bring about greater community cohesion and community identity. The Archbishop of Canterbury, at the time, focused in on this concern saying:

'We now have a major question to address, which is how to combat the deep alienation we have seen, the alienation and cynicism that leads to reckless destruction.'

The role of Christians in violent conflicts

Some Christians choose to serve in the armed forces and are therefore involved in violent conflict. As individuals, those who are part of the forces believe that their service helps to bring peace, protect innocent civilians and challenge evil in the world. The Bible calls on Christians to 'Defend the weak and the fatherless; uphold the cause of the poor and the oppressed' (Psalm 82:3). In their work Christian members of the armed forces act to carry out this commandment, and sometimes they accept that violent conflict is part of achieving this.

The relationship between religion and politics

Some Christians argue that it is wrong to get involved in politics. They believe that the authorities are appointed by God so should be respected and trusted. One basis for this belief is the views of the apostle Paul when he wrote to the Romans. As a Roman citizen Paul believed that the Roman authorities were God's servants and that as a matter of conscience believers should submit to them (Romans 13:5). Jesus commanded his disciples to go into all nations to preach the Gospel (Matthew 28:19), and some Christians say that this should be their focus rather than getting involved in politics. One example of a Christian group that does not get involved in politics and abstains from voting is the evangelical movement the Plymouth Brethren, though it does pray for good government.

Wayne

I joined the Royal Marines in October 1996. It was an exciting and scary time all rolled into one, and I knew that it was going to be the hardest thing I had ever done. Not just physically and mentally, but also, and most importantly to me, spiritually. Being a born-again Christian is to me the most important thing in my life, so I knew the test of my faith was on its way in the form of the Commando Training Centre Royal Marines (CTCRM). The Royal Marines' training barracks near Exmouth on the river Exe is where the toughest and longest recruit training in the world takes place, all to win the coveted "Green Beret".

A career in the armed forces as a Christian can be a difficult one, but it is possible if you know God has called you there. Strong influences can be a constant sidetrack, as can peer pressure, but a strong faith and belief in what you know is right will help. More importantly, though, a firm and active relationship with God is a must. He is the only one who is always with me no matter what part of the world I'm in or in what situation I might find myself. He has never left me once.

I know God wants me to be a soldier, even though at times this may mean fighting the enemy. I see this part of my role as one of protecting the weak and working for peace when nothing else has achieved it. Unfortunately, to get or defend peace we sometimes have to fight for it. I believe Jesus is the Prince of Peace, and the work I do is for him.

To discuss

a In what way was Wayne, as an individual Christian and a Royal Marine, involved in violent conflict?

b Wayne says that 'sometimes to get peace we have to fight for it or defend it'. What do you think he means by this?

To discuss

Do you think that the Church has a role to play in British politics?

Other Christians argue that there is a moral obligation for them to be involved in politics. They believe that it is important to stay informed about government decisions and to speak up if there appears to be any form of injustice. Voting is part of each Christian's involvement in politics in the UK. Christians will seek to use their right to vote in a way that best fits with Christian values. Many Christians with this view believe that actively participating in politics, or even standing as an MP, is a way to serve God and effect change.

Tasks

1 Give an example of an act of violence occurring in the Bible.

2 Describe what the Bible teaches about the use of violence.

3 Explain how many Christians interpret this teaching.

4 In what way do other Christians oppose this interpretation?

5 'A Christian should never choose to be in the armed forces.'

Discuss this statement. In your answer, you should:

- analyse and evaluate the importance of points of view of common and divergent views within Christianity
- refer to sources of wisdom and authority.

Stretch what you know

Canon J. John identifies three principles that should underpin the voting decisions of a Christian. They are:

1 Find out exactly what the candidates and parties really believe.

2 Be very wary of voting simply on the basis of what will be best for us. We should have no self-interest. A distinctive feature of Christians in the political arena should be that they consider what is best for others rather than for themselves.

3 Avoid either negative or immoral campaign methods that focus on greed, hatred and fear. Equally questionable is the sort of negative campaigning that focuses entirely on the weaknesses of the opposition.

(Adapted from:
http://christians-count.org/resources/christianVoters.cfm)

a How might these Christian principles differ from those of people who have a non-religious perspective?

b How do these principles fit with the Bible teaching on social responsibility and equality?

245

The Church of England

The Lords Spiritual in the House of Lords

The Church of England is the state Church in England. It is the established Church, meaning there is a link between the Church and the State. The monarch is the Supreme Governor of the Church and the Defender of the Faith. In this role the monarch promises to maintain the Church. The monarch has to approve the appointment of archbishops, bishops and deans, on the Prime Minister's recommendation. The Church also carries out a range of official functions, for example, the marriage of Prince William to Kate Middleton in 2011. In England the Church also has a role in law-making. In the House of Lords 26 bishops make up the Lords Spiritual, who are there to bring a spiritual consideration to the secular process of law.

Some people do not believe in this link between Church and State. As Britain has become increasingly multicultural and attendance at Anglican churches has gone into decline, questions are being raised about the relevance and fairness of having the Lords Spiritual.

The Church can also provide an opposition voice to certain government policies. In the 1980s Prime Minister Margaret Thatcher often came into conflict with certain members of the Church of England, including the Archbishop of Canterbury at that time, Robert Runcie. Despite being a committed Christian herself, Thatcher came in for criticism from senior members of the Church of England for her social policy, including policies about welfare for the poor and the closure of the coal mines. There was also conflict between them after the Falklands War (between the UK and Argentina), when the Archbishop remembered the Argentinian dead, as well as the British dead, in a service in St Paul's Cathedral.

Terrorism

The causes of terrorism

 The 2001 terror attacks in New York

Terrorism is the illegal use of violence to cause fear and intimidation for political aims. It is often carried out against civilians rather than military targets.

There are many reasons why some people choose to take terrorist action. Often those involved in terrorism feel that they have no alternative. They believe that their actions have the potential to force change and they believe that their use of terror is an appropriate response to the given situation or opposition. For example, in the 1930s Zionist groups, who were campaigning for a Jewish state to be established, bombed British targets in Palestine. The group believed that doing this would force the British community to work to create an independent Jewish state.

Terrorist groups develop over time as a result of several contributing factors. These may include social reasons, like the marginalisation of minority groups. Such groups may receive fewer rights or feel that their culture is being attacked and destroyed. Some terrorist organisations use violence in their fight for independence or for international recognition and land. There may also be religious reasons for terrorism as some extremists may choose to use violence when religious freedoms are violated, in an effort to address the issue.

To discuss

a What examples are there of terrorist activity in the world today?

b What causes for these actions are you able to identify?

c How do you think society can work together to reduce terrorism?

Islamic extremism

An example are Islamic groups who have an extremist take on jihad. This includes terrorist groups, such as those who call themselves Daesh or ISIS (Islamic State in Syria). The majority of Muslims say that these groups have distorted the Islamic teaching on jihad, which in the Qur'an is a call to put Allah first in their lives and reflects the inner, spiritual battle that has to be undertaken to achieve this. Instead, Islamic terrorist groups have interpreted the teaching on jihad to justify the use of violent methods. Using terror tactics, including suicide bombings, jihadist groups often aim to establish strict Shari'ah law and an Islamic state.

In response to this, and to all terrorist activity, Britain has a strategy called CONTEST. CONTEST aims to counter international terrorism. The CONTEST strategy works to tackle extremism, which is 'active opposition to fundamental British values, including democracy, the rule of law, individual liberty and mutual respect and tolerance of different faiths and beliefs'. People develop extremist views through the process of radicalisation. Radicalisation happens when a person's thinking becomes significantly altered from that of the majority of people within their society or community. They may seek to change the nature of society or government, which may lead to some people who have become radicalised using violent terrorist actions. The CONTEST strategy includes responses to help tackle radicalisation. One way schools are being encouraged to do this is through the promotion of British values.

Stretch what you know

Use the internet to find out more about the Government's CONTEST strategy.

a Summarise what the four responses – pursue, prevent, protect and prepare – are about.

b Create a leaflet to warn people about the dangers of extremism or a leaflet to promote British values.

❶ This poster campaign by Victus Ltd is designed to raise awareness of violent extremism and radicalisation in the UK

Different Christian attitudes towards terrorism and the causes of terrorism

The Catholic Church is opposed to terrorism. The Catholic *Catechism* teaches:

'Terrorism threatens, wounds, and kills indiscriminately; it is gravely against justice and charity.'

(Paragraph 2297)

Pope Benedict made it clear that, even if the motivation behind terrorist activity is to make a better society, acts of terrorism are never justifiable. Both the Catholic Church and the Church of England believe that the use of hatred, terror and violence by Christians is not an appropriate way to find solutions in any situation. After the attacks on America on 9/11, the Catholic Church called on America to seek a peaceful resolution to the problem, not just to retaliate violently. The Catholic Church accepts that responding to terrorists may require an act of just war. This means an act of aggression that is acceptable as a final resort to preserve innocent life in the face of the indiscriminate violence used by terrorists.

The Church of England also opposes terrorist activity and accepts the use of lethal force as a last resort in dealing with terrorists. In its report *Facing the Challenge of Terrorism* (2005) it concluded that members of the Church of England ought to promote greater understanding, reconciliation and respect within their local communities, especially where there are significant numbers from other faith traditions. The Church teaches that creating stronger communities will help to combat some of the causes of terrorism.

To discuss

a Identify the wars shown in the images here.

b What do you think were the causes of each war?

Case study: The IRA

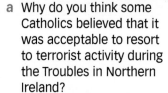
The signing of the Good Friday Agreement in 1998

Until 1920, the whole of Ireland was ruled by the British government. In 1921, 26 of the 32 counties of Ireland were given independence from Britain, and formed the Republic of Ireland. The remaining six counties in the north of Ireland were divided off from the rest of Ireland and became known as Northern Ireland. Unlike the rest of Ireland, Northern Ireland remained part of the UK. Two-thirds of the population of Northern Ireland were Protestants, who had wanted to remain part of the UK. The other one-third, however, were Catholics, who had wanted Northern Ireland to join the

Republic of Ireland and not be under British rule. The Protestant majority kept control and armed police responded to any problems. Discrimination against Catholics affected both jobs and housing.

As a result, a terrorist organisation known as the Irish Republican Army was established. The IRA made use of acts of violence and terror against the Protestants, including the police force and the British army who were present in Northern Ireland. Many thousands of people died on both the Protestant and the Catholic sides until 1998, when Sinn Féin (the political party of the Republicans) agreed to the signing of the Good Friday Agreement. This was accompanied by a ceasefire. This agreement established a government in Northern Ireland in which Catholics and Protestants shared power.

The 'Troubles' in Northern Ireland have had many repercussions. For example, in 2010 an inquiry found the Parachute Regiment of the British army guilty of 'unjustifiable firing' that injured and caused the deaths of 26 unarmed Republican protestors on Bloody Sunday in 1972. British Prime Minister David Cameron stated in response to the inquiry that the killings were 'unjustified and unjustifiable' and that he was 'deeply sorry'.

To discuss

a Why do you think some Catholics believed that it was acceptable to resort to terrorist activity during the Troubles in Northern Ireland?

b Cardinal Timothy Dolan said in 2015: 'The IRA claimed to be Catholic, they were baptised. They had a Catholic identity but what they were doing was a perversion of everything the Church stood for.' In what way could the actions of the IRA be described as a 'perversion' of Church teaching?

c Is it acceptable for Christians to fight for their rights, even if it is against other Christians?

Stretch what you know

The National Liberation Front of Tripura (NLFT) is a Christian terrorist organisation based in Tripura, India. The NLFT is a 'nationalist' organisation, which means it aims to establish Tripura as an independent state. The NLFT says that it wants to expand what it describes as the kingdom of God and Jesus Christ in Tripura. The Indian government claims the Baptist Church of Tripura provides the NLFT with weapons and financial support. Some Christian terrorist organisations, such as the NLFT are influenced by Dominion Theology. The majority of Christians in the world would argue that such theology is a dangerous misinterpretation of Bible teaching.

a Find out about Dominion Theology.

b Explain how Christians would argue against the actions of the NLFT and Dominion Theology.

Just war theory

The idea of a just war is that when a war is fought it ought to meet certain criteria in order to be justifiable. The just war theory covers three areas:

Jus ad bellum

This is the consideration of whether it is right to go to war.

Thomas Aquinas, a thirteenth-century Christian monk, thought that there were three conditions, *jus ad bellum*, that would make starting a war just.

1 The war must be started by the proper authority, e.g. the government.

2 The reason to go to war must be just, e.g. to protect a people.

3 Everything must be done to make sure good instead of evil results from the war.

Later on, the Catholic Church added two more criteria to this.

4 The war must be the last resort, every other way of solving the situation must have been tried and failed.

5 The force used must be no more than is necessary to win, and civilians or those not posing a threat should not be targeted, e.g. children.

Jus in bello

This concerns the actions taken within a war, making sure the correct conduct is followed.

A war that starts as a just war may stop being a just war if the way that it is fought becomes inappropriate. It needs to stick to these three rules to remain appropriate.

1 Civilians should not be harmed.

2 Appropriate force only should be used.

3 Internationally-agreed conventions (rules) regulating war must be obeyed.

Jus post bellum

This refers to the actions taken after the war.

This part of justice should help countries move from war to peace in a positive way. It includes:

1 Punishing war criminals.

2 Helping retrain police and military in a defeated country where a bad government has been defeated.

To discuss

a Was the Second Gulf War just?

b Work through each of the five *jus ad bellum* conditions to help you provide a written answer.

For many Christians the just war theory provides a way of accepting war when all other options have been exhausted.

Holy War

Holy war is an argument that states physical violence is sometimes necessary to defend religion. The causes of a Holy War may include the claiming of land for the religion, the spreading of the faith or the defence of religious believers. Holy Wars tend to have three elements:

- The achievement of a religious goal.
- The authorisation of a religious leader, e.g. the Pope.
- The promise of a spiritual reward for those who take part, e.g. that they will go to heaven.

Although it is the religious leader who may call for war, it is usually believed that God Himself is in favour of the Holy War. This is sometimes supported by references to accounts in the Bible when God sent His people into battle. For example, in the book of Joshua, God promises the Israelites land that other people are living in. Joshua sends out spies to see the land and then to prepare for battle. Obeying God, the Israelites fight those occupying the land, for example, the Hittites and God promises them victory. The Israelites do win and take possession of the land that they have fought for.

◑ The Crusades

Historical examples of Holy war

From 1096 to 1487, and especially between 1101 and 1271, Christianity was engaged in a series of Holy Wars known as the Crusades. The Crusades were an attempt by Christians to reclaim the Holy Land of Jerusalem from the Muslims. Many Christians took up arms and participated in the Crusades out of obedience to the Popes. The crusaders were often promised spiritual rewards for fighting. For example, in 1095 Pope Urban II promised the knights of Europe forgiveness of their sins if they went on a Crusade to win back Jerusalem for Christianity. The resulting military action later became known as the First Crusade. During this time the Muslim world was far more advanced in many ways than Christian Europe and the Crusades were largely unsuccessful. Many people were killed and the crusader knights took part in raids and looting, which was not part of their mission.

Modern day Holy War

Some Christians have drawn on parts of the Bible to support wars that they claim are fought with God on their side. In 2003 the USA and the UK declared war on Iraq, believing the country to be hiding weapons of mass destruction. Iraq is a Muslim country and was led at the time by Saddam Hussein, a cruel dictator. It has been widely reported that in the war briefings delivered to President Bush, Bible quotes were included in support of the military action. The *Guardian* newspaper reported for example '[that] one shows an image of Saddam Hussein speaking into a television camera and quotes 1 Peter 2:15: "It is God's will that by doing good you should silence the ignorant talk of foolish men"', the implication being that the US attack on Iraq was in fact God's will. Such attitudes caused much concern among some staff in the American military. President Bush, in fact, claimed that he had been told by God to invade Iraq as part of a God-given mission to bring peace to the Middle East, security for Israel, and a state for the Palestinians. Many fundamentalist American Christians supported Bush's belief that this war was in effect a Holy War.

Removal of statue of Saddam Hussein

In contrast, however, the Reverend Barry Lynn, of the US campaign group Americans United for Separation of Church and State, said US soldiers 'are not Christian crusaders, and they ought not be depicted as such'. Many Christians share this concern, since such an attitude could be used to suggest that the war was in fact an act of aggression from a Christian nation seeking to overthrow an Islamic nation. Such a view would serve to fuel conflict and increase division between Muslim nations and the USA, rather than helping to establish peace or move towards understanding and reconciliation.

Neither the Catholic nor the Anglican Church has called on believers to fight in a Holy War since the time of the Crusades.

To discuss

a Does the removal of a cruel dictator justify war?

b Why may some Christians agree with George Bush's claim that the war on Iraq was God's will?

Tasks

1 Give a definition of Holy War.
2 State an example of a Holy War in which Christians were involved.
3 Describe the three elements of a Holy War.
4 Explain why many Christians today would argue that it was not right for George W. Bush to claim that the Second Gulf War was a Holy War.

Christian attitudes to behaviours during war

International humanitarian law is also known as the law of war. Most of this law was agreed during the Geneva Conventions in 1949, and most countries have agreed to be bound by these laws. It is a set of rules that aims to limit the effects of armed conflict. It exists to protect civilians during war, and it limits the type of warfare that can take place, for example, it forbids the use of biological weapons. These laws are there to regulate the behaviour of those fighting. The rules of war aim to safeguard human life as far as is possible, along with some other human rights, for example, not allowing torture as part of war. The law of war also aims to make sure war is limited in its level of violence. This means that if a soldier surrenders during war he can expect to be taken prisoner rather than be killed by the opposing force. Also, wounded soldiers can expect to be given appropriate medical care by their enemy: once out of action a soldier has the right to be treated like a civilian.

Those involved in war, however, are often killed, and the armed forces are not then put on trial for murder. Soldiers are required to use the necessary force to overcome the enemy, but they are not allowed to kill indiscriminately or to kill when another action would stop the enemy. These principles are very important to Christians as they try to balance Jesus' teaching to 'love your enemies' (Matthew 5:43) with standing up for the oppressed, defending the weak (Psalm 82:3), and overcoming evil.

Christian attitudes to conventional warfare

Christians do not believe that war can easily be justified. Unless a proposed war meets all the criteria of a just war, then Christians usually think it should be avoided. Christians believe that the Bible teaches the need to aim for peace and to maintain justice, and at times war may be necessary to achieve this. St Augustine even went as far as to say that wars that aimed to punish evil were peaceful acts.

All Churches believe that the global community should do all it can to ensure nations coexist peacefully. Achieving this may include working on forgiveness between nations to overcome differences that may otherwise lead to war. The Catholic Church teaches that peace is possible and that Christians have a duty to aim for peace in the world – this peace must be built upon truth, justice, love and freedom.

Catholics and Anglicans agree that war is always regrettable as it means that peaceful methods of resolving a situation have failed. Christians believe that they have a responsibility to pray for, and to pray for God's guidance and wisdom to be made known to, the leaders of countries and all those involved in any war.

> 'Peace was not made for the sake of justice, but justice for the sake of peace.'
>
> (Martin Luther King)

Stretch what you know

Christian realism

Christian realism was developed in the 1920s by a Christian leader called Reinhold Niebuhr. He argued that it is completely impossible to achieve ethical perfection because sin is in everyone and in every action. This means that when people act, self-interest and the desire to control other people may be present. Such selfish desires by people in power may contribute to acts of war, for example, Hitler's desire for land and power during the Second World War.

Niebuhr thought that war was evil and the result of human sinfulness. He believed that war was also sometimes necessary, however, in order to prevent even greater evils, for example, in order to stop Hitler conquering Britain. Niebuhr believed that individual humans have the capacity to rise above selfishness, but that this was not always true of whole countries. As a result he rejected pacifism because he thought that there would always be nations that would attack other nations and therefore war would be needed to stop this. For Niebuhr, pacifism was an unrealistic position to have in a sinful world.

Case study: Royal Army Chaplains'

■ An army chaplain

The British army currently has more chaplains on active service than at any time since the Second World War. There are over 280 chaplains in the armed forces. Twelve chaplains flew out to serve the approximately seven thousand British troops in Iraq during the Second Gulf War.

Find out more about the Royal Army Chaplains' Department. You may find this link useful: **www.army.mod.uk/chaplains**

a Explain the history of army chaplains.

b Describe the current role of army chaplains.

c Explain how this vocation fits in with biblical teaching.

d Why might some Christians oppose the role of the army chaplain?

Discuss

In what way may Christians argue that war is an act of justice?

Christian attitudes to apocalyptic warfare

Apocalyptic war is war that would lead to catastrophic results and widespread destruction. The term primarily refers to the use of nuclear weapons. If a nation with nuclear weapons – such as the USA, Russia or Britain – ever launched them, the effect would wipe out whole nations. Furthermore, the effects of the radiation from the nuclear weapon would last for generations.

Excessive use of force, including the use of nuclear weapons, is something that the majority of Christians oppose and consider incompatible with their faith. Reflecting this, in 1963 Pope John XXIII said:

'It is impossible to conceive of a just war in a nuclear age.'

The Methodist Church also condemns the possible use of all weapons of mass destruction: chemical, biological and nuclear. It, however, has not condemned the possession of nuclear weapons as a deterrent. The destructive potential of nuclear weapons means many Christians believe that their use could never be justified in a war.

On 30 April 2005, a letter from five Church leaders (the Archbishop of Wales, and the Presidents/Moderators of the Baptist, Methodist and United Reformed Churches and the Church of Scotland) was published in the *Guardian* newspaper. The letter encouraged the UK to move towards nuclear disarmament. In addition, the Peace Churches (Brethren, Mennonites and Quakers) believe that there is no justification for nuclear weapons. This is in line with their teaching that Jesus advocated non-violence and their absolute pacifist beliefs.

About nuclear bombs, the Church of England writes:

'Such weapons cannot be used without harming non-combatants and could never be proportionate to the just cause and aim of war'

('The Church and the bomb' report)

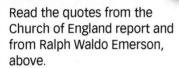

To discuss

Read the quotes from the Church of England report and from Ralph Waldo Emerson, above.

a What does each mean?

b To what extent do you agree with each? Explain your reasons.

'Peace cannot be achieved through violence, it can only be achieved through understanding.'

(Ralph Waldo Emerson)

 A nuclear explosion

Stretch what you know

a Radiation exposure might have caused 421 excess cancers. Of the 17 types of cancers considered, survivors suffered excesses in 16.

b Studies on 1600 children who were irradiated while they were in their mother's womb during the atomic bomb explosions in the two cities revealed that 30 of them suffered clinically severe mental retardation.

c Studies of children born to mothers who received whole-body radiation doses of between 50 and 100 rad following the Japanese atomic bombing showed that the children had an increased risk for small brain size and mental retardation. This was especially true for those women who were eight to 15 weeks pregnant at the time of exposure. Compared with non-exposed children, children exposed to whole-body radiation doses during this period before birth had lower intelligence test scores and performed less well in school.

d Some estimates state up to 200,000 had died by 1950, due to cancer and other long-term effects. From 1950 to 1990, roughly 9% of the cancer and leukemia deaths among bomb survivors was due to radiation from the bomb.

To discuss

a What does the information about the effects of the nuclear bomb dropped on Hiroshima lead you to think about such weapons?

b What reasons could be used to argue that the UK should keep their nuclear weapons?

c Do you think that disarmament should be considered?

Christian attitudes to technological warfare

Technological warfare means the use of developments in technology to advance weapons and means of engaging in war. An example of this is the development of drones. Drones are unmanned aerial vehicles that can be armed with weapons and operated remotely. They allow the military to launch attacks without any human involvement at the scene. Drones may be used to carry out surgical strikes – airstrikes on specific military targets that are planned to be precise and cause damage only to the planned target.

♪ An unmanned drone

Many Christians have concerns about the use of unmanned drones during war. The use of drones means that attacks can be carried out remotely. Some people, including some Christians, are concerned that this can reduce awareness of the human cost of war. It may also mean that one side involved in the war removes or reduces the death toll of its soldiers while the side without drones faces far greater death tolls.

Lord Bishop of Bath and Wells argues that the use of drones without international regulations poses a threat to a government's ability to prevent armed conflict, promote human rights and strengthen international legal regimes.

This view is reflected in concerns raised within the Catholic Church. Robert George, a Catholic scholar at Princeton University in the USA, argues that

'Having a valid military target is in itself not a sufficient justification for the use of weapons such as predator drones.'

He is concerned that the number of civilian deaths caused by drone strikes is unacceptable. This links back to the just war criteria (see p.251).

In January 2014 an article on the use of drones was published in *By Faith*, an online journal for the Presbyterian Church of America. The article acknowledges that while the use of drones does not necessarily go against the just war criteria, it is possible that they could be used in such a way that they would. The fact that drones may make going to war easier and less risky, and the way they make it harder to apply human judgement, are concerns raised by the article.

Stretch what you know

Loving yourself is a fundamental principle of Christian morality. As part of this it is therefore important to defend your own life. Accordingly, a person is not guilty of murder if they kill someone in self-defence.

'If a man in self-defence uses more than necessary violence, it will be unlawful: whereas if he repels force with moderation, his defence will be lawful.'

(Catechism of the Catholic Church)

a Explain why the Catholic Church teaches that defending your own life by killing another does not make a person guilty of murder.

b How do you think this teaching affects a Christian's view on soldiers going to war?

Legitimate defence is not only a right, but also a serious duty for those responsible for the lives of others. Defending what is good requires that an unjust aggressor be stopped so they can't cause harm. For this reason, a legitimate authority (such as the government of a country) has the right to use weapons to stop aggressors harming the civil community.

c What does the quote from the *Catechism* say is required for the defence of the common good? How does it accept that this might have to happen?

d Explain whether you agree or disagree with this teaching.

Tasks

1 List the three areas covered by the just war theory.

2 Describe why many Christians believe it is important for a government to follow the just war criteria.

3 Explain the relationship between the Christian teaching on war and peace and the just war theory.

4 Explain how Christians may respond to the behaviour of combatants during war, including the use of drones.

5 'A just war is no longer possible in the world today.' Discuss this statement. In your answer you should:

- draw on your learning from across your course of study, including reference to beliefs, teachings and practices within Christianity
- explain and evaluate the importance of points of view from the perspective of Christianity.

'Sometimes considerations of justice to noncombatants forbid their [drones] use, even if that means that grave risks must be endured by our own forces in the prosecution of a war.'

(Robert George of Princeton University)

Bible bitz

'Proclaim this among the nations:
   Prepare for war!
Rouse the warriors!
   Let all the fighting men draw near and attack.
Beat your ploughshares into swords
   and your pruning hooks into spears.
Let the weakling say,
   "I am strong!"
Come quickly, all you nations from every side,
   and assemble there.
Bring down your warriors, Lord!'

(Joel 3:9–11)

"Then the Lord said to Joshua, "Do not be afraid; do not be discouraged. Take the whole army with you, and go up and attack Ai. For I have delivered into your hands the king of Ai, his people, his city and his land.""

(Joshua 8:1)

'You have heard that it was said, "Love your neighbor and hate your enemy." But I tell you, love your enemies and pray for those who persecute you.'

(Matthew 5:43–44)

'I pursued my enemies and overtook them;
   I did not turn back till they were destroyed.
I crushed them so that they could not rise;
   they fell beneath my feet.
You armed me with strength for battle;
   you humbled my adversaries before me.'

(Psalm 18:37–39)

'He will judge between many peoples

and will settle disputes for strong nations far and wide.

They will beat their swords into ploughshares

and their spears into pruning hooks.

Nation will not take up sword against nation,

nor will they train for war anymore.'

(Micah 4:3)

'Blessed are the peacemakers, for they will be called children of God.'

(Matthew 5:9)

Link it up

a How have these Bible verses been used to support Holy Wars such as the Crusades?

b In what way can these Bible verses be applied to the teaching on just war?

c Why might some Christians argue that it is possible to support a just war but still be acting as a 'peacemaker'?

Peace and peacemaking

U Anti-war protest

The value of peace

Peace helps to limit suffering and develop harmony and it provides opportunities to promote mutual respect between peoples. As conflict and war are reduced so too are the negative impacts of war, including poverty, homelessness and broken families. The Dalai Lama believes that compassion is at the very heart of peace. He says that through compassion for all living beings, people become better able to respond to the suffering of others and to seek solutions in a peaceful way. In the Sermon on the Mount, Jesus taught that 'blessed are the peacemakers' (Matthew 5:9). Christianity supports the high value that can be placed upon peace. This is peace between God and humans through salvation, peace between people – including love for enemies (Matthew 5:44) – and peace between nations. The Bible speaks of a time in the future when absolute peace will once again be restored (Isaiah 11:6).

To discuss

a Look up the lyrics for the song 'Fragile' by Sting. What do you think Sting meant when he wrote that 'nothing comes from violence'?

b Do you agree with this view? Explain your reasons.

Stretch what you know

Since 1982, every year on 21 September there has been an International Day of Peace, also known as World Peace Day. It is a day that is intended to focus thoughts and attention particularly on stopping war and conflict. Anyone who wants to be involved and take action is invited to do so. This may involve a simple action, such as lighting a candle and taking some time for silent meditation, or something larger like a march for peace. There have even been temporary ceasefires agreed in conflict zones on this day in order to allow humanitarian aid into such regions. In 2015 the General Assembly of the United Nations dedicated World Peace Day to peace education. The charity UNICEF defines peace education as:

'the process of promoting the knowledge, skills, attitudes and values needed to bring about behaviour changes that will enable children, youth and adults to prevent conflict and violence...; to resolve conflict peacefully; and to create the conditions conducive to peace, whether at an intrapersonal, interpersonal, intergroup, national or international level.'

Use the internet to find out more about the actions taken in the most recent World Peace Day.

a Discuss whether you think it is worthwhile to have a World Peace Day.

b What 'attitudes and values' do you think are needed to bring about greater peace in the world?

c Identify, plan and carry out an event or 'action' in your school that would help promote peace or the skills and values associated with peace.

Pacifism

For some people, including some Christians, a commitment to achieving peace means a rejection of violence, conflict and war. Pacifism is the belief that any use of violence is wrong, including any act of war. Many people choose to be pacifists because they believe there is always a way to solve a problem without the need to resort to violence. Pacifists believe that violence and aggression should not be tolerated, but they do not believe that further violence is the way to achieve this. Pacifists aim to use peaceful methods to resolve conflicts instead of war. These methods may include sanctions, protests and boycotts. Some Christians are pacifists because they believe that God requires us to love one another and the Bible includes our enemies in this.

Absolute pacifism

Absolute or total pacifism is the belief that there should be no use of military force whatsoever – whether or not the cause is just. Christians who hold this view focus on Jesus' teaching to:

'Love your enemies and pray for those who persecute you.'

(Matthew 5:44)

When faced with his own enemies, the Romans, Jesus gave himself up to death. Furthermore, when one of Jesus' followers slices off the ear of the servant of the High Priest in the Garden of Gethsemane to try and prevent Jesus being arrested, Jesus heals the servant and criticises his follower for using violence to interfere with God's plans (Luke 22:49–51). Later in the New Testament, Paul teaches that governments should be respected as they carry God's authority to rule (Romans 13). According to this, any rebellion against the state is seen as an act of rebellion against God.

◑ Quakers campaigning for peace

Some Christian denominations – such as the Brethren, the Amish and the Quakers – advocate pacifism. These Churches teach that Jesus himself was a pacifist. This view is based on the way Jesus lived, for example, his choice to accept the violence put upon him before his crucifixion without fighting back, his teaching regarding loving enemies and praying for persecutors and his promise that peace-makers would be blessed. Consequently these Churches argue that followers of Jesus should also be pacifists.

Conditional pacifism

An alternative view to absolute pacifism is conditional pacifism. From this perspective it is the negative consequences of war and violence that make them unacceptable. But people who believe in conditional pacifism would argue that there are times when the consequences of an act of war are less bad than the alternative. In such cases the act of war is considered necessary, though from this perspective ideally no civilian should be killed. Some Christians may hold this view.

Christian teachings, beliefs and attitudes to pacifism

As you have learnt, both the Catholic and the Anglican Churches accept that war is sometimes necessary to achieve peace. Neither of these Churches promotes the use of violence but they recognise that there are times, such as in self-defence, when it may be necessary to use force as a last resort. There are several entries in the Old Testament of God telling His people to prepare for war, for example, when God tells His people to destroy those tribes who are living in the land that He has promised to them (Joshua 8:1). The Bible does, however, give Christians the task of aiming for peace and seeking a time when people will not fight against each other anymore. The Catholic and Anglican Churches aim to reflect this in their teaching.

> ## Stretch what you know
>
> Peace is a very part of the Quaker movement, whilst not all Quakers are pacifists, many are. George Fox, the founder taught that God does not call his people to war with outward weapons. They believe that God wants peace and that he gives his believers his Spirit of peace. However each individual Quaker has to search their own conscience and decide if it is right to be a pacifist.
>
> Explore the Quaker response to war by looking at their website **www.quaker.org.uk.** Look at their online exhibition 'Matter of Conscience: Quakers and Conscription'. Produce a summary of the way Quakers in the past have been caused to act at times of war due to their belief in pacifism.

Tasks

1 Describe the difference between absolute and conditional pacifism.

2 Outline the reasons why some Christians believe that it is right to be pacifists.

3 Explain why other Christians argue that sometimes violence is necessary and justifiable. Aim to include Bible evidence.

4 Explain which of these two views do you think is the strongest.

Christians working for peace

In Luke 1:79 it says that Jesus came to Earth to guide people to live in peace. Jesus' teaching in the Sermon on the Mount includes the promise of God's blessing on peacemakers, and the command that people should love their enemies and pray for those who oppose them. Developing this emphasis on peace, it says that people should:

'Make every effort to live in peace with everyone.'

(Hebrews 12:14)

These teachings inspire many Christians to work hard for peace.

Christians believe that they should work for peace in different ways. Many, because of their pacifist beliefs (see p.262), work for peace using non-violent methods, such as protests, boycotts and negotiations. Others believe that sometimes, when all else fails, violence becomes a necessary approach to achieve peace. This reflects the just war approach (see p.251), but may also include other acts of violence, such as terrorism and assassination attempts.

The Campaign for Nuclear Disarmament

One organisation that works to bring greater peace in the world is CND, an organisation that campaigns for unilateral nuclear disarmament by the United Kingdom. This means it wants the UK to get rid of its nuclear weapons, even though other countries have not done so. It also wants to see nuclear disarmament happen internationally. Christian CND (CCND) is a specialist section of the Campaign for Nuclear Disarmament, which enables Christians to campaign against nuclear weapons and other weapons of mass

⟩ This CCND protest was to send a message to the government to use money on education and social needs rather than on nuclear weapons

destruction on the basis of their faith. The CCND also campaigns for peace. It does this through conferences, peaceful protests, petitions and services at military sites.

Other Christian groups also work for peace in this way, for example, Pax Christi, an international Catholic peace movement. The main aim of Pax Christi is to reflect the peace of Christ in the life of the people and to promote what it believes is the Christian duty of non-violence. The work of the organisation includes holding public debates on the morality of nuclear weapons and criticising the government's defence policy, for example, the way money is spent on weapons. Pax Christi also holds regular days of prayer and fasting, calling on God to bring peace in troubled areas around the world.

Using violence to achieve peace

Sometimes Christians will support the use of violence to help achieve peace, for example Nelson Mandela in his struggle against apartheid (see p.280). Dietrich Bonhoeffer was a minister in the German Lutheran Church during the Second World War. He was firmly against the Nazi dictatorship and was involved in a plot to assassinate Adolf Hitler, but the plot was discovered and he was executed for his involvement. Bonhoeffer did not try to justify his planned use of violence. He believed that God, in His grace, would judge him fairly and he felt clear in his own conscience about what he was doing. He was committed to justice and believed that his actions demonstrated this.

Case study: Archbishop Desmond Tutu

■ Archbishop Desmond Tutu

Desmond Tutu is the Archbishop of the Anglican Church in South Africa. He is a pacifist and in 1984 was awarded the Nobel Peace Prize for his non-violent work to help end apartheid (the racial segregation of black and white people) and bring equality to people in South Africa. His work is underpinned by his firm belief in 'The Rainbow People of God'. Archbishop Tutu uses this phrase to refer to his belief that all people are God's children, regardless of their race, gender, age, health or any other factor. He believes that people should therefore treat one another with grace and compassion, just as Jesus did. He wants to help create a world where there are opportunities for everyone to receive an education, to have access to healthcare and clean water, to have a house and to be able to live with dignity. He believes that diversity should be celebrated, not used as a reason for war. Archbishop Tutu continues to work to help bring about fair human rights for all people.

Link it up

Find out more about the Archbishop Desmond Tutu's work by investigating the Tutu Foundation.

Case study: Peace Jam

■ The Peace Jam logo

Peace Jam (http://peacejam.org) is an organisation that develops young leaders and engages adults and youths in local and global communities. In doing so it aims to promote peace. The work is supported by Nobel Peace Laureates including Archbishop Desmond Tutu and the Dalai Lama. The organisation does its work through education programmes, through the inspirational stories of Nobel Peace Prize winners and through campaigns. For example, the 'One Billion Acts of Peace' Campaign is led by the Nobel Peace Laureates and youth ambassadors. Through the campaign they seek to get the world's population to create a billion acts of peace linked to the ten biggest issues facing the planet, for example, global health. People can get inspiration from the work others are doing via the website and they can then select an area that interests them. Having selected an area of focus it is simple to click to join an act and then share that act to inspire others.

Link it up

a Find out about the work of the 2011 Nobel Prize Laureate Leymah Gbowee. Explain how her work with Muslims and Christians helped bring about peace in Liberia.

b In what way is the work of Gbowee similar to the work of Archbishop Desmond Tutu?

c Read some of the One Billion Acts of Peace actions and summarise three that you read about. Explain how campaigns like this may make a difference in the world.

d Explain whether you think Christians would support the work of Peace Jam.

Case study: The Anglican Pacifist Fellowship

The Anglican Pacifist Fellowship (http://anglicanpeacemaker.org.uk) is a body of people within the Anglican Communion who reject war as a means of solving international disputes and who believe that peace and justice should be sought through non-violent means. Central to Jesus' teaching is the message of love for God, neighbours and even enemies. He taught that Christians should do good to

♬ Anglican Pacifist Fellowship

those who hate them, and not respond to violence with violence. The urgency of this message is all the greater in today's world, with its weapons of mass destruction, its flourishing arms trade, and its intractable conflicts. Violent means fail to bring lasting solutions and humanity itself is increasingly at risk of extinction.

The Anglican Pacifist Fellowship believes that:

● Jesus' teaching is incompatible with the waging of war

● a Christian Church should never support or justify war

● Christians should oppose the waging or justifying of war.

Link it up

a Find out about one of the projects led by the Anglican Pacifist Fellowship (APF) and provide a summary to share with your class.

b Produce a written challenge to the views of the APF from an alternative Christian perspective.

Should working for peace be the most important activity for Christians?

Peace is obviously a central teaching in Christianity. Before he ascended to Heaven, Jesus told his followers it was his peace that he left with them. The reconciliation between God and individuals as they seek His forgiveness is a step towards inner personal peace. The Christian teaching on salvation makes it clear that forgiveness for sins brings a peace from God that 'passes all understanding' (Philippians 4:7). Peace achieved through personal salvation has an eternal effect as Christianity teaches that those who are in a relationship with God will spend eternity in heaven. Furthermore, the impact of this personal relationship with God is meant to cause a person to live a good life that is pleasing to God.

Living in this way means obeying the commands of Jesus and following his example. Jesus taught people to aim for peace. So it may be argued by some Christians that the most important thing for a Christian to do is to follow the great commission – that is, Jesus' command to 'go and make disciples of all nations, baptising them in the name of the Father and of the Son and of the Holy Spirit, and teaching them to obey everything I have commanded you' (Matthew 28:19). This would mean that a Christian's priority would be evangelism and the spreading of the gospel in order to bring people to faith. In doing this, many Christians would say they are working for peace in an indirect way.

Other Christians may argue that Jesus' teaching calls them to work for peace on a larger scale. They believe that in order to obey Jesus' command to be peacemakers and love their enemies, they need actively to work to bring peace where there is none. This is important as an act of service, continuing Jesus' work. For these Christians it is through their actions to promote peace and end conflict that they believe God's love for people is best shown. Responding to injustice and meeting the needs of those affected by war – for example the poor, the displaced and the injured – is seen as obeying the two greatest commandments: loving God and loving your neighbour (Matthew 22:36–40). Some Christians therefore argue that working for peace is in fact the most important activity for Christians as it fulfills these two commandments.

Task

'All Christians should be pacifists.' Discuss this statement. In your answer, you should:

- draw on your learning from across your course of study, including reference to beliefs, teachings and practices within Christianity
- explain and evaluate the importance of points of view from the perspective of Christianity.

To discuss

'Forgiveness does not mean ignoring what has been done or putting a false label on an evil act. It means, rather, that the evil act no longer remains a barrier.'

(Martin Luther King)

Can you identify examples from history, or the world today, in which forgiveness can be seen in the way Martin Luther King describes?

Forgiveness and reconciliation

Forgiveness means making a choice to let go of the wrongs that have been done. That does not mean that they are forgotten, but that they are not held as a grudge or put up as a barrier to reconciliation. Reconciliation is the restoring of relationships between former enemies and the creation of trust and understanding between them, rather than hostility and hatred.

Forgiveness and reconciliation help to end disputes and allow for the restoration of relationships. This may be between individuals but it can also happen between communities and even between countries. This restoration can properly happen if there is a willingness, from both sides, to listen.

Stretch what you know

The Rwandan civil war occurred in the 1990s between different groups in the country. During this conflict the 1994 genocide took place, in which up to a million people were murdered, and around a quarter of a million women were raped. It left the country's population traumatised and its infrastructure destroyed. Since then, Rwanda has been working on a justice and reconciliation process. The aim of the process is for all Rwandans to learn to live side by side in peace. To facilitate this process the National Unity and Reconciliation Commission was set up in 1999. The Commission has five approaches to achieving its aims:

1 Ingando: a programme of peace education.
2 Itorero: cultural school where Rwandans would learn language, patriotism, social relations, sports, dancing, songs and defence of the nation.
3 Seminars: a training programme for various leaders.
4 National summits.
5 Research.

a Research what happened in the Rwandan genocide.

b Find out more about two of the Commission's approaches. You may find it useful to look at the United Nations' website:
www.un.org/en/preventgenocide/rwanda/about/bgjustice.shtml

c Produce a leaflet based on the research you have done.

d Explain what you think it is that enables humanity to find ways to forgive and reconcile with one another, even after the most atrocious circumstances.

■ The Rwandan civil war

To discuss

'That's the basis of the Truth and Reconciliation Commission – that it is possible for the perpetrator of even the most gruesome atrocity to become a better person. Each one of us has the capacity for great good, we each of us have the capacity to become a saint.'

(Archbishop Desmond Tutu)

a To what extent do you agree with what Archbishop Tutu says about perpetrators of 'even the most gruesome atrocity'?

b How does his belief that 'we each of us have the capacity to become a saint' fit with Christian teachings?

Christian teachings and beliefs about justice, forgiveness and reconciliation

Jesus' teachings make it clear that forgiveness is very important. In John 8:3–11 there is an account of the Pharisees (Jewish religious leaders) bringing an adulterous woman to Jesus. They refer to the Old Testament law that required her to be stoned to death. Jesus turns this back on the Pharisees, however, saying, 'If any one of you is without sin, let him be the first to throw a stone at her.' Jesus is redirecting the judgement of the Pharisees back on to them. The same happens in Matthew 7:5, when Jesus tells the people first to deal with the wrongdoing in their own lives before pointing out the wrongs in the lives of others. When people reflect on their own lives and identify their own sins, Jesus teaches through the Lord's Prayer that forgiveness must be sought by the individual from God (Matthew.6:15). In the Catholic Sacrament of Reconciliation, a person can confess their sins to the priest and they are given absolution, this frees them from their blame and guilt before God. Jesus teaches that restoration of relationships between people requires dialogue and a willingness to listen. Many Christians believe that this reconciliation between humans and God then allows people to deal with others more compassionately and with an attitude of reconciliation rather than condemnation.

In Romans, Paul teaches that Christians should avoid responding to any situation with an attitude of revenge. Revenge belongs to God. Instead, Christians should act with loving kindness, even towards their enemies.

In the book of Amos there is a clear command from God that the nation of Israel should uphold justice and that evil should be hated. God promises them that if they do these things then He will be present. However, they don't obey God's commandand He is angry and says to them:

'I hate, I despise your religious festivals; your assemblies are a stench to me.'

(Amos 5:21)

It is clear that religious behaviour is meaningless and hypocritical in the absence of justice and where corruption is permitted. This passage teaches that God is disgusted by such behaviour.

To discuss

Read the parable of the Prodigal (lost) Son in Luke 15:11–32.
a Who do you think the lost son and the Father represent?
b What message is the parable offering about forgiveness?

To discuss

'…an act of forgiveness is a relationship between humans requiring action from both sides. But you cannot go to the 6 million. They are dead; I cannot speak for them. Nor can I speak for God.'

(Rabbi Albert Friedlander)

This quote was made about the Holocaust.

a What do you think the Rabbi means when he describes what forgiveness requires?

b Explain what the Rabbi is suggesting about forgiveness for those responsible for killing.

c How may a Christian respond to this view?

The parable of the unmerciful servant

'Then Peter came to Jesus and asked, "Lord, how many times shall I forgive my brother or sister who sins against me? Up to seven times?" Jesus answered, "I tell you, not seven times, but seventy-seven times.

"'Therefore, the kingdom of heaven is like a king who wanted to settle accounts with his servants. As he began the settlement, a man who owed him ten thousand bags of gold was brought to him. Since he was not able to pay, the master ordered that he and his wife and his children and all that he had be sold to repay the debt. At this the servant fell on his knees before him. 'Be patient with me,' he begged, 'and I will pay back everything.' The servant's master took pity on him, cancelled the debt and let him go.

"But when that servant went out, he found one of his fellow servants who owed him a hundred silver coins. He grabbed him and began to choke him. 'Pay back what you owe me!' he demanded.

"His fellow servant fell to his knees and begged him, 'Be patient with me, and I will pay it back.'

"But he refused. Instead, he went off and had the man thrown into prison until he could pay the debt. When the other servants saw what had happened, they were outraged and went and told their master everything that had happened.

"Then the master called the servant in. 'You wicked servant,' he said, 'I cancelled all that debt of yours because you begged me to. Shouldn't you have had mercy on your fellow servant just as I had on you?' In anger his master handed him over to the gaolers to be tortured, until he should pay back all he owed.

"This is how my heavenly Father will treat each of you unless you forgive your brother or sister from your heart."'

To discuss

a How does the reaction of the king to the servant compare to the reaction of the servant to his debtor?

b Who is being represented by the king? What causes you to come to this conclusion?

c What practical applications can Christians draw from this parable about forgiveness?

Link it up

Create a Christian guide on forgiveness and reconciliation based on the verses in the 'Bible bitz' box.

Bible bitz

'Seek good, not evil,
  that you may live.
Then the Lord God Almighty will be with you,
  just as you say he is.
Hate evil, love good;
  maintain justice in the courts.'

(Amos 5:14–15)

'I hate, I despise your religious festivals;
  your assemblies are a stench to me.'

(Amos 5:21)

'For the Lord is righteous,
  he loves justice;
    the upright will see his face.'

(Psalm 11:7)

'For if you forgive other people when they sin against you, your heavenly Father will also forgive you.'

(Matthew 6:14)

'Do not repay anyone evil for evil. Be careful to do what is right in the eyes of everyone. If it is possible, as far as it depends on you, live at peace with everyone. Do not take revenge, my dear friends, but leave room for God's wrath, for it is written: "It is mine to avenge; I will repay," says the Lord.'

(Romans 12:17–21)

The impact of teachings about justice, forgiveness and reconciliation

The impact of this teaching on the lives of individuals is significant, as it enables relationships to be restored in even the most extreme of cases. An example of forgiveness in action is the case of Mary Johnson, whose son Laramium was murdered in 1993, aged 20. As a committed Christian, Mary asked to meet her son's killer. They met regularly at his prison and once he was released she helped him get a flat right next door to her. She says that God's forgiveness in her life has enabled her to forgive her son's killer.

Through Christian teachings people are able to see that no one is beyond forgiveness. This can be a hard teaching to apply, but when it happens the effects can be widespread and can affect whole communities.

A Christian group called the Dialogue Club was set up in the aftermath of the Rwandan genocide in 1994. The club brought together the victims and perpetrators, helping them to talk, forgive and reconcile. One victim, Patricia, found her brother and his whole family dead in the genocide. Aloys was one of the men involved in her brother's killing. Through the Dialogue Club he found a way to ask Patricia for her forgiveness. Today Patricia and Aloys are friends and there are many similar examples of this in their community. Although the Rwandan community still has difficulties and division, gradually some communities are rebuilding their lives. Similarly, the process of restorative justice in Northern Ireland, led in part by Desmond Tutu, has helped improve community relations between Catholics and Protestants. As communities are affected in these ways, societies can become stronger.

🔈 In Northern Ireland restorative justice was used to improve relations between the Catholic and Protestant communities

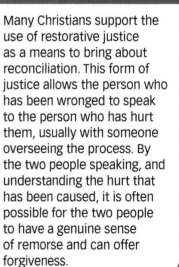

Stretch what you know

Many Christians support the use of restorative justice as a means to bring about reconciliation. This form of justice allows the person who has been wronged to speak to the person who has hurt them, usually with someone overseeing the process. By the two people speaking, and understanding the hurt that has been caused, it is often possible for the two people to have a genuine sense of remorse and can offer forgiveness.

Is forgiveness always possible or desirable?

Some people do not agree that forgiveness is always possible. Forgiveness requires repentance, which is a recognition and acceptance by the person in the wrong that their actions were not acceptable. When people are unable to come to a point of repentance for their own actions, forgiveness by others can be said to be impossible. This matches the teaching in Luke that

'if your brother sins, rebuke him; if he repents, forgive him.'

(Luke 17:3)

A person who does not see that they are in the wrong will see no need for forgiveness.

Furthermore, the word 'repent' comes from the Greek word *metanoeo*, meaning to think differently. So when the Bible says that repentance is necessary for forgiveness, it means much more than simply saying the word 'sorry'. It actually requires the person in the wrong to change their thinking and their actions. Forgiveness is therefore tied in with a change in the person at fault.

For certain acts some people would argue that forgiveness is in fact impossible. For example the Rabbi Albert Friedlander spoke about the atrocities of the Holocaust, saying:

'...an act of forgiveness is a relationship between humans requiring action from both sides. But you cannot go to the 6 million [Jews murdered by the Nazis]. They are dead; I cannot speak for them. Nor can I speak for God.'

The Rabbi's point is that those who were killed are the ones who have been wronged, but once dead they are unable to offer forgiveness and no one can offer it on their behalf. He also points to the belief that ultimately God is the judge of humans – and no human is, in the Rabbi's view, able to speak for God. Obviously Catholics would reject this argument as they believe that priests serve God in this way on Earth.

Tasks

1 Do you think that forgiveness is always possible or desirable?
2 How would you support your argument?
3 How would Christians respond to this question? What biblical support might they refer to?

Justice and injustice

Justice is the fair and equal treatment of all people within a society. This includes the appropriate use of punishments and rewards within society. Injustice is when unfair action is allowed and can often lead to people's rights being interfered with.

The Bible teaches Christians about God's justice. Psalm 97:2 says that righteousness and justice are central to the nature of God. It is against a perfect standard that God measures all human acts so that He can respond with justice. The Bible teaches that humans are unable to lead lives of perfection, but that forgiveness is part of God's system of justice. Any penalty for failing to meet God's standard of perfection is paid for through the acceptance of Jesus' sacrifice on the cross.

In the Bible, God judges, condemns and punishes those who abuse others. He has compassion for those who suffer injustice, defends the weak and afflicted and sets the oppressed free. He intervenes in human history by using His people to speak out for the oppressed and on behalf of those who are suffering (Exodus 6:6). Christians are required to show a sacrificial love to those who are in need as they seek God's justice on Earth (James 1:27). The Bible tells Christians to plead for the weak, to speak for the voiceless (Proverbs 31:8) and defend the rights of the afflicted (Proverbs 31:9), to loosen the bonds of wickedness, and to let the oppressed go free (Isaiah 58:6).

Christian justice is not simply about love and forgiveness, it demands that wrongdoing is appropriately punished and that forgiveness is offered only if the wrongdoer is repentant. In Christian justice, someone who has repented is given the chance to reform and move on. This approach to justice is a reflection of the way Christians believe God deals with the wrongdoings of humans against Him. Christians believe this to be the perfect example of justice.

Christians attempt to apply the Biblical teaching on God's justice in the world. This affects their attitudes towards crime and punishment, violence, war and acts of social injustice.

⊂ God will judge people on their actions but will also offer forgiveness if the wrongdoer is repentant

Social justice and injustice

Social justice is defined as 'justice in terms of the distribution of wealth, opportunities, and privileges within society' (© Oxford English Dictionary). Social injustice results in unequal wealth, unfair treatment of individuals because of their race, sexuality or religion and laws that support segregation.

The relationship between peace and a just society

When a society is just – valuing all people and providing fair opportunities – there are fewer reasons for people to be drawn into conflict. Even in diverse communities, there is no need for conflict if there is dialogue and mutual respect. Many people value the chance to experience diverse cultures, beliefs and traditions. In these conditions people are less likely to feel marginalised or disempowered, and so the likelihood of acts such as terrorism taking root is also reduced. Therefore there is a significant link between a just society and peace. Crime is punished appropriately in a just society, which adds to the community's sense of safety and reliance on the systems of laws that are in place. If the law can be trusted then people feel able to report concerns, rather than deciding to take the law into their own hands.

The chances of peace being disrupted become quite high, however, if social injustice is not dealt with when it begins to develop. For this reason many people, including Christians, work to oppose social injustice.

The ways Christians work for social justice

Christians believe that it is important to work for social justice and towards achieving fair treatment for all people as equal and valuable before God. Christians work towards this end in many ways. For example, many Christians support the Fair Trade movement. Fair Trade ensures fair prices are paid to producers in developing countries and many Christians choose to buy Fair Trade products as part of their action for social justice.

Many Christians also work to raise awareness about human trafficking and may support the work of groups such as the Salvation Army, which has projects dedicated to rescuing those caught up in human trafficking.

Tasks

1 Investigate one product that is Fair Trade.
2 Where does it come from and how does Fair Trade impact upon those producers?

Case study: Salvation Army

■ The Salvation Army

The Salvation Army is a Christian denomination that 'exists to save souls, grow saints and serve suffering humanity' (www.salvationarmy.org.uk/about-us). It was founded in 1865 by Catherine and William Booth. Their aim was to bring salvation to the poor, destitute and hungry. They set about achieving this by working to meet the physical, as well as the spiritual, needs of these people. The Salvation Army works in 127 countries around the world and is very involved in helping to achieve social justice. It has a whole range of programmes to help people, including those involved in trafficking, the homeless, and older people. It runs activities to help older people avoid becoming isolated by providing clubs, cafes and day centres. Through the work of the Salvation Army, the elderly are recognised and valued as part of society. The Salvation Army tries to meet the immediate needs of people who are homeless, with many of its churches offering night shelter during cold weather. But it does more than this: it also works with councils to help get individuals into accommodation and off the streets.

Tasks

1 Explain how the work of the Salvation Army is an example of Christians putting into practice their belief in social justice.

2 Find out more about one of the ways the Salvation Army helps people by going to their website at www.salvationarmy.org.uk or by visiting a Salvation Army church near you and interviewing one of its members.

3 Produce a report on your findings.

4 Does the Salvation Army's work to bring salvation to people have a positive impact upon society?

5 Define justice and injustice.

6 How does the Christian teaching on justice reflect the character of God?

7 In what way does justice help to create greater peace in society?

8 Christian beliefs on social injustice may effect the way they live. Explain how the Salvation Army put their beliefs into practice.

How Christians view social injustice

Christians believe in the value and dignity of all human beings, including those who are weak, immigrants and members of other minority groups. Christians do not accept that any human should possess fewer rights or values than another. For this reason all Christians are opposed to any form of social injustice. Christians believe that the value of every human is equal in the eyes of God and in response to this belief Christians aim to achieve justice for all people.

🔾 Martin Luther King

🔾 Mother Teresa

🔾 Jackie Pullinger

Each of the Christians photographed above has stood up for the weak or the oppressed. They all believed that injustices in society should not be left unchallenged. Martin Luther King was assassinated for his views, even though he carried out all his protests in a non-violent manner.

Stretch what you know

Pick one of the people photographed.

a Find out which group of people they stood up for and why they did this.

b Write a speech explaining why history must never forget them.

Link it up

1 Explain what each of these Bible quotes means.

2 What evidence is there in these quotes to suggest all people should be treated fairly?

Bible bitz

'When an alien lives with you in your land, do not ill treat him … Love him as yourself, for you were aliens in Egypt.'
(Leviticus 19:33)

'Do not take advantage of one another, but fear your God.'
(Leviticus 25:19)

'Seek justice, encourage the oppressed. Defend the cause of the fatherless.'
(Isaiah 1:17)

'Suppose a man comes into your meeting wearing a gold ring and fine clothes, and a poor man wearing shabby clothes also comes in. If you show special attention to the man wearing fine clothes and say "Here's a good seat for you", but say to the poor man … "Sit on the floor by my feet," have you not discriminated among yourselves and become judges with evil thoughts?'
(James 2:2–4)

Case study: Amnesty International

Amnesty International is an organisation that helps any person who has been wrongly imprisoned. It is not a Christian organisation but many Christians support its work.

Amnesty works internationally to draw attention to prisoners of conscience in order to achieve justice for them. The campaigns that Amnesty runs are non-violent and may include such things as letter-writing. Christians may also support the work of the organisation through prayer.

To discuss

The sculpture around this candle is based on the symbol of Amnesty International. What do you think it represents?

■ The Light shines in the darkness and darkness cannot overcome it' (John 1:5): the Amnesty Candle in Trinity Chapel at Salisbury Cathedral

To discuss

a What kind of social injustice does Lorraine say she observed in Romania, and how did she respond to it?

b How else might a Christian respond to this type of injustice?

Lorraine

In December 2001, my husband, a friend and I drove to Romania to deliver shoeboxes full of presents to orphans. I chose to go to Romania not just to take Christmas gifts to orphans, but also to show the children that they, as people, are of immense value and that I was just one of a large number of people from around the world who cared about them and wanted to encourage them. I wanted them to see that God cares for each individual, even those whom the rest of society may reject.

Many of the orphans I visited still had living parents, but because of severe poverty they had been unable to care for their children and so had had to abandon them. Many of these abandoned children had severe disabilities and had not been supported by the community they were born into. Orphanages and hospitals were in a state of disrepair, wards were old and damp, and there was a complete lack of resources.

In contrast to this situation, the city, with its shops and festive lights, gave me the impression of a generally tolerant society. The disabled, however, were treated as a different, lower class of citizen, and were stared at when we took them into the city for the first time.

As a Christian I believe that God made people in His image and that He is able to give hope to all people. I felt the responsibility to share God's message of love, equality and hope with some of the rejected people I met in Romania. I will always remember their courage and determination, and the joy that simple gifts brought into their lives.

(© Lorraine)

Liberation theology

According to liberation theology, God has the power to change situations in the world that are unjust. Some Christians have taken this belief to mean that it is right to stand up against governments that oppress their people, or authorities that misuse their powers. In response to liberation theology, Christians may take part in peaceful protests or actively support those who are harmed by injustice. Some supporters of liberation theology have been killed for speaking out against such injustice, for example, Oscar Romero. Some followers of liberation theology – like those in the following case studies – believe that it is important to fight for humans rights if it becomes necessary to do so. This may result in the use of violence when peaceful methods fail.

Case study: Oscar Romero

■ Oscar Romero

In 1977, Oscar Romero became the Catholic Archbishop of El Salvador in Central America. At that time there was a great deal of social injustice in the country: a tiny, powerful and wealthy minority owned most of the land, while the majority of the population was poor and oppressed.

Small Christian groups used to meet to worship and to seek comfort in the Bible regarding their situation in El Salvador. Each group had its own priest and an elected leader. The landowners were worried that these groups might challenge their power and rights, so the wealthy and powerful started campaigns against these groups. Some Christians were kidnapped, persecuted and murdered – they vanished without trace.

It was this kind of injustice that Romero spoke out against. He defended another priest, Father Grande, who had spoken out against the unfair treatment of 30,000 peasants in his own area. Grande was murdered in 1977. Romero was sent to see his corpse in order to show him what happened to priests who challenged the powerful. Rather than serve to silence Romero, however, Grande's murder spurred him on to stand up for the poor and speak out more than ever before.

The government did not investigate Grande's death. The Sunday after the murder a Catholic mass service was held in Romero's church. Thousands of Christians attended, united as one people who would not be put down. Romero asked churches to record all the injustices they observed and these were passed on to the Pope. These actions brought together Christians in El Salvador and helped them to speak out against the oppression in their country.

In March 1980 Romero was killed by a single bullet to the chest, shot from the back of his own church as he was performing mass. Romero himself believed that murder did nothing to kill the work of God. His words and actions have continued through the work of others.

To discuss

a What does Oscar Romero's work reflect about his views on justice?

b How do you evaluate the value of Oscar Romero's death?

Case study: Camilo Torres Restrepo

■ Camilo Torres Restrepo

Camilo was born into a rich upper-class family in Bogotá, the capital of Colombia, on 3 February 1929. He grew up and became a Roman Catholic priest. The Columbian government was corrupt and as a result the poor were left without proper food or shelter. Camilo Torres became involved in using violence on behalf of the poor. In fact he became known as the 'revolutionary priest'. He said that

'People don't happen to be poor; their poverty is largely a product of the way society is organised.'

Starting in 1964, he began to organise a movement known as the United Front of the People, which held large meetings, demonstrations and campaigns. Many supporters came from universities or were factory workers. The state tracked many of these activists down, however, and they simply 'disappeared'. Torres became convinced that force was the only way that they were going to bring about change and an end to the injustice. So in 1964 he joined the National Liberation Army. In February 1966, he died during his first involvement in combat against the state army. He death was mourned by thousands of peasants, who put up flowers and crosses in his honour. Torres' actions were met with disapproval from many in authority in the Catholic Church.

Tasks

1 Compare the case studies of Romero and Torres.

2 What do they have in common?

3 What is the most significant difference between these two activists?

4 In what way may Torres have been considered a terrorist?

5 Why do so many people, even today, believe that he was a freedom fighter?

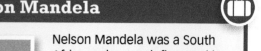

Tasks

1 Explain Mandela's reasons for resorting to violence in order to stand up to the government and its unjust system of apartheid.

2 Do you agree with Margaret Thatcher that Mandela was a terrorist or with David Cameron, who accepts Mandela's use of violence to bring about change?

3 What are the different responses that Christians may have to the actions of someone like Nelson Mandela? How may such views be supported by the teachings in the Bible?

'Freedom is a sweet word but freedom without justice is a freedom for the few who have brought the right to tell us that their freedom lie is true.'

(Fat and Frantic, lyrics)

To discuss

a Look up the lyrics for the song 'Freedom is a sweet word' by Fat and Frantic. What do you think the lyrics mean?

b Can you think of any examples, either in the present or in history, where 'freedom without justice is a freedom for the few' can be shown to be true?

Case study: Nelson Mandela

■ Nelson Mandela

Nelson Mandela was a South African who was influenced by his Christian upbringing to seek change by non-violent means. He tirelessly worked for an end to apartheid (the segregation of and discrimination against black people) in South Africa. He is celebrated by many people in the world today for what he achieved in his lifetime, including an end to apartheid in April 1994. Nelson Mandela became the first black president of South Africa. Despite starting out with a non-violent approach to campaigning against apartheid, his approach shifted. He explained this in his opening statement in his defence case before the Pretoria Supreme Court in April 1964:

'At the beginning of June 1961, after a long and anxious assessment of the South African situation, I, and some colleagues, came to the conclusion that as violence in this country was inevitable, it would be unrealistic and wrong for African leaders to continue preaching peace and non-violence at a time when the Government met our peaceful demands with force.

This conclusion was not easily reached. It was only when all else had failed, when all channels of peaceful protest had been barred to us, that the decision was made to embark on violent forms of political struggle, and to form Umkhonto we Sizwe [Spear of the Nation]. We did so not because we desired such a course, but solely because the Government had left us with no other choice. In the Manifesto of Umkhonto published on 16 December 1961, which is Exhibit AD, we said:

"The time comes in the life of any nation when there remain only two choices – submit or fight. That time has now come to South Africa. We shall not submit and we have no choice but to hit back by all means in our power in defence of our people, our future, and our freedom."'

(Nelson Mandela's statement at the opening of the defence case in the Rivonia Trial, Pretoria Supreme Court, 20 April 1964)

At his trial he had pleaded guilty to 156 acts of public violence, including mobilising terrorist bombing campaigns that planted bombs in public places, such as the Johannesburg railway station. During the time of apartheid the British prime minister, Margaret Thatcher, referred to Mandela as a terrorist. In 2006, however, David Cameron, the current prime minister, said that this perception was wrong and that his own view was 'not how violent the armed struggle [led by Mandela] or Soweto uprisings were, but how restrained'. Mandela remained firm in his own conviction that if necessary he was prepared to die for the cause to end injustice and inequality.

Let's Revise

a State three ways in which Christians might work for social justice. (3 marks)

- Bullet point three different ways that Christians might work for social justice. For example, you could include Christian support of Fair Trade.

b Describe different Christian attitudes towards terrorism. (6 marks)

- Answer this question in clear paragraphs.

- Make clear links between Christian beliefs, Bible evidence and church teaching.

- Describe the opposition to terrorism from the Catholic Church and the Church of England.

- Describe the way that these churches believe that acts of terror go against the Christian teaching on justice and love.

- In contrast describe how some Christians have taken up terrorist activities because they believed there was no alternative. You could include an example such as Nelson Mandela.

c Explain why some Christians reject pacifism. (6 marks)

You should refer to sources of wisdom and authority in your answer.

- Answer this question in clearly written paragraphs. Include links to relevant Bible passages. For example, you may refer to the book of Joshua in which God commands his people to go to war.

- Start by explaining that some Christians accept that war was used by God in the Bible to bring about his will and that this leads them to accept that war in the modern world may sometimes be needed, thus pacifism is not a realistic or biblical position to hold.

- You could explain the Christian realist attitude to war that recognises in a sinful world peaceful solutions may not always be possible. That the evil of war is sometimes necessary to overcome a greater evil.

- You could explain that some Christians support a 'Just' war. For some Christians this theory, based on the teaching of St Thomas Aquinas, is a source of wisdom and authority. This means every other means of resolving the situation has been tried and has failed, for this reason peaceful solutions are not going to work and so violence is ultimately needed.

- Extend your answer to explain the difference between absolute pacifists and conditional pacifists.

d 'Working for peace should be the most important activity for Christians.'

Discuss this statement. In your answer, you should:

- explain and evaluate the importance of points of view from the perspective of Christianity

Let's Revise contd.

- draw on your learning from across your course of study, including reference to beliefs, teachings and practices within Christianity. (15 marks)

Spelling, punctuation and grammar (3 marks)

- You must evaluate this statement from different Christian perspectives.

- Jesus said that his followers should be peacemakers and this is supported by his teaching in the Sermon on the Mount about loving enemies.

- Explain how some Christians would argue that to bring peace injustice has to be combated and that sometimes on the route to peace there may need to be war. There are examples of this in the Bible for example in Micah and Joel.

- Other Christians may say that 'the peace that Christians should focus on working for is the peace achieved through salvation'. As a result they may say that the most important role for Christians is evangelism and discipleship.

- The Great Commission could support this argument.

8 Dialogue within and between religious and non-religious beliefs and attitudes

Topic checklist ✔

✔ The **challenges for religion** in modern British society, including the role of the Church in public life and the potential clashes between religion, secular values and scientific developments.

✔ **Dialogue within and between religious groups,** including how Christians view other religious groups and the value of interfaith dialogue.

✔ **Dialogue within and between religious and non-religious groups,** including values that are shared by Christians and non-religious groups and values that might cause disagreement between them.

Key concepts 🔑

There are many people who think that the United Kingdom is a Christian country. The proportion of the British population that is Christian is getting smaller, however, and the number of people who have no religious faith is growing. Some people therefore believe that British society is secular. If this is true, it means that there are potential clashes between Christianity and secular values.

Christianity, of course, is a religion that comprises a number of groups or denominations and there are areas of disagreement between them. There are also potential tensions between Christian groups and other religions. It is important for many Christians, and for people of other faiths, to recognise common elements of their faith, while respecting differences.

In the same way, many Christians and people of no religious faith feel it is important to engage in constructive debate over differences of beliefs and attitudes.

Challenges for religion

The importance of Christian traditions in British society

The history of Christianity in Britain goes back almost two thousand years, when it was introduced by the Romans. The Church of England itself can trace its origins to the early seventh century. The teachings of Christianity and the Christian Church are therefore deeply embedded in British traditions and culture, and elements can still be seen in everyday British life. For example:

- School terms are arranged around the Christian festivals of Christmas and Easter.
- The Christian calendar influences other British traditions, like Valentine's Day (a Saint's day), Pancake Day (or Shrove Tuesday) and Hallowe'en (the day before All Saints' Day).
- The week has seven days. Some people think this may reflect the biblical story of the creation of the universe.

- There are restrictions on the hours shops are allowed to be open on Sundays, the Christian day of rest. Large stores are not allowed to open on the Christian festivals of Christmas Day and Easter Sunday.
- Some popular superstitions have Christian origins: the number 13 is considered unlucky because thirteen men sat down to the last meal Jesus ate before his death.
- Many popular names come from the Bible, such as Daniel, Sarah, Aaron and Hannah.

Stretch what you know

As far back as the seventh century the Church of England was the English branch of the Roman Catholic Church. However, in the sixteenth century, King Henry VIII took the English Church from Rome. The Act of Supremacy, declaring the Monarch to be Supreme Head of the Church of England, became law in 1534. It also established the independence of the Church of England.

Around the same time, some Christians in Europe started to protest about the power and corruption of the Catholic Church (Protestants). Protestantism spread in England, and, under Queen Elizabeth I, the Church of England broadened its appeal to satisfy both Catholics and reforming Protestants.

Nevertheless, for over a century, Catholics did not enjoy equal civil rights with Protestants. They were not allowed to vote or sit in Parliament, and no Catholic could succeed to the throne. Still today, the reigning Monarch is Supreme Head of the Church of England, which is the established or official Church in England. Anglican Bishops sit in the House of Lords as Lords Spiritual. Although there are Catholic MPs and Lords in Parliament, the Catholic Church itself forbids its bishops to take part in politics.

To discuss

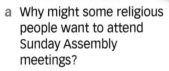

a Why might some religious people want to attend Sunday Assembly meetings?

b Why might some non-religious people want to attend?

Case study: The Sunday Assembly

The Sunday Assembly was started by Sanderson Jones and Pippa Evans, two comedians who were on their way to a gig in Bath when they discovered they both wanted to do something that was like church but totally secular and inclusive of all – no matter what they believed.

The first ever Sunday Assembly meeting took place on 6 January 2013 in Islington. Almost 200 people turned up at the first meeting and 300 at the second and soon people all over the world asked to start one.

Now there are 68 Sunday Assembly chapters in eight different countries, where people sing songs, hear inspiring talks and create community together.

The charter of the Sunday Assembly can be found at: www.sundayassembly.com/story#charter.

↻ Sunday Assembly meeting

The Church of England: the established religion in a country of diverse religious traditions

Although the traditions and values of Britain derive from Christian beliefs and teachings, many different religions are practised. Polls and surveys conducted in Britain consistently show that Christianity is the largest religion, with Christians making up over half of the population.

The 2011 Census for England asked the question, 'What is your religion?' Responses are set out in the table below.

◑ Census responses for the question, 'What is your religion?'

	Number	Percentage
Christianity	31,479,876	59.4
Islam	2,660,116	5.0
Hinduism	806,199	1.5
Sikhism	420,196	0.8
Judaism	261,282	0.5
Buddhism	238,626	0.5
Other religion	227,825	0.4
No religion	13,114,232	24.7
Religion not stated	3,804,104	7.2

The Census showed that Christianity was the largest religion in England and the UK in 2011 by a significant margin, but it also showed that the number of Christians had fallen by 12 per cent since 2001. At the same time, the number of Muslims had increased, as had the number of people who said they had no religion.

The 2011 Census did not ask Christians which denomination they belonged to, but it is thought that more than half identify themselves with the Church of England.

The Church of England is the established Church in England, This means more than simply being the biggest. 'Establishment' means that the Church has strong links with the State, that is, with the government and government institutions like the law, education and the military. Establishment also means that the reigning Monarch is both Head of State and Supreme Governor of the Church of England.

'Across Britain, Christians don't just talk about "loving thy neighbour", they live it out … in faith schools, in prisons, in community groups. And it's for all these reasons that we should feel proud to say, "This is a Christian country." The Church is not just a collection of beautiful old buildings. It is a living, active force doing great works across our country. Yes, we are a nation that embraces, welcomes and accepts all faiths and none, but we are still a Christian country.'

(David Cameron)

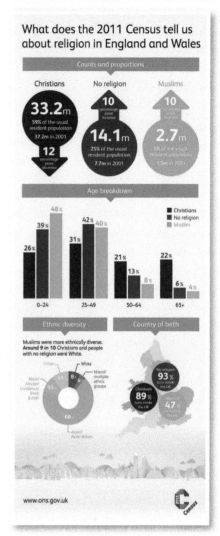

◑ Information on religion in England from the 2011 Census

The Monarch as the head of the Church of England

The monarch is Head of State of the UK and 15 other Commonwealth countries. The official title is 'His/Her Majesty [Name], by the Grace of God, of the United Kingdom of Great Britain and Northern Ireland, and of His/Her other Realms and Territories King/Queen, Head of the Commonwealth, Defender of the Faith'. So, the Monarch is Head of State and Defender of the Faith. The faith of which he or she is defender is not Christianity in general, but the Church of England in particular.

The Monarch is crowned by the Archbishop of Canterbury, who is Primate (first bishop) of the Church of England. During the ceremony, the Monarch is asked:

'Will you to the utmost of your power maintain in the United Kingdom the Protestant Reformed Religion [i.e. the Church of England] established by law? Will you maintain and preserve inviolably the settlement of the Church of England, and the doctrine, worship, discipline, and government thereof, as by law established in England?'

The Monarch replies: 'All this I promise and do.'

As well as being Defender of the Faith, the Monarch is the Supreme Governor of the Church of England.

Although the Church of England can trace its origins back to the seventh century, its links with the State date back only to the Reformation in the sixteenth century. Up until then, the Church of England was a Catholic Church under the leadership of the Pope in Rome. But in the 1530s, King Henry VIII passed laws that made him head of the Church of England as well as Head of State.

☊ The Queen is crowned by the Archbishop of Canterbury

The role of the Monarch today

The current Monarch's role as Supreme Head is rather different from that of Henry VIII. Henry VIII made decisions on his own, appointing bishops and making laws for the Church. Today, the Monarch makes decisions within parliament.

As Supreme Governor of the Church of England, the King or Queen:

- approves the appointment of senior clerics (archbishops, bishops and deans of cathedrals), on the recommendation of the Prime Minister, who considers a list provided by the Church. These clerics take an oath of loyalty to the Monarch on appointment and may not resign without his or her authority (Parish priests also swear allegiance to the Monarch)
- opens new sessions of the General Synod (the Church's governing body). Since 1919, the Synod has had the power to propose laws on any matter concerning the Church of England. These laws are called Measures. The Measures are taken to both Houses of Parliament to be passed. Following acceptance of the Measures by both Houses of Parliament, they are submitted for Royal Assent (agreement by the Monarch) and become law
- keeps the vow made at his or her coronation to maintain the Church.

In a speech made in her jubilee year, Queen Elizabeth II explained what she understood by 'maintaining' the Church:

'The concept of our established Church is occasionally misunderstood and, I believe, commonly under-appreciated. Its role is not to defend Anglicanism to the exclusion of other religions. Instead, the Church has a duty to protect the free practice of all faiths in this country.'

'It certainly provides an identity and spiritual dimension for its own many adherents. But also, gently and assuredly, the Church of England has created an environment for other faith communities and indeed people of no faith to live freely. Woven into the fabric of this country, the Church has helped to build a better society – more and more in active co-operation for the common good with those of other faiths.'

(Her Majesty the Queen)

⌒ ELIZABETH II D.G.REG.F.D on a pound coin stands for *Elizabeth II Dei Gratia Regina Fidei Defensor*, which means Elizabeth II, by the grace of God, Queen and Defender of the Faith

The Church in Wales

The Anglican Church in Wales was part of the Church of England since the time of Henry VIII when Wales was absorbed into England. However, during the nineteenth century, Welsh Anglicans and other Protestants felt that the Church of England was marginalising the Church in Wales. As a result, it was disestablished in 1920.

The Church in Scotland

The Church of Scotland is the national established Church in Scotland, though it is Presbyterian, not Anglican. The Anglican Church in Scotland is the Scottish Episcopal Church, though, unlike the Church in Wales, it has never had any connection with the Church of England.

The Church in Northern Ireland

The Roman Catholic Church of Ireland is the largest single Christian denomination in Ireland, though there are slightly more Protestants than Catholics in that part of the United Kingdom. The Church of Ireland is the Anglican Church in Northern Ireland. After Henry VIII declared himself to be head of the Church of England in the sixteenth century, the Irish Parliament declared him to be head of the Church of Ireland, and thus the Church of Ireland became the established Church in Ireland. However, in 1870, the UK Parliament passed the Irish Church Act, which disestablished the Church of Ireland and separated it from the Church of England. It also gave the Church independence from the Monarchy and the state.

The role of religion in public life

In his Christmas message in 2015 the Prime Minister, David Cameron, described Britain as a Christian country. He said:

'I believe that we should … reflect on the fact that it is because of [these] important religious roots and Christian values that Britain has been such a successful home to people of all faiths and none.'

Christianity, then, plays a significant part in the public life of Britain.

Bishops in the House of Lords

Parliament is where all British laws are made – it is made up of two parts, the House of Commons, which consists of elected Members of Parliament (MPs) and the House of Lords. The role of the House of Lords includes holding the government to account for its actions and its spending, and making laws. New laws have to be approved by both the House of Commons and the House of Lords.

The House of Lords consists of 26 Lords Spiritual and a variable number of Lords Temporal. Unlike MPs in the House of Commons, none of the Lords is elected. The Lords Temporal are people who have a title, such as Duke or Earl. The Lords Spiritual are all bishops of the Church of England. This means that bishops of the Church of England can play a significant role in the governance of this country.

Bible bitz

Jesus said to them, 'Render to Caesar the things that are Caesar's, and to God the things that are God's.'

(Mark 12.17)

Let every person be subject to the governing authorities. For there is no authority except from God, and those that exist have been instituted by God. Therefore whoever resists the authorities resists what God has appointed, and those who resist will incur judgment.

(Romans 13.1–2)

Be subject for the Lord's sake to every human institution, whether it be to the emperor as supreme, or to governors as sent by him to punish those who do evil and to praise those who do good.

(1 Peter 2.13–14)

He changes times and seasons; he removes kings and sets up kings; he gives wisdom to the wise and knowledge to those who have understanding.

(Daniel 2.21)

Tasks

1 Describe the way in which the church and the state are linked in Britain.

2 What reasons does the Queen put forward to defend the role of The Church of England as the Established Church?

3 Outline the impact of this relationship between the church and the state on public life.

4 Explain whether you believe that there should be this kind of link in modern British society.

🎧 Twenty-six Anglican bishops make up the Lords Spiritual in the House of Lords

More religious representation in the House of Lords report says

A report published in December 2015 recommends that there should be greater religious representation in the House of Lords. This would mean fewer Anglican bishops, but more representatives of other religions. The report, compiled by The Commission on Religion and Belief in Public Life (Corab), maintains that religious belief is still central to the lives of people, but not just Christian belief. It says, 'The pluralist character of modern society should be reflected in national forums such as the House of Lords, so that they include a wider range of world views and religious traditions, and of Christian denominations other than the Church of England.' Dr Ed Kessler, vice-chair of Corab, told *The Independent* newspaper: 'It's an anomaly to have 26 Anglican bishops in the House of Lords. There needs to be better representation of the different religions and beliefs in Britain today' (**https://corablivingwithdifference.files.wordpress.com/2015/12/living-with-difference-online.pdf**).

National Secular Society calls for no religious representation in the House of Lords

The National Secular Society, which sees religion as irrelevant to lives of most people, believes that no faith has a role to play in politics and government. It says that that there should be no religious representation at all in the House of Lords.

The Society criticised the Corab report's findings. 'They failed to call for the removal of the bishops from the House of Lords, Westminster being the only parliament in the world to have them,' said its director Keith Porteous Wood.

'They even want even more clerics appointed there from minority faiths in a country where the majority are not religious … Disestablishing [i.e. taking away establishment status from] the Church of England should be a minimum ambition for a modern Britain in the twenty-first century' (**www.bbc.co.uk/news/uk-politics-35022517**).

Church of England defends Anglican bishops in the House of Lords

The Church of England has always maintained that Anglican bishops in the House of Lords represent people of all faiths, providing a religious perspective to political issues.

'Their presence in the Lords is an extension of their general vocation as bishops to preach God's Word and to lead people in prayer. Bishops provide an important independent voice and spiritual insight to the work of the Upper House and, while they make no claims to direct representation, they seek to be a voice for all people of faith, not just Christians'

(**www.churchofengland.org/our-views/the-church-in-parliament/bishops-in-the-house-of-lords.aspx**).

Task

Summarise the views shown in the three boxes from Corab, the National Secular Society and the Church of England on the presence of Anglican bishops in the House of Lords. What are the strengths and weaknesses of each view?

Christian services to mark key events

There are milestones in almost everyone's life when important changes take place. These are usually marked in ways that bring people together to share thoughts and feelings. Rites of passage are ceremonies that mark these events. Christianity and other religions have developed traditions over hundreds of years to commemorate these important occasions.

Christian rites of passage include:

- Baptism, which celebrates the birth of a baby and welcomes it into the Church (see p.71–73).
- Marriage, a ceremony that marks the coming together of two people to start a new family (see p.74–76).
- Funerals, at which the lives of dead people are remembered and loved ones can say goodbye (see p.78–79).

⚭ First World War war memorial; Wales UK

These rites of passage are not confined to Christians. Many non-Christian couples choose to marry in a church and many non-Christians arrange Christian funerals for deceased relatives.

Christian services also mark key events in British public life. For example, early in November each year, the National Service of Remembrance is held in London to remember the contributions of service personnel in the two World Wars. The service includes Christian prayers and hymns. Services are also held at war memorials, across the country.

Given the close relationship between the State and the established Church, it is not surprising that meetings in both Houses of Parliament begin with prayers. The prayers are Christian.

Stretch what you know

Tony Blair was Prime Minister of the United Kingdom from 1997 until 2007. He is a Christian and has said that his Christian faith influenced some of the political decisions he made as Prime Minister. In a speech made in 2011, he said:

'Those of us inspired by our faith must have the right to speak out on issues that concern us and in the name of our beliefs. At the same time our voice cannot predominate over the basic democratic system that functions equally for all, irrespective of those of faith or of none.'

(© The Tony Blair Faith Foundation)

a Explain what two points Tony Blair is making.

b Is it reasonable or possible to take religion out of politics altogether?

Public holidays based on Christian celebrations

Public holidays are days when most businesses close so that employees may spend their time away from work. The occasions that are marked by public holidays have been decided over time by custom and tradition and some of those traditions are Christian.

There are eight public holidays in England and Wales over the course of a year, four of which mark Christian occasions:

- Good Friday remembers the death of Jesus. ('Good Friday' means God's Friday.)
- Easter Monday is the second day of Easter. It emphasises the importance of Easter Sunday, which celebrates the Christian belief in the resurrection of Jesus, by allowing workers an extra day off work.
- Christmas Day celebrates the birth of Jesus.
- Boxing Day is also the Feast of St Stephen, a Christian Saint, and marks the day on which workers were traditionally given a Christmas 'box', or gift, by their employer.

Whit Monday was a public holiday in the UK until the late 1960s. This marked Whit Sunday, or Pentecost, for Christians, which remembers when the Holy Spirit came to Jesus' disciples. It was replaced in 1971 by a spring bank holiday.

In addition, Sunday is traditionally a holiday in celebration of the Christian belief that Jesus' resurrection took place on a Sunday.

Church schools

The first schools in England were founded by the Church and attached to cathedrals and monasteries. After Henry VIII moved away from Catholicism and became the head of the Church of England, these schools became Church of England schools and Roman Catholic schools had to move abroad.

There were very few schools in Britain until the nineteenth century. The Church of England was responsible for most of the educational establishments that there were, until the State became involved in the education of children in the 1830s.

Today, about one third of state-funded schools in England and Wales are faith schools. This means that, although their income comes from public funds, these schools have a 'religious character'.

Of the 7,000 faith primary and secondary schools in England and Wales, 98 per cent have a Christian character. Sixty-eight per cent are Church of England schools and 30 per cent are Catholic.

A school with a religious character has formal links with a faith organisation, though most of them are almost entirely funded by the government. One in six selects some or all of their pupils by their religion. The religious organisation may appoint a large proportion of governors of their schools, and the governors may choose to appoint teachers and leaders who share their faith.

♬ Religious education is compulsory in all schools whether or not they are faith schools

Case Study: Church of England schools in numbers

- Approximately one million children attend C of E schools.
- There are 4,500 C of E primary schools and over 200 C of E secondary schools in England.
- A quarter of state-funded schools are Church of England.
- One in ten C of E schools is an academy.
- Over 500 private schools declare themselves to be Church of England.

Case Study: Catholic schools in numbers

- There are over 2,000 state-funded Catholic schools in England and Wales, including nearly 350 secondary schools.
- One in ten state-funded schools is a Catholic school.
- There are 150 private Catholic schools.

Whether a school has a religious character or not, all pupils must, by law, be taught religious education and all schools should provide a daily act of worship. Religious education should reflect the fact that the traditions of England are, in the main, Christian. For state schools without a religious charter, more than half of the acts of worship should be Christian.

Some people and organisations are against the principle that religious groups should be able to use public money to run schools. These organisations include the National Secular Society and the British Humanist Association. They say:

- If the Churches want faith schools, they should fund them themselves.
- It is wrong that children should not be allowed to attend their local school because of their (or their parents') religious views.
- Faith schools select pupils from the wealthiest families and so do not represent their local communities.

Religious groups may argue:

- Since they contribute 10 per cent of the costs of some faith schools, they are actually paying for public education.
- If some religious families are wealthy, this means they pay higher taxes and so contribute more than most people to state education in general, including non-faith schools.
- Parents should be able to choose schools for their children that share their own values.

Tasks

Carry out the following:

- Divide your table group into two.
- One half of the group need to create a campaign to defend keeping Church schools in Britain.
- The other half of the group need to create a campaign to get rid of Church schools in Britain.
- Each campaign needs to produce a speech, a promotional advert for TV or radio (this could be acted live or recorded).
- Present the campaigns to the whole class and discuss the issue.
- Have a class vote to establish which side has been most successful.
- Write up your own conclusion, supporting your view with reasons.

To discuss

a Should the State fund schools with a religious character?

b Should religious education be compulsory in state schools?

Secularisation

Secularisation is the idea that religious beliefs, practices and organisations are becoming less important in society. This means secularisation is a process that happens over time as the influence of religion weakens.

Max Weber, one of the founders of sociology, described secularisation as 'the disenchantment of the world'. He meant that, as society modernises and becomes more industrialised and scientific in its outlook, people have less need to rely on ideas that cannot be proved.

Those who argue that secularisation is taking place include sociologists Bryan Wilson and Steve Bruce. They say that there is observable evidence that it is happening:

- Religious teachings and organisations are no longer respected.
- People can rely on material comforts for happiness and so have less need to believe in supernatural ideas.
- Religion has become a private matter and has less influence in public life.
- People are increasingly less committed to religious values and practices such as prayer and worship.
- Religion has become a 'leisure pursuit' rather than a deep commitment.

To discuss

What examples can you give of secularisation in your own community or in the wider world?

☊ Max Weber (1864–1920), one of the founding fathers of sociology

---

Case study: The National Secular Society

The National Secular Society stands against the promotion of religion and privileges for religious institutions, and opposes the link between the Church of England and the State. It is not, however, against religion and some religious people support its aims. It states that secularism is about tolerance and that people of different religions (including those of no religion) and beliefs are equal before the law.

The Society aims to promote freedom of belief, expression and practice.

- Freedom of belief: Secularism seeks to ensure and protect freedom of religious and other belief for all citizens. Secularism is not about restricting religious freedoms, it is about ensuring that the freedoms of thought and conscience apply equally to all, to believers and non-believers alike. Secularism ensures that the right of individuals to freedom of religion is always balanced by the right to be free *from* religion.

- Freedom of expression: Religious people have the right to express their beliefs publicly, but so do those who oppose or question those beliefs. Religious beliefs, ideas and organisations must not enjoy privileged protection from the right to freedom of expression. In a democracy, all ideas and beliefs must be open to discussion. Individuals have rights; ideas do not.

- Freedom of practice: Secularism seeks to defend the absolute freedom of religious and other belief, and protect the right to practise religious belief – so long as it does not affect the rights and freedoms of others.

The charter of the National Secular Society can be found at:
www.secularism.org.uk/secularcharter.html.

The place of religion in a secular society

The British Social Attitudes Survey, published in May 2015, shows that the proportion of people in Britain who say they belong to a religion has fallen over the last 30 years, and particularly during the last decade.

The Church of England has suffered the biggest decline, falling from 40 per cent of the population in 1983 to 17 per cent in 2014. The drop between 2004 and 2014 alone was 12 per cent. At the same time, the proportion of people who say they are Catholics and other Christians has remained fairly stable at 25 per cent.

Religions other than Christianity have grown. In particular, the proportion of people who are Muslim increased from 0.5 per cent in 1983 to 5 per cent in 2014.

The fastest-growing group consists of those who say they have no religion. This group comprised 49 per cent of the population in 2014, up from 31 per cent in 1983.

The majority of the population, however, still agrees that: 'The Church of England should keep its status as the official established Church in England.' When presented with this statement by the British Election Study in the spring of 2011, most English people agreed.

‑ Percentages of people who agreed that 'The Church of England should keep its status as the official established Church in England'

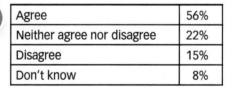

Agree	56%
Neither agree nor disagree	22%
Disagree	15%
Don't know	8%

The effects of secularisation on religion

Sociologists Wilson and Bruce have argued that three processes that lead to the decline of religion occur as society develops and modernises:

- Rationalisation: People use science to explain the universe and the place of human beings in it. They reject religion, which cannot be proved.
- Differentiation: The Church used to control or influence large parts of people's lives (education, hospitals and government, for example). Today these are all run by different non-religious organisations.
- Decline of community: As means of communication and the exchange of information have improved, the world seems bigger. People no longer live in small communities, which used to be held together by the Church.

On the face of it, it seems fairly obvious that religion has decreasing power and authority in our society. In spite of the fact that the Church of England is the established Church in England, people are more influenced by non-religious institutions, such as the media. In particular:

To discuss

a What conclusions can you draw about the place of religion in society in the twenty-first century?

b Is the place of Christianity in British society different from that of religion in general?

- Fewer people attend church services.
- Fewer people are willing to work in the Church.
- Many churches are being closed or sold off.
- Fewer people get married now than in the past.
- Fewer people are baptised into the Church of England and even fewer are confirmed into the Church.
- The great Christian festivals of Christmas and Easter have lost their Christian significance in British society. People like to have time off work to spend with their families, but most do not go to church.

Stretch what you know

'God is dead. God remains dead. And we have killed him. How shall we comfort ourselves, the murderers of all murderers? What was holiest and mightiest of all that the world has yet owned has bled to death under our knives: who will wipe this blood off us? What water is there for us to clean ourselves? What festivals of atonement, what sacred games shall we have to invent? Is not the greatness of this deed too great for us? Must we ourselves not become gods simply to appear worthy of it?'

(Friedrich Nietzsche)

a When Nietzsche says that 'God is dead', he means that Christian beliefs and teachings no longer have relevance in society. To what extent do you agree with him?

b Find out more about Nietzsche and think about how his ideas relate to different views about secularisation.

c Do you think that there will come a time when there is no religion in the world?

Not everyone agrees, however, that secularisation is taking place. They would say that there is evidence that religion still has importance in society, but that the nature of its importance is changing.

- Even though traditional religious beliefs and organisations have lost their appeal, most people do still hold religious beliefs.
- Religion is very important in the lives of many social groups, particularly minority ethnic groups (e.g. Muslims).
- Some new religious movements and eastern religions have experienced considerable popularity.
- Even if religion is becoming less important in Western Europe, it is still strong in other parts of the world, for example, in many sections of the Muslim world, Latin America and Africa.
- In some very modern countries religion is still very important, for example, in the USA.

'Dare to know! Have courage to use your own reason!'

(Immanuel Kant)

The rise of humanism

Humanism is way of seeing and reacting to the world using science, logic and reason, and rejecting religious beliefs and ideas.

Before the middle of the eighteenth century, the Christian Church dominated European thinking. Gradually, however, things began to change. Thinkers started to question the authority of the Church and to challenge its teachings. In 1689 John Locke, an English philosopher, published his book *An Essay Concerning Human Understanding*, in which he argued that human knowledge came through experience of the world, not from some outside truth. Writers in other European countries and America were coming to the same conclusions.

THERE'S PROBABLY NO GOD.
NOW STOP WORRYING AND ENJOY YOUR LIFE.

www.humanism.org.uk
www.richarddawkins.net
www.atheistcampaign.org

◑ The British Humanist Association supported a 2008 campaign to promote the idea that God does not exist

At the same time, the idea developed that human goodness and ethics came from human reason rather than from some external power. The word 'humanism' began to be used to describe a view of the world that focused on human beings rather than on organised religion.

Although the first humanists challenged the authority of the Church, many still maintained their Christian faith. Over time, the Church adapted so that Christian humanists were accepted and humanism became a completely non-religious movement.

Today, humanists share three central principles:

- A scientific view of the universe that rejects supernatural beliefs, including religious beliefs.
- A concern for the welfare of other human beings and animals based on reason, not on divine authority.
- The need for each person to create meaning in their own life without a belief in life after death.

In 1967, several humanist organisations in Britain merged to become the British Humanist Association. The guiding principle of the Association is: 'this is our world, our responsibility, our possibility'. Among other things, it campaigns to disestablish the Church of England, to remove the right of Anglican bishops to sit in the House of Lords and to abolish faith schools.

The aims of the British Humanist Association can be found at: https://humanism.org.uk/about/our-aims.

Tasks

1 What is secularisation?
2 What are the differences between secularisation and humanism?
3 What evidence is there that secularisation is happening in Britain?
4 Is a decline in religious belief an argument against the existence of God?

'Modernity is not necessarily secularising; it is necessarily pluralising. Modernity is characterised by an increasing plurality, within the same society, of different beliefs, values, and world views. Plurality does indeed pose a challenge to all religious traditions; each one must cope with the fact that there are "all these others," not just in a faraway country but right next door. This challenge, however, is not the one assumed by secularisation theory.'

(Peter Berger)

5 Berger says that the modernisation of society does not necessarily bring about secularisation. Instead it brings about a larger number of different, perhaps smaller, religious groups in competition with each other. At the same time, religion becomes a private matter, and people start to develop their own spiritual beliefs and practices.

Do you think Berger makes a good case against secularisation?

Potential clashes between religious and secular values in education

We have seen that about half of the British population says they have no religious associations, yet a third of state-funded schools are faith schools. It is not surprising that there is potential for conflict between religious and secular values in English schools.

Religious education is compulsory in all state schools. In some faith schools, the faith organisation may decide on what and how it should be taught.

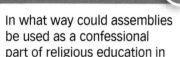

To discuss

In what way could assemblies be used as a confessional part of religious education in Church schools?

♦ One third of state-funded schools are faith schools

Christian faith schools are clear that some of the aims of religious education are confessional, in other words they are designed to reinforce the faith of pupils and promote a Christian world view.

The aims of religious education in Church of England schools include:

- Reflecting critically on the truth claims of Christian belief.
- Seeing how the truth of Christianity is relevant today and facing the challenge of Jesus' teaching in a pluralist and post-modern society.
- Recognising that faith is not based on a positive balance of probabilities but on commitment to a particular way of understanding God and the world.
- Understanding how religious faith can sustain pupils in difficult circumstances and in the face of opposition.

The aims of religious education in Catholic schools include:

- Enabling pupils continually to deepen their religious and theological understanding and to be able to communicate this effectively.
- Enabling pupils to relate their Catholic faith to daily life.
- Provoking a desire for personal meaning as revealed in the truth of the Catholic faith.
- Making pupils aware of the demands of religious commitment in everyday life.

The National Secular Society is not against religion or teaching about the religions represented in Britain. It is, however, against the idea of the State promoting religion. It opposes the confessional teaching of Christianity in Christian schools.

Tasks

Summarise the views presented by the National Secular Society for why it:

- opposes confessional teaching of Christianity in Church schools
- believes all worldviews, including religious worldviews, should be taught alongside one another.

'We regard it as unjustifiable that VA [faith] schools and most religiously designated academies, all publicly funded, are still permitted by law to teach RE solely from their own exclusive viewpoint, and in a confessional way. Such a situation not only undermines the integrity of a state education system, it also undermines young people's religious freedom. It is worth noting that not all pupils at such schools are admitted on religious grounds in accordance with their parents' stated religion. Some choose a school because of its proximity – often the Church of England school is the only one in the area. In other areas, a shortage of school places means many parents have no option other than to send their children to a faith school.'

(© National Secular Society http://www.secularism.org.uk/ uploads/religious-education-briefing-paper.pdf)

'In a religiously plural democracy it is inappropriate for any belief system to be privileged in state schools. The law, however, privileges Christianity… This legal position reflects the desire of the Church of England, which believes that religious education teaching in England should have a "central focus on Christianity". The Church recognises that with church attendance in decline, schools provide the only real opportunity to reach children with its message.'

(© National Secular Society http://www.secularism.org.uk/ uploads/religious-education-briefing-paper.pdf)

In non-faith state schools, religious education must be taught according to a locally agreed syllabus that should 'reflect the fact that the religious traditions in Great Britain are, in the main, Christian while taking account of the teaching and practices of the other principal religions represented in Great Britain.'

The National Secular Society believes that non-religious and humanist world views should be taught alongside religions, and that no religion or world view should have greater importance than any other.

In addition to religious education, schools without a religious character should provide daily acts of collective worship, most of which should be 'of a broadly Christian character'.

The aims of collective worship in schools

'Collective worship in schools should aim to provide the opportunity for pupils to worship God, to consider spiritual and moral issues and to explore their own beliefs; to encourage participation and response, whether through active involvement in the presentation of worship or through listening to and joining in the worship offered; and to develop community spirit, promote a common ethos and shared values, and reinforce positive attitudes.'

(Department for Education: Circular 1/94 Religious Education and Collective Worship)

The British Humanist Association opposes religious worship in state schools:

'In demanding Collective Worship in schools that will typically have pupils from a wide variety of religious backgrounds and none, the law is incoherent: a school can do many things collectively but, lacking a shared religious faith, it cannot worship collectively. It also ignores the right of children below the sixth form to freedom of belief and conscience by giving only to parents the right to have a child excused from worship or to withdraw the child from school for an alternative form of worship.'

(© British Humanist Association https://humanism.org.uk/ campaigns/schools-and-education/collective-worship/, 2016)

'Every state-funded school must offer a curriculum which is balanced and broadly based, and which: promotes the spiritual, moral, cultural, mental and physical development of pupils; and prepares pupils at the school for the opportunities, responsibilities and experiences of later life.'

'All state schools ... must teach religious education ... All schools must publish their curriculum by subject and academic year online.'

(National Curriculum in England: Framework Document)

'Every agreed syllabus [for religious education] shall reflect the fact that the religious traditions in Great Britain are in the main Christian whilst taking account of the teaching and practices of the other principal religions represented in Great Britain.'

(Education Act 1996 Section 375 (3))

'All pupils in attendance at a maintained school shall on each school day take part in an act of collective worship ... The collective worship required in the school shall be wholly or mainly of a Christian character ... Collective worship is of a broadly Christian character if it reflects the broad traditions of Christian belief without being distinctive of any particular Christian denomination.'

(Education Reform Act 1988 Sections 6 and 7)

Tasks

1 Why must schools without a religious character provide an act of worship?

2 What reasons do the Churches give to support confessional religious education in schools?

3 In your opinion, should religious education be compulsory for all students in English state schools? Give your reasons, and give reasons why someone may have a different view.

4 Since 2004, schools in France have had to display posters that contain a number of principles designed to keep religion out of schools. When it was introduced, Education Minister Vincent Peillon said his secular charter was designed to promote 'absolute respect for freedom of conscience'.

Does a charter like this promote freedom of belief and expression, or does it restrict them?

The articles of the charter include:

'Secularism guarantees freedom of conscience for all. Everybody is free to believe or not to believe. This allows the freedom of expression of one's convictions, in respecting the convictions of others and while remaining within the limits of public order.'

'Secularism in schools offers students the conditions necessary to develop their personalities, to exercise their own free will, and to be a student of what it means to be a citizen. It protects them from all attempts at religious conversion and pressure which would stop them making their own choices.'

'Secularism allows the freedom of expression of students, within the bounds of the normal running of schools.'

'Staff are required to maintain a strict neutrality: they must not express their personal convictions (religious or political) while exercising their role.'

'No one can use their belonging to a religion as a reason to refuse to conform to the rules of the school.'

'The wearing of signs or clothing conspicuously expressing a religious affiliation is forbidden.'

(Ministère de l'Éducation Nationale)

Potential clashes between religion, tradition and secular law

Even though the Church of England is represented in parliament and many Members of Parliament have religious backgrounds, British law is secular and has no religious basis. When judges are sworn in, they take a judicial oath to 'do right to all manner of people after the laws and usages of this realm, without fear or favour, affection or ill will'. This means that all people are treated equally under the law, regardless of religious belief or lack of it.

Marriage

For Christians, marriage is a special relationship between a man and woman that is created by God. Therefore, when a couple gets married, they make promises before God that their relationship will be faithful and permanent, regardless of circumstances.

Marriage in the Church of England

'...according to our Lord's teaching, marriage is in its nature a union permanent and lifelong, for better or worse, till death do us part, of one man with one woman, to the exclusion of all others on either side, for the procreation and nurture of children, for the hallowing and right direction of the natural instincts and affections, and for the natural society, help and comfort which one ought to have of the other, both in prosperity and adversity.'

(Canon B30.1)

Marriage in the Roman Catholic Church

'The matrimonial covenant, by which a man and a woman establish between themselves a partnership of the whole of life and which is ordered by its nature to the good of the spouses and the procreation and education of offspring, has been raised by Christ the Lord to the dignity of a sacrament between the baptised.'

(Canon 1055.1)

'The essential properties of marriage are unity and indissolubility, which in Christian marriage obtain a special firmness by reason of the sacrament.'

(Canon 1057)

Civil marriage

A civil marriage is a legal contract between two people that sets out rights and duties between them. A civil ceremony must be secular. Regulations do not allow a civil ceremony to be religious, to contain any form of worship, or to be conducted by a minister of any religion.

⋂ Civil marriages are not allowed to have religious content

Clashes between secular and Christian views on marriage include:

- Civil marriage is a legally recognised union of two people. It is recognised as this by the Church of England and, although the Roman Catholic Church accepts the marriage of non-Catholics through a civil ceremony, it does not recognise that Catholics can be married in this way. For them, marriage is a spiritual bond and must take place in a church according to the laws of the Church.
- Same-sex marriage is legal in the United Kingdom, except in Northern Ireland, and is legally recognised through a civil ceremony. The Church of England is opposed to same-sex marriages in church. It teaches that marriage can only take place between a woman and a man. Nevertheless, Anglicans recognise the validity of civil same-sex marriages. The Roman Catholic Church, on the other hand, is completely opposed to same-sex partnerships and does not recognise marriage between two people of the same sex.
- Marriage can be legally dissolved through a divorce. Individuals are free to remarry after they have been granted a divorce. Although the Church of England sees marriage as a 'permanent and lifelong union', it recognises that there may be circumstances in which couples cannot stay together and that divorce may be inevitable. If a divorced person wishes to marry again in a church, they may do so if their vicar agrees. The Catholic Church maintains that the permanency of marriage cannot be broken. Therefore, even though a divorce may legally be allowed, the Catholic Church does not recognise it. Marriage is a relationship made by God and human beings cannot break it. Divorcees are therefore not allowed to remarry in a Catholic church.

Annulment

Although divorce is forbidden in the Catholic Church, it is possible to get an annulment. An annulment is a procedure that cancels a marriage: it effectively wipes it out as if it never existed. One of three strict conditions that must be met for an annulment to take place:

- The marriage was not conducted by a Catholic priest.
- There was an 'impediment', which means that the couple should not have been allowed to marry. Examples include being underage or being closely related.
- There was a 'defect' in the couple's consent to marry. This means that one or both of the partners was not in a position to agree to the marriage. Examples include not being mentally fit to make the decision, not having sufficient time to make the decision, making the decision under the influence of drugs or alcohol, or getting married because the female partner is pregnant.

To discuss

a Should marriage be permanent? What does marriage mean if it is not permanent?

b What is the difference between being married and just living together?

Tasks

1 What is the difference between a civil marriage and a Christian marriage?

2 Identify the potential clashes between secular and Christian views on marriage.

3 Explain which of these clashes could be considered most significant from a Christian perspective.

Responses to forced, arranged and child marriages

An arranged marriage is a marriage that is planned by the families of the two partners and not by the partners themselves. Indeed, the partners may not even meet until the marriage takes place. Many cultures have traditionally approved and encouraged arranged marriages that bring economic or social benefits to families, or political benefits to countries. The wishes of individuals about whom they should marry were hardly considered.

Christian societies practised arranged marriages to establish peaceful relationships between families and clans until the twelfth century. In 1140, a Christian monk called Gratian produced a book of Catholic law entitled *Decretum Gratiani*. In it, he introduced the idea of consent in marriage. It was no longer enough for marrying couples simply to be present at the marriage ceremony, they had to agree formally to it.

Roman Catholic Church law still requires consent to be a condition of marriage. Indeed, not giving consent to a marriage is grounds for its annulment. Consent is an important factor in the Anglican marriage ceremony.

The Church of England strongly affirms the principle that forced marriages are legally and morally wrong. This view is reflected in the Forced Marriage Act 2007.

The idea of consent is key for the Christian understanding of marriage and for the very foundation of the concept of marriage in English law.

The Church of England states that:

'The Church's view is founded on the principle that non-consensual marriage should be dealt with on the same basis as non-consensual sexual relations, as an issue of fundamental human rights.'

> 'A marriage is brought into being by the lawfully manifested consent of persons who are legally capable. This consent cannot be supplied by any human power.'
>
> 'Matrimonial consent is an act of will by which a man and a woman by an irrevocable covenant mutually give and accept one another for the purpose of establishing a marriage.'
>
> *(Code of Canon Law 1057) – this is part of the legal principles of the Catholic Church*

➲ Couples must agree to marry each other in a church wedding ceremony

Non-Christian and historical attitudes to forced, arranged and child marriage.

Some non-Christian cultures still practise arranged marriages. In the UK, they are legal, provided that both partners agree to the marriage. When one or both of the partners does not consent to the marriage, it is called a forced marriage. Marriage may be forced by emotional pressure or threats of physical violence. Forced marriages are illegal in the UK.

Although forced marriage exists in some religious communities, all the major religions condemn it. Since the Christian Churches teach that consent is an important condition of marriage, they oppose forced marriage absolutely.

As ideas about arranged marriages have changed through history, so have ideas about the age to marry. In biblical times, it was common for girls to marry when they hit puberty. It is indeed probable that Jesus' mother, Mary, was a girl of about 14 when she gave birth to him. In a sense, this is not too surprising considering that the age at which people were likely to die at that time was about 45.

Laws about marriage in the UK today

Today, the laws about the age for marriage are not consistent in the UK. In England and Wales, a couple can marry when they are 16, providing their parents agree. They can marry when they are 18 without parental agreement. In Scotland, marriage is permitted at 16 without parental consent.

Roman Catholic Church law allows males to marry when they are 16 and females when they are 14. The Church, however, allows bishops in individual countries to set ages for their own countries. In the United Kingdom, both the Catholic and Anglican Churches set the minimum ages for marriage in line with UK laws.

To discuss

Why is consent such an important factor in marriage?

Tasks

1. How have Christian attitudes to arranged marriages changed over time?
2. What are the benefits of this change in attitude?
3. Arranged marriages are legal in the UK, why do you think some families have this approach to marriage?
4. Explain what you think is the most important consideration for a couple who are thinking about whether to marry or not.
5. How does your view compare to Christian teachings?

Christian attitudes to equality and potential clashes with equality laws

Christianity teaches that all people are equal, regardless of sex, ethnicity, nationality, sexuality, class or disability. This is because:

- God created the human race.
- God plays a part in the creation of each individual.
- God loves each person and accepts them as they are.
- God created human beings in His image, which means each human being shares characteristics of spirituality, creativity and love.

Bible bitz

'From one man he made every nation of men, that they should inhabit the whole earth.'

(Acts 17:26)

'You shall love your neighbour as yourself.'

(Matthew 22:39)

'There is neither Jew nor Greek, slave nor free, male nor female, for you are all one in Christ Jesus.'

(Galatians 3:28)

Stretch what you know

Find out more about Martin Luther King's struggle with the secular authorities, including the actions taken against him and his thoughts about them.

History throws up examples of Christians who have fought against secular authorities to establish equality in the face of injustice. Martin Luther King in the USA and Trevor Huddleston in South Africa campaigned against racial inequality, challenging laws that they saw to be unfair.

⊙ Trevor Huddleston worked for racial equality in South Africa

The role of women in the Church

In spite of all this, to some people the Bible itself provides examples of inequality. For instance, St Paul writes:

'Women should remain silent in the churches. They are not allowed to speak, but must be in submission, as the Law says. If they want to enquire about something, they should ask their own husbands at home; for it is disgraceful for a woman to speak in the church.'

(1 Corinthians 14:34,35)

And:

'He [the man] is the image and glory of God; but the woman is the glory of man.'

(1 Corinthians 11:7)

The Church of England, after many years of debate, allows women to be ordained as priests and bishops. The Roman Catholic Church, however, teaches that it against the will of God for women to have leadership roles in the Church.

The Equality Act of 2010 requires equal treatment of men and women in access to employment. Priests, monks, nuns and ministers of religion, however, are exempt from the provisions of the Act.

'I declare that the Church has no authority whatsoever to confer priestly ordination on women and that this judgement is to be definitively held by all the Church's faithful.'

(Pope John Paul II)

ᴖ The Church of England allows women to become priests, but the Roman Catholic Church forbids it

Same-sex marriages

Similarly, the Marriage (Same Sex Couples) Act 2013 makes the marriage of same-sex couples lawful in England and Wales in civil ceremonies. We have seen that the Christian Churches are generally opposed to the religious marriage of people of the same sex. The Act, therefore, ensures that no religious organisation can be made to allow same-sex marriages to happen on their premises and no religious organisation or representative can be made to conduct religious ceremonies for same-sex couples.

Bible bitz

'Jesus said to them, "Render to Caesar the things that are Caesar's, and to God the things that are God's." And they marvelled at him.'

(Mark 12:17)

'Let every person be subject to the governing authorities. For there is no authority except from God, and those that exist have been instituted by God.'

(Romans 13:1)

To discuss

a If secular laws conflict with a person's religious beliefs or principles, should that person break the law?

b Is breaking the law wrong in itself? Would breaking the law conflict with Christian principles? Use the quotes in the 'Bible bitz' box above to help you answer this question.

Tasks

1 Should the Christian Churches be exempt from some laws? Give examples and evidence in your answer.

2 Do Christians really believe in equality? Present two different points of view in your answer.

3 Is the Marriage (Same Sex Couples) Act about creating equality in marriage or about changing the definition of marriage?

Scientific development in medical ethics

We have seen that one of the reasons for secularisation is the development of science and technology. This seems to some people to leave religious world views behind, and to leave those who hold them out of touch with the modern world. In this section, we shall examine how these developments may conflict with Christian values.

Euthanasia

Euthanasia is the deliberate act of ending someone's life to relieve them of suffering. There are different types of euthanasia and two ways of classifying it:

1 • **Voluntary euthanasia:** when a person requests that their life be ended, perhaps because they have a terminal illness that is causing them a lot of pain.
  • **Involuntary euthanasia:** when a person is unable to request that their life be ended, maybe because they are in a coma, so a doctor or relative makes the decision.
2 • **Passive euthanasia:** withholding treatment that, if administered, would keep the person alive.
  • **Active euthanasia:** deliberately ending a person's life, for example, with lethal drugs. Active euthanasia is regarded as either murder or manslaughter under British law.

Assisted suicide, when a terminally ill patient asks someone to help them take their own life, is a form of active euthanasia. It is illegal under the Suicide Act of 1961 (though it is not illegal for someone to take, or to attempt to take, their own life).

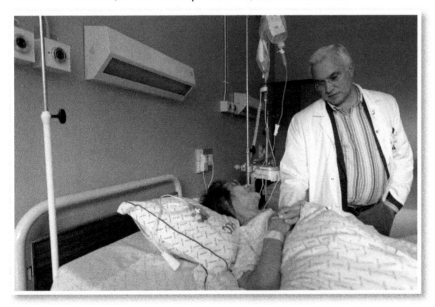

ᘯ Euthanasia is illegal in Britain, even if a patient requests it

Public opinion is strongly in favour of euthanasia. A poll conducted by YouGov in January 2013 revealed that 70 per cent of people support the principle. Yet a vote among MPs in the House of Commons in September 2015 saw a proposal to legalise assisted suicide defeated, by 330 votes to 118. In addition, a YouGov survey of Anglican clergy conducted in September 2014 showed that 70 per cent of them believe that the law in relation to assisted suicide should not be changed.

Christian teachings about euthanasia

Most Christians believe that euthanasia is wrong. For them:

- life is precious; it is sacred because it was created by God. Christians refer to the sanctity of life
- euthanasia is deliberate killing; in other words it is murder and murder is forbidden by the Ten Commandments
- Christians have a duty to care for those who are suffering.

The Catholic Church

The Roman Catholic Church teaches that the deliberate killing of an 'innocent' human being is always unacceptable morally. Life, as a gift from God, has unqualified value. Life is always preferable to death, and does not depend for its value on how much pleasure or well-being it brings. Therefore, euthanasia must always be wrong, even if it is conducted to relieve a human being from pain and suffering.

The Church teaches that assisted suicide is also wrong, since it too is the deliberate killing of a God-given life which human beings do not have the right to do.

The Church of England

In considering euthanasia, the Church of England recognises the importance of 'personal autonomy', or the right to make independent decisions about one's own life. However, it also recognises that this puts an unwelcome burden on someone else to carry out euthanasia or assist a suicide.

Stretch what you know

The hospice movement was founded in the 1950s by Cicely Saunders. She was a doctor who worked in the field of pain relief. She developed a system of giving pain relief to patients in regular doses, rather than waiting for them to complain that they were in pain. In 1967 she opened the first hospice, a special hospital whose aim was not to cure patients (hospice patients have incurable illnesses), but to care for them and their families. Hospices are involved in research into pain control, ways of caring, and teaching.

■ Cicely Saunders (1918–2005), founder of the hospice movement

Dame Cicely Saunders was a devout Christian and her Christian principles underlay her vocation to work to help people die with dignity.

- Find out more about the work of the hospice movement and the religious reasons why many Christians support it.

It says that to end the life of a human being implies that their life no longer has meaning, and this goes against the Christian principle of the sanctity of life. The Church maintains that it is also better to protect life than protect the autonomy of the individual. Therefore, instead of assisting the suicide of a dying person, society should offer compassionate care.

Attitudes to euthanasia

There are, in addition, non-religious reasons for opposing euthanasia:

- A doctor's duty is to preserve life, not to end it.
- Medical advances mean that pain control is very effective, and cures for illnesses more likely.
- Some patients, particularly elderly ones, may agree to euthanasia against their will so as not to be a burden on relatives.

Those who agree with euthanasia, however, say that it is not murder. Murder is committed through anger and hatred, whereas euthanasia is performed out of love and compassion as it stops a person suffering. It is possible to put controls in place to ensure that the patient really wants their life to end. It is their life, after all, so they should be able to decide how and when it ends.

The right to die

Some people believe that a person's life is their own and that they should have the right to self-determination. This means that they should have the right to decide the course of their own lives without interference from anyone else. It follows, then, that they should be able to decide to end their life if they wish.

Christians, however, believe that a person's life is not their own. Each life is created by God and only God has the right to take it away. Therefore no one has the right to end their life or have it ended by someone else.

Under the Suicide Act of 1961, it is not illegal in Britain to commit suicide, but voluntary euthanasia and assisting suicide remain illegal. A patient has the right, however, to refuse medical treatment, even if that treatment would save their life. Many people – including some Christians – agree with this, provided the person has the mental capacity to make such a decision. These Christians would say that if the death of the patient is God's will, then it would be wrong to interfere.

In the eighteenth century, the Scottish philosopher David Hume argued that committing suicide does not go against Christian principles. He maintained that God created human beings with certain mental powers that can be used for their 'ease, happiness, or preservation'. If these mental powers lead a person to take their own life for their ease or happiness, then suicide is allowable.

To discuss

a What does Hume mean by what he says?

b How would Christian respond to this view?

Tasks

1 Create a letter for a problem page which sets out the reasons that someone might give for wanting euthanasia.

2 Provide two different Christian responses for the problem page to this letter.

'The life of man is of no greater importance to the universe than that of an oyster ... I thank [the] Providence [of God], both for the good which I have already enjoyed, and for the power with which I am endowed of escaping the ill that threatens me.'

(David Hume)

Case study: The Samaritans

The Samaritans was set up by a London vicar called Chad Varah. He used to see people every day in his parish who were distressed but who had no one to turn to who would listen to them. He wanted to do something to help these people, and this was how the Samaritans started. The charity was initially called 'Good Samaritans' by the *Daily Mirror* in 1953, linking Chad's organisation to the Good Samaritan whom Jesus speaks of in the Bible. In the story, a Samaritan stops to help a Jew who has been robbed, even though they come from very different backgrounds.

Today, the Samaritans offers a round-the-clock listening service, nearly every day of the year – the service is run by over 20,000 volunteers. People talk to Samaritans any time they like, in their own way and off the record, about whatever's getting to them. They do not have to be suicidal.

The Samaritans has a three-point vision for a society in which:

- fewer people die by suicide
- people are able to explore their feelings
- people are able to acknowledge and respect the feelings of others. Many Christians support the on-going work of the Samaritans either by volunteering themselves or through financial donations.

To discuss

a Look at the Samaritans' advert. Who do you think it is targeted at?

b Do you think a Christian would agree with the Samaritan vision for society?

Lorraine

I find the question of whether euthanasia is right really hard to answer. I don't think I'd ever want to end my life early and miss out on time with my friends and family. But I don't really know what it must be like to be terminally ill or in terrible pain. Maybe in that situation it would be different. When my nan was ill with cancer she went to a hospice. The nurses there were great and she seemed to be comfortable, but she wasn't really herself. I do believe that God is with us always, and that he won't leave us without the strength to cope, whatever situation we are in. I guess continuing to live despite our suffering is an act of faith. Sometimes though I do wonder if euthanasia is actually wrong. After all, some people say it is an act of love to help end a person's suffering, and God is love.

To discuss

Read Lorraine's account.

a What does she believe about euthanasia? Explain whether you agree or disagree with what Lorraine says.

'True compassion leads to sharing another's pain; it does not kill the person whose suffering we cannot bear.'

(Pope John Paul II, Evangelium Vitae, 1995)

b Do you think killing can ever be compassionate? Why?

What Quakers believe

The Quakers, also known as the Society of Friends, are not united on the subject of euthanasia. Some believe that people who are suffering greatly should be allowed to die if they want to. Others believe that people should care for one another and support each other's pain so that euthanasia is not needed. Some Quakers work in hospices, helping patients to receive the necessary pain relief to die naturally, but still with dignity.

In the past when other Christian denominations would not bury suicide victims in holy ground, the Quakers did. The Quakers believe that love and support should be made available to people who feel that suicide is their only option. Some Quakers are members of the Samaritans and they provide support for many people who are struggling to find a solution to their problems.

Abortion

Christianity teaches that life begins at conception – the moment that sperm meets egg – and that the fertilised egg is a sacred God-given life, with the same rights as a baby, child or adult.

Medical science tells us that about 70 per cent of fertilised eggs do not become implanted in a woman's womb and that a large proportion of those that do are lost naturally through miscarriage (estimates suggest around 25 per cent). As a result, some people do not believe that fertilisation is a good point at which to mark the beginning of a sacred life.

Some people believe that a foetus' rights should increase as it develops. Others believe that it is the end of pregnancy and the birth of the baby that marks the beginning of a new life and the point at which it has rights.

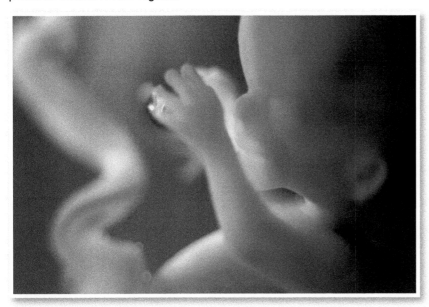

♁ People disagree about when human life starts

Attitudes to abortion

A survey conducted by YouGov and the University of Lancaster in January 2013 showed that more Christians than people of no religion believe that life starts at conception.

☋ Beliefs about when life starts

	Anglican	Catholic	No religion
Human life starts at conception	50%	60%	34%
Human life starts at some point during pregnancy	27%	21%	36%
Human life does not start until the baby is born	16%	13%	21%

Abortion is the deliberate termination or ending of a pregnancy through a medical process. In most cases, the termination must take place before the 24th week of pregnancy. This is because, after this time, a foetus is able to survive independently outside its mother's body.

Those who believe that the moment of conception marks the beginning of life must also believe that abortion is always wrong. These people are known as 'pro-life' and include most Christians.

Some people believe that a woman should have an absolute right to decide whether or not to continue with her pregnancy. As it is her body and her life that will be affected by pregnancy, childbirth and motherhood, no one else should have the power to force her to continue with an unwanted pregnancy. They believe that women should have the right to choose safe, legal abortion. These people are called 'pro-choice'.

Others believe that a balance must be struck between the rights of the foetus and the rights of the woman, and that the rights of the foetus increase as it develops in the womb. These people may believe that abortion is acceptable in some circumstances, for some reasons and/or at some stages of pregnancy.

Although the Churches teach that abortion is wrong, Anglicans and Catholics broadly support it, according to the 2013 survey.

☋ Support for and opposition to abortion

	Anglican	Catholic	No religion
In favour of abortion	78%	69%	78%
In favour of banning abortion	5%	14%	3%

Bible blitz

'For you formed my inward parts; you knitted me together in my mother's womb.'

(Psalm 139:13)

'Do not murder.'

(Exodus 20:13)

'The Church of England combines strong opposition to abortion with a recognition that there can be – strictly limited – conditions under which it may be morally preferable to any available alternative.'

(Church of England)

'Life must be protected with the utmost care from the moment of conception; abortion and infanticide are the most abominable of crimes.'

(Roman Catholic Church Second Vatican Council, Encyclical Gaudium et Spes)

Christian attitudes towards abortion

Christian teachings

Christian teaching on abortion is not simple. Generally Christians' belief in the sanctity of life means they have concerns about abortion, but their attitudes towards it differ.

No Christian Church believes that abortion should be encouraged, and most agree that it should only be used in the most serious circumstances.

The Catholic Church

The Catholic Church believes abortion is never acceptable. It is strongly against abortion in every situation. However, it does accept abortion if it is to save the life of the mother. This is because the intention behind this action is not to end the pregnancy, but to care for the woman's life and health. The end of the pregnancy is an unfortunate side-effect.

The Catholic Church teaches that the foetus is a human being from the moment of conception. As the Church believes that all human life is sacred the foetus has a right to life.

The Church of England

Other Christian denominations including the Church of England are generally opposed to abortion, although some believe that in certain situations it can be justified. These situations include if the continued pregnancy will lead to the mother's death, or if the foetus is so badly disabled that after being born it would only live for a short period of time.

The Church recognises that, in trying to respond to severe situations with compassion, individuals within the Church may arrive at different decisions on how best to respond to pregnancy as the result of rape, or when a baby is likely to be born with a disability. Some Anglicans may conclude that in these situations abortion is morally acceptable, and that they are acting in the way described in Matthew 7:12.

The Church believes that alternatives to abortion, such as adoption, should be available and that parents in difficult situations should be supported.

> 'You shall not kill by abortion the fruit of thy womb.'
> *(From The Didache, an early Christian writing)*

To discuss

a What does the quote from *The Didache*, shown above, mean?

b Would all Christians agree with this idea in every situation?

c Do you agree with the quote from *The Didache*? Give reasons for your answer.

Bible bitz

'Before I formed you in the womb I knew you, before you were born I set you apart.'
(Jeremiah 1:5)

'You shall not murder.'
(Exodus 20:13)

'So in everything, do to others what you would have them do to you, for this sums up the Law and the Prophet.'
(Matthew 7:12)

'For you created my inmost being; you knit me together in my mother's womb.'
(Psalms 139:13)

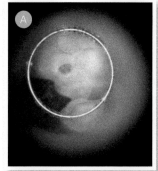
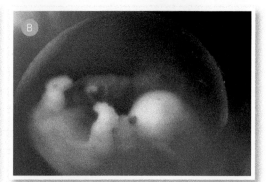
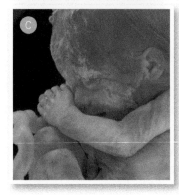
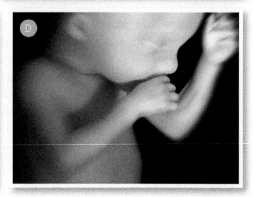

These four images show the foetus in the womb at different stages of fetal development: (a) 1 week, (b) 7 weeks, (c) 12 weeks, and (d) 20 weeks.? In the UK, abortion is legal up to 24 weeks.

Tasks

1. How might someone who is PRO-LIFE (anti-abortion) use these images to argue against abortion?

2. What might a counter-argument be? Explain your answer.

3. Why might some Christians be in favour of abortion is some circumstances?

4. Should people always follow the teachings of their religion? Give reasons for your answer, and reasons why someone may hold a different view.

5. Does the fact that many Christians appear to disagree with the teachings of their Church make organised religion meaningless?

Rosetta

I am totally against abortion. I am pro-life. Abortion to me means killing the innocent and everyone has the right to life.

A foetus cannot speak for itself. Mothers are given choices that are not always given to the unborn child. The rights of the unborn child are ignored, even by their mothers!

I believe that every member of the human family, whether foetus, infant or adult, is made in the image of God and is totally irreplaceable.

For this and other reasons I support the Roman Catholic Church when it rejects not only abortion but also IVF, which can also be used to eliminate life. I think it is wrong that pregnant mothers are given tests to determine the health of their babies and are given the option to abort if the baby is found to be disabled. As a Christian, I believe that all human life has to be cherished, protected and respected.

To discuss

How may other Christians respond to the beliefs about abortion that Rosetta has?

Issues of genetic manipulation

DNA (deoxyribonucleic acid) is a molecule that contains the biological instructions that make each species unique. DNA is passed from adult organisms to their offspring during reproduction. An organism's complete set of DNA is called its genome. Genetic manipulation (or genetic engineering) involves making changes to an organism's genome, either by adding DNA or isolating it, to produce particular characteristics.

Scientists can use genetic manipulation for many purposes. For example, it is possible to make copies of cells that can be grown and used to cure someone of a serious medical condition. This is called 'therapeutic cloning'. It involves taking a cell from someone's body and removing the nucleus that contains the person's entire DNA. The nucleus is then placed into an egg that is stimulated to start growing. The resulting embryo contains stem cells. These are cells that can grow into any type of cell so that, in theory at least, damaged cells – or even complete organs – can be replaced.

The Roman Catholic Church is absolutely opposed to therapeutic cloning. Since it teaches that life begins at conception, it sees the embryo that is created for this purpose as a human being. The deliberate destruction of such embryos after stem cells have been removed is therefore wrong absolutely.

The Church of England is more cautious. It acknowledges the view that an embryo could be seen as a human being, but recognises also the view that while it has the potential to be a human being, it is not one yet.

The creation of life

It is not uncommon for a couple to be unable to have a baby naturally. If this is the case, they may turn to fertility treatment to help them.

Some Christians may take the view that their ability to have children is a matter for God to decide. They would argue that to opt for fertility treatment is to interfere with God's plan. However, the Churches' objections to fertility treatment are largely to do with the method used rather than with the idea of fertility treatment itself.

There are two methods of fertility treatment:

1 Artificial insemination (AI), also referred to intrauterine insemination (IUI), involves collecting a man's sperm and inserting it directly into a women's uterus through non-sexual means. The Church of England teaches that conception should occur in a loving sexual relationship, but if this is not possible then AI is acceptable. The Roman Catholic Church, on the other hand, believes that conception should happen only though sexual union and that AI is therefore unacceptable.

🎧 DNA is a double-stranded structure that stores biological information

To discuss 💬

a Is it acceptable to manipulate the genes of a foetus to prevent a baby being born with a serious illness?

b Is it acceptable to manipulate the genes of a foetus to prevent a baby being born with low intelligence?

c Is it acceptable to manipulate the genes of a foetus to prevent a baby being born male, or to prevent a baby being born female?

'It is gravely immoral to sacrifice a human life for therapeutic ends.'
(Dignitas Personae)

'Therapeutic cloning may be thought of as ethical, as it does not result in another human being.'
(Church of England)

🎧 IVF is the fertilisation of an egg in laboratory conditions

2 In vitro fertilisation (IVF) brings sperm and egg together outside a woman's body in laboratory conditions. Several eggs are fertilised, creating several embryos and usually two are inserted into the woman's uterus. The remainder are frozen, to be used if the first attempt does not result in pregnancy, or to be donated to another couple (though very few are), or to be used for research, including research into genetic manipulation. The 'spare' embryos remain frozen for ten years, after which many are destroyed.

The Roman Catholic Church opposes IVF because conception does not take place through an act of love. In addition, there is concern about the use of the spare embryos. Since the Church sees embryos as independent, sacred human lives given by God, it is therefore absolutely opposed to research being conducted on them and their destruction is seen as a 'crime against their dignity as human beings' (*The Gospel of Life*, Paragraph 63).

The Church of England accepts IVF treatment, but understands why some Anglicans may be opposed to it. It even accepts the use of embryos for medical experimentation, so long as it is carried out within 14 days of fertilisation. After 14 days it believes that the embryo becomes a unique, human being. In reality, stem cells are removed from embryos five or six days after fertilisation and research can legally take place on embryos only up to 14 days.

It is possible to use genetic manipulation to select embryos based on certain characteristics. Screening can show gender or inherited disorders and doctors can select healthy embryos for implanting into the womb. Embryos can also be selected in order to produce so called saviour siblings – babies born to provide tissue to a brother or sister suffering from a serious medical condition, who could be treated by receiving this tissue.

Some people worry that selecting embryos in this way produces what are sometimes called 'designer babies', where parents are able to select embryos for intelligence or looks.

Tasks

1 What do Christians mean by the 'sanctity of life'?
2 Explain why the Christian Churches oppose abortion.

My husband and I have been married for ten years. We started trying to have a child shortly after we were married. When we didn't conceive on our own we went to the doctor. Nothing worked. I was sure I would never become pregnant. Finally, we decided to try IVF. We made the decision that if IVF didn't work that was it. We only had the money to try once.

When five of the eleven eggs fertilised, I felt that was a huge accomplishment. In my mind, I had five children! Three of them were transferred and twelve days later I found out that I was pregnant.

I gave birth to a healthy, beautiful baby girl. She is the most wonderful thing I've ever created in my life. She has just started walking, and today when she was sitting on my lap she leaned over and kissed my cheek for the first time.

All those years I used to wonder and try to imagine what my child would look like. I still look at her and think, 'So this is what my child looks like.' After a year, it's still hard to believe she is actually mine.

Dialogue within and between religious groups

Different teachings, beliefs and attitudes of Christians towards each other and towards other religious groups

Although, as we have seen, the influence of organised religion on people in Western Europe is declining, religion is still a strong feature of human life in a global context. It is estimated that around 84 per cent of the world's population identifies in some way with a religion.

Even in Britain, it is thought that somewhere between 50 and 75 per cent of the population is religious to some extent. And, although most of these identify themselves with Christianity, British culture is nevertheless characterised by diversity of ethnic, cultural and religious background.

In a very general way, what separates religions from each other are different beliefs about spiritual and ethical issues. Religions have different views on spirituality in terms of:

- the nature of God
- the origins of the universe
- the meaning and purpose of life
- good and evil
- the afterlife.

And on ethics:

- sexual relationships
- marriage
- sexuality
- gender roles
- medical ethics
- money
- war
- justice
- equality
- human rights
- the environment
- alcohol and food.

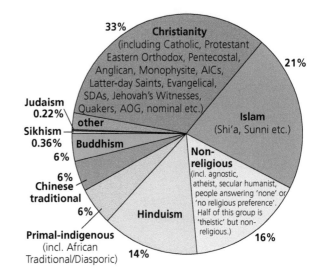

⋂ Major religions of the world

Given that there is no consensus or collective view on these issues, the question naturally arises as to where the truth can be found. And, if each religion claims to possess the truth or special understanding, what are their attitudes to other religions that also have claims to the truth?

Of course, there is a good deal of diversity of belief within each faith, too. How do members of a faith regard others of the same faith?

Exclusivism

Exclusivism is the view that only one religion is true and that the others are therefore false. As far as Christianity is concerned, exclusivists believe that salvation is possible only through faith in Jesus Christ. Furthermore, they see those who follow other religions, those who reject Christianity or even those of other Christian denominations, as being destined for hell or, at best, not heaven.

Three quotations from the Bible are often used by Christian exclusivists to support their view:

'For God so loved the world, that he gave his only Son, that whoever believes in him should not perish but have eternal life.'

(John 3:16)

'Jesus said to them, "I am the Way, the Truth, and the Life. No one comes to the Father except through me".'

(John 14:6)

'Whoever believes and is baptised will be saved, but whoever does not believe will be condemned.'

(Mark 16:16)

Inter-faith exclusivism

For most of its existence, the Roman Catholic Church has maintained an exclusivist outlook on non-Catholic Christians and people of other faiths. In the thirteenth century, Pope Innocent III wrote:

'There is but one universal Church of the faithful, outside of which no one at all can be saved.'

Similarly, in the fifteenth century, Pope Eugene IV wrote:

'[The Church] firmly believes, professes, and proclaims that those not living within the Catholic Church ... cannot become participants in eternal life, but will depart into everlasting fire which was prepared for the devil and his angels.'

Bible bitz

'Everyone who trusts in the Lord will be saved. But before people can pray to the Lord for help, they must believe in him. And before they can believe in the Lord, they must hear about him. And for anyone to hear about the Lord, someone must tell them. And before anyone can go and tell them, they must be sent. As the Scriptures say, "How wonderful it is to see someone coming to tell good news!"'

(Romans 10:13–16)

'All authority in heaven and on earth is given to me. So go and make followers of all people in the world. Baptise them in the name of the Father and the Son and the Holy Spirit.'

(Matthew 28:18,19)

⮕ Missionaries in the nineteenth century believed that only Christianity could bring salvation to people. Robert Moffat (1795-1883) giving a sermon to congregation in South Africa

These negative views of non-Christian religions lay behind much of the missionary work carried out by the Church in the nineteenth century. Missionaries were individuals who were sent into Africa, Asia, the Americas and the Far East to convert people to Christianity. They believed that followers of other religions needed to hear the Christian Gospel in order to be saved for eternity.

Some Protestants, too, have held exclusivist views of other religions, and some still do. A recent survey of Evangelical Protestants in America shows that a substantial majority believes that there is only one God and that Muslims do not pray to the same God as they do.

Intra-faith exclusivism

Throughout the history of the Christian Church, some Christians have held exclusivist views on the validity of Christians who believe differently. For example, during the Reformation in the sixteenth century, Protestants persecuted Catholics, and vice versa. The Catholic queen, Mary, believed that, if England were Protestant, all her subjects would be destined for hell.

The Catholic Church's view, however, has softened over time. The Second Vatican Ecumenical Council (known as Vatican II) was held in Rome from 1962 to 1965. One of the pronouncements that came from the Council stated:

'The Catholic Church professes that it is the one, holy catholic and apostolic Church of Christ; this it does not and could not deny. But in its Constitution the Church now solemnly acknowledges that the Holy Ghost is truly active in the churches and communities separated from itself.'

As far as non-Christians are concerned, Vatican II declared:

'The non-Christian may not be blamed for his ignorance of Christ and his Church; salvation is open to him also, if he seeks God sincerely and if he follows the commands of his conscience.'

In 2000, however, a document entitled *Dominus Iesus* was published by the Church. It was written by Cardinal Ratzinger (later to become Pope Benedict VI) and signed by Pope John Paul II. It attempted to clarify the Church's position in relation to other Christian organisations by stating:

'The Church of Christ, despite the divisions which exist among Christians, continues to exist fully only in the Catholic Church.'

It goes on to claim that some other Christian groups, including the Church of England and Protestant Churches, 'are not Churches in the proper sense', describing them as 'imperfect' and 'defective'.

With regard to followers of other religions, Ratzinger said:

'They are in a gravely deficient situation in comparison with those who, in the Church, have the fullness of the means of salvation.'

'Exclusivism maintains that the central claims of Christianity are true, and that where the claims of Christianity conflict with those of other religions, the latter are to be rejected as false. Christian exclusivists also characteristically hold that God has revealed himself definitively in the Bible and that Jesus Christ is the unique incarnation of God, the only Lord and Saviour. Salvation is not found in the structures of other religious traditions.'

(Harold A. Netland Christ on Campus Initiative, 2008)

Inclusivism

Exclusivists would argue that their position is entirely logical. If Jesus really is God in human form, then it would follow that Christianity is the true faith.

Some Christians, however, take issue with this view. They point out that Christians have other beliefs that make exclusivism less straightforward. They say that:

- Christians believe that God is omnibenevolent and loves all of His creation. A loving God would not give salvation to only Christians, nor to only a particular group of Christians.
- People who lived before Jesus could not have been saved. Yet there are passages in the Old Testament that suggest they were.
- God is good and fair. It would not be fair to condemn people who have not heard of Jesus.
- In the parable of the Sheep and the Goats (Matthew 25:31–46), Jesus says 'the righteous [will go] into eternal life', but mentions nothing about faith or belief being necessary for salvation.

It was beliefs like these that gave rise to inclusivism. Christian inclusivism is the view that Christianity is the only true religion, that Jesus was God embodied as a human and that his death was a sacrifice for the sins of the world. Inclusivists, however, also believe that non-Christians can go to heaven; that faith in Jesus and being a member of the Church are not necessary.

Inclusivism is most closely associated with the Catholic thinker Karl Rahner. Rahner developed the idea of the 'anonymous Christian'. He argued that God has the power to save anyone, through His grace. Grace came into the world through the sacrifice of Jesus on the cross and the death of Jesus is essential for the salvation of humankind. Individuals do not have to be conscious of God's grace, however, for it to affect them. The anonymous Christian is someone who is not a Christian, but who has been given God's grace, even though they are not aware of it. The anonymous Christian behaves ethically, *like* a Christian without *being* a Christian.

Rahner says that anonymous Christianity only applies to someone who is unaware of Christianity. If someone is aware of Christianity but refuses to accept it, then they cease to be an anonymous Christian.

Critics of inclusivism say that is really a form of exclusivism. It still has the view that Christianity is the only true religion. It does not take seriously any other religion.

To discuss

Would it be possible to be an anonymous Christian in Britain?

Tasks

1 Describe the diversity of religious belief in the world today. Use the diagram on page 319 to help you complete this task.

2 Outline what it means to say that Christianity is an exclusivist religion.

3 Explain the way in which the Bible can be used to support the view of Christian exclusivists.

4 Ratzinger said that those in the Church "have the fullness of the means of salvation" Using your work on salvation explain what he meant by this. Discuss how other Christians and people of a different faith may evaluate this claim.

5 'Christian inclusivism is the only logical view to hold.'

Discuss this statement. In your answer, you should:

● draw on your learning from across your course of study, including reference to beliefs, teachings and practices within Christianity

● explain and evaluate the importance of points of view from the perspective of Christianity.

Stretch what you know

Catholic theologian Hans Küng said that:

'It would be impossible to find anywhere in the world a sincere Jew, Muslim or atheist who would not regard the assertion that he is an "anonymous Christian" as presumptuous.'

a What do you think Hans Küng meant by this? Do you agree with him?

b How do you think Rahner would respond?

Pluralism

Pluralism rejects the idea that God has revealed himself only through Jesus Christ and that salvation can be obtained only through him. So pluralists disagree with both exclusivists and inclusivists. They maintain that God reveals Himself through all the world's religious traditions and that the Christian faith is just one of many valid responses to God.

Bible bitz

'There are many rooms in my Father's house. I would not tell you this if it were not true.'

(John 14:2)

The person most closely associated with pluralism is the English theologian John Hick.

'Christianity understands itself as the absolute religion, intended for all men, which cannot recognise any other religion beside itself as of equal right.'

(Karl Rahner)

'The Christian religion ... has a beginning point in history; it did not always exist but began at some point in time. It has not always and everywhere been the way of salvation for men.'

(Karl Rahner)

'A non-Christian religion can be recognised as a lawful religion (although only in different degrees) without thereby denying the error and depravity contained within it.'

(Karl Rahner)

Hick says that all the major faiths have two things in common:

- None can prove that it is the one and only true religion.
- Individuals of all faiths have experiences they say come from God.

Hick concludes that all religions have truth in them, or are equally close to the truth, and deserve the same respect.

Hick accounts for the differences between the religions by saying that they arise from different cultures. Just as people from different cultural backgrounds have different ideas about dress codes, food or music, so their religious experiences are different. Cultural differences also mean that the different religions teach different things about God. However, the God they all experience is the same God.

> 'It seemed evident to me that essentially the same thing was going on in all these different places of worship, namely men and women were coming together under the auspices of some ancient, highly developed tradition which enables them to open their minds and hearts "upwards" toward a higher divine reality which makes a claim on the living of their lives.'
>
> *(John Hick An Autobiography, 2005, ©Oneworld Publications)*

> 'Can we then accept the conclusion that the God of love who seeks to save all mankind has nevertheless ordained that men must be saved in such a way that only a small minority can in fact receive this salvation?'
>
> *(John Hick)*

↻ A religious pluralist might claim that religions are like different paths that lead to the same God

Hick strongly challenges the exclusivist view that only Christianity can lead to salvation. Since a person's religious beliefs are largely determined by the culture into which they are born, it seems unfair that someone should be denied salvation simply because they were born into a non-Christian culture. On the other hand, a person born into, say, a Muslim culture could reasonably claim that only Islam can offer salvation.

Furthermore, Hick says that if Christianity were the only true religion, then Christians should be obviously better people than anyone else. He says:

> 'Can we be so entirely confident that to have been born in our particular part of the world carries with it the privilege of knowing the full religious truth?'
>
> *(John Hick)*

'If we take literally the traditional belief that in Christ we have a uniquely full revelation of God and a uniquely direct relationship with God ... then surely this ought to produce some noticeable difference in our lives. Christians ought to be better human beings than those who lack these inestimable spiritual benefits.'

Stretch what you know

Pope Francis wrote the following statement in an Italian newspaper in 2013:

'You ask me if the God of the Christians forgives those who don't believe and who don't seek the faith. I start by saying – and this is the fundamental thing – that God's mercy has no limits if you go to him with a sincere and contrite heart. The issue for those who do not believe in God is to obey their conscience.

'Sin, even for those who have no faith, exists when people disobey their conscience. To listen and to follow your conscience means that you understand the difference between good and evil.'

Is the Roman Catholic Church exclusivist, inclusivist or pluralist? Give reasons and evidence for your answer.

Critics of pluralism point out that Hick ignores genuine differences between religions. Religions actually contradict each other in some of the beliefs they hold, so they cannot be different versions of the same truth. Religious followers hold their beliefs to be completely true. None considers them to contain some truth or to be 'close to' the truth.

Ecumenicalism and intra-faith communication

It is estimated that there are somewhere between 30,000 and 45,000 different Christian groups or denominations in the world. All Christians believe that there is one God, and that Jesus is the Son of God and the saviour of humankind. Aside from that, each denomination has its own particular combination of beliefs and teachings that give it its own distinctiveness and identity.

We have seen that different denominations have different ways of looking at others:

- some are exclusivist, holding that there is the one true Church
- some are inclusivist, claiming that, while their Church is the true Church, others may also be able to achieve salvation
- some are pluralist, believing that all denominations share the truth of God, but express it in different ways.

A number of Christian denominations believe that it is important to emphasise their common beliefs and histories, while recognising and respecting their differences. This is achieved through dialogue across the Churches but within the faith. It may be called intra-faith communication. An example of how intra-faith communication may work is ecumenicalism.

Ecumenicalism comes from the Greek word 'oikoumene', which means the whole world. It refers to the attempt to bring about unity of the Christian Churches. Unity does not necessarily mean uniformity and there is no attempt to merge all denominations into one great Christian Church. Rather, it is about the different Christian Churches cooperating in worship and working together to serve humanity.

🎧 The logo of the World Council of Churches incorporates the word *oikoumene* – the whole world

> 'You are joined together with peace through the Spirit. Do all you can to continue as you are, letting peace hold you together. There is one body and one Spirit, and God chose you to have one hope. There is one Lord, one faith, and one baptism. There is one God and Father of us all, who rules over everyone. He works through all of us and in all of us.'
>
> *(Ephesians 4:3–6)*

The ecumenical movement started at the beginning of the twentieth century, when the devastation brought about by the First World War generated a feeling that the Churches together could bring hope to the world. In 1948, 147 Churches assembled in Amsterdam to form the World Council of Churches (WCC) (see p.81). The Roman Catholic Church did not join.

Today the World Council of Churches consists of almost 350 Churches, representing over half a billion Christians worldwide. It works in three areas:

- Setting up a community of different Churches across the world through dialogue and increased understanding of each other.
- Working together for peace in the world by helping people in need.
- Training people to continue intra-faith communication.

Although the Roman Catholic Church is still not a member of the WCC, the WCC welcomes Catholic observers to its meetings.

Not all Christians are in favour of ecumenicalism:

- Christian exclusivists find it hard to accept other denominations on equal terms.
- Some Churches are happy to remain distinct from other Christian groups.
- Some Churches are concerned that ecumenicalism will make them less distinct from other Christian groups.

> 'The aim of the World Council of Churches is to pursue the goal of the visible unity of the Church. This involves a process of renewal and change in which member churches pray, worship, discuss and work together.'
>
> *(World Council of Churches)*

Tasks

1 When asked, 'Why is the Roman Catholic Church not a member of the World Council of Churches?' the WCC replies (on its website): 'There is no constitutional reason why the Roman Catholic Church (RCC) could not join; in fact it has never applied. The RCC's self-understanding has been one reason why it has not joined.'

   What reasons might the Roman Catholic Church have for not joining the WCC? What does the WCC mean by 'the RCC's self-understanding'?

2 How is pluralism different from inclusivism and exclusivism?

3 Present the key beliefs of pluralism in the form of an information poster.

4 What problems do some Christians have with pluralism?

Inter-faith dialogue

The differences between the religions of the world can lead to tensions between them. These tensions can take the form of intolerance, prejudice and discrimination. They can develop into violence and war.

Those who promote inter-faith dialogue believe that tension between religious groups can be reduced through communication and that communication can bring about peace.

↻ (L to r) – Rabbi Shulamit Ambalu of the North London Central Synagogue, Omar Khalid of Finsbury Muslim Centre, Sikh Shivcharan Singh of the Guru Ramdas Centre and Halima Chergur of the North London Central Mosque in conversation at a memorial service for North London residents who died in the July 2005 blasts in London. The memorial was held on 22 September 2005 in the Union Chapel in Islington

Inter-faith dialogue is not an attempt to remove difference between religions, but rather to understand the differences and respect them, while remaining true to one's own faith. The aims of interfaith dialogue include:

- Enabling members of different faiths to form friendships and strengthen social ties.
- Providing opportunities to learn about each other's beliefs, values and practices.
- Promoting multi-faith events in local communities.
- Engaging in practical projects locally, nationally or internationally to help other people.

Tasks

1 Identify the religions represented by their leaders in the photo.
2 Explain what message you think these leaders wanted to give to the nation by having a joint memorial service.
3 Explain what you think the benefits within a community might be of joint inter-faith acts. Do you think there are any negatives to such acts?

> 'There will be no peace among the nations without peace among the religions. There will be no peace among the religions without dialogue among the religions.'
>
> (Hans Küng)

> 'Interreligious dialogue is a necessary condition for peace in the world.'
>
> (Pope Francis)

> 'Tolerance implies no lack of commitment to one's own beliefs. Rather it condemns the oppression or persecution of others'.'
>
> (John F. Kennedy)

In the UK, differences between religious groups have resulted in conflict. According to a study by the Pew Research Center in February 2015, the UK as a country has high levels of social hostilities involving religion. Examples include the following:

- A report published by the Islamic Human Rights Commission in November 2015 reports rising levels of abuse and violence against Britain's Muslims. It says that the media is creating an atmosphere of hatred. Half of Muslims have experienced or witnessed violent attacks and many report job discrimination.
- A report published by the Department of Communities and Local Government of Britain in December 2015 says there has been a 25 per cent increase in anti-Jewish incidents on social media.
- A report by the Equality and Human Rights Commission (EHRC) published in March 2015 gives examples of people in the UK who have experienced misunderstandings or discrimination at work because of their religious beliefs or lack of them.

Commenting on the EHRC report, former Archbishop of Canterbury Lord Carey concluded that 'a knowledge of religion is an ever more important key to understanding the world around us.'

The Roman Catholic Church has promoted inter-faith dialogue since the Second Vatican Council (1962–65), which encouraged more open relations with other faiths and Christian denominations. One of the outcomes of this was the setting up of the Pontifical Council for Interreligious Dialogue (PCID). The aims of the PCID are:

- To promote mutual understanding, respect and collaboration between Catholics and the followers of other religious traditions.
- To encourage the study of religions.
- To promote the formation of persons dedicated to dialogue.

They do this through welcoming visitors from other faiths, visiting others, organising meetings and publishing articles about interfaith dialogue.

The Church of England runs a Presence and Engagement programme to engage with people from different faiths. It follows four principles of inter-faith dialogue set out by the British Council of Churches:

- Dialogue begins when people meet each other.
- Dialogue depends upon mutual understanding and mutual trust.
- Dialogue makes it possible to share in service to the community.
- Dialogue becomes the medium of authentic witness (telling others about the Christian faith).

Margaret

When I was a child in Dorset, I didn't know anyone who held a different faith from Christianity. I heard sermons about Christians working with people of other faiths, but there were no opportunities to get to know those people myself, and the Religious Education syllabus at my school in the 1960s did not cover any faiths other than Christianity. In my ignorance, I viewed people who belonged to other faiths warily, but with curiosity.

However, through my job as an RE teacher, I have loved meeting members of the Jewish community and local Muslims, getting to know them as friends, and understanding what their faith is and how it affects how they live.

Inter-faith dialogue is enormously important. There are beliefs and values which we share together, and there are also major differences we need to appreciate. Talking together is such an important

way to build relationships, understand each other's way of life and why our differences matter. Dialogue means really trying to listen, being open to different ways of looking at life, and being willing to express what is important to us while respecting other people's right to disagree.

As a Christian, I believe that God's love is given for everyone and that, as a Christian, I have to find a way to show that love in all my words, actions and relationships. Inter-faith dialogue will always be demanding!

To discuss

Read Margaret's account.

a What benefits from meeting people of different faiths does Margaret identify?

b Margaret says that 'inter-faith dialogue will always be demanding'. What do you think she means by this?

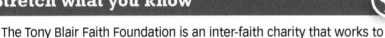

Stretch what you know

The Tony Blair Faith Foundation is an inter-faith charity that works to 'prevent religious prejudice, conflict and extremism.'

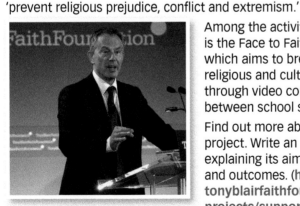

Among the activities it promotes is the Face to Faith project, which aims to break down religious and cultural differences through video conferencing between school students.

Find out more about the project. Write an article explaining its aims, methods and outcomes. (**http://tonyblairfaithfoundation.org/projects/supporting-next-generation**).

■ Tony Blair is a former Prime Minister of the UK. He is founder of the Tony Blair Faith Foundation, which aims to stop religious conflict by building understanding

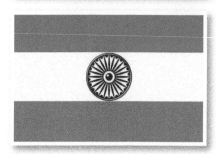

↻ Some countries have flags that show the religious identity of their people as well as their national identity

The relationship between religion and society

Religion and national identity

The history of the human race shows that religious beliefs and practices are closely linked with ethnic groupings and national borders. To belong to a people meant sharing their beliefs and living in the same geographical location as them. The modernisation of societies may have challenged this state of affairs, but it has not really changed it. As states became more powerful, they used religion to provide stability and ethical leadership.

Today, religions are still associated with some countries.

- The state of Israel is defined as a Jewish state. In reality, 'Jewish' refers to the ethnicity of its inhabitants, rather than to their religion. In fact, Israel has no official religion. Nevertheless, there are strong connections between Israel, the Jewish people and the Jewish faith.
- A theocracy is a country that is ruled by religious leaders. A modern example is Iran, which has Shi'a tradition of Islam as its official religion and whose Supreme Leader is a Muslim cleric.
- Other countries may be associated with religions by tradition, even though they are secular states. For example, the constitutions of Sri Lanka and Thailand identify Buddhism as their foremost religion, having the greatest number of followers among their populations, though Buddhism is not their state religion.

England is often spoken of as a Christian country, even though, as we have seen, fewer people practise the faith as each decade passes. Nevertheless, most British people identify themselves with Christianity. On the other hand, research shows that Sikhs and Muslims in Britain identify themselves with being British more strongly than white Britons do.

The British Social Attitudes survey shows that, since 1995, the proportion of the population who think that being a Christian is either a very important, or a fairly important, part of being British has gone down, from just under a third in 1995 to less than a quarter in 2013.

⊃ The proportion of the population who think being a Christian is an important part of being British, 1995–2013

	1995	2003	2008	2013
Very important	18.5%	15.1%	6.2%	12.5%
Fairly important	13.5%	15.6%	17.4%	12.0%
Not very important	27.3%	23.7%	37.3%	26.2%
Not at all important	35.1%	39.0%	37.7%	45.0%
Can't choose/not answered	5.7%	6.6%	1.4%	4.4%

When presented with nine factors that might define what it means to be British, the most popular answers were an ability to speak English (95 per cent), having British citizenship (85 per cent) and respecting British institutions and laws (85 per cent). Being a Christian was the least popular (24.5 per cent).

Proselytisation

The Bible records the last words of Jesus as,

'Go and make followers of all people in the world. Baptise them in the name of the Father and the Son and the Holy Spirit. Teach them to obey everything that I have told you to do.'

(Matthew 28:19,20)

From the early days of Christianity, Christians have taken this to mean that they should tell others about their faith and convert them so that they too become Christians. This is called proselytisation.

Proselytisation is controversial. There is a fine line between sharing one's faith with others and imposing it on them. Christians who proselytise may call themselves Evangelists. An Evangelist is, literally, someone who spreads good news. As far as Evangelical Christians are concerned, the aim of proselytisation is to pass on to another person the joy and happiness that Christianity has brought them. The person who receiving the proselytisation may feel that evangelism is an invasion of their privacy and does not respect the views they already hold. The Evangelist may understand that it is their religious duty to pass on their faith. The person who is being evangelised may feel that they have no duty to be part of it. There is tension, then, between freedom of expression on the one hand and freedom of belief on the other.

The tension that proselytisation may cause has resulted in disciplinary and legal cases:

- A Christian nurse was disciplined because she encouraged patients to pray to get better.
- Another nurse was disciplined for praying with a colleague, giving her a Christian book and inviting her to church events.
- A nursery worker was sacked because she told a co-worker, who was a lesbian, that she was a sinner, even though she added that everyone is a sinner and that God accepts people as they are.

Stretch what you know

In June 2014, a Christian health worker was accused of 'bullying' a Muslim colleague by presenting her with her Christian views. Compare the account recorded at **www.telegraph.co.uk/news/ health/news/10933206/NHS-worker-who-bullied-Muslim-by- praying-for-her.html** with that published at **www.secularism.org. uk/blog/2015/04/the-christian-fired-for-praying-at-work--heres- the-other-side-of-the-story**.

- If you were chairing the industrial tribunal at which this case was being heard, what would your verdict have been? Write a paragraph to explain your decision.

Tasks

1 Why do some Christians believe they have a duty to proselytise?

2 Why is inter-faith dialogue important for some Christians?

3 'Religion is a private matter. Religious believers have no right to tell others about their beliefs.'

Draw on your learning from across your course of study, including reference to beliefs, teachings and practices within Christianity. Explain and evaluate the importance of points of view from the perspective of Christianity.

Dialogue within and between religious and non-religious groups

Different Christian views and attitudes towards non-religious worldviews

Non-religious people believe the existence of the universe can be explained without God. Science and technology have helped us understand how the world was created and God is no longer required to understand it. So there is no point in having religious faith.

Religious people may well think that the universe exists with and because of God, and that it is impossible to know or understand the universe without God. They may say that those who say they have no religious beliefs actually have very strong religious beliefs, the central one being that there is no God.

People who are not religious can be divided into two groups:

- Atheists are people who believe that there is no God. They would say that those who believe in God should be able to prove His existence, but they have not and they cannot.
- Agnostics are those people who say it is impossible to know if God exists. They would say that believers have not proved and cannot prove God's existence, but also that atheists have not proved and cannot prove He does *not* exist.

⋂ Atheists and humanists do not believe that God created the universe

Some atheists and agnostics are secularists. Secularists say that everyone has the right to freedom of belief, whether that belief is religious or not. Secularists, however, maintain that beliefs are private and should not affect other people if they do not want to be affected by them. They say, too, that religions and religious beliefs and practices should not have special status, nor receive special treatment by the State.

Some atheists and agnostics are humanists. Like secularists, humanists believe in the equal treatment of everyone, whether religious or not. They do not, however, accept any religious view of the universe. They think that the universe can be explained entirely by science, and that people find their own meaning in life and behave with compassion and dignity without need of a god.

Atheists and agnostics maintain that human beings use their reason and respect for others to work out what is right and wrong. The British public agrees. A survey conducted in 2014 shows that nearly two-thirds (63 per cent) think that atheists are just as moral as, or more moral than, religious people. Christianity teaches that morality comes from God and that behaving morally means acting in accordance with God's laws. The same survey, however, reveals that 60 per cent of Christians believe atheists are just as moral as religious people.

Christian values and ideals shared with atheism, agnosticism, humanism and secularism

Christians, atheists and agnostics, humanists and secularists all agree that human beings have a moral sense and have the capacity to behave in a moral way. The point on which they disagree is the Christian teaching that morality is not possible without God, and that positive values come from the teachings of Jesus. A non-religious view is that these values are not *Christian* values, they are instead *human* values.

There is, nevertheless, agreement about what those values are.

Compassion

- For Christians, compassion comes from God, whose own compassion is revealed in the passage from the Bible that says:

'God loved the world so much that he gave his only Son, so that everyone who believes in him would not be lost but have eternal life.'

(John 3:16)

Christians believe that Jesus showed in his own life and teachings the importance of compassion. He summarises the Christian view of compassion with the words:

'You shall love your neighbour as yourself.'

(Matthew 22:39)

He teaches that love for one's neighbour should extend to loving those who wish you harm:

'Love your enemies and pray for those who persecute you.'

(Matthew 5:44)

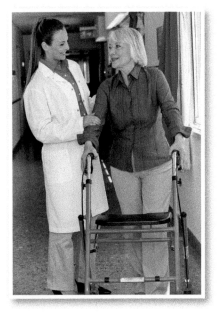

🎧 Non-religious people would argue that compassion isn't a Christian value, but a human value

Support for those in need

- Christians believe they have a religious as well as a moral duty to help those who need it. The Parable of the Good Samaritan (Luke 10:25–37) teaches this, as do the following quotations:

'Give to the one who begs from you, and do not refuse the one who would borrow from you.'

(Matthew 5:42)

'Heal the sick, raise the dead, cleanse lepers, cast out demons. You received without paying; give without pay.'

(Matthew 10:8)

'Whoever has two coats must share with anyone who has none; and whoever has food must do likewise.'

(Luke 3:11)

The promotion of peace over war

- In the Old Testament of the Bible, the Book of Isaiah describes the desirability of using technology for creative, peaceful purposes, not for war:

'And He [God] shall judge among the nations … and they shall beat their swords into ploughshares, and their spears into pruning hooks: nation shall not lift up sword against nation, neither shall they learn war any more.'

(Isaiah 2:4)

Jesus, too, teaches about the value of peace:

'Blessed are the peacemakers, for they shall be called children of God.'

(Matthew 5:9)

The protection of the environment

- For Christians, the environment is the creation of God. Human beings are stewards – God's representatives – charged with the duty of caring for it. The Old Testament explains that the world is God's:..

'The earth is the Lord's, and everything in it, the world, and all who live in it....'

(Psalm 24:1)

The World Council of Churches says,

'The dignity of nature as creation needs to be bound up with our responsibility for the preservation of life.'

To discuss

What values and ideals are being expressed in the sculpture by Yevgeny Vuchetich?

⮥ This sculpture by Yevgeny Vuchetich stands outside the United Nations' headquarters in New York. Its name – Let Us Beat Swords into Ploughshares – comes from a quotation in the Bible, but the values and ideals it expresses are likely to be shared by atheists and agnostics, too

Potential areas of disagreement and difference between Christianity and atheism, agnosticism, humanism and secularism

Although there are important values and ideas that Christians share with atheists and agnostics, there are differences. Many Christians are concerned that traditional values, which they may call 'Christian values', no longer seem important in a secular society. For example:

- The impermanence of marriage: Christianity teaches that marriage should be lifelong. Jesus says:

'What God has joined together, man must never separate.'

(Matthew 19:6)

Some Christians believe that it is too easy for married couples to divorce, and that many do not work hard enough at making relationships successful.
- Sex before marriage: The Christian ideal is that sex is an act of love and procreation that should only occur within a married relationship. Sex before marriage, however, is now socially acceptable. Cohabitation – living together without being married – is accepted. Some Christians disapprove of this.
- Parenting outside marriage: Christianity teaches that marriage is the relationship within which a couple should have children. Many Christians would say that in order to thrive children need the stability of family life with committed, married parents.
- Single parenthood: Although single parenthood is sometimes unavoidable, Christians would see the ideal family as being led by two parents, who act as role models and examples of a loving relationship.
- Same-sex partnerships: Although many Christians support same-sex relationships (and, of course, some Christians are gay), some still believe that homosexuality is wrong. Some recognise civil same-sex marriages but do not agree with them being celebrated in a Christian marriage ceremony.
- Materialism: Secular society seems to value wealth and celebrity over spiritual and moral values. Christians believe that there is life after death in which wealth and celebrity have no meaning. Wealth and celebrity are shallow and have no lasting significance.

◔ Society seems to be becoming more materialistic, but Christians believe wealth and status won't be important after death

Should secular or religious views take precedence?

There are, however, areas in which religious values and institutions seem to have special protection or privilege. Humanists and secularists believe that this should not be the case. For example:

- Establishment: Both the National Secular Society and the British Humanist Association campaign against the establishment of the Church of England. This means that they are against the Queen being Head of State and Supreme Governor of the Church of England, and they oppose the presence of Anglican bishops in the House of Lords. They also believe that religious groups play too great a role in advising governments and being involved in making decisions of state.
- Education: Secularists and humanists oppose the involvement of religious groups in publicly funded education. They believe that parents of pupils and students should be able to choose openly which school to send their children to, without having to share the faith of their local school. As well as being against faith schools, secularists and humanists believe that religious education should cover a variety of religious and non-religious world views (like secularism and humanism) equally.
- Religious exemption: Employment law in Britain allows religious organisations to discriminate against people who wish work for them but who do not share their faith. Humanists and secularists do not object to the right of religious groups to choose group members to be faith leaders. They are, however, against public services that are run by religious groups selecting employees and clients on the grounds of faith.
- Blasphemy: Until 2008, blasphemy (insulting religious faith) was illegal in Britain. This only applied to blasphemy against Christianity, and was scrapped because the government introduced a new law that made encouraging religious hatred a criminal offence. Most Christians and all secularists and humanists agreed that the blasphemy law was unfair. Blasphemy laws still exist in other countries, however, to protect believers from discrimination. Secularists and humanists believe, though, that they protect religious beliefs and give them special importance.

Let's revise

a Describe one Christian attitude towards abortion.　　(3 marks)

- Choose one Christian attitude to abortion and describe it in three clear sentences.

b Describe the role of Christianity in public life.　　(6 marks)

In your response you must consider that religious traditions in Great Britain are diverse, but mainly Christian.

- Answer this question in clear paragraphs.

- Make sure that you acknowledge that whilst there are many religious traditions in Great Britain it is mainly Christian. For this reason the Church is very involved in the public life of the country. However, other religious groups are represented.

- You could describe the involvement of the established church through the Lords Spiritual.

- You could also describe the use of Christian services to mark key events such as the marriage of Prince William to Princess Katherine.

- Public holidays are also based on Christian celebrations for example, Christmas Day, Boxing Day and Good Friday.

c Explain the different Christian attitudes to proselytisation.
　　(6 marks)

You should refer to sources of wisdom and authority in your answer.

- Answer this question in clearly written paragraphs. Include links to relevant Bible passages. For example you may refer to the Great Commission which commands the disciples to spread the gospel and make disciples of all people.

- Start by explaining what proselytisation is and why Christians seeks to share their faith and help people to convert to Christianity.

- However, in a multi-faith culture Christians need to take care about how and when they evangelise. For example when in a professional capacity it may be considered wrong, and result in disciplinary action, to act in a way that is considered proselytising. You could support this with an example that you have learned about.

- Some Christians continue to share their faith believing that is what they are called to do, even though the law may be used to challenge them. This could be linked back to Paul being imprisoned for proselytising (Acts).

d 'Christians should be involved in inter-faith dialogue.'

Discuss this statement. In your answer, you should:

- draw on your learning from across your course of study, including reference to beliefs, teachings and practices within Christianity

- explain and evaluate the importance of points of view from the perspective of Christianity.　　(15 marks)

Let's Revise contd.

Spelling, punctuation and grammar　　　(3 marks)

- You must evaluate this statement from different Christian perspectives.

- Many Christians who promote inter-faith dialogue argue that it is an effective way of bringing peace rather than tension between different religious groups in society. Jesus spoke with people of all faiths and none and this is a pattern that some Christians aim to follow through inter-faith dialogue.

- You could explain the positive impact that inter-faith dialogue is believed to have as a reason why some Christians believe they have a duty to participate in it. For example engaging in shared social action projects that help other people. For Christians this is showing Jesus' love in action both by the practical project and by working with people of other faiths.

- You could demonstrate your knowledge about the Catholic and Church of England support for inter-faith dialogue.

- Other Christians may argue that their duty is to share the gospel. That this is the truth and the most essential message; to share. Inter-faith dialogue is not the forum for evangelism and so some Christians find it hard to engage with people who have conflicting religious beliefs. You might refer back to the teaching about Salvation through Christ alone in Part 1. Many Christians may find a lack of willingness to engage with inter-faith dialogue, by some Christians, as unhelpful in establishing peace and the opportunity for deeper faith discussions once genuine friendships have been formed.

Glossary

Adhan the call to prayer five times a day

Agape Christian love

Akhirah belief in life after death

Al-Kiswah the black cloth that covers the Kaaba in Makkah

All-loving all-compassionate, benevolent

All-merciful ever-forgiving and not vindictive

Al-Ma'ad the belief that the body will be resurrected in the life to come

Al-Qad'r predestination of the will of Allah; the belief that Allah has decreed everything that is to happen in the universe

Amr-bil-Maroof commanding what is just

Anglican another term for Church of England

Apostles' Creed a statement of Christian belief from the Early Church

Ascension Jesus being taken up to heaven forty days after his resurrection

Atonement the action of making amends for wrongdoing; the idea of being at one with the self

Baptism a ceremony to welcome a person into the Christian religion

Believer's baptism a ceremony to welcome an adult into the Christian religion using full emersion

Benevolence an act of charity or kindness in an effort to do good for others

Cafod a charity, the Catholic Agency for Overseas Development

Caliph a successor of Muhammad ﷺ as the spiritual leader of Islam

Catechism of the Catholic Church a summary of Roman Catholic teaching

Christian Aid a charity working in the developing world, providing emergency and long-term aid

Confirmation an initiation ceremony carried out by a bishop bestowing the gift of the Holy Spirit

Conventional War waging war in a manner which does not use nuclear, biological or chemical weapons.

Corrymeela a Christian community based in Northern Ireland that promotes peace and tolerance

Crucifixion a capital punishment used by the Romans, which nails a person to a cross to kill them

Denomination the names for the different branches of the Christian Church

Ecumenical relating to the worldwide Christian church

Eucharist bread and wine ceremony in the Anglican Church

Evangelism preaching of the faith in order to convert people to that religion

Food banks charity groups collecting donated food to distribute to the poor in Britain

Gospel the names of the books about the life of Jesus in the Bible: Matthew, Mark, Luke and John

Grace unconditional love that God shows to people who do not deserve it

Hadith the teachings of Muhammad ﷺ

Hajj pilgrimage to Makkah and the Fifth Pillar of Islam

Hijra Muhammad's ﷺ escape journey from Makkah to Medinah

Holy Communion the bread and wine ceremony in the Church of England

Ihram the white clothing worn by pilgrims on hajj in Makkah

Imamate leadership

Immanence the belief that God is closer to us than our heartbeat and is involved in the world

Infant baptism ceremony to welcome a child into the Christian religion

Iona an island in Scotland with a fourth-century monastery; used by Christians today as a religious retreat as it is a place of tranquillity and peace

Jihad the greater or lesser striving for the way of Allah

Jumu'ah Friday prayers where the khutbah (sermon) is read

Justice fairness in society or the right thing to do

Khums tax in Shi'a tradition of Islam

Khutba the name for the sermon on Friday in mosques

Liturgical worship a church service with a set structure of worship

Lord's Prayer the prayer Jesus taught his disciples to show them how to pray

Lourdes a town in France where the Virgin Mary appeared; now a place of pilgrimage

Mass the bread and wine ceremony in the Roman Catholic Church

Makkah holy city of Islam in Saudi Arabia, with the great mosque housing the Kaaba

Medinah holy city in Saudi Arabia; the place where Muhammad ﷺ set up the first Muslim community and the place where he is buried

Merciful showing forgiveness and compassion to those who do wrong

Messiah the anointed one who is seen as the saviour by Jews and Christians

Methodist a Protestant Christian group founded by John Wesley in the eighteenth century

Mihrab indented archway in the mosque showing the direction of the Kaaba

Minaret tower on the outside of the mosque used for the call to prayer (adhan)

Miracles events that have no logical or scientific explanation; these were used by Jesus and described in the Gospels

Mission an organised effort to spread the Christian message

Monotheistic a religion that teaches that there is only one God

Nahi Anil Munkar forbidding what is evil

Nicene Creed a statement of faith used in Christian services

Night of Power the night Muhammad ﷺ received the first revelations of the Qur'an

Omnipotence the belief that God is all-powerful

Oneness of God the idea that God is 'One'

Orthodox Church a branch of the Christian Church with its origins in Greece and Russia

Predestination the idea that everything that happens has been decided already by God

Protestant a branch of the Christian Church that broke away from the Roman Catholic Church

Psalms the books written by David

Qibla the direction of Makkah

Quakers the Society of Friends Christian group

Rak'ah a sequence of prayer containing actions and recitations

Ramadan the holy month of fasting for 30/31 days

Reconciliation the process of making people in conflict friendly again

Resurrection the physical return of Jesus on the third day after he died

Risalah communication between man and God in the form of books, angels and prophets

Roman Catholic the largest Christian group; based in Rome with the Pope as its leader

Rosary a set of beads used to count prayers, especially in the Roman Catholic Church

Sacrament the external and visible sign of an inward and spiritual grace

Salah compulsory prayer five times a day and the Second Pillar of Islam

Salvation the saving of the soul from sin

Sawm month of fasting

Seal of the Prophets Muhammad 醬, the last prophet chosen by Allah and who was given the Qur'an

Shahadah Declaration of Faith – to believe in One God and Muhammad 醬 as the Prophet of Allah

Shari'ah Law a legal system that comes from the religious rules of Islam

Shi'a Muslims who adhere to the Shi'a branch of Islam, followed by about a tenth of all Muslims

St Paul a man who taught the teachings of Jesus – originally Saul of Tarus before his conversion

Sunna the way of life of Muhammad 醬 as an example to follow

Sunni Muslims who follow the Sunnah, the Way of the Prophet

Surah the name for chapters in the Quran

Tabarra expressing hatred towards evil

Tawalla expressing love towards good

Tawhid the belief in the Oneness of Allah and the unity of His being

Tearfund a Christian charity working to relieve poverty in developing countries

Torah the revelations given to Musa (Moses)

Transcendence God is outside the world, beyond everything and outside time

Transubstantiation the change in the bread and wine to become the actual body and blood of Christ

Trinity the belief in God the Father, God the Son and God the Holy Spirit

Ummah the brotherhood/community of Islam

Usul ad-Din the foundations of faith in Shi'a tradition of Islam

Wudu the symbolic washing and purification of the mind and body before salah

Zakah almsgiving to the poor, which benefits the Muslim community

Index

A

abortion 100–102, 313–16
abstinence 173
Adam 104
adultery 29
Advent 64
agnostics 332, 333, 335
Amish community 6, 185, 219
Amnesty International 277
angels (malaikah) 114–15
Anglican Pacifist Fellowship 266
Anglican worship 47
annulment 303
anthropic principle 212
apocalyptic warfare 256–57
Apostles' Creed 3, 9, 36
Aquinas, Thomas 208
Arafat 143
arranged marriage 304, 305
ascension 35, 36
Ashura 148–49
assisted suicide 309–10
atheists 332, 333, 335
atonement 37
Augustinian theodicy 23

B

baptism 52–53, 71, 73
  believer's 53, 73
  in Holy Spirit 233
  infant 53, 71
Barzakh 119
Beatitudes 28
Bible 2–3
  God revealed in 218–20
  teaching on violence 243
blasphemy 336

Boethius 6
British Social Attitudes Survey 294, 330

C

Campaign for Nuclear Disarmament 264–65
celebrations 64–70, 291
celibacy 171
challenges for religion 283–318
charismatic
  experiences 233
  worship 50
child marriage 304, 305
children, religious upbringing 184
Christian aid agencies 89
Christian Feminist Network 192
Christian realism 255
Christian traditions in society 283–84
Christian values, non-religious views of 333–34, 335
Christianity 1–92
  beliefs and teachings 2, 5–42
  practices 4, 43–92
Christmas 64–65
Church of England
  abortion 315
  as Church of state 246, 286, 336
  civil partnerships 165–66
  contraception 172
  divorce 177, 303
  Eucharist 51, 238
  euthanasia 310–11
  inter-faith dialogue 328
  IVF (in vitro fertilisation) 318
  marriage 158, 302, 304
  marriage service 161
  Monarch as head of 286

origins 3, 284
  religious upbringing of children 184
  same-sex marriage 64, 167, 169
  schools 291, 292, 298
  secular campaign against establishment of 336
  sexual relationships 170
  sources of authority 3
  terrorism 249
  therapeutic cloning 317
  women, role of 183, 307
Church schools 291–92, 298
Churches Together Movement 86
civil marriage 302, 303
civil partnerships 165–66
cohabitation 170
colour, church and use of 45
community, role of Church in local 71–80
compassion 333
confession 239
confirmation 72, 184
conscience 214, 215, 218
contraception 172
conversions 228–30
cosmological argument 213
Creation
  Biblical accounts 12–16, 200
  God's goodness revealed 203
  interpretations of story 19–20, 199
creation of life 317–18
Creationists 19, 20
crucifixion 34, 36, 38, 69

D

Darwin, Charles 211
Dawkins, Richard 205, 211

Dawud 106–7
Day of Judgement 99, 114, 119–20
dedication 72
denominations
    Christian 3–4, 42, 325–26
    of Islam 96
design argument 210
dialogue
    between religious and non-religious
        groups 332–36
    between religious groups 319–31
Divine Justice (Al-Adl) 99, 117
divorce 29, 174–79, 303
Du'a' (Supplication)` 133
E
Easter 65–70
Easter Sunday 70
ecstatic experiences 233, 234–35
ecumenical communities 86
ecumenicalism 85, 325–26
education
    faith schools 291–92, 298
    religious and secular values 298–301,
        336
    worship in schools 300
environment, protection of 334
Episcopal Church 168, 169
equality
    Christian attitudes and laws on 306–8
    Christian understandings of 186–91
    and family roles of men and women
        181–82
    and gender discrimination 191–92
eschatological beliefs 40, 116–18
ethical living 216–17
Eucharist 51–52, 237–38
Eucharistic service 46, 47, 48, 66
euthanasia 309–13
Euthyphro dilemma 204
Evangelical Christians 232, 321, 331
evangelism 81, 82–83, 190, 267, 331
evil 21–24, 207
evolution, theory of 19, 211
exclusivism 320–21
F
families 80, 155–56, 184
    role of men and women in 180–82
fertility treatment 317–18
festivals and special days, Muslim
    145–49
first cause argument 213
Five Pillars of Islam 124–44
forced marriage 304, 305
forgiveness 39, 204, 268–80, 272
free will 22, 23, 116, 117–18, 207
fundamentalists 219
funerals 77–79
G
gender and prejudice 191–92
Genesis 1 12–13, 14
Genesis 2 13, 15
Genesis 3 17–18
genetic manipulation 317, 318
glossolalia 58, 233
God 195–241

arguments for existence of 209–14
experiencing 218–39
the Father 9, 196, 198
as good 203–5
the Holy Spirit 9–10, 196, 198
human suffering, relationship with
    206–8
humanity, relationship with 200–201,
    202
love shown through Jesus 201
nature of 5
question of 195–208
the Son 9, 26, 196, 198
as a Trinity of persons 8–11, 196,
    197–98
world, relationship with 199, 202
Good Friday 69
grace 38
H
Hadith 95, 113
Hajj 139–44
heaven 41, 120
hell 41, 121
Hick, John 215, 323–25
Holy Saturday 70
Holy Spirit
    baptism in 233
    being filled with 234
    God the 9–10, 196, 198
    role in Creation 15
Holy Trinity 8–11, 196, 197–98
Holy War 251
Holy Week 65–70
hospices 310
House Church 83
House of Lords, bishops in 288–89
human suffering
    and evil 21–24, 207
    and relationship with God 206–8
humanism 296–97, 332, 333, 335
    and precedence of religious views 336
    worship in state schools 300
humanitarian law 254
humanity, God's relationship with
    200–201, 202
I
Ibrahim 104–5, 139, 140, 143
Id-ul-Adha 145
Id-ul-Fitr 146
Id-ul-Ghadeer 147
ihram 139–40
imams 98–99
incarnation 34, 36
inclusivism 322–23
individual worship 50, 56
inspirational people 226–27
inter-faith dialogue 327–29
intra-faith dialogue 325–26
IRA 250
Iraq War 253
Irenaean theodicy 23
Isa 19, 107
Islam 93–152
    beliefs and teachings 94, 97–123
    practices 96, 124–52

Islamic extremism 247
Isma'il 105
Israfil 115
IVF (in vitro fertilisation) 318
Izra'il 114
J
Jehovah's Witnesses 197
Jerusalem 61
Jesus 2, 25–33
    ascension 35, 36
    crucifixion 34, 36, 38, 69
    example of 32–33
    forgiveness, teaching on 269–70
    God revealed through 32, 221
    God the Son 9, 26, 196, 198
    God's love shown in life and death of
        201
    incarnation 34, 36
    as Lord and Saviour 27
    resurrection 34–35, 36, 40, 70
    and role of women 181
    Sermon on the Mount 28–32
    violence and conflict, teaching on
        243–44
Jibril 114
jihad 121, 125, 150–51, 248
judgement, God's 203, 215
Jumu'ah prayer 124, 131
just society, peace and 274
just war theory 251
justice and injustice 273–77
K
Kaaba 140–41
khums 125, 135
Kingdom of God 33
L
Last Supper 46, 68, 238
law
    God's goodness in provision of 203
    Jesus and 29–30
    religion and secular 302–8
    and salvation 38
    Shari'ah 95, 113
Lent 65
liberation theology 278–80
life after death
    in Christianity 40, 215
    in Islam 97, 119–23
liturgical worship 44, 237
Lord's Prayer 30, 54–55
Lourdes 60, 224–25, 231
M
Mackie's inconsistent triad 22
Mandela, Nelson 280
marriage 155, 157–59, 302–5
    services 74–75, 76, 160–63
martyrdom 121
Maundy Thursday 68
meaning of 'Church' 85–86
medical ethics 309
men and women
    role in Christian communities 183,
        307
    roles in Christian family 180–82
Messiah 2, 26, 27, 34, 107, 119

Methodist Church 49, 58, 72, 157, 216, 256
Mika'il 114
Mill, John Stuart 210
Mina 143–44
miracles 222–25
mission 81–84
Monarch 286, 287
moral argument 214
Mothers' Union 156
Muhammad 95, 103, 108–11
Musa 105–6
Muslims, British 94, 285, 294, 328
mystical experiences 230–31

N
national identity and religion 330
National Liberation Front of Tripura (NLFT) 250
National Secular Society 289, 293, 299
new forms of Church 83–84
Nicene Creed 3, 11, 198
Night of Power 109
non-conformist Churches 4, 49, 52, 72, 73
  Eucharist 238
  marriage services 161
non-liturgical services 49
Northern Ireland 86, 303
  Church 288
  IRA 250
  restorative justice 271
nuclear weapons 256–57

O
oaths 29
Orthodox Churches
  baptism 71
  Christmas celebrations 64–65
  Eucharist 238
  Holy Trinity 198
  marriage ceremonies 76, 160
  Requiem Mass 79
  sources of authority 3
  worship 48–49

P
pacifism 262–63
Paley, William 210
Palm Sunday 67
parable of sheep and goats 7, 215, 322
parable of unmerciful servant 270
Parousia (Second Coming) 40, 64, 99
peace and peacemaking 261–67
  promotion over war 334
  relationship between just society and 274
Peace Jam 266
Pentacostalists 234–35
persecuted Church 87–88
pilgrimage
  Christian 60–63, 224–25
  Hajj 139–44
pluralism 323–25
Plymouth Brethren 7
politics, relationship between religion and 245–46, 288–89
prayer

Christian 30, 54–59
  Muslim 127–32, 133
predestination (al-Qad'r) 97, 116–18
prejudice 191, 219
prophethood (Risalah) 97, 103–11
proselytisation 331
Protestants 3–4
public holidays 291
public life, role of religion in 288–92
purgatory 42

Q
Quakers 53, 263
  euthanasia 313
  marriage services 162
  worship 48
Qur'an 95, 103, 109, 112

R
Rahner, Karl 322, 323
rak'ahs 124, 130
Ramadan 136–38, 146
reality, nature of 209–17
reconciliation and forgiveness 268–80
redemption 38
Reformation 3–4, 284, 286
Relate 176
relationships 154–79
religious discrimination 328
religious exemption 336
religious experiences 228–36
religious traditions, diverse 285, 319
repentance and forgiveness 39, 272
Requiem Mass 79
restorative justice 271
Restrepo, Camilo Torres 279
resurrection 34–35, 36, 40, 70
right to die 311
rites of passage 71, 290
Roman Catholic Church 160, 249
  abortion 315
  annulment 303
  baptism 71
  celibacy 171
  Christmas celebrations 64
  civil partnerships 165
  contraception 172
  divorce 177, 303
  Eucharist 48, 51, 238
  euthanasia 310
  exclusivism 320–21
  family roles of men and women 181
  inter-faith dialogue 328
  IVF (in vitro fertilisation) 318
  marriage 159, 302, 304, 305
  marriage service 160
  purgatory 42
  relationship between God and humanity 202
  religious upbringing of children 184
  Requiem Mass 79
  Sacrament of Penance 239
  sacraments 51–53, 238, 239
  salvation 39
  same-sex marriage 168
  schools 291, 292, 298
  sexual relationships 170

sources of authority 3
terrorism 249
therapeutic cloning 317
unequal rights with Protestants 284
women's roles in 183, 307
and World Council of Churches 326
worship 48
Rome 63
Romero, Oscar 278
Royal Army Chaplains 255
Rwandan civil war 268, 271

S
Sacrament of Penance 239
sacraments 51–53, 237–38, 239
Sadaqah 135
Salah (prayer) 124, 127
salvation 7–8, 37–39, 204, 324
Salvation Army 53, 65, 82, 275
Samaritans 312
same-sex marriage 167–69, 303, 308
Sawm 136–38
sa'y 142
Scotland 86, 168, 288
Seal of the Prophets 103, 111
Second Coming 40, 64, 99
secular
  and Christian shared values 333–34
  and Christian values and areas for disagreement 335
  law and religion 302–8
  and religious values in education 298–301, 336
  or religious views taking precedence 336
secularisation 293–97
self-defence 259
Sermon on the Mount 28–32
sexual relationships 163–64
  pre-marital 170, 335
Shahadah 124, 126
Shari'ah law 95, 113
Shi'a Muslims 96, 111, 125
  Divine Justice (Al-Adl) 99
  imams 98–99
  Usul ad-Din 98
Shi'a prayer 132
sin
  evil and 22, 207
  original 18
  punishment for human 27, 34
  and salvation 38
Six Articles of Faith 97
slavery 189
social justice and injustice 274–77
society, relationship between religion and 330
soul 40
soul-making argument 215
sources of authority
  Christianity 2–3
  Islam 95, 112–13
speaking in tongues 58, 233
state, church and 246, 286, 336
Stoning of Iblis 143
suicide 311

Sunday Assembly 284
Sunday School 184
Sunna 95, 113
Sunni Muslims 96, 111, 125
    Divine Justice (Al-Adl) 99
    imams 98
    Six Articles of Faith 97
T
tawaf 141–42
Tawhid (oneness) 97, 100–102
Taylor, James Hudson 227
Tearfund 89, 217
technological warfare 258
teleological argument 210
Teresa, Mother 226
Teresa of Avila, Saint 231
terrorism 247–49
the Fall 17–18, 23
the Word 16, 46
Theistic evolution 19

therapeutic cloning 317, 318
Toilet Twinning 217
Tony Blair Faith Foundation 290, 329
Toronto Blessing 235
transubstantiation 48, 51, 238
Tutu, Archbishop Desmond 265
U
Unitarianism 197
Usul ad-Din 98–99
V
Vatican City 63
violence and conflict 243–60
visions 231–32
W
Wales, Church in 287
Walsingham 62
war
    Christian attitudes to 254–60
    Christian teaching on 243
promotion of peace over 334

wealth 31, 190
women
    Jesus and role of 181
    role in Church 183, 307
world
God's relationship with 199, 202
    religions 319
    role of Church in 85–90
World Council of Churches (WCC) 81,
    85, 326
worship
    Christian 44–50
    Muslim 126–32, 133
    prayer in congregational 54–55
    and sacraments 237–38
    in schools 300
wudu 124, 128–29
Z
Zakah 134–35

The publishers would like to thank the following individuals, institutions and companies
for permission to reproduce copyright illustrations in this book:

Cover © Viktoria Rodriguez/EyeEm/Getty Images; **pp1, 12, 13, 17, 62, 202** © Stuart Aylmer/Alamy; **p19** © RosaIreneBetancourt 8/Alamy Stock Photo; **p21** tl, © Philippe Huguen/Afp/Getty Images; **p21** br, © REX/Shutterstock; **p21** bl, © Images & Stories/Alamy; tr, ml, © Andrew Findlay/Alamy; tr, © Eye Ubiquitous/Alamy; **p22** © Stephen Barnes/Europe/Alamy; **p23** © Zvonimir Atletic/123RF; **p24** © Kevin Carter/Ap/Press Association Images; **p26** © shufu/123RF; **p33** ©Kathryn Reali/KRT/Newscom; **p36** t, © Artur Tomasz Komorowski/123RF; b, © PanjarongU/iStock/Thinkstock; **p44** © Peter Noyce GEN/Alamy; **p45** © Washington Imaging/Alamy; **p46** © WorldPhotos/Alamy; **p47** © Dmitry Naumov/Alamy; **p50** © Ben Stansall/AFP/Getty Images; **p52** © Pascal Deloche/Corbis Documentary/Getty Images; **p55** © adam korzeniewski/Alamy; **p60** © Prisma Bildagentur AG/Alamy; **p61** © Kobby Dagan/123RF; **p63** © Vito Arcomano/Alamy; **p65** © Dmitry Naumov/Alamy; **p66** © imageBroker/Alamy; **p67** © Vojtech Vlk/123RF; **p68** © SuperStock/Alamy; **p69** © World History Archive/Alamy; **p70** © imageBROKER/Alamy; **p71** © TerryHealy/E+/Getty Images; **p72** © Godong/Alamy; **p73** © Marmaduke St. John/Alamy; **p76** © maximkabb/123RF; **p78** tl, © OJO Images Ltd/Alamy; bl, © OJO Images Ltd/Alamy; tr, © Phil Noble/AFP/Getty Images; br, © Paul Doyle/Alamy; **p79** l, © Stephen Barnes/Religion/Alamy; tr, © Sally and Richard Greenhill/Alamy; br, © Art Directors & TRIP/Alamy; **p81** © World Council of Churches; **p82** t, © Jack Sullivan/Alamy; m, © Jacob Ford|Odessa American/AP/Press Association Images; b, © ZUMA Press Inc./Alamy; **p86** l, © Lynne Sutherland/Alamy; r, © Arthur Edwards - Pool/Getty Images; **p90** t, © Logo used by permission of tearfund.org; b, © Kumar Sriskandan/Alamy; **pp93, 144** b, © Aidar Ayazbayev/123RF; **p95** t, © Marco Secchi/Alamy; b, © Cliff Hide Local/Alamy; **p96** t, © Radharc Images/Alamy; b, © Yuri_Arcurs/Getty Images; **p99** © Majid Saeedi/Getti Images News; **p100** © azat1976/123RF; **p101** l, © ISP Photography/Alamy; m, © Acorn 1/Alamy; r, © Peter Titmuss/123RF; **p102** © Abstract art calligraphy painting by hamid iqbal khan (http://fineartamerica.com/featured/1-allah-name-abstract-painting-hamid-iqbal-khan.html); **p103** © robertharding/Alamy; **p108** © Ozkan Bilgin/Anadolu Agency/Getty Images; **p110** © Mahmud Hams/AFP/Getty Images; **p112** © sowari/123RF; **p113** © Shaun Curry/AFP/Getty Images; **pp116, 137, 144,** t, **222, 251** t, **271, 289** © epa european pressphoto agency b.v./Alamy; **p117**

© Gandee Vasan/Stone/Getty Images; **p122** © Graham Hardy/Alamy Stock Photo; **p132** © Paula Bronstein/Getty Images; **p133** © hskoken/123RF; **pp138, 142** © Art Directors & TRIP/Alamy; **p139** © JTB Media Creation, Inc./Alamy; **p140** © rasoul ali/Moment Open/Getty Images; **p143** © epa european pressphoto agency b.v./Alamy Stock Photo; **p144** b, © Aidar Ayazbayev/123RF; **p145** © Asianet-Pakistan/Alamy; **p146** © Velar Grant/ZUMA Press, Inc./Alamy; **p148** t, © Peter Macdiarmid/Getty Images; b, © Janine Wiedel Photolibrary/Alamy; **p149** t, © Yoray Liberman/Getty Images; b, © Hani Mohammed/AP/Press Association Images; **p153, 209** bl, © Nigel Cattlin/FLPA; **p158** © Eydfinnur Olsen/123RF; **p159** © RealyEasyStar Fotografia Felici/Alamy; **p160** © maximkabb/123RF; **pp162, 163, 178, 182, 228, 229, 230, 244, 277** b, **312** b, supplied by author; **p164** tl, © REX/Shutterstock; **p164** tr, © REX/Shutterstock; b, Jack Hobhouse/Alamy Stock Photo; **p165** ©Lisa Young/123RF; **p167** ©Sarah L. Voisin/The Washington Post/Getty Images; **p169** ©Gareth Fuller/PA Wire/Press Association Images; **p170** © warrengoldswain/123RF; **p171** l, © Paco Ayala/123RF; r, © FSergio/123RF; **p172** ©Lusoimages – Fotolia; **p174** © dpa picture alliance archive/Alamy; **p175** tl, © Tetra Images/Alamy; tml, ©Leung Cho Pan/123RF; bml, ©Elena Elisseeva/123RF; bl, © itanistock/Alamy; tr, © preve beatrice/123RF; mr, © Ace Stock Limited/Alamy; br, © piksel/123RF; **p183** © Heathcliff O'Malley/REX/Shutterstock; **p184** © Design Pics Inc./Alamy; **p185** © RosaIreneBetancourt 8/Alamy; **p191** © Lev Kropotov/123RF; **p192** © This is the CFN logo and we give you full permission to use it for Hodder Education; **p197** © The Holy Spirit with a Model of Ptolemy's World, 1610 (oil on panel), Han, Hermann (1574–1627/8)/© Muzeum Narodowe, Gdansk, Poland/Bridgeman Images; **p199** © Cathy Keifer/123RF; **p200** © GraphicaArtis/Archive Photos/Getty Images; **p204** © Heritage Image Partnership Ltd./Alamy; **p206** © Dinodia Photos/Alamy; **p207** © Baloo/Cartoonstock.com; **p208** © Granger, NYC./Alamy; **p209** tr, © Prof. P. Motta/Dept. Of Anatomy/University "La Sapienza", Rome/Science Photo Library; tmr, © Volker Steger/Science Photo Library; tm, © Scott Camazine/Science Photo Library; br, ©Alex Hinds/123RF; bm, © Scott Camazine/Science Photo Library; **p213** l, ©George Diebold/Stockbyte/Getty Images; m, © Sharon Montrose/Iconica/Getty Images; r, © Sipa Press/REX/Shutterstock; **p215** © designpics/123RF;

p216 © Mark Boulton/Alamy; **p217** © Vernon Kinglsey/Toilet Twinning; **p218** © skhoward/E+/Getty Images; **p219** © Ksenia Ragozina/123RF; **p221** ©DEA/G. Nimatallah/Getty Images; **p225** © REX/Shutterstock; **p226** © Linda Schaefer/Alamy; **p227** © Print Collector/Hulton Fine Art Collection/Getty Images; **p231** © Adam Eastland/Alamy; **p233** © Homer W Sykes/Alamy; **p235** © Kevin Weaver/REX/Shutterstock; **p237** © Imagestate Media Partners Limited – Impact Photos/Alamy; **p239** © RyersonClark/Getty Images; **p242** © zabelin/123RF; **p243** © Fine Art Images/Heritage Images/Getty Images; **p246** © PA/ROTA PA ROTA/PA Archive/Press Association Images; **p247** © Spencer Platt/Getty Images; **p248** © This poster campaign by Victvs Ltd is designed to raise awareness of violent extremism and radicalisation in the UK'; **p250** © Dan Chung/AFP/Getty Images; **p249** m, © Bettmann/Getty Images; rt, © J. A. Hampton/Topical Press Agency/Getty Images; rb, © Pete Holdgate Crown Copyright. IWM via Getty Images; l, © Laurent Van Der Stockt/Gamma-Rapho via Getty Images; **p251** b, © APAImages/REX/Shutterstock; **p252** © Timewatch Images/Alamy; **p253** © Trinity Mirror/Mirrorpix/Alamy; **p254** © 615 collection/Alamy; **p255** ©Greg Gibson/AP/Press Association Images; **p257** © Stocktrek Images, Inc./Alamy; **p258** ©NASA Photo/Jim Ross; **p261** © Washington Stock Photo/Alamy; **p262** © Bjanka Kadic/Alamy; **p264** © Lana Rastro/Alamy; **p265** © Gary Doak/Alamy; **p266** t © The PeaceJam Foundation; b © By permission of the Anglican Pacifist Fellowship'; **p268** © Scott Peterson/Hulton Archive/Getty Images; **p273** © photo5963/123RF; **p275** © MediaWorldImages/Alamy; **p276** l, © Library of Congress Prints and Photographs Division Washington, D.C. 20540 [LC-USZ62-126559]; m, © Allstar Picture Library/Alamy; r, © Art Directors & TRIP/Alamy; **p277** t, © Art Directors & TRIP/Alamy; **p278** © Bettmann/getty Images; **p279** © AP/Press Association Images; **p280** © Eye Ubiquitous/Alamy; **p284** © Roger Parks/Alamy; **p285** © Office for National statistics; **p286** t © Fox Photos/Getty Images; b © Fox Photos/Hulton Royals Collection/Getty Images; **p287** © Oleg Dudko/123RF; **p290** © Graham Morley Alamy; **p291** © Petar Paunchev/123RF; **p293** © INTERFOTO/Alamy; **p296** © Jon Worth/British Humanist Association/REX/Shutterstock; **p298** © World Religions Photo Library/Alamy; **p302** © Tatiana Chekryzhova/123RF; **p304** © ice/123RF; **p306** © Paul Popper/Popperfoto/Getty Images; **p307** © Pontino/Alamy; **p309** © Sergio Azenha/Alamy; **p310** © Johnny Green/PA Archive/Press Association Images; **p312** © Samaritans 2016 (permission sought); **p313** © Dopamine/Science Photo Library; **p316** tl, © Alexander Tsiaras/Science Photo Library; tr, © Edelmann/Science Photo Library; bl, © James Stevenson/Science Photo Library; br, © Mediscan Alamy; **p317** © ktsdesign/123RF; **p318** t, © helenap2014/123RF; **p318** b, © ImageWorks/TopFoto; **p320** © Dea Picture Library/Getty Images; **p326** © World Council of Churches; **p327** © Andrew Stuart/PA/PA Archive/Press Association Images; **p329** t, supplied by author; b, © Spencer Platt/Getty Images; **p330** t, © Aravind Teki/123RF; m, © issumbosi/123RF; b, © Aravind Teki/Alamy; **p332** © Pop Nukoonrat/123RF; **p333** © stylephotographs/123RF; **p334** © Patti McConville/Alamy; **p335** © maksym yemelyanov/123RF.

The Publishers would also like to thank the following for permission to reproduce material in this book:

p58 www.24-7prayer.com; **p81** World Council of Churches; **p86** Churches Together in England. © The Congregational Federation. http://www.congregational.org.uk/who-we-work-with/churches-together-in-england; **p186** © Benjamin Zephaniah; **p208** © Kevin C Knight http://www.newadvent.org/cathen/05649a.htm; **p212** With thanks to the LASAR (Learning about Science and Religion) Research project; **p224** © Benny Hinn; **p225** © Dr Raj Persaud; **p253** Iraq war briefings headlined with biblical quotes, reports US magazine by Daniel Nasaw. Copyright Guardian News & Media Ltd 2016; **p256** 'The Church and the bomb' report - Church of England. © The Archbishops' Council; **p258** Catholics Should Criticize Indiscriminate Drone Use. © Robert George; **p261** Definition of social justice. © Oxford English Dictionary; **p275** © The Salvation Army; **p277** © Lorraine; **p289** l, Report compiled by The Commission on Religion and Belief in Public Life (Corab). © The Woolf Institute; **p289** r, Keith Porteous Wood, executive director of the National Secular Society. ©National Secular Society; **p289** b, Bishops in the House of Lords - The Lords Spiritual. The Church of England. © The Archbishops' Council; **p290** Tony Blair, speech in 2011. ©The Tony Blair Faith Foundation; **p299** t, b, © National Secular Society http://www.secularism.org.uk/uploads/religious-education-briefing-paper.pdf; **p300** © British Humanist Association (https://humanism.org.uk/campaigns/schools-and-education/collective-worship/2016); **p304** Forced marriage. The Church of England. ©The Archbishops' Council; **p321** Harold A. Netland, "One Lord and Savior for All? Jesus Christ and Religious Diversity" (Christ on Campus Initiative, 2008); **p324** t, An Autobiography by John Hick, 2005, © Oneworld Publications; b, John Hick 'The Next Step Beyond Dialogue', in The Myth of Religious Superiority: A Multi-Faith Exploration, ed. Paul F. Knitter, © Orbis Books, 2005; **p325** Pope Francis reaches out to atheists and agnostics. © The Telegraph Media Group Limited; **p326** World Council of Churches.

Bible quotes are from The Holy Bible, New International Version®, NIV® Copyright © 1973, 1978, 1984, 2011 by Biblica, Inc.® Used by permission. All rights reserved worldwide.